STUDIES ON THE PERSONAL NAME
IN LATER MEDIEVAL ENGLAND
AND WALES

STUDIES ON THE PERSONAL NAME

IN LATER MEDIEVAL ENGLAND

AND WALES

Edited by

Dave Postles and Joel T. Rosenthal

2006
Studies in Medieval Culture XLIV
Medieval Institute Publications

WESTERN MICHIGAN UNIVERSITY

Kalamazoo, Michigan, USA

Library of Congress Cataloging-in-Publication Data

Studies on the personal name in later medieval England and Wales /
edited by Dave Postles and Joel T. Rosenthal.
    p. cm. -- (Studies in medieval culture ; 44)
Includes bibliographical references.
  ISBN 1-58044-025-8 (alk. paper) -- ISBN 1-58044-026-6 (pbk. : alk. paper)
  1. Names, Personal--England--History. 2. Names, Personal--Wales--History.
3. Great Britain--History--Medieval period, 1066-1485. 4. Great Britain--History--Anglo-Saxon period, 449-1066. 5. Wales--History--1063-1536. I.
Postles, David. II. Rosenthal, Joel Thomas, 1934- III. Series.
  CB351 .S83 vol.44
  [CS2503]
  929.4'0942--dc21

2002007485

ISBN 1-58044-025-8 (casebound: alk. paper)
ISBN 1-58044-026-6 (paperbound: alk. paper)

Cover design by Linda K. Judy

Cover photograph by Chafe Hensley. MS 10, *Ordinarium Ecclesie Sancte Marie de Biloca*, fol. 5^r, Flanders, s. XV^{in} from The Obrecht Collection, Gethsemani Abbey, at the Institute of Cistercian Studies Library, Western Michigan University. Used with permission.

Printed in the United States of America

CONTENTS

PART IV—CHRONOLOGIES AND IMPACTS

ACKNOWLEDGMENTS

Dave Postles expresses his gratitude to the Marc Fitch Fund for its support and to members of its Council, Jenny Kermode and Richard Smith, as well as to its Secretary, Roy Stephens. Similarly, he is grateful to Judith Bennett for many helpful comments on naming processes and to Paul Griffiths for ideas on labeling processes. It has also always been a great help to be able to reflect ideas with Kate Parkin. Both editors wish emphatically to record their gratitude to their colleagues working at Medieval Institute Publications: Tom Seiler, Patricia Hollahan, and especially Julie Scrivener and Candace Porath.

ABBREVIATIONS

AN	Anglo-Norman
A-NS	*Anglo-Norman Studies*
ANorse	Anglo-Norse
AS	Anglo-Saxon
AScand	Anglo-Scandinavian
CG	Continental-Germanic
CIPM	*Calendar of Inquisitions Post Mortem*
CPR	*Calendar of the Patent Rolls*
EHR	*English Historical Review*
e.s.	extra series
IG	Insular Germanic
LPS	*Local Population Studies*
MDu	Middle Dutch
ME	Middle English
ModE	Modern English
MP	*Medieval Prosopography*
NFr	Norman French
NG	Nomina Germanica
OBret	Old Breton
OCFr	Old Central French
ODan	Old Danish
OE	Old English
OFr	Old French
OHG	Old High German
OIr	Old Irish
ON	Old Norse

ONFr	Old Northern French
OSax	Old Saxon
OSwed	Old Swedish
Oxon.	*Oxoniensia*
n.s.	new series
PP	*Past and Present*
PL	Patrologia Latina
Sc	Scandinavian
VCH	*Victoria History of the Counties of England*
WG	West-Germanic

PART I—INTRODUCTION

NAMES AND NAMING PATTERNS
IN MEDIEVAL ENGLAND:
AN INTRODUCTION

Joel T. Rosenthal

When my students are at a loss for the opening of a paper, they often resort to citing *Webster's Collegiate Dictionary*. This allows them to begin on safe if unadventurous ground and it helps chew up a bit of the assigned length. On the idea that learning should be a two-way process, I will follow their lead in setting up the nine-pins for this collection of papers on names and naming patterns—mostly forenames or Christian names, but with some attention to family names—in medieval England.

A name (as a noun), the good book says, is "a word or phrase that constitutes the distinctive designation of a person or thing." And as a verb we simply roll over a bit: "to give a name" or "to mention or identify by name." This is certainly basic and well within the grasp of those of us who come—as I do—with little prior work in, or serious knowledge of, scholarship about names and naming patterns. Names, as a mark of distinction, and naming as a form of activity, are so basic to human society—denoting deep waters regarding power, social and familial continuity, and identity—that most historians have tended to accept naming as just one of those givens, much as we once did for aspects of life such as diet, clothing, leisure activities, and child rearing. The paradox is that it has been the central importance of names and naming, rather than any peripheral status, that has put them among those easily-overlooked aspects of a past society. Of course, as the papers below illustrate, names contain and are part of a code, or a series of

1

codes, to decipher and interpret before we can talk with confidence about what they tell us and the directions in which they (seem to) point. We can certainly agree that names (as common and proper nouns) and naming (as an active verb) imply agency and individuation. The power to name all other living creatures was one of the signs of Adam's dominion over life in the first week of creation. It was a reassuring or recurring indication that he indeed was made in God's image. That he eventually used this power to designate or categorize his partner only served to confirm his special gender-driven and gender-bestowed power, just as his use of this power helped legitimate a pervasive cultural heritage of sexism, male chauvinism, and hierarchy. But the universal lesson—that most of us *are* named by another, rather than at some time in our own life span as we ourselves might choose—is part of the baggage we carry for having a pre-assigned niche within a family structure, both in its micro- or domestic form and in its larger, more symbolic and constructed form.

In some ways historical name studies are reminiscent of research in physics. In physics new findings result from the interplay of theoreticians, who speculate on what might happen and why, and of experimentalists, concerned with what does happen. For any given historical universe, be it a village in the midlands or the fens, or jurors in Domesday, or women in the eleventh century, we have the names; the experiment has yielded data. Now what we want to know is why we have those particular names, and for how long have others of the community, or family, or ethnic stock, or linguistic stock, or social class, etc., had these names (or other names)—and what is the rate of change, and to how many identifiable social forces are the names linked in some causal fashion. The papers below, with adjustments for detail, length, and the wayward nature of my metaphor, can be thought of as offering a mix-and-match of experimental data (the names) and theory (the why, when, whence, and whither).

The arrangement of the papers in this volume reflects decisions we made, mostly to guide our own thinking, when we organized what we wished to present. We have tried to offer the papers so as to maximize common approaches and focus: an introduction to name studies and naming, social groups or delineated communities, a focus on place or locale, and chronology or the impact of events on naming patterns. The extent to which this arrangement is arbitrary soon becomes evident, especially as many papers touch on more than one theme and employ a variety of methods and approaches.

Drawing on the lessons of the papers that follow, and going beyond the organization displayed in the table of contents, three lines of interpretation or analysis present themselves in trying to assess degrees of similarity or unity of conceptualization. These three lines run—as we are wont to explain historical development and change these days—in diverging directions. And it is in our inability to offer unity or closure that some of the fascination behind this kind of research lies. Our limited analytical vision also reminds us of the extent to which a society—past and present—is a complex entity upon which we impose some degree of unity for our own explanatory and heuristic purposes.

We like to think our interpretations are in conformity, or at least not badly out of sync, with those of that society about itself. This, however, is a one-sided game, though we try to honor the rules and to give some thanks to the dead for their contributions. That we impose patterns on medieval behavior of which "they" were unaware does not vitiate their value or aesthetic appeal, but it should warn us about caution and humility.

Let us turn to what I term the three lines of assault upon the culture and practices revealed by way of an analysis of names and naming patterns. One is the micro-social or family dynamic. It focuses on the small social group—parents and other close relatives, godparents, family friends and patrons and servants, and perhaps localized traditions about patron saints of nearby churches and popular festivals—and it traces naming patterns as explained by such links. The papers of Niles, Bennett, and Haas give us an entree to this line of discussion, with an element of disagreement, principally revolving around the centrality and decision-making autonomy of godparents. The core of the discussion offers a scholarly case study in the use of data and their interpretation that begs for inclusion within a single cover. We are happy to oblige.

A second line of analysis straddles village life and some wider and more open-ended stretches of the cultural landscape. It touches on radical as well as evolutionary socio-political change, as revealed by names, as well as on all matter of contacts and interactions among languages, racial stocks, and classes. I refer to the papers that track the wide range of larger influences that emerge in naming patterns. Name studies provide an opportunity to trace the consequences of the Norman Conquest as a political turning point, or the sustained identity of Scandinavian tongues and peoples in East Anglia or the North, or the gap between social and cultural roles ascribed to men and to women, or the assimilation of French and Bretons and Normans into their new land, to point out but some of the elements our papers trace.

The diversity, or multiplicity, of the traditions and vectors we can trace is an arresting feature of the papers. It reminds us of how many currents simultaneously flow within a given culture or "nation state" or society, *and* of the way in which name studies provide a method of tracing them. The obvious top-down movement of names is to be expected, and we might say the same about the cyclical popularity of names associated with ecclesiastical traditions and themes. Nor are we surprised at comparable findings when we consider intermarriage and the quest for roots and sense of community on both sides of the historical divide—for winners as well as losers— of 1066. But we can also take into account long-term cycles of Welsh (and/or non-Welsh) names, and of links between village and peasant society at one level, and at the fashions and hegemonic patterns set by the lords and ladies who towered over this world from their lofty heights. So if the discourse over baptismal naming patterns at the micro-level is one line of approach, another is represented by the many vectors that talk to these and similar questions as we move into a vast panorama of lordship and assimilation and marriage, cutting across political and ethnic and cultural boundaries. We can examine ramifications of the Norman Conquest: papers by Lewis, Clark (in *Speculum*, 1978), Christelow. Or we can find comparable or parallel work for the peasantry and in local studies: Franklin, Insley, Jones, and Postles wrestle with big problems but on the reduced scale of village and peasant culture.

A third line of analysis has to do with the very limited name stock that confronts us when we tally the range of names that served the bulk of the populace. Such findings—reported both early and late, and at almost any and every social level—invariably indicate a small, oft-used name stock. As such, these findings open yet another room in Clio's mansion, as we now have to come to imaginative grips with a world where identity and individuality were usually defined through a resort to small dimensions and limited variations—a scenario running contrary to some of the themes we have broached about borrowing, diffusion, and the mimetic face of vicarious identification.

But the reality of our data has to be the master (or mistress), and we cut our cloth accordingly in regard to our speculation about the "medieval imagination" and the desire, or the lack thereof, to stand apart. Though it seems trite to suggest that the heavy reliance on *John, Thomas, William, Richard,* and *Robert* that we find all over the place indicates an anti-individualized way of staking a claim to one's place in the world, such a conclusion does force itself upon us.[1] Davis and Franklin both support this peculiar picture of medieval society.

The phenomenon or problem of a small name stock is familiar to anyone who has worked with prosopographical materials or the men and women of a closed community or universe. In this area, at least, I can offer data to support what more expert inquiries have assured me is the norm. A brief analysis of jurors' names as found in the Proof of Age proceedings for the reign of Henry IV—material I have been reading for other purposes—brings this point home quickly and clearly.[2] In a universe of 1,151 jurors, the "usual suspects" are *John, William, Thomas, Robert,* and *Richard.* These names comprise no less than 79.6% of the group, with *John* alone making up 36.7%. Nine other names (*Nicholas, Henry, Walter, Roger, Simon, Ralph, Hugh, Stephen,* and *Adam*) reached double figures, in terms of their incidence; the first four appear between twenty and thirty-one times, the others between ten and twenty times. Eleven other names are found more than once (though never more than nine times); nineteen men carried unique names as far as this collection went.

What does this relentless return to the common pool of names tell us about the narrow boundaries of imagination, or of differentiation, within which men lived? To us the answer seems to be an argument for provincialism, a heavy hand of tradition (of family, or village, or class and culture), and by our standards a grievous lack of imagination. To the many Johns and Thomases there must have been comforts of tradition, continuity of some sort, and *nominal* links, either tangible or intangible, with spiritual guardians and men of substance. If the educated and socially ambitious Pastons thought it "the thing" to name the first two sons John in the first half of the fifteenth century, we just have to accept that their antennae were sensitive to what passed muster in their world. Maybe we should think of this narrow name stock as a check upon, or balance to, the social forces—explicated in many of these papers—that worked toward diversity and multiculturalism.

So "what's in a name?" is, and should properly remain, an open-ended question. The papers we present are intended to point in various directions

---

[1]Scott Smith-Bannister, *Names and Naming Patterns in England, 1538–1700* (Oxford, 1997), tables on pp. 100, 108–09, 191–93.

[2]PRO, *CIPM*, 18: *1–6 Henry IV,* ed. J. L. Kirby (London, 1987), and *CIPM*, 19: *7–14 Henry IV* (London, 1992).

in pursuit of this question, but never to touch base at a given meeting ground. This collection grew from a suggestion by Dave Postles that *Medieval Prosopography* devote a special issue to onomastics. Negotiations among the editors convinced us that a separate volume was more likely to do justice to the importance and interest of the topic. Furthermore, assembling a volume from scratch gave us the opportunity to offer a mix of already-published papers and newly commissioned ones. It is our hope that the mix of old ("old" being relative; we go as far back as Cecily Clark's paper of 1978) and new, of English and British (and some written by "Americans"), of aristocratic and ecclesiastical and common, and of men and women—to list but some of the polarities and contrasts—indicates how many topics can be approached by way of name studies, how many questions can be asked (if not answered). We have not mentioned gender as a distinct line of force, and we point to work by Clark as showing the value of this type of inquiry. We also offer a mix of methodologies, ranging from the statistical analysis of Jones to work growing out of peasant and regional studies.

In concluding this brief introduction, a few more acknowledgments: The support and advice of George Beech, who withdrew from co-editorship because of other commitments, some involving work with Continental scholars on these very issues, was very useful as we began. As always when publishing with Medieval Institute Publications, the encouragement and labors of Tom Seiler (and now Patricia Hollahan), Julie Scrivener, and Candy Porath (and the easy lead of Paul Szarmach) and the many hands in editorial, production, design, and marketing carry a goodly share of the credit for this volume. From early endorsement through the triumphant end, they make such a volume possible.

And, since the author of the introduction has the last word, I want to say that this volume really is Dave Postles' project. I have had the pleasure of helping expedite it, but Dave has been the guiding force. He has done the bulk of the work. I wish to express my gratitude, as well as my pleasure, at being his colleague in what we hope is an intriguing, puzzling, and oft-used contribution to English medieval history.

Joel T. Rosenthal
State University of New York at Stony Brook

ENGLISH PERSONAL NAMES CA. 650–1300: SOME PROSOPOGRAPHICAL BEARINGS

†*Cecily Clark*

Prosopography and anthroponymy are complementary.[1] The more precisely the former defines any individual, the better the evidence available to the latter for national or social characterization of his or her name. Reciprocally, anthroponymical commentary may orient or enrich a prosopographer's analysis of a career or a personality. However, because anthroponymy uses evidence and methods of its own, for a prosopographer to profit from it and appreciate the degrees of precision attainable requires some technical understanding. This is the theme of the present paper, explored specifically with reference to the Old and Early Middle English periods.

This essay, originally published in *MP* 8/1 (Spring 1987), 31–60, is reprinted here with minor changes, with the permission of G. R. Anderson, Peter Jackson, and the editors of *Medieval Prosopography*.

[1] I am happy to have this opportunity of expressing my gratitude to Peter McClure, University of Hull, for his generous and constructive criticism of this paper in successive drafts; whatsoever inaccuracies and oversights may remain are my sole responsibility. Some definitions of the technical terms used here may be helpful: "anthroponymy" = (study of) personal naming; "byname" = a non-hereditary qualifying element, of whatsoever kind, that is coupled with a baptismal name, usually to make identification more secure; "blood," "nationality," and "race" refer to the geographical origins of a name-bearer's family, usually with implications of cultural affinity.

For periods before about 1100, "personal name" means, predominantly, "baptismal name," because nicknames and bynames of other types, although current, are too sparsely recorded for systematic study.[2] Partly for that reason and partly to preserve some unity of theme, this paper will touch on bynames only—and then briefly—insofar as they stem from baptismal names.

Baptismal names were drawn from conventional stocks and in every community reflected influences at work there. In medieval times, cultural influence implied human contact and, therefore, human movement, whether for conquest, settlement, or trade. A study of naming reveals more about the cultural attitudes of a community at large than about those of any particular individual,[3] because the latter may, through fashion or godparents' whims, have been labeled in a style superficially at odds with his or her own affinities, whether racially or linguistically defined. Yet every name chosen must in some way have symbolized influences impinging upon, and welcomed by, that family as well as by the community as a whole. Personal-name studies can, therefore, help to define more closely the national, familial, and cultural background of an individual—and often, too, his or her socioeconomic status.

---

[2]For early English usages of this sort the standard treatment remains that in Gösta Tengvik, *Old English Bynames*, NG 4 (Uppsala, 1938); but this work, now outdated, was also from the outset ill-conceived, with deliberate under-recording of women's names and inadequate distinction between pre- and post-Conquest materials (see the review article by Olof von Feilitzen in *NoB* 27 [1939], 116–30). So, useful though it is as a quarry, Tengvik's work is not authoritative. For some particular forms, more reliable treatments may be found in, for instance, Olof von Feilitzen, "Some Old English Uncompounded Personal Names and Bynames," *Studia Neophilologica* 40 (1968), 5–16, and "The Personal Names and Bynames of the Winton Domesday," in Martin Biddle and Frank Barlow, eds., *Winchester in the Early Middle Ages: An Edition and Discussion of the Winton Domesday* (Oxford, 1976), pp. 143–229, esp. 207–17. [N.B. the List of Abbreviations on p. 28.—Eds.]

[3]For socio-onomastic studies of medieval English name corpora, see, e.g., Cecily Clark, "People and Languages in Post-Conquest Canterbury," *Journal of Medieval History* 2 (1976), 1–33 (some etymological detail here now needs revision); "Clark's First Three Laws of Applied Anthroponymics," *Nomina* 3 (1979), 13–19; "Battle c. 1110: An Anthroponymist Looks at an Anglo-Norman New Town," in *Proceedings of the Battle Conference on Anglo-Norman Studies II, 1979*, ed. R. Allen Brown (Woodbridge, 1980), pp. 21–41 and 168–72; "The Early Personal Names of King's Lynn: An Essay in Socio-Cultural History," pt. 1, *Nomina* 6 (1982), 51–71, and pt. 2, *Nomina* 7 (1983), 65–89 [hereafter "King's Lynn" 1 and 2]; "On Dating The *Battle of Maldon*," *Nottingham Medieval Studies* 27 (1983), 1–22, esp. 8–14.

Status and "race" are frequently interdependent. "Nationality" is thus a basic concept; but defining it in onomastic terms is complex. For Western Europe generally, the evidential value of personal names is both created and limited by the linguistic and cultural characteristics of the stocks from which they were drawn. Throughout this area (with the partial exception of the Celtic lands), two name stocks were dominant during the Middle Ages: the Germanic, spread by the Great Migrations,[4] and the "Christian," taken from saints and from biblical characters.[5] With the former, and to some extent with the latter, sound changes followed the usual dialect patterns—that is, the major split between North- and West-Germanic and, within each

---

[4]For a general introduction see H. B. Woolf, *The Old Germanic Principles of Name-Giving* (Baltimore, 1939); see also Adolph Bach, *Deutsche Namenkunde*, 3 vols. in 5 (Heidelberg, 1952–56), vol. 1, *Personennamen*, and Gottfried Schramm, *Namenschatz und Dichtersprache. Studien zu den zweigliedrigen Personennamen der Germanen* (Göttingen, 1957). For specific reference to OE see *OEPN* and Bo Seltén, *The Anglo-Saxon Heritage in Middle English Personal Names*, 1, LSE 43 (Lund, 1972), pp. 23–24, 70–81. For Continental styles, the many works that may be consulted include, especially, Ernst Förstemann, *Altdeutsches Namenbuch*, rev. ed., 3 vols. (Bonn, 1900–16), vol. 1, *Personennamen* [hereafter cited as Förstemann], together with Henning Kaufmann, *Altdeutsche Personennamen, Ergänzungsband* (Munich, 1968) [hereafter, *Ergänzungsband*]; *Polyptyque de l'abbaye de Saint-Germain des Prés,* ed. Auguste Longnon, 2 vols. (Paris, 1886–95) [hereafter, Longnon], esp. 1:259–382; Joseph Mansion, *Oud-gentsche Naamkunde; bijdrage tot de kennis van het oud-nederlandsch* (The Hague, 1924) [hereafter, Mansion], and C. Tavernier-Vereecken, *Gentse Naamkunde van ca. 1000 tot 1252. Een Bijdrage tot de kennis van het oudste Middelnederlands* (Tongres, 1968); Schlaug I and II; Henning Kaufmann, *Untersuchungen zu altdeutschen Rufnamen* (Munich, 1965); Morlet I; Heinrich Tiefenbach, *Xanten, Essen, Köln: Untersuchungen zur Nordgrenze des Althochdeutschen an niederrheinischen Personennamen des neunten bis elften Jahrhunderts* (Göttingen, 1984) [hereafter, Tiefenbach], with extensive bibliography. Much anthroponymical information has lately been emerging also from the study of commemorative documents being carried out at Freiburg and at Münster, e.g., *Liber memorialis von Remiremont*, ed. Eduard Hlawitschka, Karl Schmid, and Gerd Tellenbach, MGH, Libri memoriales 1, 2 pts. (Dublin, 1970); *Die Klostergemeinschaft von Fulda im früheren Mittelalter,* ed. Karl Schmid, 3 vols. in 5, Münstersche Mittelalter-Schriften 8 (Munich, 1978), with extensive bibliography; *Das Verbrüderungsbuch der Abtei Reichenau,* ed. Johanne Autenrieth, Dieter Geuenich, and Karl Schmid, MGH, Libri memoriales et necrologia, n.s. 1 (Hanover, 1979).

[5]See, e.g., Longnon 1:254–58 and Morlet II; but in this sector the appropriate reference book is often a dictionary of saints. The balance between Germanic and "Christian" naming varied by social class and by date. In Frankish Gaul, for instance, the latter receded until ca. 1000 but then recovered ground, never again to lose it (see also below, p. 20 and n. 50.)

sector, the manifold subdivisions into regional and tribal dialects. OE *Ēadgār*, for instance, corresponds to Continental West-Germanic (CG) *Audger/Otger* and to the fairly rare Sc *Auðgeirr*.[6] Many forms can in this way be tied dialectally to specific peoples or areas. Dialect apart, individual items varied in distribution, some peculiar to certain areas and others characteristic of certain social ranks. (For the "Christian" stock, "item" means "name." For the Germanic stock, it primarily denotes one of the "themes" or elements used—as will be explained more fully below—in forming the characteristic compound names, and so only secondarily does it denote a "full name," of whatever structure.)

Distribution or phonology, and with luck both, should thus allow an item, or at least a given form of it, to be localized. Happily, this is often so, but uncertainties occur. Varied pronunciations are masked by latinized documentary spellings. Some Germanic items, and proportionately more "Christian" ones, were so widespread as to be scarcely localizable, especially when only latinized forms are available. A recent attempt more closely to define some apparently Continental name forms recorded in twelfth- and thirteenth-century King's Lynn encountered a barely differentiated Low-German usage current from Flanders to the Baltic coast.[7] Yet, despite falling short of ideal precision, name study offers some modest certainties. As the term "Continental" has just implied, medieval England had, within the West European context, a distinctively "Insular" name usage, reflecting its separate history.

Political and cultural isolation joined with sound change to differentiate English naming from that of any continental Germanic people. Whereas in parts of the Continent, in Frankish Gaul especially, "Christian" names were current from early times on, in England they remained—except among churchmen—rare until after the Norman Conquest.[8] The early name stock here was almost purely West-Germanic, as brought over by the "Angles, Jutes and Saxons." Just a few fresh items, such as *Cǣd-* (= British *Catu-* "battle"), were adopted from the Britons and integrated into the traditional

---

[6]For OE *Ēadgār* see *OEPN*, pp. 12–13, 165, and *PNDB*, p. 229. For CG *Audger/Otger* see Förstemann, cols. 192–93; Longnon 1:286, 313; Schlaug II, p. 136; and Morlet I, 43b. For Sc *Auðgeirr* see *SPLY*, p. 38.

[7]See "King's Lynn" 1, pp. 56–58, and "King's Lynn" 2, p. 77.

[8]See *PNDB*, pp. 30–31, and n. 5 above.

Germanic patterns.[9] The OE system deployed, as did all Germanic systems, names of several types, the most characteristic formation being a two-element ("dithematic") compound. The elements ("themes") were based on substantival and adjectival roots originally carrying "heroic" meanings,[10] some figuring equally as first element ("prototheme") or as second ("deuterotheme"), others confined to a single function. The prototheme stock was richer and more open to innovation than that of deuterothemes. Typical OE themes included: *Ælf-* "elf," *Æðel-* "noble," *Beorht-/-beorht* "radiant," *Beorn-/-beorn* "warrior," *Burg-/-burg* (f.) "defense," *Cūð-* "renowned," *Cyne-* "royal," *Ēad-* "wealth," *Ealh-* "temple," *-flǣd* (f.) "beauty," *Gār-/-gār* "spear," *-gifu* (f.) "gift," *Gūð-* "battle," *-gȳð* (f.) "battle," *Helm-/-helm* "protection," *Hild-/-hild* (f.) "battle," *Ōs-* "god," *Rǣd-/-rǣd* "counsel," *Sige-/-sige* "victory," *Wīg-/-wīg* "battle," and so on.[11] Women's names, hardly distinguished from men's semantically, were characterized by second elements that were feminine (or feminized) in grammatical gender.[12] From this element stock, name forms were generated by permutation and recombination. Some elements, like *-flǣd*, had by OE times lost nearly all linkage with current vocabulary; most became, in time, divorced from their "dictionary meanings," which played little part in the name-creating permutations. In addition, deuterothemes became obscured by lack of stress. (In OE, as in all Germanic languages, word accent fell mainly on initial syllables.)

What governed name creation and name choice was family relationship, for, although in the settlement period and for at least seven or eight centuries afterwards hereditary surnames were unknown,[13] kinship by no means

---

[9]See, e.g., K. H. Jackson, *Language and History in Early Britain* (Edinburgh, 1953), p. 244.

[10]See, e.g., Woolf, *Principles*, passim; *OEPN*, pp. 4–43; Schramm, *Namenschatz*, passim; and Seltén, *Anglo-Saxon Heritage* 1:70–81.

[11]See further, on this and other topics, the chapter on onomastics to be contributed by the present writer to vol. 1 of the projected *Cambridge History of the English Language.* For current work on all aspects of Old and Middle English personal naming, see the annual bibliographies published in *Nomina.*

[12]See Maria Boehler, *Die altenglischen Frauennamen*, Germanische Studien 98 (Berlin, 1930), and Schramm, *Namenschatz*, pp. 120–43.

[13]For a conspectus of the rise of English family names see P. H. Reaney, *The Origin of English Surnames* (London, 1967; reissued 1980); but, for some reservations as to the authoritativeness of this, see the review in *Nomina* 4 (1980), 88–90. Detailed treatments, from historical rather than etymological points of view, are offered by the county volumes

went unmarked. A family of any pretension adopted a characteristic proto-theme: when the *ASC* annal for 755 tells of a feud between the princes Cynewulf and Cyneheard, the shared *Cyne-* emphasizes their cousinhood. Elements from both sides of an ancestry might be re-combined, bringing several protothemes into play. Sometimes a range of alliterating protothemes was adopted: in later centuries, the royal house of Wessex, for instance, permutated *Ælf-*, *Æðel-*, *Ēad-*, and *Ecg-*, all alliterating on mid-front vowels. Such patterns offer pointers to and confirmation of possible kinship.

With so flexible a system, name fashions tended gradually to change, so that, to a limited extent, name forms may also suggest or confirm approximate datings of their bearers and of documents in which they figure. As yet, however, the trends have not been fully documented. It has been said, of English and of Continental usages alike, that by the eleventh century the original variety of elements and of combinations had been much reduced, so that late OE naming had become more stereotyped than that of the settlement period.[14] Among aristocrats this may have been true, but for English people of more modest rank it was not: late OE and early post-Conquest records reveal that the name choices of peasantry and towns-people were varied and innovative, within traditional patterns.[15]

In other ways, too, questions of rank and of dating prove awkwardly entangled. Alongside the "full" dithematic names other types were current, some based on a single element, perhaps with a diminutive or other suffix,

---

of the English Surnames Series, those so far available being: George Redmonds, *Yorkshire, West Riding* (Chichester, 1973); R. A. McKinley, *Norfolk and Suffolk Surnames in the Middle Ages* (Chichester, 1975), *The Surnames of Oxfordshire* (London, 1977), *The Surnames of Lancashire* (London, 1981), and *The Surnames of Sussex* (forthcoming [published Oxford, 1988]).

[14]See F. M. Stenton, "Personal Names in Place-Names," in *Introduction to the Survey of English Place-Names*, ed. Allen Mawer and F. M. Stenton, English Place-Name Society 1/1 (1924), pp. 165–89, esp. 176–79. For Continental fashions see, e.g., P. Aebischer, "L'anthroponymie wallonne d'après quelques anciens cartulaires," *Bulletin du dictionnaire wallon* 13 (1924), 73–168, esp. 132–41, and G. T. Beech, "Les noms de personne poitevins du IXe au XIIe siècle," *Revue internationale d'onomastique* 26 (1974), 81–100, esp. 86–87, 90–91.

[15]See Olof von Feilitzen, "Some Unrecorded Old and Middle English Personal Names," *NoB* 33 (1945), 69–98; P. H. Reaney, "Notes on the Survival of Old English Personal Names in Middle English," *Studier i Modern Språkvetenskap* 18 (1953), 84–112; and Seltén, *Anglo-Saxon Heritage*, 2, RSL 73 (Lund, 1979). Landholders' names recorded in the 1066 stratum of Domesday Book (*PNDB*) likewise fail to bear out Stenton's assertion.

others derived from nicknames of various kinds.[16] Some were shortened "pet" forms or childish simplifications based on dithematic names. Occasionally, use of alternative names for one individual reveals the connection, as with the *Saba* used of their father by sons of the early seventh-century King Sǣbeorht of Essex, and the *Totta* found alongside *Torhthelm* for a mid-eighth-century bishop of the Mercians.[17] In early OE times not even kings disdained public use of such forms; but in later documents nobles normally figure under dithematic ones. Peasant nomenclature, as shown in manumission records, continued to make free use of short forms and nicknames as well as of dithematic names.[18] A one-time belief that any short form referring to a noble must date from pre-Alfredian times has lately been challenged on the grounds that informality cannot be assumed to be peculiar to the lower classes.[19] That said, some differences between upper- and lower-class naming remain likely, with non-noble nickname formations based not on the "heroic" elements but on roots with pejorative implications (such as *Dod-*, usually taken to mean "heap; clod").[20]

Formal and distributional criteria thus together define certain name usages as OE and as characteristic of certain periods and certain ranks; but neither criterion is absolute. Phonological rules for determining etymology

---

[16]See Mats Redin, *Studies on Uncompounded Personal Names in Old English* (Uppsala, 1919), now, however, outdated. See also Boehler, *Frauennamen*, pp. 206–39; *PNDB*, passim; *OEPN*, pp. 58–79; and von Feilitzen, "OE Uncompounded Personal Names."

[17]*Bede's Ecclesiastical History of the English People*, ed. Bertram Colgrave and R. A. B. Mynors (Oxford, 1969), p. 152; John Earle, *A Hand-Book to the Land-Charters, and Other Saxonic Documents* (Oxford, 1888), pp. 38, 307 (I wish to thank Catherine Coutts for help with documenting *Totta* and other OE short forms). See also Redin, *Uncompounded Personal Names,* pp. 70–71, and *OEPN*, pp. 37, 76.

[18]Relevant published manumission lists include those in Earle, *Hand-Book*, pp. 276–77. See further Woolf, *Principles*, pp. 139–42, and A. R. Rumble, "The Status of Written Sources in English Onomastics," *Nomina* 8 (1984), 41–56, esp. 50–51.

[19]See Redin, *Uncompounded Personal Names*, pp. 184–89, and cf. Gillian Fellows Jensen, "Some Problems of a Maverick Anthroponymist," in *The Study of the Personal Names of the British Isles*, ed. Herbert Voitl, Klaus Forster, and John Insley (Erlangen, 1976), pp. 43–55, esp. 47–49, and intervention by von Feilitzen on pp. 57–58. Calculations based on *PNDB* likewise counsel skepticism towards the older view.

[20]Not a definitive interpretation, but see, e.g., *PNDB*, pp. 223–25, s.n. *Dod(d)a*, and Seltén, *Anglo-Saxon Heritage* 1:73.

are, as will appear, complicated by tendencies to anglicize alien introductions. As for distributions—whether geographical, social, or chronological —the incompleteness of extant records, Insular and Continental alike, forbids dogmatism. OE naming offers, nonetheless, some certainties and many strong probabilities.

In pre-Conquest times, the main foreign element injected into English naming was Scandinavian. From the late ninth century on, the OE stock was supplemented and variegated, in some districts rivaled, by forms and styles introduced by the Vikings who settled in the Danelaw.[21] Phonologically and in other ways, the Vikings' North-Germanic language differed from Old English. Name fashions also differed. Although many elements were shared (but with each language having its distinctive forms), some that were particularly favored by Scandinavians had been unknown in pre-Viking England, *Þór-* and *Ketil-/-ke(ti)ll* being prime examples. Sc fashions also ran far more to short single-root names, especially those of nickname type, such as *Krákr* "raven" and *Nebbi* "nose."[22] Discrimination between the two stocks is not always as straightforward as such a summary makes it sound. Some items were, like some everyday vocabulary, common to both languages and therefore ambivalent, at least in late or latinized spellings. Thus *Siward(us)* and *Wimund(us)* can, with equal propriety, be referred either to OE *Sigew(e)ard* and *Wīgmund* or to Sc *Sigvarð* and *Vígmundr*.[23] Anglicizing tendencies blurred the pattern further. Because the two languages allowed some mutual comprehensibility, English speakers could deduce the native equivalents for many Sc items and use them to replace the latter. This practice—apparently

---

[21]See *NPE* and *ZEN*; Olof von Feilitzen, "Notes on Some Scandinavian Personal Names in English Twelfth-Century Records," *Anthroponymica Suecana* 6 (1965), 52–68; and *SPLY*. For Sc personal naming in general see Magnus Lundgren and Erik Brate, *Svenska Personnamn från Medeltiden* (Uppsala, 1892–1915), now being superseded by *Sveriges Medeltida Personnamn* (Stockholm, 1967–); E. H. Lind, *Norsk-isländska Dopnamn och Fingerade Namn från Medeltiden* (Uppsala, 1905–15, supplement Oslo, 1931) and *Norsk-isländska Personbinamn från Medeltiden, samlade och utgivna med förklaringar* (Uppsala, 1920–21); Gunnar Knudsen, Marius Kristenssen, and Rikard Hornby, *Danmarks gamle Personnavne*, pt. 1 (2 vols.) *Fornavne* (Copenhagen, 1936–48), and pt. 2 (2 vols.) *Tilnavne* (Copenhagen, 1949–64).

[22]*SPLY*, pp. 181, 201–02.

[23]See *PNDB*, pp. 361–63, 413; *SPLY*, pp. 236–39, 337–38; and Seltén, *Anglo-Saxon Heritage* 2:147, 167. See also n. 57 below.

almost *de rigueur* in the less heavily settled Southern Danelaw—meant that Sc *Ás-* was replaced by OE *Ōs-*, *Geir-/-geirr* by *Gār-/-gār*, *Ketil-/-ke(ti)ll* by *Cytel-/-cytel*, *Stein-/-steinn* by *Stān-/-stān*, and so on, even though several of these items had functioned in previous OE usage only as common vocabulary, not as name elements.[24] Sc endings often gave way to OE equivalents: Sc *Feggi*, for instance, gave AScand *Fegga* (Middle English *Fegge*); OE *Sǣlida* probably represents AScand *Sǽliði*; and so on.[25]

A Danelaw name corpus, especially one from the south of that area, usually offers many ambivalent forms, some originally alike in both languages, others anglicized, as is illustrated by some names preserved in *Liber Eliensis*. Almost one quarter of the stock concerned (about one hundred names, all masculine and all belonging to late tenth-century landholders within Ely's sphere of influence) consists of Sc forms which, far from occurring in self-contained groups, constantly appear in families also using OE ones. Cited in normalized spelling, examples would be as follow: *Ælfnōð* (OE) was a son of *Áni* (Sc), *Ásketill* (Sc) a son of *Saxferð* (OE), and *Grím* (Sc) a son of *Wine* (OE); each of two *Oswīgs* (OE) had a brother with a Sc name, one being *Ulf* and the other *Úfi*, and *Bóndi* (Sc) had brothers with the OE names *Ælfstān* and *Æðelstān*, showing a shared second element.[26] Ambivalent forms amount to 12% of the stock; given the bicultural background, Danelaw families might, on occasion—like some present-day bilinguals— have consciously chosen such names. Once the first generation of settlement was past, name etymology, however unambiguous, had only a limited bearing on an individual's "race" or "blood" and a greater one on the cultural milieu in which his or her family lived. On the other hand, any family that used a succession of purely or even predominantly Sc names may, without too much danger, be presumed likely to be of actual part-Viking descent.

Thus, in an English context of the tenth century or after, a Sc name implies for its bearer and his or her kin at the very least a Viking-influenced

---

[24]See, e.g., *SPLY*, pp. lxxi, lxxii–lxxiii, lxxx.

[25]See *SPLY*, pp. xcix–c. The related range of possibilities in both languages, plus anglicizing tendencies, can make particular etymologies matters of opinion; for *Fegga* see von Feilitzen, "Notes on Some Scandinavian Personal Names," p. 54, and *SPLY*, p. 81; for *Sǣlida*, alternatively to be taken as a case of element substitution, see *PNDB*, p. 353, and Seltén, *Anglo-Saxon Heritage* 2:134.

[26]See Clark, "*Maldon*," pp. 9–14, based on *Liber Eliensis*, ed. E. O. Blake, Camden 3rd ser., 92 (London, 1962), pp. 72–142.

cultural background; that in turn implies—at all events until after the more diffuse Cnutian settlement[27]—an origin somewhere in the Danelaw. Certain forms suggest narrower localizations, because regionalized studies beginning to be undertaken show them as geographically limited in currency. For instance, *Anand*, *Bóndi*, and *Tóki* were, until well into ME times, used frequently in Norfolk but seldom at any period in Lancashire (the former two being rare also in Lincolnshire). On the other hand, *Orm*, *Steinolf*, and *Walþeof* were common in Lancashire but rare in Norfolk.[28] Distributions partly followed settlement patterns, with East Anglia colonized mainly by Danes but the Northwest largely by Norwegians, many of whom had come via Dublin; but English usage was by no means governed by such factors, and its details have to be established empirically. Some Sc names were correlated with social ranks: a delicate matter to investigate, depending as it does upon chronology of fashions. In the immediate aftermath of the Viking settlements, Sc names recorded in England usually—like those found in *Liber Eliensis*—belonged to landholders, hence the part that they played in place-name creation. From the 1020s on, forms whose spellings suggest pronunciations that developed only after ca. 1000 marked people recently arrived from the Sc homelands, whether as conquerors and colonists or as traders.[29]

Of special interest to prosopographers are cases where name study can help assess the authenticity of doubtful materials and traditions.[30] Such cases include, for instance, the legend of three hermits—two brothers and a sister—supposedly martyred during a Viking attack of ca. 870 on the site later to be that of Thorney Abbey.[31] The only extant Life which mentions

---

[27]As yet, the cultural repercussions of the Cnutian hegemony remain obscure, but see John Insley, "Some Scandinavian Personal Names from South-West England," *NoB* 70 (1982), 77–93, esp. 77–78, and "Some Scandinavian Personal Names from South-West England from Post-Conquest Records," *SAS* 3 (1985), 23–58, esp. 44–53.

[28]See John Insley, "Regional Variation in Scandinavian Personal Nomenclature in England," *Nomina* 3 (1979), 52–60.

[29]See Insley, "Regional Variation," pp. 57–58; also his articles in *NoB*, pp. 80, 82, and *SAS*, pp. 45–46.

[30]See Olof Brattö, *L'Anthroponymie et la diplomatique*, Göteborgs Universitets Årsskrift 62/3 (Gothenburg, 1956).

[31]See Cecily Clark, "Notes on a *Life* of Three Thorney Saints: Thancred, Torhtred and Tova," *Proceedings of the Cambridge Antiquarian Society* 69 (1979), 45–52.

them dates from the late eleventh century and claims as its main authority Thorney's foundation charter, a difficult document dating at best from the 970s and now accessible only in late medieval copies. All three are named in *The Resting-Places of English Saints,* but that compilation, datable after 1013, presumably recorded uncritically each house's claims as to the relics it possessed. A skeptic might therefore accuse these thinly documented "saints" of being Thorney Abbey's answer to neighboring Crowland's St. Guðlac and his sister Pege. Their names at first sight certainly look odd. The least so is *Torhtred*: the element *Torht*- seems to have been an exclusively OE one, and names involving it are adequately recorded (one is the *Torhthelm* cited above) and, apart from one doubtful case in Domesday Book (DB), appropriately early.[32] *Þancred* is more dubious: not only does it resemble the CG *Tancred* current in eleventh-century Normandy and thereabouts, but OE names in *Þanc*- are in general poorly evidenced.[33] The sister's name, *Tova*, is most suspect of all, insofar as its obvious etymon appears to be Sc *Tófa*, impossible in a pre-Viking English context.[34] Poor documentation makes it less feasible to establish a full list of OE women's names than of men's, but short name forms were current for both sexes (St. Guðlac's sister was called *Pege*, as already noted, and his mother, *Tette*), and they often represented playful abbreviation of dithematic ones.[35] Within a family group, as we have observed, a set of elements might be permutated; the brothers' names here share the element *-rǣd*/*-red*. In this light *Tova*, or rather an un-latinized OE **Tofe*, could represent reduction of a name combining *Torht*- with a feminine deuterotheme containing *-f-*, perhaps **Torhtflǣd* or **Torhtgifu*.[36] Speculative though this possibility is, it warns us against lightly dismissing the name *Tova,* and *Torhtred* and *Þancred* with it, as impossible for the 870s.

---

[32]See the relevant entries in W. G. Searle, *Onomasticon Anglo-Saxonicum* (Cambridge, 1897), for the shortcomings of which see Olof von Feilitzen, "Planning a New Old English Onomasticon," in *Personal Names,* ed. Voitl, pp. 16–39; also Boehler, *Frauennamen,* pp. 120–21, and *PNDB,* p. 387. The element *Torht*- seems peculiar to OE name styles; see *OEPN,* p. 37.

[33]See, e.g., Searle, *Onomasticon.*

[34]See *NPE,* pp. 140–41, and *ZEN,* p. 83.

[35]See Boehler, *Frauennamen,* pp. 206–39, esp. 227, 231–32.

[36]See Boehler, *Frauennamen,* pp. 120–21.

Other foreign elements also appeared sporadically in pre-Conquest English naming. "Christian" names occurred mainly among churchmen, such as Archbishop Theodore and Alfred's adviser, John the Old Saxon. CG names were rather more frequent and, because of the close kinship between the WG dialects, now provoke philological problems analogous to those besetting AScand names. Some are revealed as Continental not simply by distributional or phonological criteria but, more conclusively, by their bearers' biographies. For example, the first abbot of Winchester's New Minster (Hyde Abbey), bearer of the un-English name *Grimbald*,[37] was Flemish by birth and a former monk of Saint-Bertin.[38] Two goldsmiths and die-cutters flourishing in England from the mid- to late eleventh century are identifiable as "German" partly by their names, *Theodoric* and *Otto*—the latter with its specifically CG consonant pattern,[39] and the former probably non-English in distribution[40]—but also by the style of coin dies they produced.[41] CG names were, in general, frequent among the moneyers of AS England and, in particular, among those responsible for the so-called "St. Edmund memorial coinage."[42] No definitive explanation has yet been ad-

---

[37]See Förstemann, col. 670; Longnon 1:325; Mansion, p. 63; Schlaug II, p. 97; Morlet I, 115a; and Tiefenbach, p. 359. There seems no evidence for *Grīm-* as a native OE prototheme.

[38]Janet Bately, "Grimbald of St Bertin's," *Medium Ævum* 35 (1966), 1–10.

[39]Spelled in Domesday Book and elsewhere as *Otho/Otto* (see *PNDB*, p. 334 and n. 1), this form is distinct both from Late OE *Od(d)a* (which *PNDB*, p. 333, refers to multiple origins) and from the latinized French *Odo* (Morlet I, 45b); the unvoiced and geminated medial consonant is typical of Low-German hypocoristics (see Kaufmann, *Rufnamen*, pp. 15, 17, 21, 118; also Mansion, pp. 62, 64; and C. Marynissen, *Hypokoristische Suffixen in oudnederlandse Persoonsnamen inz. de -z- en -l-suffixen*, 2 vols. [Diss. Leuven, 1971], 1:296–307, esp. 301–03).

[40]This compound, although common throughout the CG area (see Förstemann, cols. 1445–48, and esp. Erik Rooth, *Saxonica: Beiträge zur niedersächsischen Sprachgeschichte*, RSL 44 [Lund, 1949], pp. 143–61), occurred in OE usage, if at all, only in early times; see *PNDB*, pp. 383–84, and *OEPN*, p. 36 (examples cited in *ELPN* refer to the moneyer).

[41]See A. E. Packe, "The Coinage of the Norman Kings," *Numismatic Chronicle*, 3rd ser., 13 (1893), 129–45, esp. 140–41, and F. Spicer, "The Coinage of William I and William II," *Numismatic Chronicle*, 4th ser., 4 (1904), 144–79 and 245–87, esp. 148–49, 247. I am grateful to Dr. Fran Colman, University of Edinburgh, for bringing these names to my notice.

[42]See V. J. Smart, "Moneyers' Names on the Anglo-Saxon Coinage," *Nomina* 3 (1979), 20–28, esp. 22; "The Moneyers of St Edmund," *Hikuin* 11 (1985), 83–90; and "Scandi-

vanced, and any acceptable one will need to use numismatic as well as onomastic evidence.

Two further CG names found in late eleventh-century England belonged to master masons (or architects). A man called *Teinfrith* was described in the Confessor's writ which invested him with certain estates connected with Westminster Abbey as a "churchwright"—presumably a master mason employed to work on the abbey church.[43] His is evidently a CG name: familiar though the common noun *þegn* was in OE, the corresponding prototheme, current though not frequent from Saxony to Frankish Gaul, cannot confidently be claimed also for England.[44] Given the Norman affinities of the abbey's architecture, at variance with the evidently OE names, *Leofsige Duddesunu* and *Godwine Greatsyd*, borne by the other master masons known there,[45] a Continental background for *Teinfrith* would be appropriate. An analogous case concerns a name variously spelled *Blitherus, Blittære,* or *Blvtere,* whose bearer, alternatively called *Blize,* was described in a late eleventh-century narrative from St. Augustine's Abbey, Canterbury, as "praestantissimus artificum magister, templique spectabilis dictator."[46] Although opinions have differed, evidence for an OE name element

---

navians, Celts and Germans in Anglo-Saxon England: The Evidence of the Moneyers' Names," in *Anglo-Saxon Monetary History: Essays in Memory of Michael Dolley*, ed. M. A. S. Blackburn (Leicester, 1986), pp. 171–84.

[43]See Richard Gem, "The Romanesque Rebuilding of Westminster Abbey," in *Proceedings of the Battle Conference on Anglo-Norman Studies III, 1980*, ed. R. Allen Brown (Woodbridge, 1981), pp. 33–60 and 203–07, esp. 39 and 204–05; I am grateful to Dr. Gem for bringing this name to my notice.

[44]See Olof von Feilitzen, "Some Continental-Germanic Personal Names in England," in *Early English and Norse Studies Presented to Hugh Smith*, ed. Arthur Brown and Peter Foote (London, 1963), pp. 46–61, esp. 57–58. For CG names in *Thegan-/Thegin-* see Förstemann, cols. 1406–08; Mansion, p. 169; Tavernier-Vereecken, *Gentse naamkunde*, pp. 74–75; Schlaug I, p. 82, and II, p. 159; Morlet I, 66a; no forms in *-frid(us)* seem noted.

[45]For *Godwine* and *Lēofsige*, both among the most frequent of Late OE names, see *PNDB*, pp. 269–73, 315. The patronymic *Duddesunu*, latinized as *filius Duddi*, involves the obscure, probably plebeian OE *Dudd(a)* (see n. 20 above). For Godwine's byname, the spelling *Greatsyd* varies with *Gretsið*, the latter being interpretable as "long journey"; but see the Winchester name *Godwinus Gretsud*, where von Feilitzen took the byname to mean "big purse," from OE *sēod* "money-bag" ("Winton Domesday," p. 212).

[46]Goscelin, *Historia translationis S. Augustini*, in Migne, PL 115, col. 17; *The Domesday Monachorum of Christ Church, Canterbury*, ed. D. C. Douglas (London, 1944), p. 90. Dr.

Bliδ- is thin,[47] whereas the corresponding CG item is well attested, the particular compound *Blit-harius/-herus* being recorded from many areas, including northern France and Flanders.[48] The short form *Blize* suggests a similar derivation, because diminutives in *-z-*, frequent in Flanders,[49] were unknown in native OE forms.

The Norman Conquest and settlement rapidly swelled the proportion of Continental forms current in English naming, because the prestige associated with the settlers' customs and fashions inspired widespread imitation. The Normans and their followers, recruited from the whole area extending from Brittany to Flanders, mainly favored Frankish names, in speech often gallicized. Following Continental fashion, they used "Christian" names somewhat more freely than the pre-Conquest English had done.[50] The Normans themselves also used Sc forms reflecting the Viking element in their ancestry,[51] together with a few Irish forms introduced by Northmen previously based in Dublin.[52] The Bretons partly retained their Celtic names, some of which had passed into wider French use.[53]

Gem, to whom I am again grateful for bringing the name to my notice, has a study of the personage concerned in *Romanesque and Gothic: Essays for George Zarnecki*, 2 vols. (Woodbridge, 1987), 1:83–101.

[47]See von Feilitzen, "Winton Domesday," p. 151, n. 3. The sole possible instance noted of a pre-Conquest English *Blīδ-here* is preserved only in a late medieval copy. (The form cited by Ekwall, *ELPN*, p. 22, is irrelevant because it shows French effacement of the intervocalic dental.)

[48]Förstemann, cols. 313–16, esp. 314–15, and *Ergänzungsband*, p. 64; Longnon 1:294; Morlet I, 58b–59a; and Tiefenbach, p. 350.

[49]Marynissen, *Hypokoristische Suffixen*, pp. 124–25, cites a form *Blizo*, referring to a man from Bruges; see von Feilitzen's comments on the gallicized *Blizot* in "CG Personal Names," p. 48.

[50]Men's names listed in the index to *Recueil des actes des ducs de Normandie de 911 à 1066*, ed. Marie Fauroux (Caen, 1961), include about a score of "Christian" forms; cf. the more exiguous list in *PNDB*, pp. 30–31. See also n. 5 above.

[51]See Jean Adigard des Gautries, *Les noms de personnes scandinaves en Normandie de 911 à 1066*, NG 11 (Lund, 1954).

[52]See, e.g., Lucien Musset, "Pour l'étude comparative de deux fondations politiques de Vikings: Le royaume d'York et le duché de Rouen," *Northern History* 10 (1975), 40–54, esp. 48.

[53]See, e.g., André Chédeville, "L'immigration bretonne dans le royaume de France du XIe au début du XIVe siècle," *Annales de Bretagne* 81 (1974), 301–43, esp. 304.

Ampler survival of contemporary documentation makes post-Conquest processes of change more accessible to investigation than those consequent on the Viking settlements. Only for a short while did correlation between name and "nationality" survive to any degree which would allow us to assume that bearers of Continental names were, for the most part, recent settlers. During this time, name patterns revealed interplay between the two camps. Although little specific evidence survives to confirm general assertions of frequent Norman intermarriage with the English, several baronial and knightly couples do appear in which one (usually the husband) has a Continental name but the other an Insular (that is, OE or AScand) one.[54] Two of Henry I's numerous mistresses had the unambiguously English name *Edith* (OE *Ēadgȳð*); one, a daughter of the Cumbrian magnate Forne (the name is AScand), subsequently married into the d'Oilly family that furnished the hereditary castellans of Oxford.[55] In other spheres, too, name patterns reflected AN cooperation. The Northumbrian monastic revival of the 1080s, for instance, was led by three monks from Evesham, one of whom, described as a former knight, bore the CG name *Reinfrid(us)*; the other two had the typically OE names *Aldwine* and *Ælfwīg*.[56]

As with pre-Conquest Sc and CG introductions, various overlaps and ambiguities occurred: *Wimundus* again constitutes a prime example.[57] Problems and some possible approaches to them are illustrated by the late eleventh-century form *Aiulfus*, of interest to prosopographers because it was borne by a sheriff about whose background little is known.[58] The name is

---

[54]See Cecily Clark, "Women's Names in Post-Conquest England: Observations and Speculations," *Speculum* 53 (1978), 223–51, esp. 227–30 (repr. below, pp. 65–102).

[55]See G. E. C[okayne] et al., *Complete Peerage*, 13 vols. in 14 (London, 1910–59), 9:108–09, appendices. For the name *Ēadgȳð* see Boehler, *Frauennamen*, pp. 58–59, and *PNDB*, pp. 231–32; for *Forne* (Sc *Forni*) see *SPLY*, pp. 84–85.

[56]*Symeonis monachi opera omnia,* ed. Thomas Arnold, 2 vols. (London, 1882–85), 1:108–09. For *Reinfrid(us)*, among the most frequent of CG names, see Förstemann, cols. 1227–28; Longnon 1:358; and Morlet I, 184ab. For OE *Ælfwīg* and *Aldwine* (West-Saxon *Ealdwine*) see *OEPN*, pp. 5–6, and *PNDB*, pp. 157–58 (s.n. *Al-wig*) and 242.

[57]See n. 23 above, and, further, Förstemann, col. 1587; Morlet I, 223b; and Adigard des Gautries, *Les noms de personnes scandinaves*, pp. 236–38, 368–69.

[58]See Cecily Clark, "Starting from *Youlthorpe* (East Riding of Yorkshire): An Onomastic Circular Tour," *Journal of the English Place-Name Society* 16 (1983–84), 25–37. See also Judith Green, "The Sheriffs of William the Conqueror," in *Anglo-Norman Studies V, Pro-*

uncommon: at one time usually ascribed to OE or AScand origins, it also possessed close CG parallels.[59] Apart from references in DB and elsewhere specifically to the sheriff, English examples also occur, mainly in both strata of DB, without byname or other qualifier. At first sight, its being borne by a post-Conquest sheriff seems to favor a CG etymology, especially as this Aiulf had a brother called *Hunfridus*, a name which at this date was fairly certainly CG.[60] Yet not all the Conqueror's sheriffs had Continental names;[61] and the picture is further complicated by pre-Conquest instances of the name *Aiulf*, at one point connected with lands later linked with the sheriff's estates. The Aiulf in question had a son called *Edmund*, with the prototheme *Ēad-* noted as specifically English. This context, although explaining the attempts to devise an English, or at least AScand, etymology for *Aiulf*, is onomastically irrelevant, because various landholders *tempore regis Edwardi* bore CG names,[62] and in pre-Conquest times such men, even though themselves of Continental birth, would have had little reason to avoid giving a son a traditional OE name. (A goldsmith with the CG name *Witso* had a son called *Lēofstān*, who in turn named his own sons *Witso* and *Edward*.[63]) The OE etymology once proposed for *Aiulf* is, at all events, exposed

---

ceedings of the Battle Conference, 1982, ed. R. Allen Brown (Woodbridge, 1983), pp. 129–45, esp. 130, 140. I am grateful to Dr. Green, University of Belfast, and Dr. Brian Golding, University of Southampton, for bringing this name to my notice.

[59]For the AScand etymology suggested see *NPE*, p. 36, and *ZEN*, p. 31; also *SPLY*, p. 77. For the OE etymology see *PNDB*, p. 191, s.n. *Æðelwulf*. For the well-attested CG *A(g)iulf(us)* see Förstemann, cols. 26–27, with *Ergänzungsband*, pp. 20–22; also Longnon 1:278; Mansion, p. 159; Schlaug II, p. 39; Morlet I, 22a; and, further, Clark, "*Youlthorpe*," pp. 27–28 and related notes on p. 34.

[60]For the OE prototheme *Hūn-* see *OEPN* and *PNDB*, p. 295; but the instances of *Hūnfrið* listed by Searle all antedate the mid-ninth century. For the better attested CG *Hunfrid* and *Hundfrid* see Förstemann, cols. 929, 932; Longnon 1:339; Morlet I, 140b, 141b; and Tiefenbach, p. 368.

[61]Green, "Sheriffs," pp. 130–33.

[62]*PNDB*, pp. 26–29.

[63]*Chronicon abbatiae Rameseiensis*, ed. W. D. Macray (London, 1886), p. 245. For the OE names *Ēadw(e)ard* and *Lēofstān* see *PNDB*, pp. 237, 316; for CG *Witso/Wizo* see Förstemann, col. 1627, with *Ergänzungsband*, pp. 411–12; also Mansion, p. 95; Kaufmann, *Rufnamen*, pp. 155–57; Morlet I, 22b; Tiefenbach, p. 387; and Marynissen, *Hypokoristische Suffixen*, pp. 363–64, 366, 369.

as untenable. Partly on distributional grounds, the AScand etymology acceptable for the form *Eiulf* is less acceptable for *Aiulf*, and most instances of the latter therefore seem best referred to CG origins.

The early post-Conquest period soon saw the native English copying the new settlers' Continental name styles so enthusiastically that by about 1200 the original Insular forms had become rare except among the peasantry, and even among them were falling rapidly from favor. Statistics can be used to demonstrate this.[64] Particular instances underline the point. A typical family of respectable but far from aristocratic standing was that of St. William of Norwich, an apprentice furrier "martyred" in 1144. His parents were called *Wenstan* (OE *Wynstān*) and *Elviva* (OE *Ælfgifu*), and his aunt and her husband were called *Liviva* (OE *Lēofgifu*, showing a deuterotheme shared with her sister's name) and *Godwine Stert* (OE *Godwine*; the byname, whatever its etiology or implications, is OE by etymology). But the latter couple's son had, like William himself, a Continental name, although of a different type, *Alexander*. The story also presents another young lad, a baker's son called *Robert*.[65] In that urban milieu, therefore, name fashions had shifted between, approximately, the opening of the twelfth century and the 1130s. What social pressures might then impinge upon anyone bearing an Insular, and therefore out-of-date, name are apparent in the Life of another saint, the hermit best known (from the name he took in religion) as Bartholomew of Farne. Born at Whitby, probably about 1120, he had been given by his parents the AScand name *Tósti*. As a boy, however, he was constrained by his playmates' mockery of its desuetude to change it for the more modern, already almost banal, name *William*.[66]

---

[64]See, e.g., Clark, "Women's Names in Post-Conquest England," pp. 238–45, and "King's Lynn" 1, pp. 55–56. For this shift of fashion, see further *ELPN*, passim; Reaney, *Origin*, pp. 101–07 and 128–56; and, in due course, the chapter to be contributed by the present writer to vol. 2 of the projected *Cambridge History of the English Language* (see n. 11 above).

[65]*The Life and Miracles of St William of Norwich*, ed. and trans. Augustus Jessopp and M. R. James (Cambridge, 1896), pp. 10, 16, 40. For the OE names *Ælfgifu, Godwine, Lēofgifu*, and *Wynstān*, see *PNDB*, pp. 173–74, 269–73, 312, 429; for *Robert* and *William* see, e.g., Morlet I, 136a, 225a, and *PNDB*, pp. 439–50, 415; and for *Alexander* see Morlet II s.n. P. H. Reaney, *Dictionary of British Surnames*, 2nd ed. (London, 1976), derives the modern surname *Start/Sturt* from OE *stēort* "tail" in its topographical sense; if this is so here, then at this date the absence of a connecting preposition looks anomalous.

[66]*Symeonis monachi opera* 1:296. For the Sc name *Tósti* see *SPLY*, p. 291.

This shift of fashion means that soon the evidential value of names comes to bear upon rank or role rather than "blood." This is especially so for certain minor categories. A certain type of "learned" name was characteristic of clerical families, such as the *Quintilian* and *Cyprian* (father and son) found among twelfth-century canons of St. Paul's, and, likewise, Henry of Huntingdon's grandson, Master Aristotle.[67] CG names innocent (as far as documentary evidence allows us to judge) of gallicization sometimes marked those engaged in the North Sea trade.[68] So, in mid-twelfth-century England, names were fair social pointers. Insofar as Continental forms were fast becoming too widespread to be informative, the main significance attaches to Insular forms, now a mark of the elderly and of those of humble station. Some late twelfth-century records—such as, for instance, those in Lincoln Cathedral's *Registrum antiquissimum*—show peasant occupiers of land as mostly still bearing Insular names, whereas witnesses bear Continental ones which now indicate little more than middling social rank.[69] The pre-Conquest regional limitations of certain items, AScand ones especially, persisted as long as the items themselves remained current. Continental names too showed some regional variations, partly due to the settlement patterns by which Bretons and other special groups of people tended to cluster together. To the social and geographical dimensions are added chronological ones: not only were people with Insular and therefore old-fashioned names likely to be, within any given group, older than those with Continental ones,[70] but inside this latter category itself, some CG names that had been popular ca. 1100 fell from favor over the following two centuries, while names with specifically Christian associations grew in frequency.[71]

---

[67]John Le Neve, *Fasti ecclesiae Anglicanae 1066–1300*, 1: *St Paul's, London*, ed. Diana E. Greenway (London, 1968), pp. 18, 45; Charles Clay, "Master Aristotle," *EHR* 76 (1961), 303–08. For the names *Cyprian* and *Quintilian* see Morlet II, pp. 34, 95.

[68]See n. 7 above.

[69]The volume examined is *The Registrum Antiquissimum of the Cathedral Church of Lincoln*, 8, ed. Kathleen Major, Lincoln Record Society 51 (Hereford, 1953).

[70]See "King's Lynn" 1, pp. 55–56.

[71]As yet, there is no systematic account of the impact made in England by this shift of fashion; but see, e.g., Reaney, *Origin*, pp. 129–33, where *John* in particular is noted as rare in the twelfth century yet accounting for almost one quarter of the names occurring in some fourteenth-century documents.

By the thirteenth century a new set of social markers was beginning to appear. Much as in pre-Conquest times, the peasantry continued to favor shortened name forms, but with the difference that now these were based on the most frequent among names of Continental type: for instance, *Rick*, *Dick*, and *Hick* or *Hitch* for *Richard*, of which the North-French form was *Rikard*; *Robb*, *Dobb*, *Hobb*, and probably also *Nobb* for *Robert*; *Dodge* and *Hodge* for *Roger*; *Dawe* for *David*; and so on. (Because the prevailing latinization of baptismal names largely masks the incidence of such forms, evidence for them comes mainly from patronymics.[72]) Thus, at every stage of English medieval history, inspection of name usage can help towards social classification of individuals.

Indeed, medieval baptismal naming continues to illuminate family history up to the present day, through the part that it played in producing patronymic and metronymic family names. From the early twelfth century on, administrative records commonly specified individuals in terms of parentage, usually expressed by means of Latin formulas based on *filia/filius.* At first representing actual personal descriptions, not hereditary surnames, these bynames often reveal bearers of Continental names as children of people with Insular ones: for instance, a Battle rent roll of ca. 1110 lists a Robert *filius Siflet* (OE *Sigeflǣð* f.),[73] and by mid-century similar collocations were frequent everywhere, giving valuable pointers to name fashions and to the sources and cultural structure of the population as well as to individual family histories. The vernacular styles underlying such latinized forms were various. The oldest seems to have been simply appositional (sometimes called "asyndetic"), as in the form *Robertus Thein*, conventionally latinized as *Robertus filius Thein*.[74] Only later did suffixal formations appear as the vernacular norm; when they did, forms in -*s* were typically southern and those in -*son* northern. Therefore such bynames, and the present-day family names derived from them, offer a rough basis for geographical discrimination.[75] A patronymic or metronymic byname implies, furthermore, some

---

[72]See, e.g., Reaney, *Origin*, pp. 149–51; and also Karl Sundén, *Contributions to the Study of Elliptical Words in Modern English* (Uppsala, 1904), where the OE and ME clipped forms are argued to reflect a permanent tendency of colloquial English.

[73]Clark, "Battle c. 1110," p. 30.

[74]"King's Lynn" 2, p. 70.

[75]See Redmonds, *West Riding*, pp. 26–31, 36–41; McKinley, *Norfolk and Suffolk*, pp. 129–38, *Oxfordshire*, pp. 216–35, and *Lancashire*, pp. 313–34.

likelihood of modest family origins: not everyone possessed a settled residence or a distinctive trade, but few can have been without known kin, and so this basic sort of byname was often used for the humble. (Among a group of late thirteenth-century bondmen, for instance, the most frequent type of byname consists of familial ones, which amount to some 30%, against the 15% found for freemen listed in the same record.[76])

Outside the nobility and gentry, it was only after about 1200 that personal bynames began to develop into hereditary family names; and they did so in slow and irregular ways much affected by social class and by geography, as well as by family circumstances.[77] To this day, family names continue to carry the same sorts of social and geographical implication as did the bynames from which they are derived, except that they project these implications not onto the immediately preceding generation but onto an indefinitely distant ancestry. To such general indications, the particular baptismal name involved may add more specific clues. Although by the "surname-creating period" names of the various Continental types were so widespread as in themselves to carry little information, patronymics based on their monosyllabic short forms—*Dobbs/Dobson, Hobbs/Hobson, Hodges/Hodgson, Dawes/Dawson*, and so on—imply origins in the humble milieux where these were current. An OE or AScand patronymic or metronymic—such as *Edrich* (OE *Ēadrīc*), *Goodeve* (OE *Gōdgifu* f.), *Gunnell* (AScand *Gunnild* f.), *Tooley* (AScand *Tóli*), and so on—implies ancestors unfashionable enough, rustic enough, still to have been using such forms after ca. 1200 (or, exceptionally, ancestors whose family name became fixed well before that date). The geographical bearings noted for baptismal names, Insular ones especially, likewise persist in the family names to which they gave rise. In particular, AScand forms remain characteristic of the Danelaw, so that a surname like *Gamble* (Sc *Gamall*), *Orme/Ormesson* (Sc *Ormr*), *Thurkell/Thurkettle* (Sc *Þorke[ti]ll*), or *Swaine* (Sc *Sveinn*) implies family origins somewhere in that wide area. Sometimes a narrowly localized name may focus the possibilities: *Ormesson* and *Orme*, for instance, are predominantly Lancashire names, whereas *Tooley* seems more characteristic of the Eastern

---

[76]McKinley, *Oxfordshire*, pp. 199–200; cf. *Norfolk and Suffolk*, pp. 147–48.

[77]McKinley, *Norfolk and Suffolk*, pp. 3–22, *Oxfordshire*, pp. 7–30, and *Lancashire*, pp. 9–57; see also "King's Lynn" 2, pp. 66–69.

Danelaw.[78] In this sphere, however, often it is the anthroponymist who has to rely on the findings of the prosopographer and the genealogist.

Anyone using name material as prosopographical evidence must constantly bear in mind the limitations of the reference books. To say that is not in the least to denigrate their compilers: the documents surviving from medieval Western Europe record only small fractions of the actual populations, so neither the complete name stocks nor the true distributions and frequencies of the items that are known can ever be definitively established. The warmest gratitude of the whole scholarly community is indeed due to the compilers of our reference books for their achievements in locating, analyzing, and excerpting the source materials; but that must not mislead us into taking their works for bibles. In all such works the commentary is necessarily provisional: name etymologies, even more than those of common vocabulary, represent no more than modern hypothesis—informed and systematic, but for all that, hypothesis rather than fact. As this paper has tried to show, there is great need for re-appraisal, for replacement of outdated views by fresh perspectives better founded. Prosopographers and genealogists, so well placed for noting the name patterns of particular families, have much to contribute to this process. The more often they bring to anthroponymists' attention the phenomena they observe and the problems to which these give rise, the more precise will become the interpretations that the latter can offer in return.

---

[78]See the surname distributions tabulated by McKinley, *Lancashire*, p. 337, and cf. the review by John Insley in *Nomina* 6 (1982), 93–98, esp. 94.

ABBREVIATIONS

ELPN	Eilert Ekwall, *Early London Personal Names*, RSL 43 (Lund, 1947)
LGF	Lunder Germanistische Forschungen
LSE	Lund Studies in English
Morlet I	*Les noms issus du germanique continental et les créations gallo-germaniques*, vol. 1 of Marie-Thérèse Morlet, *Les noms de personne sur le territoire de l'ancienne Gaule du VIe au XIIe siècle*, 2 vols. (Paris, 1968–73)
Morlet II	*Les noms latins ou transmis par le latin*, vol. 2 of Marie-Thérèse Morlet, *Les noms de personne sur le territoire de l'ancienne Gaule du VIe au XIIe siècle*, 2 vols. (Paris, 1968–73)
NoB	*Namn och Bygd*
NPE	Erik Björkman, *Nordische Personennamen in England in alt- und frühmittel-englischer Zeit. Ein Beitrag zur englischen Namenkunde*, StEP 37 (Halle, 1910)
OEPN	Hilmer Ström, *Old English Personal Names in Bede's History: An Etymological-Phonological Investigation*, LSE 8 (Lund, 1939)
PNDB	Olof von Feilitzen, *The Pre-Conquest Personal Names of Domesday Book*, NG 3 (Uppsala, 1937)
RSL	Acta Regiae Societatis Humaniorum Litterarum Lundensis
SAS	*Studia Anthroponymica Scandinavica*
Schlaug I	Wilhelm Schlaug, *Studien zu den altsächsischen Personennamen des 11. und 12. Jahrhunderts*, LGF 30 (Lund, 1955)
Schlaug II	Wilhelm Schlaug, *Die altsächsischen Personennamen vor dem Jahre 1000*, LGF 34 (Lund, 1962)
SPLY	Gillian Fellows Jensen, *Scandinavian Personal Names in Lincolnshire and Yorkshire*, Navnestudier 7 (Copenhagen, 1968)
StEP	Studien zur englischen Philologie
ZEN	Erik Björkman, *Zur englischen Namenkunde*, StEP 47 (Halle, 1912)

IDENTITY AND IDENTIFICATION: SOME RECENT RESEARCH INTO THE ENGLISH MEDIEVAL "FORENAME"

Dave Postles

Who am I? But this can't necessarily be answered by giving name and gene-alogy.—Charles Taylor[1]

Once again, the privilege accorded the proper names assigned to humans has to do with their subsequent role in confirming their identity and their selfhood. —Paul Ricoeur[2]

Nevertheless, Ricoeur acknowledges that "identifying by naming states more than individualizing," for it situates the individual within wider social organization.[3] As Charles Taylor reminds us above, however, individuality expressed through the naming process reflects not selfhood as a disengaged phenomenon, for rather naming is some form of identity refracted through

---

[1]Charles Taylor, *Sources of the Self: The Making of Modern Identity* (Cambridge, 1992 ed.), p. 27.

[2]Paul Ricoeur, *Oneself as Another*, trans. Kathleen Blamey (Chicago, 1992), p. 29. I console myself that I am not the first to approach the *nomen* from the perspective of "identity": see Françoise Zonabend, "Prénom et identité," in *Le prénom. Mode et histoire. Entretiens de Malher, 1980*, ed. Jacques Dupâquier, Alain Bideau, and Marie-Elizabeth Ducreux (Paris, 1984), pp. 23–27.

[3]Ricouer, *Oneself*, p. 29 n. 4.

social and cultural experience.[4] Names are, and were, of course, conferred by others onto us. Identity, as it occurs through naming, is thus not a realization of John Locke's punctual person but rather a social act exercised by others on the self.[5] The naming process is thus constitutive of individuation and identification, and also identity, the latter less as selfhood as within the social sphere.[6] The identity involved in the naming process is thus not

---

[4]Stanley Lieberson and Eleanor O. Bell, "Children's First Names: An Empirical Study of Social Taste," *American Journal of Sociology* 98 (1992), 511–54.

[5]Throughout, I try to adopt the term *nomen* to represent what might *loosely* be conceived as "forenames" or "first names." It is accepted here because it surmounts confusion when an individual has a single name for identification without a byname (*cognomen*) or surname. In this, I unashamedly follow the practice of some recent anthroponymical research on the European continent; whilst *Genèse médiévale de l'anthroponymie moderne*, ed. Monique Bourin (Tours, 1990), tended to employ the terms *nom seul* or *prénom*, in *Genèse médiévale de l'anthroponymie moderne*, t. 2/1: *Persistances du nom unique*, ed. Monique Bourin and Pascal Chareille (Tours, 1992), p. 2, *nomen proprium* was predicated. Second, without theorizing too much, my discussion will address three levels of "identity" identified by sociologists: personal (perhaps "selfhood"); social; and cultural. Third, I recognize fully that these three levels are in fact inextricable and that it is artifice to separate them, but I indulge in their abstraction for heuristic reasons. Fourth, I admit that there is something of a distinction, as some sociologists have propounded, between social rôles and identities, but these again seem to me to be inextricably confused and I may then refer to identities and rôles somewhat indiscriminately. Although I was already engaged in introspective consideration of such issues, I have benefited from reading work by Kate Parkin of the Department of English Local History, University of Leicester. Finally, I should acknowledge many intellectual debts, incurred over recent years whilst thinking about the issues of names and some of the attendant problems (such as women and gender), to Judith Bennett, Joel Rosenthal, and Richard Smith, one of whom has also been empathetic co-editor.

In 1984, Jacques Dupâquier maintained that "l'étude des prénoms semble revenir à la mode," in *Le prénom*, "Introduction," p. 5. As will be apparent below, whilst research on the European continent has progressed remarkably, the pursuit of the significance of the *nomen* in medieval England has depended largely on the valuable work of a small number of individuals.

[6]On the vexed question of identity/selfhood/individuation in the Middle Ages see Caroline Walker Bynum, "Did the Twelfth Century Discover the Individual?" in eadem, *Jesus as Mother: Studies in the Spirituality of the High Middle Ages* (Berkeley, 1982), pp. 82–109; for the cultural contingency of individuality, T. C. Heller, M. Sosna, D. E. Wellberg, et al., *Reconstructing Individualism: Autonomy, Individuality, and the Self in Western Thought* (Stanford, 1986), in particular Stephen Greenblatt, "Fiction and Friction" at pp. 30–52, and Natalie Zemon Davis, "Boundaries and the Sense of Self in Sixteenth-Century France" at

selfhood, that is, personal identity, but social and cultural identity, and it is precisely in this context that it has something to offer to historians of social organization and cultures.[7]

Investment with names is equally part of the process of socialization, not only in the conferment of the name but also in its attendant ritual. Nevertheless, there is not simply a single act, but rather processes. In fact, the name may be reconstituted on several occasions within the social domain. For example, the conferment of the baptismal name in the past might have invoked a formal name and related the child to kinship or spiritual kinship. The selection of the name might, in some circumstances of gender, have comprised part of parents' socialization of the child, particularly when the name was invested with some lexical or symbolic value (see further below). The name may be reconstituted later as a hypocorism, perhaps within the family, but just as likely within a peer group, as part of socialization within that peer group, and in which the subject of the hypocorism need not be just a passive recipient but may exercise some agency—some limited sort of self-fashioning (see further below).[8] These are the social and cultural worlds of the *nomen*.

It is perhaps in these realms—the social and cultural—that most recent medieval English anthroponymical research has been conceived. Demographers, in contrast, have emphasized the question of identification, in the sense that demographic increase, in their perception, was one cause of homonymy; so Richard Britnell seems to infer that homonymy amongst the early twelfth-century English peasantry, with the repetition of IG personal

---

pp. 53–63. I am struck by Greenblatt's notion that "initial representations of individuality appear in the interstices" (see the editors' commentary at p. 4), which seems to me to have some pertinence for those families who selected unusual *nomina* for their children when there was an immense concentration of *nomina* in use—i.e., rejecting the popularity of a small nucleus of *nomina*. It is equally apposite, however, that "boundaries of the self were always redefined in relation to existing, collective institutions" (editors' comments on Natalie Davis at p. 4) to some extent, although in the case of women's names leaps of creativity which were not simply appropriations were potential, for which see below.

[7]Ian Burkitt, *Social Selves: Theories of the Social Formation of Personality* (London, 1991).

[8]Stephen Greenblatt, *Renaissance Self-fashioning: From More to Shakespeare* (Chicago, 1980), introduced the notion of self-fashioning, within cultural constraints; it is recognized here that the adoption of a hypocorism is not truly self-fashioning, but it might be something of a reflexive action with some imagined consequences.

names, to some extent reflected demographic increase.[9] Other research, by anthroponymists and historians influenced by anthropology, has exhibited a different concern, one for kinship structures and cultures, so bringing into focus the issue of "identities" to kinship and wider social organizations. Thus Cecily Clark has discussed the same homonymy of the IG *nomen* amongst the late eleventh-century peasantry as a result of recursive or repetitive selection of some commonly used *nomina*, that is, names as cultural items.[10] In this latter sense, names can be posited as warps in the webs of significance which the actors themselves have woven, although it should be noted that those webs of significance need not have the same meaning for all participants.[11]

Both identification and identity remain ambivalent in naming. As we shall see, despite variation in the width of the name stock, the corpus of names has always been insufficient for precise and unambiguous identification. In terms of identity, disregarding selfhood, the relationship was

---

[9]Richard H. Britnell, *The Commercialisation of English Society, 1000–1500* (Cambridge, 1993), pp. 5–6; my reduction does not fully represent Britnell's position. I am more pertinently reminded of the notion of the rôle of demography in producing homonymy because I was asked by the editors of *LPS* to insert this element into a paper which I wrote.

[10]Cecily Clark, "*Willelmus rex? vel alius Willelmus?*" *Nomina* 11 (1987), 9–12, repr. in *Words, Names and History: Selected Writings of Cecily Clark*, ed. Peter Jackson (Cambridge, 1995), pp. 283–87 (hereafter all references to Clark's papers are to reprinted versions where appropriate).

[11]Clifford Geertz, *The Interpretation of Cultures: Selected Essays* (New York, 1973); Geertz does not argue for a completely homologous culture but for a minimum degree of coherence to ensure that the culture is intelligible: "Thick Description: Toward an Interpretive Theory of Culture," ibid., pp. 17–18. Some of his other research suggests that culture *within* a society is homologous and that the meaning of codes and symbols *is always predetermined*; see, e.g., "Deep Play: Notes on the Balinese Cockfight," ibid., pp. 412–53. Below, I intend to illustrate that within one society the culture of naming is not homologous, but that there are cultures of naming; that the cultures are heteroglossia; and that how they will turn out is unpredictable. Consequently, I partly follow M. M. Bakhtin, but disagree with his notion of cultural integration or conflation. For a brief introduction to Bakhtin's philosophy of action see Alan Swingewood, *Cultural Theory and the Problem of Modernity* (London, 1998), pp. 108–35. I have some empathy with William Sewell's notion of cultural "thin coherence," which allows for resistant, residual, or oppositional cultures on the lines of cultural materialism: "The Concept(s) of Culture," in *Beyond the Cultural Turn*, ed. Victoria E. Bonnell and Lynn Hunt (Berkeley, 1999), pp. 35–61.

never with all other holders of the same name but with specified individuals of significance who bore the name.

The same ambivalence pervades the situating of names within language. If any real lexical content ever inhered in the *nomen*, certainly by the late OE period it was attenuated or almost non-existent.[12] Yet names remained as codes and symbols and so might still be included within a broader definition of language, of how we construct the world.

One of the most interesting properties of the *nomen* as a cultural item is the potential for change with every generation or the "repeated chance of choice," so that *nomina* are thus "the most malleable elements of linguistic culture."[13] Recursive selection could have resulted from two cultural explanations: from structured thought patterns (thus constrained in a negative fashion) and from action (positive agency), although the two modes might not be dichotomous or exclusive, but interrelated and involved. The former mode might reflect the *habitus* of Pierre Bourdieu, in which there is a repertory of responses and actions, but which are still constrained or limited.[14] The repetition of *nomina*, in some contexts, nevertheless might have constituted a "rhetoric of re-enactment," actively perpetuating some symbolic values.[15] It might be important too that such repetitive action occurred within an oral context, for the *nomen* was rarely seen by its bearers in

---

[12]On the decline of the lexical content of "variation" in the formation of IG *nomina*: Bo Seltén, *The Anglo-Saxon Heritage in Middle English Personal Names: East Anglia 1100–1399* (Lund, 1972). Clark, in fact, suggests that the selective repetition of "whole names" (as opposed to repetition of marked elements within dithematic *nomina*) "had, in short, come to oust permutation as the chief means of marking familial links" ("*Willelmus rex?*" p. 287). Here we re-encounter the notion of names as symbols or codes within language, as marked linguistic items, for which see Roman Jakobson, *On Language*, ed. L. R. Waugh and Monique Monville-Burston (Harvard, 1990), pp. 134–40, although this original explanation of marking of language might be considered to fall within a structuralist, dichotomous paradigm.

[13]Robert Bartlett, *The Making of Europe: Conquest, Colonization and Cultural Change, 950–1350* (London, 1994), p. 271.

[14]Pierre Bourdieu, *The Logic of Practice*, trans. Richard Nice (Cambridge, 1992), pp. 52–65, esp. p. 56; see also idem, *Outline of a Theory of Practice*, trans. Nice (Cambridge, 1977). Names, when the active corpus is concentrated, might thus be included within the "accumulated capital" which constitutes the *habitus*.

[15]I borrow this term from Paul Connerton, *How Societies Remember* (Cambridge, 1989), pp. 66–68.

written form; it was essentially part of an oral discursive practice.[16]

A crucible for the potentiality for discursive or dialogic[17] change was distinctively introduced in and from the late eleventh century, so it is important to assess anthroponymists' conceptualization of that period; to that conceptualization, important further evidence is adduced in this volume. From that time on, the processes of naming affected, and were affected by, notions of what has recently been conceived in terms of "ethnicity," that is, different traditions of a vanquished indigenous population and its new immigrant overlords; of gender; of difference of social group; and of the infusion of a new ethos of naming, "Christian" names *stricto sensu*, that is, saints' and biblical names. How this cultural *bricolage* was worked through, negotiated, and contested from the twelfth century through the subsequent four centuries is the present theme, to provide an overview of previous research, for the new contributions to this volume, many of which are specialized case studies, and along with the suggestions in these other case studies for an agenda for further research.

> Childebert—Dagobert—Chilpéric—Clotaire—Thierry—Childéric— Pépin—Charles Jean—Jean—Sisinnius—Constantin—Grégoire—Grégoire— Zacharie—Étienne—Paul—Étienne—Paul—Étienne—Adrien—Adrien—Léon. Voici deux listes de l'époque qui précède l'an Mil: celle des rois francs et celle des papes du VIIIe siècle. Les rois francs portent sans exception des noms Germaniques, les papes, sans exception eux aussi, des noms latins ou grecs. Tout semble parfaitement en ordre.[18]

Notions about the boundary between sacred and profane were thus observed at this highest level, although kingship inherently involved the sacred as well as the profane, sometimes as a dualism, sometimes as syncretism.[19] At

---

[16]For the problematic of oral and literate see Brian Stock, *The Implications of Literacy: Written Language and Models of Interpretation in the Eleventh and Twelfth Centuries* (Princeton, 1983); James Fentress and Chris Wickham, *Social Memory* (Oxford, 1992), pp. 92–114 ("Peasant Memories"); for the English late Middle Ages, Stephen Justice, *Writing and Rebellion: England in 1381* (Berkeley, 1994).

[17]Mikhail Bakhtin's term.

[18]Jörg Jarnut, "Avant l'an mil," in *L'Anthroponymie. Document de l'histoire sociale des mondes méditerranéens médiévaux*, ed. Monique Bourin, Jean-Marie Martin, and François Menant (Rome, 1996), p. 7.

[19]The foremost statement about the separation of sacred and profane, which has influenced

its highest level, Christianity in the early Middle Ages depended on the separation of sacred and profane in terms of personal naming: Christian names were reserved for the spiritual and ecclesiastical sphere and names of ethnic origin for the lay realm.

What was the position in England at lower social and ecclesiastical levels? Caedwalla, who undertook pilgrimage to Rome where he was baptized and where he adopted the *nomen Peter*, was an exception.[20] Although the host of saints of Rome was familiar in the liturgical environment of the English, Christian names remained exotic before the middle of the twelfth century.[21] In Ireland, the same separation seems to have been observed. Although in the pre-Norman era a small number of males bore saints' and biblical names, it has been suggested that these were not baptismal names but rather names "assumed at some point in a religious career." The more expansive use of saints' and biblical names did not occur until after the AN colonization of Ireland.[22]

By the twelfth century on the Continent, Christian names exerted great pressure on ethnic (predominantly Germanic) names in the identification of the laity. In England, however, although Christian names were introduced into the naming of the laity, the extent of their influence continued to be more attenuated, with the exception of a single name, *John*. The explanation for this transformation is polysemic. It seems unlikely that the displacement of Germanic language by a universal register of Latin can conceivably provide an explanation, although it has been invoked.[23] Despite the undoubted fact that protothemes and deuterothemes lost their lexical meaning, causing confusion in the process of *variation* in the formation of OE dithematic

---

some writing of medieval history, particularly about the boundary between orthodoxy and heterodoxy, was made by Mary Douglas, in *Purity and Danger: An Analysis of the Concepts of Pollution and Taboo* (London, 1966), but see the criticism, e.g., by Malcolm Hamilton, *Sociology and the World's Religions* (Basingstoke, 1998), pp. 156–58.

[20]Cited by Jarnut, "Avant l'an mil," p. 10.

[21]For these saints in England before the Conquest see Veronica Ortenberg, *The English Church and the Continent in the Tenth and Eleventh Centuries: Cultural, Spiritual and Artistic Exchanges* (Oxford, 1992).

[22]Brian Ó Cuív, "Aspects of Irish Personal Names," *Celtica* 18 (1986), 164–65, but bearing in mind the selectivity of the sources, annals, and genealogies, so that it is impossible to recover the names of "the more lowly members of society" (ibid., p. 155).

[23]Jarnut, "Avant l'an mil," p. 16.

names, the introduction of Latin as a *higher* register surely cannot account for the displacement of Germanic names. Consider, for example, that the Insular language continued as the lower register, the *parole* of the speech community, as well as being incorporated in the writing of governance, in the boundary clauses in diplomas produced by beneficiaries, and in the writs which were complementary to this purpose.[24]

Two other, interrelated considerations might be adduced. In societies which depend heavily on symbols, codes, and ritual, names assume meaning, even if the lexical content has been debased; they perform the function of code. Around the millennium, and slightly later in England because of its insularity, there was a transition in the "webs of significance" of meaning, not a radical transformation but certainly an attenuation of the *mores* within some social groups.[25] Relating that alteration in a social environment to the transformation in naming, however, is extremely difficult for us at this time. Even partially to satisfy the condition would involve analyzing very closely the changes in the naming of the nobility against similar changes amongst the peasantry.

Another cause is potentially the spiritualization of the laity from the twelfth century, through interior inspiration—the attraction of an interior spirituality and participation in religious practice—and external motivation —the exhortation of the universal church, culminating in the Fourth Lateran Council of 1215, which was inextricably responding and innovating.[26]

It has been cogently recognized that the (Catholic) church did not *formally* intervene in the naming process before the Council of Trent.[27] There nevertheless existed sufficient informal pressure for conformity to an ecclesiastical *praxis* on naming. First, there is the closer association between name-giving and the sacrament of baptism. It is evident that universal prac-

---

[24]Susan Kelly, "Anglo-Saxon Lay Society and the Written Word," and Simon Keynes, "Royal Government and the Written Word in Late Anglo-Saxon England," both in *The Uses of Literacy in Early Mediaeval England*, ed. Rosamond McKitterick (Cambridge, 1990), pp. 36–62 and 245–55.

[25]John Gillingham, "1066 and the Introduction of Chivalry into England," in *Law and Government in Medieval England and Normandy*, ed. George Garnett and John Hudson (Cambridge, 1994), pp. 31–55.

[26]The classic statement is André Vauchez, *Les Laïcs au Moyen Âge. Practiques et expériences religieuses* (Paris, 1987).

[27]Dupâquier, "Introduction," in *Le prénom*, p. 5.

tice before at least the tenth century involved the name being given within the context of the family before the baptismal ceremony.[28] The stronger interposition of the clergy thereafter in a sacramental process, especially after the Fourth Lateran Council, provided the opportunity for clerical pressure in the naming process. Naming was thus transferred from a secular environment to a liturgical and sacramental one, and this transference introduced new covert, sometimes overt, pressure for conformity to a Christian code of naming.

This suggestion is problematized, of course, by the lack of positive evidence because of the nature of the sources. At one level the process is visible. When the child of William of Avalon was baptized in the cathedral at Grenoble, the boy's uncle was insistent that the child be named after himself, Peter. Hugh, bishop of Lincoln, intervened successfully so that the boy received the name of the patronal saint of the cathedral, John. It seems, moreover, that the baptism occurred on one of the feast days of the saint, the patronal feast day, presumably the Nativity rather than the Decollation.[29] This event is compounded by the uncle's name being a Christian one, but the transferral was undoubtedly a secular connection whilst Hugh was demanding the influence of the Christian code in naming. If we consider that the patronal saint of the sacrament of baptism was the Baptist, it is not surprising that the name *John*, certainly in England, penetrated most deeply into the corpus of personal naming of the laity.

Just how far did the secular clergy, at parochial level, follow the example of the great bishop? It is impossible to deduce. What we do know is that the higher clergy became frustrated at some aspects of naming in the late thirteenth century; this frustration is reflected in the exhortation (rather than instruction) by Archbishop Pecham to the lower clergy: "Attendant etiam sacerdotes, ne lasciva nomina que scilicet mox prelata sonant lasciviam, imponi permittant parvulis baptizatis, sexus precipue feminini. Et si contrarium fiat, per confirmantes episcopos corrigatur."[30] In this context, which is discussed in more detail below, the higher clergy was concerned

---

[28]Jarnut, "Avant l'an mil," p. 11.

[29]Adam of Eynsham, *Magna vita Sancti Hugonis*, ed. and trans. Hugh Farmer and Decima Douie, 2 vols. (London, 1961–62), pp. 83–84.

[30]*Councils and Synods, with Other Documents Relating to the English Church*, 2/2: *1265–1313*, ed. Frederick M. Powicke and Christopher R. Cheney (Oxford, 1964), p. 897 (cap. 3).

to exert an influence in the propriety of the naming of the laity within its pastoral care.

It has been fairly conclusively demonstrated that there appears to be no correlation between local naming and local patronal saints of parish churches.[31] That inconsistency might come as no surprise, for it is acknowledged that the laity's search for a personal expression of lay devotion during the later Middle Ages sometimes led to the relative neglect of the patronal saint of parishes, as a profusion of other saints invaded the parish church.[32]

That association with saints did not escape ambiguity. The child of Emelota de Wideslade had a swollen body, but invocation to a specific religious person provided the cure. That religious person was Godric of Finchale, and in reciprocity she named the child Ralph Godric. In this case, the spiritual association resulted in the conferment not of a Christian name but that of a local merchant who had assumed the life of a hermit and continued to bear his IG *nomen*.[33]

There is evidence from the later Middle Ages for the attachment of people to their name saints, a spiritual "friendship."[34] What is not clear is whether the attachment of a lay person to a namesake saint was instituted at baptism or later in life, that is, whether association led to name or name led to association. General associations are visible: for example, *Margaret* became a common female *nomen* from about the time of the canonization of St. Margaret and the inauguration of her feast day in the English calendar at the Council of Oxford in 1222.[35] We have another intimation of a general regional association in the poll tax for the West Riding of Yorkshire, for in this area of a higher incidence of dedications to St. Helen, 3% of all named

---

[31]Peter Franklin, "Normans, Saints, and Politics: Forename-Choice among Fourteenth-Century Gloucestershire Peasants," *LPS* 36 (1986), 19–26 (repr. below, pp. 177–88); *Saints and Their Cults: Studies in Religious Sociology, Folklore and History*, ed. Stephen Wilson (Cambridge, 1983), pp. 12, 15, 40.

[32]Eamon Duffy, *The Stripping of the Altars: Traditional Religion in England, c.1400–c.1580* (New Haven, 1992), p. 162, although the evidence is for the later Middle Ages.

[33]*Libellus de vita et miraculis S. Godrici, heremitae de Finchale*, ed. Joseph Stevenson, Surtees Society 20 (1847), pp. 434–35 (no. clxxvii).

[34]Duffy, *Stripping of the Altars*, p. 162, cites a couple of examples.

[35]Bella Millett and Jocelyn Wogan-Brown, eds., *Medieval English Prose for Women: Selections from the Katherine Group and the Ancrene Wisse*, rev. ed. (Oxford, 1992), p. 153.

women in the poll tax of 1379 had the *nomen Helen* (Lat. *Elena*).[36] Whilst 3% does not seem a terribly high proportion, it would appear to be an unusually high figure for this *nomen*, although it must be admitted that there are, at this stage, no regional comparative data.

Such associations between the laity and spiritual persons and saints were probably not dissimilar to social networks amongst the laity. Reciprocity was the store of social capital in both cases, and therefore the emphasis is on a sort of horizontal social relationship, if one imbued with spirituality.[37]

To some extent, whether one accepts the demise of "feudalism" as a descriptive term or not, some form of vertical relationship existed in medieval England, if lordship is rescued as a form of social and tenurial relationship.[38] Whether or not lordship informed the process of naming is an interesting question, which has been investigated only embryonically. Focusing on the late eleventh century, Clark surmised that "Among the peasantry, acquaintance with the styles characteristic of the foreign settlers must have come from two main sources: from the lords of their own and of neighbouring vills; and from rumours of magnates further afield."[39] Her detailed examination of the survey of the knights and tenants of the abbey of Bury St. Edmunds leads her to infer that local lordship was not instrumental in the naming process, although she requested further studies to substantiate what processes were happening in localities.[40] Taking a later period, in the High Middle Ages, Franklin reached the same negative conclusion.[41] It is by no means clear that this line of approach has been completely exhausted,

---

[36]The total number of females is 20,939, but 8,682 are not attributed a *nomen* (i.e., in some wapentakes wives were attributed *nomina*, but not in others); amongst daughters, the proportion bearing the *nomen Helen* was 3.5% ("Rolls of the Collectors in the West Riding of the Lay-Subsidy [Poll Tax] 2 Richard II," *Yorkshire Archaeological Journal* 5:1–51, 241–66, 417–32; 6:1–44, 129–71, 287–342; 7:6–31, 145–86 [1879–84]).

[37]Duffy, *Stripping of the Altars*, pp. 155–205, for associations with saints being a process, in constant flux, and, in the late Middle Ages, construed as "friendship."

[38]Susan Reynolds, *Fiefs and Vassals: The Medieval Evidence Reinterpreted* (Oxford, 1994), esp. pp. 323–95, although Reynolds might be reluctant for lordship to be retained as a paradigm. Compare *Cultures of Power: Lordship, Status, and Process in Twelfth-Century Europe*, ed. Thomas N. Bisson (Philadelphia, 1995).

[39]Clark, *"Willelmus rex?"* repr. in *Words, Names and History*, p. 281.

[40]Clark, *"Willelmus rex?"* p. 290.

[41]Franklin, "Normans, Saints, and Politics."

and it is possible that different local traditions might have been in operation. One of the problems of such research is the matching of taxpayers or tenants to the correct generation of lordship, that is, including in the analysis the *nomina* of the previous lords as well as of those contemporaneous.

Such encounters should perhaps warn us about the acceptance of a single homologous culture of naming. It is instructive to consider again the cultural *milieux* (the plural is used advisedly) of England in the twelfth century and to be cautious about the rate of displacement of Insular naming cultures by imported CG and Christian name forms. The most important work on the replacement of IG personal names by newly introduced forms of name, associated with the French male aristocracy, has been produced by Cecily Clark.[42] Inferences based on research by her and Olof von Feilitzen have entered into the mainstream historical literature:

> One reason why it was difficult to decide who was Norman and who was English by Fitz Nigel's time [the 1170s] was that most freemen by then used non-English personal names like "Richard" and "Robert." Striking evidence of this comes from Winchester, where information is available for the years 1066, 1110, 1148 and 1207. [This section, of course, refers to von Feilitzen's research.[43]] At the time of the Norman Conquest 29 per cent of property-owners in Winchester had foreign names. This proportion increased to 62 per cent by 1110, 66 per cent by 1148 and 82 per cent by 1207. Comparable rates of increase occur at Canterbury, where about 75 per cent of the names listed in the rent surveys of the 1160s are non-English and this increases to about 90 per cent by 1206. . . . What is most significant in these figures is the increase in the twelfth century. Evidently each new generation gave a larger proportion of its children foreign names, as Norman rule and French fashions became more normal, until by 1200 the great majority of freemen in southern England at least had ceased to bear English names. This information, because it is derived from a large number of individuals, is a better indicator of attitudes to foreign rule than are isolated statements in chronicles. A fact of comparable significance is that "William" became and remained the single most common recorded name in the twelfth century. . . . Peasant families in the

---

[42]Clark, "Women's Names in Post-Conquest England: Observations and Speculations," repr. in *Words, Names and History*, ed. Jackson, pp. 117–43 and below (pp. 65–102); eadem, "*Willelmus rex?*"; eadem, "People and Languages in Post-Conquest Canterbury," ibid., pp. 179–206; eadem, "Battle c.1110: An Anthroponymist Looks at an Anglo-Norman New Town," ibid., pp. 221–40.

[43]Olof von Feilitzen, "The Personal Names of the Winton Domesday," in *Winchester in the Early Middle Ages, an Edition and Discussion of the Winton Domesday*, ed. Martin Biddle and Frank Barlow, Winchester Studies 1 (Oxford, 1976), pp. 143–229.

countryside (most of whose names are unrecorded), as distinct from householders in cities like Winchester and Canterbury, were presumably much slower to adopt foreign names although they can be found doing so by the thirteenth century.[44]

Questions about this radical transformation of personal naming remain to be answered, although Clark made astonishing progress towards their resolution. As the quotation above illustrates, her work on Canterbury and Battle (and also King's Lynn) provided considerable explanation of the process of change in the urban context. In her paper on women's names, reprinted below, she explored the naming of the peasantry in the context of her overall discussion of whether women's personal names continued as the repository of traditional (OE) culture. From various twelfth-century estate surveys Clark produced a chronology of the transition from IG to new forms of personal name amongst the English peasantry.[45] By the 1160s, on the Ramsey manors, IG personal names accounted for merely 30% of male tenants and on the Glastonbury manors in 1189 for less than a quarter.[46] Clark has thus elucidated some of the rate of the transition. During the third quarter of the twelfth century, therefore, Insular personal names had been substantially displaced amongst the English peasantry.[47] When one is considering this displacement, the potential for change in naming processes should be taken into the equation, the potential mutability within one or two generations. At least a hundred years had transpired since the arrival of the new overlords and their name forms. It is perhaps necessary, then, to attempt an

---

[44]M. T. Clanchy, *England and Its Rulers, 1066–1272: Foreign Lordship and National Identity* (London, 1983), p. 57. I do not want to enter into the debate about whether nation, nationhood, and nationalism are or are not constructions of modernity: see Anthony D. Smith, *Nationalism and Modernism: A Critical Survey of Recent Theories of Nations and Nationalism* (London, 1998); David McCrone, *The Sociology of Nationalism: Tomorrow's Ancestors* (London, 1998); Craig Calhoun, *Nationalism* (Buckingham, 1997); Benedict Anderson, *Imagined Communities: Reflections on the Origin and Spread of Nationalism*, rev. ed. (London, 1993), are all recent expositions of the general problem. I therefore simply problematize the continuity or discontinuity of personal names as a question of continuity or discontinuity of a traditional culture in the context of a newly introduced higher cultural register.

[45]Clark, "Women's Names in Post-Conquest England," pp. 130–32.

[46]Clark, "Women's Names in Post-Conquest England," p. 131.

[47]Clark, "Baptismal Naming: Rates and Processes of Change," in *The Cambridge History of the English Language*, 2: *1066–1476*, ed. Norman Blake (Cambridge, 1992), pp. 558–63, has less on the peasantry.

even more refined chronology of the change, and perhaps also to investigate regional differences in the transition.

In fact, Clark indicated that in the late eleventh-century survey of the estate of Bury St. Edmunds the new forms of naming had made little impact on the naming of the East Anglian peasantry, over a generation later. In the surveys of the Burton Abbey estate in the northwest Midlands in the second quarter of the twelfth century, less than a fifth of the tenants had acquired the new name forms—after about two generations from 1066.

If we consider the survey of the bishopric of Worcester estate in 1170x 1182, a rather different pattern emerges, for here over 50% of the male tenants still retained IG personal names. On some manors the homonymy of tenants with IG personal names is remarkable; for instance, encountered at Alvechurch are Edwi Piteman, Edwi *de lacte*, Edwi *carpentarius*, Edwi de la Quolle, Edwi *privignus*, Edwi *filius Aluric* [sic], and Edwi Patric, all ostensibly different tenants on that manor.[48] As well as the chronological dimension, the regional dimension may also need to be investigated further, not least a re-consideration of the North of England. Geoffrey Barrow cryptically indicated the persistence of IG personal names amongst the peasantry of the North, and such an investigation would repay more detailed exploration.[49] There also it is not simply a question of the persistence of peasant naming, but of the *bricolage* of naming at higher social levels, of the *mélange* of Breton, Goidelic, AScand, IG, and other name forms, as John Insley has indicated for one part of the North in the late eleventh century.[50] Moreover, Chris Lewis has demonstrated the persistence of a stratum of middling English personnel, on which the continuation of administration depended, not just in the North, marked out by the persistence of IG personal names.[51]

---

[48]Dave Postles, "Cultures of Peasant Naming in Twelfth-Century England," *MP* 18 (1997), 33. An attempt is made in this article for a provisional re-evaluation of the whole question of the transformation of the naming of the twelfth-century peasantry.

[49]Geoffrey W. S. Barrow, "Northern English Society in the Twelfth and Thirteenth Centuries," *Northern History* 4 (1969), 1–28.

[50]John Insley, "Some Aspects of Regional Variation in Early Middle English Personal Nomenclature," in *Studies in Honour of Kenneth Cameron*, ed. Thorlac Turville-Petre and Margaret Gelling, Leeds Studies in English, n.s. 18 (1987), pp. 183–99 (repr. below, pp. 191–210).

[51]C. P. Lewis, "The Domesday Jurors," *Haskins Society Journal* 5 (1995), 17–44 (repr. below, pp. 307–39).

What is emerging therefore is an extremely complex pattern of acculturation.

If it seems probable that there was for some considerable time longer a *bricolage* of cultures of naming, how then should we conceive of the transformation of naming? A simple diffusionist model, given the timescale, seems inappropriate. Perhaps it is necessary now to recognize an element of tension and friction which was more intense in some regions than in others, depending not simply on a core-periphery model but equally on perduring regional cultural traditions. We may thus be confronted with a dominant ideology and, it is important to note, resistance. That resistance, it might seem, was a sort of "hidden transcript" of the kind described by James Scott, in this case conveyed through names, or, perhaps more pertinent, the tactical resistance suggested in other contexts by Michel de Certeau—tactics of resistance rather than strategies.[52] Whilst in many regions of the south and middle of England Insular personal names were superseded in large measure by new forms of name, other kinship groups in other regions clung more effectively to Insular name forms. Perhaps then we should ask some questions: Did the displacement of Insular names in the south and Midlands represent a cultural conversion—ready acceptance of new cultural forms— or was it compliance with a dominant culture? Where some peasants in the south and middle of the country persisted with Insular name forms—and perhaps 25% of peasant tenants in these regions retained Insular name forms even in the third quarter of the twelfth century—is this too an expression of resistance? Or had the symbolism of Insular name forms been eroded?

This question of "identity" is further problematized by those pre-Conquest French in England who selected Insular names for their sons.[53] These immigrants came to identify with the country of their domicile, and it has indeed been suggested that the post-Conquest Normans regarded the pre-Conquest French as English.[54]

---

[52]James C. Scott, *Domination and the Arts of Resistance: Hidden Transcripts* (New Haven, 1987); Michel de Certeau, *The Practice of Everyday Life*, trans. Steven Rendall (Berkeley, 1984); my inclination is towards de Certeau's "tactics"—what is achievable in a coercive (practically and discursively) situation.

[53]Christopher P. Lewis, "The French in England before the Norman Conquest," in *Anglo-Norman Studies XVII. Proceedings of the Battle Conference, 1994*, ed. Christopher Harper-Bill (Woodbridge, 1995), pp. 123–44.

[54]Lewis, "The French in England," pp. 136–37. Note also Godwin the Frenchman, a burgess of Winchester in the early twelfth century: ibid., p. 132. Von Feilitzen's work has been prob-

Gendered differences in naming have become the site of some discussion recently, but one may also note that Archbishop Pecham in the late thirteenth century exhibited some consternation about the naming of females. Cecily Clark raised the prospect that women may have been the repository of a traditional culture of naming in the twelfth century; that whilst IG personal names were displaced at a much faster rate by CG names, IG names persisted longer amongst females.[55] Clark invoked either a pragmatic social context or cultural practice as explanation for this difference:

> That time lag could be explained by a paucity of women, and so of feminine name models, among the post-Conquest French settlers, and, if not so explained, would imply among twelfth-century English parents some otherwise unrecorded feeling that daughters were, in a way that sons were not, vessels of the native tradition.[56]

Judith Bennett also brings to our attention cultural differentiation in naming, reflected in a greater concentration of male forenames and more exotic female names in the thirteenth- and fourteenth-century countryside at Brigstock:

> The greater value that inheritance customs gave to male children is reflected in the naming practices of the medieval peasantry. Parents chose forenames for their sons from a limited range of personal names that were reused generation after generation. The repetition of a few names like John, William, Richard, and Robert emphasized the male infant's importance to his family; identified with the forename of his father or grandfather, such a child was designated as a person of consequence to his family's past and future. Less vital to both family and community, female children were named more freely and idiosyncratically. Among females, one encounters not only standard names such as Matilda, Agnes, Alice, but also a large number of unusual ones such as Tibia, Lucia, Leticia, Nute, Mariaunt, Ivette,

---

lematized by Christopher P. Lewis, "Joining the Dots: A Methodology for Identifying the English in Domesday Book," in *Family Trees and the Roots of Politics: The Prosopography of Britain and France from the Tenth to the Twelfth Century*, ed. Katharine S. B. Keats-Rohan (Woodbridge, 1997), pp. 69–88.

[55] Clark, "Women's Names in Post-Conquest England"; see the earlier suggestion of this pattern by Kenneth Cameron, in the introduction to *Documents Relating to the Manor and Soke of Newark-on-Trent*, ed. Maurice W. Barley, Thoroton Society Record Series 16 (1956), p. xii. I owe a great debt to Judith Bennett for discussion of this point about women's names in the twelfth century.

[56] Clark, "Women's Names in Post-Conquest England," p. 142.

Strangia, and Sibilla. Although these forenames were charming and evocative, they carried no familial importance. Medieval parents may have loved their daughters as much as their sons, but they also expected daughters to contribute less than sons to the family's continuation in the next generation.[57]

This stimulating, if brief, discussion, has become celebrated, but it is also provocative.[58]

Certainly, more research into the question of gender differences in naming is required. Some impressionistic material is provided here, a sort of agendum, but it is no substitute for considerable detailed and localized research into naming in various social groups. In fact, some of the new studies published below make an initiative in that direction. At some times, women's names remained the repository of traditional culture, yet at other times they allowed more creativity than male names.[59] Whilst some male names might have reflected position within the kinship, female names might have expressed other values—symbolic of virtues associated with females.[60] This difference was manifested perhaps in the greater proportion of Christian —saints'—names amongst women.[61] Possibly some of this transformation

---

[57]Judith M. Bennett, *Women in the Medieval English Countryside: Gender and Household in Brigstock before the Plague* (Oxford, 1987), p. 69.

[58]The epistemological issues in a historical context are discussed by Judith Bennett in "Confronting Continuity," *Journal of Women's History* 9 (1997), 73–94, and also in her earlier "Feminism and History," *Gender and History* 3 (1989), 251–72. I am grateful for her advice over many years on these matters, more particularly so recently. It is also perhaps important to consider philosophical discussions of female subjectivity, such as Judith Butler, *Gender Trouble: Feminism and the Subversion of Identity* (London, 1990), and, perhaps in some contrast, recent pragmatic accounts of gender issues such as Lynne Segal, *Why Feminism?* (Cambridge, 1999).

[59]For the first position, Clark, "Women's Names in Post-Conquest England"; for the second, Dave Postles, "The Distinction of Gender? Women's Names in the Thirteenth Century," *Nomina* 19 (1996), 79–89.

[60]Clark, "Women's Names," *Cambridge History of the English Language* 2:585, further developed by Postles, "The Distinction of Gender?"

[61]Clark, "Women's Names," *Cambridge History of the English Language* 2:585; Postles, "Cultures of Peasant Naming," pp. 42–44. Note also the interesting comment of Béatrice Weis: "Les noms chrétiens sont d'abord introduits par le canal des noms féminins; un peu plus tard, les noms masculins suivront" ("Répartition des noms de personnes en Alsace au XIIe siècle selon les porteurs et leur situation sociale," in *Actes du XVIe Congrès international des sciences onomastiques, 1987*, ed. J.-C. Boulanger [Quebec, 1990], p. 581).

of women's names, particularly by the early thirteenth century, was associated with the significant adoption of female virginal saints, confirming the association between names and attributed values.[62] More amongst women than men, the revival of names from Classical Antiquity was important, and it is even more significant that the female names might have retained a residue of lexical meaning, as in *Constancia*, *Preciosa*, and *Prudencia*, for example.[63]

It is not always clear how difference was conceived,[64] for some of the creativity in female naming occurred precisely in a familial context or in relation to males. Although it is completely exotic and specific to a high social group, there is the example of the eldest daughter of John Arundel, lord of Sandford (Somerset). John and his wife, Isabella, had two daughters and a son, the two youngest siblings, John and Joan, receiving rather nondescript names, which, however, reiterated the paternal name. The eldest, a daughter, who later married Richard Crispin, was named Arundella, a seemingly entirely created and intimately personal name associated with the family.[65]

The further aspect of this creativity of female names, but related to male naming, is the development of apparently new forms of cross-gender names, that is, the construction of female forms of male names (excluding here the traditional forms like *Johanna* and *Dionisia*). Thus in London wills in the early fourteenth century are enumerated as legatees women with the *nomina Elicia* (*Elisia, Elycia*), *Nicholaa*, *Egidia*, *Benedicta*, and *Philippa*.[66] In the mid-thirteenth century *Laurencia* survived her husband, Reiner *Prepositus* of Portsmouth, and their daughter was another *Laurencia*, so here, in this urban context, there is not only the creation of an ostensibly new cross-

---

[62]This suggestion is related to the context by Postles, "Cultures of Peasant Naming" and "The Distinction of Gender?"

[63]Postles, "The Distinction of Gender?" p. 87.

[64]For difference as an epistemological issue see Rosemarie Tong, *Feminist Thought: A Comprehensive Introduction* (London, repr. 1997), pp. 217–38.

[65]Postles, "The Distinction of Gender?" p. 80, where also is cited the case of Carbonella, a daughter of the Carbonel family. Such were my thoughts about Arundel at the time of writing that article, but I must admit that I have since encountered John *filius Arundel' de Hilderthorp'* in the cartulary of Bridlington Priory: London, British Library, MS 40,008, fol. 22r.

[66]Postles, "The Distinction of Gender?" pp. 86–87.

gender name but also its transmission from mother to daughter, daughter named for mother.[67]

These names are not unproblematical, for they largely occurred in socially specific contexts, amongst the burgess families of London or gentry families. It is therefore necessary to undertake more detailed studies of the peasantry to obtain a fuller understanding of how differences of naming by gender might have been culturally specific to different social groups. The conferment of such types of name had at least two implications: the position of females within the kinship, and the way in which values were attributed to females and how females were socialized. It might also be reiterated that, as codes and symbols in this context, *nomina* were still an essential part of language, and it might be useful then to place the naming of females within the general context of sociolinguistic usage, however contested that field might be in terms of use of language by gender.[68]

It is interesting, therefore, that medieval Irish society had a contingency in gender-neutral names, or so it seems. In the case of an unborn—and presumably at-risk—child, some prescriptive literature suggests: "Either Flann or Cellach should be given as a name to it for they are both common to male or female."[69]

The final question of "identity," which is interrelated with the issue of kinship, is whether names acted as kinship markers and how they might have done so, at all social levels. The eloquent discussion of this issue was instigated by examinations of naming patterns and processes amongst both the peasantry and the gentry in the High and late Middle Ages. Whilst some have emphasized the importance of spiritual kinship (*compaternitas*)—the horizontal ties constituted between parents and *cummater* (cummer) and *compater*, as well as between godparent and godsib—others have regarded linear kinship as more significant. The former involves the principal god-

---

[67] *The Cartularies of Southwick Priory*, pt. 2, ed. Katharine Ann Hanna, Hampshire Record Series 10 (1989), p. 202 (no. III 535) (and also p. 212, no. III 556).

[68] Janet Wolff, *Feminine Sentences: Essays on Women and Culture* (Oxford, 1990); Janet Holmes, *Women, Men and Politeness* (London, 1995); Jennifer Coates, *Women, Men and Language*, 2nd ed. (London, 1993), but now also Jenny Cheshire and Penelope Gardner-Chloros, "Code-Switching and the Sociolinguistic Gender Pattern," *International Journal of the Sociology of Language* 129 (1998), 5–34.

[69] Ó Cuív, "Aspects of Irish Personal Names," p. 157 (citing the fourteenth-century *Leabhar Breac*).

parent—of the same sex as the child—conferring the name at the font, consistently the principal godparent's name, it has been maintained. By contrast, there is an argument for the repetition of names that are traditional within the family. Since the literature has largely addressed male naming, in this case it is the repetition of the father's or grandfather's name. That sort of intrafamilial repetition has been discerned in medieval Irish naming processes, the norm (if such it was) of the *ainm chine*.[70] The essence of these different explanations is reprinted below.[71]

Of necessity, the matter of godparenthood is confined to higher social levels, principally the gentry, with the evidence predominantly the proofs of age at inquisitions *post mortem*. The influence of spiritual kinship on naming is contested or, at the least, ambiguous; Haas has revealed that in his sample of Yorkshire gentry, the name being conferred was not only the principal godparent's but also the father's—that is, that a father selected a principal godparent with the same name as his own in order to confer the father's name.

The relationship between godparents' and godsibs' names can also be detected in an urban context, in the wills of testators in late medieval Bury St. Edmunds, where 34% of testators who mentioned godchildren were homonymous with those godsibs.[72] It is, indeed, possible to discover earlier, if random, evidence of this correlation between the names of godparent and godsib. Thus, by a charter of ca. 1220, William, vicar of Marston-on-Dove, provided land for his godsib, William, the son of Stephen *clericus* of Eggington.[73]

---

[70]Ó Cuív, "Aspects of Irish Personal Names," pp. 172–74, but it should be noted that spiritual kinship (godparenthood) is not considered at all here.

[71]Michael J. Bennett, "Spiritual Kinship and the Baptismal Name in Traditional European Society," in *Principalities, Powers and Estates: Studies in Medieval and Early Modern Government and Society*, ed. L. O. Frappell (Adelaide, 1979), pp. 1–13 (repr. below, pp. 115–46); Philip Niles, "Baptism and the Naming of Children in Late Medieval England," *MP* 3/1 (Spring 1982), 95–107 (repr. below, pp. 147–57); and Louis Haas, "Social Connections between Parents and Godparents in Late Medieval Yorkshire," *MP* 10/1 (Spring 1989), 1–21 (repr. below, pp. 159–75).

[72]Robert Dinn, "Baptism, Spiritual Kinship, and Popular Religion in Late Medieval Bury St Edmunds," *Bulletin of the John Rylands University Library* 72 (1990), 103.

[73]*The Cartulary of Dale Abbey*, ed. Avrom Saltman, Historical Manuscripts Commission JP 11 (1967), pp. 314–17 (nos. 461 and 464).

It has been mentioned above that the relationship might be ambivalent and might yet be further problematized by the question of social group. Does it necessarily follow that because spiritual kinship played some role at higher social levels, it necessarily applied also at lower social levels? Is it possible that horizontal social ties were more important for those of the status of gentry than for the peasantry, for whom familial concerns might have been paramount?[74] It is easy enough to find amongst the peasantry examples of the transmission of the paternal *nomen*, and the same process can be observed in some of the wills of burgesses.[75] Nevertheless, we are still confronted by the issues of typicality, quantification, and alternative naming processes within the burgess and peasant social groups.

What we may consequently need are more detailed studies of the naming of the peasantry, constituted from manorial court rolls, including, wherever possible, the reconstruction of peasant genealogies. This volume presents new examinations of this sort of data, in an attempt to build upon (for example) the foundation established by Edwin DeWindt in his analysis of the peasant tenantry of Ramsey Abbey on its manor of Holywell-cum-Needingworth.[76]

Returning to higher social groups, there is some evidence of a *nomen* associated with lineage in the twelfth and thirteenth centuries. Take, for example, the FitzWarins, lords of Whittington and Alberbury in the Welsh Marches.[77] From the middle of the twelfth century, the head of the family bore the *nomen Fulk*: Fulk I (d. 1171); Fulk II (d. 1198); Fulk III (d. 1258); Fulk IV (d. 1264); and Fulk V (d. 1314). The perpetuation of this *nomen*

---

[74]For horizontal ties of the gentry see now Philippa Maddern, "'Best Trusted Friends': Concepts and Practices of Friendship among Fifteenth-Century Norfolk Gentry," in *England in the Fifteenth Century*, ed. Nicholas Rogers, Harlaxton Medieval Studies 4 (Stamford, 1994), pp. 100–17. The literature on naming and spiritual kinship, and the later developments, are now summarized by Scott Smith-Bannister, *Names and Naming Patterns in England, 1538–1700* (Oxford, 1997), pp. 25–54.

[75]Postles, "Personal Naming Patterns of Peasants and Burgesses in Late Medieval England," *MP* 12/1 (Spring 1991), 36–52, cites many examples.

[76]Edwin Brezette DeWindt, *Land and People in Holywell-cum-Needingworth: Structures of Tenure and Patterns of Social Organisation in an East Midlands Village, 1252–1457* (Toronto, 1972); in these examinations of peasant naming processes and patterns, English studies have advanced further than Continental research, it must be said.

[77]What follows is based on Janet Meisel, *Barons of the Welsh Frontier: The Corbet, Pantulf, and FitzWarin Families, 1066–1272* (Lincoln, NE, 1980), pp. 34–54.

might have owed something to the fact that the family was inconsequential before the 1140s and that it was the alliance of Fulk I with Henry Plantagenet which initiated its ascent. In this case, the impulsion to continue the *nomen* probably relates to the combined influences of the importance of the *antecessor*, a rhetoric of the lineage, and the transmission of the paternal *nomen.* Such considerations might also have informed the continuation of the *nomen* Marmaduke with the lesser lords, the de Tweing family of Yorkshire. In the cartulary of Warter Priory we are introduced to "Robertus de Tweing filius Marmeduci de Tweing. Et Marmeducus primogenitus filius et heres predicti Roberti," but brought to our attention[78] also is "Marmeducus filius domini Marmeduci de Tweing."[79] In this instance, the association is between a distinctive and unusual *nomen* transmitted within a minor seignorial family. Such associations of the *nomen* and lineage are visible in the twelfth and early thirteenth centuries, but how far were they compromised by religious and social changes in the early thirteenth century?

Whatever the processes by which it was produced, the concentration of the use of the *nomen* in all social groups of late medieval England has been remarked upon by most commentators. Some *nomina* were employed repetitively, that is, were extremely common and popular, whilst others were used infrequently.[80] The distribution of the *nomina* within a local society is thus likely to be a very skewed curve, with high usage of up to ten *nomina*, and a long tail of less frequently used *nomina*. Indeed, it is quite often the case that the two most popular *nomina* account for a sizeable proportion of the population listed.[81] Most of our accounts on the concentration of the

---

[78]For the importance of the lineage as much as the paternal name, see Jean Dunbabin, "What's in a Name? Philip, King of France," *Speculum* 68 (1993), 949: "In part the name had come to be associated with the office held by the eldest males in the family, and the giving of it strengthened the child's claim to hold that office. For example, the counts of Blois called their eldest sons either Thibauld or Eudes as a means of equipping them for their high destiny. Names therefore articulated, but also reinforced, family identity."

[79]Oxford, Bodleian Library, Fairfax MS 9, fols. 42r–43r.

[80]For this concentration in Ireland in the thirteenth to sixteenth centuries: Ó Cuív, "Aspects of Irish Personal Names," p. 116, with this rank order: *Seaán* (from the AN import *Jehan*); *Tomas*; and *Uilliam.*

[81]I use *population* here in the demographers' sense of the number of people listed in a record, for our medieval records are usually exclusive to some degree and do not encompass the whole population; the lists might comprise simply taxpayers with a level of exemption

nomen have been directed to the thirteenth and fourteenth centuries, but it was not, as has been indicated above, restricted to that *époque*. Ó Cuív, for example, has suggested that male *nomina* in Ireland were already concentrated by 1100, although further concentration occurred later.[82] Similarly, Clark revealed a degree of concentration of male *nomina* in the late eleventh century in the survey of the estates of Bury St. Edmunds.[83] It is quite clear from evidence already available, much of it reprinted in this present volume, that the process of concentration became yet more exaggerated in the late Middle Ages. Indeed, it persisted into the early modern period.[84] Further studies could attempt to discern patterns of regional variation below the consistently common names, intruders in local and regional naming patterns that might suggest some regional or local tradition.

In this final section, a return to personal identity seems not unwarranted. For, whilst the *nomen* is an enactment on the unconscious infant, hypocorisms and nicknames (here strictly nicknames as substitutes for "forenames") are received in adolescent and adult life.[85] Not only are they received, but we may collude in their adoption and reception; their formation may actively involve us as agents. At the extremes, we may, indeed, be responsible for their formation, or we may simply be recipients, but hardly always completely passive recipients. Superficially, such an area of investigation may seem trifling, but its importance has been intimated by both

---

(lay subsidies) or tenants (manorial surveys) or taxpayers with an age criterion (poll taxes). We are unlikely to be perceiving more than a selective sample of the total population.

[82]Ó Cuív, "Aspects of Irish Personal Names," pp. 156, 158, and 166. For some form of concentration in Lotharingian *nomina* caused by the repetition of protothemes and deuterothemes in dithematic name forms, see Régine le Fran, "Entre maîtres et dépendants: Réflections sur la famille paysanne en Lotharingie, aux IXe et Xe siècles," in *Campagnes médiévales. L'homme et son espace. Études offertes à Robert Fossier*, ed. Elisabeth Mornet (Paris, 1995), pp. 277–96.

[83]Principally in "*Willelmus rex?*" repr. in *Words, Names and History*, pp. 283–86. In fact, the names which she detailed were examples of a much wider homonymy on the estate ca. 1065x1098: see Postles, "Cultures of Peasant Naming," p. 31 n. 26.

[84]Smith-Bannister, *Names and Naming Patterns*, pp. 135–82 and Appendix C at pp. 191–201.

[85]For the literature about the psychological impact of names see Andrew M. Colman, David J. Hargreaves, and Wladyslaw Sluckin, "Psychological Factors Affecting Preferences for First Names," *Names* 28 (1980), 113–29.

Cecily Clark and Peter McClure, not precisely in a medieval context but in a wider perspective.[86] Perhaps a consideration of the medieval evidence can be deemed worthwhile. It is, of course, our misfortune that the usage of such designations is largely confined to the speech community and that medieval records, whatever their provenance, are still to some extent formal, and thus predominantly exclude these more colloquial forms—but not exclusively, it must be added.[87] Whether court rolls or taxation lists, the records are formal to the extent that their writers employed the highest register of language, Latin, and the *nomen* is almost universally inscribed in its Latin form.

In fact, it is quite apparent that hypocorisms were widely used in ME personal naming, from the evidence of bynames and surnames derived from personal names and in patronymic forms, which almost exclusively incorporate as an element a hypocorism, and from the evidence of literary texts.

> And þat a wiste by Wille to Watekyn he tolde hit
> And al þat he wiste by Watte tolde hit Wille aftur. . . .[88]

Further on, Langland described alliteratively:

> Dawe þe dikere, with a dosoyne harlotes
> . . . .
> Hicke þe hackenayman hit his hod aftur
> And bade Bitte þe bochere ben on his syde
> . . . .
> Robin þe ropere aryse they bisouhte.[89]

Consequently, the formal Latin, even at its lowest level, largely conceals the hypocorisms of the speech community—or apparently so.[90] In an entirely

---

[86]Peter McClure, "Nicknames and Petnames: Linguistic Forms and Social Contexts," and Cecily Clark, "Nickname Creation: Some Sources of Evidence, 'Naive' Memoirs Especially," both in *Nomina* 5 (1981), 63–76 and 83–93.

[87]See Alexander Rumble, "The Status of Written Sources in English Onomastics," *Nomina* 8 (1984), 41–56, esp. 47.

[88]William Langland, *Piers Plowman: The C-text*, ed. Derek Pearsall (Exeter, 1994), p. 112 (Passus VI, lines 70–71).

[89]Langland, *Piers Plowman*, ed. Pearsall, pp. 126–27 (Passus VI, lines 369, 378–79, and 387).

[90]It would be foolhardy here to attempt to establish a chronology of the use of hypocorisms on the lines of Jean Germain, "Les prénoms à Namur (Wallonie) de la fin du XVe siècle au

male context, admissions to the freedom of the borough of Leicester, the local clerks, although employing Latin (but also some French in a lower register), did employ some hypocorisms. In 1196, in the first extant roll, the admissions or pledges included Wilke Waterman, Wilke Smalbon, *Colinus* de foleuille (thus a latinization of the French hypocorism *Colin*), in 1198 Wilke Ouernon, Hiche de Sadint', Viel *filius Ailvin* [*sic*] *de derbi* (*Viel* being a hypocorism of *Vitalis*), in 1208 Wilke Ston, in 1210 Wilke *filius Rogeri clerici*, and in 1219 Coste Sanne.[91] Although exceptional in their incidence in the rolls, these hypocorisms reflect more accurately the naming of people within the speech community. Occasionally, the formal register of the rolls adopted latinized forms of hypocorisms, so that on Merton College's manor of Kibworth Harcourt in the late thirteenth century, the peasant Robert Sibile the younger was constantly identified in the court rolls as *Paruus Robertus*.[92] More expansively, the rental of 1251 of Cockersand Priory contains numerous hypocorisms in what would, at least further south, have been a record of some formality, so that the profusion of hypocorisms perhaps suggests, as with the Wakefield court rolls below, less reluctance to use hypocorisms in written records in the North. Amongst the male tenants of Cockersand in 1251 thus occurred eleven incidences of *Dobbe*s, two each of *Hudde/Houde* and *Hulle*, three of *Dik(k)e/Dikre*, and single incidences of *Goppe, Alecok, Beke, Bimme, Kitte, Doge, Gille, Willekin, Lawe,* and *Gibbe*.[93] Inadvertent introductions of hypocorisms might intrude into quite formal records. For example, the survey of the estate of the bishop of Ely compiled in 1222 is engrossed into a volume and written in a very well-formed charter hand. The formal Latin text renders the *nomina* in extended Latin form. When, however, a marginal memorandum was added in an early fourteenth-century hand, it reverted to an informality not exhibited in the original engrossment: "De Hicche uenatore .xv.s." The formal *Ricardus* of

---

XVIIe siècle," in *Actes du XVIe Congrès international des sciences onomastiques*, ed. Boulanger, p. 279.

[91] *Records of the Borough of Leicester*, 1: *1103–1327*, ed. Mary Bateson (Cambridge, 1899), pp. 12–14, 16–17, 20, 22, and 24.

[92] Postles, "Notions of the Family, Lordship and the Evolution of Naming Processes in Medieval England: A Regional Example," *Continuity and Change* 10/2 (1995), 187.

[93] *The Chartulary of Cockersand Abbey of the Premonstratensian Order*, ed. William Farrer, 3/3, Chetham Society, n.s. 64 (1909), pp. 1219–29.

the original text is counterpoised against the transgressive hypocorism of the addition.[94]

The most frequent occurrence of hypocorisms occurs in the court rolls of the manor of Wakefield in the late thirteenth century. Depending on which clerk wrote the rolls, there is some proliferation of these colloquial forms. Distinctive amongst the repeated hypocorisms are *Hanne* and *Han(ne)cok*, reflecting colloquial forms of *Henry*, as indicated in the tabulation below.

Hypocorism	Byname	Date	Litigation	Page[95]	Comment
Hanne	de Wlvedale	1274	leased mill	3	
	de Goukethorp	1275	took land	30	
	de Nortwode	1277	pledge, timber	161, 165	
	de Bothemley	1277	battery	165	
	prepositus	1277, 1285	pledge	165, 199	
	Packe	1277	false measure	179	
	garcio	1284		183	
	Sossan	1284	pledge	184	
	de Hyperun	1286	pledge	213	
	de Holgate	1296	trespass	245	
	le Pinder	1297	pledge	281	Henry le Pinder 1297 in battery, p. 282
	Bassard	1297	theft of sheep	287	
	molendinarius	1297	transferred land	290	

---

[94]London, British Library, Cotton MS Tiberius B II, fols. 86v–89r [Somersham].

[95]*Court Rolls of the Manor of Wakefield*, 1: *1274–1297*, ed. W. P. Baildon, Yorkshire Archaeological Society Record Series 29 (1901).

Hypocorism	Byname	Date	Litigation	Page	Comment
Hannecok	(le) Nonne	1285–86, 1297	pledge, transferred land, brushwood	203, 223, 225, 266, 292	Henry le Nonne: leased land, trans- ferred land, juror, 1286, 1297; pp. 204, 216, 225, 279–80
	ultra rivulum	1286	plaintiff	211	
	le Harpor	1286	defendant	211	Henry le Harpor in the same case: pp. 212, 214
	Coltenote	1297	*licencia concordandi*	297	

Other frequent male hypocorisms in the Wakefield court rolls include: *Nelle*; *Alcok*; *Hycke*; *Geppe*; *Luvecok*; *Gelle*; *Hudde*; and *Bate*; whilst there was occasional usage of *Heyne, Hulle, Hebbe, Huchun, Wilkoc, Jacke, Hudde, Hobbe, Watte, Nik, Wylle,* and *Dande*.[96] The Wakefield court rolls of the late thirteenth century thus reveal that hypocoristic forms of address were rife amongst the peasantry, such that some of the clerks of the rolls felt compelled frequently to record those forms rather than the more formal *nomen*. What remains unclear is whether these more colloquial forms were employed throughout all social groups or were confined to the peasantry.

---

[96] *Wakefield Court Rolls*, 1, for example: Nelle le Syur, de Wynter, de Soureby, *ad boscum*, de Thorneleye (pp. 2, 12, 21, 162); Alcok de Dundreland, *carpentarius*, de Litilwode, de Wlvedale, del Clif (pp. 6, 13, 17, 33); Hycke Schym, *garcio, serviens* (pp. 8, 204, 262); Geppe de Wytewrth, de Litelwode, le Sahar, del Dene, John son of Geoffrey de Littelwode who paid an entry fine of 12d. for two acres of land from his father Geppe in 1286, thus associating Geppe with Geoffrey, de Aula, le Folur, le Colier (pp. 12, 27, 42, 178, 184, 216, 222, 268, 272, 275); Gelle *molendinarius*, Pymerige, Cussing, de Stanley, Quintin (pp. 78, 216–17, 220–22, 228, 274, 290, 294, 299, 301, 303); Gille Quintin appeared also as Gilbert Quintin when he carried off seven cartloads of wood in 1297 (p. 301), thus associating hypocorism and formal *nomen*. The hypocorism *Hebbe* is connected to *Herbert* in the person of Hebbe de Botterlye a juror in 1286, but described as Herbert de Butterlay when a pledge in the same year (pp. 210–11). In the same manner, Nik Keneward, a pledge in 1286, must have been the father of Adam son of Nicholas Keneward, involved in an action of trespass in 1296 (p. 241).

Is it possible that the peasantry, by some inverse form of cultural independence, marked themselves off by this continuous use of hypocorisms and that these colloquial forms of address were distinctive of an independent peasant cultural tradition which was not emulative?[97]

Here, however, gender is reasserted, for, in some records at least, there seems to be less reluctance to attribute hypocorisms to females than to men, although it must be stated that the proportion of females assigned such hypocorisms is still small and the Wakefield court rolls and the Cockersand rental illustrate that male hypocorisms were not totally excluded from written records, at least in the North. If, for example, we take the poll tax of 1379 for the West Riding of Yorkshire, very few men indeed are identified by hypocorism, but hypocorisms are not unusual amongst females. *Magota* is by far the most common, but not isolated.[98] For example, in the borough of Pontefract there are twelve *Magota*s, two *Sibota*s, four *Emmota*s, a *Flissota*, two *Ibota*s, two *Cissota*s, a *Diota*, and an *Elisota*; and thus the poll tax enumerated there Emmota *Seruiens*, Magota *Seruiens*, Cissota Tresch, Cissota Seymster, and Diota de Bougate. Most of these women were not singletons, but married.[99] In general, the corpus of these female hypocorisms in the West Riding poll tax seems to include *Cissota, Diota, Elisota, Elota, Emmota, Evota, Flissota, Gillota, Ibota, Isota, Magota, Mariota, Phillipota, Senota, Sibota,* and *Tillota*.

In this introduction to recent research into the *nomen* in medieval England, the earlier work of (Scandinavian) linguists has not been evaluated or discussed, although it is listed below. It was invaluable in its time in addressing the issues of the *nomen*, in attempting to differentiate the contours of differing contributions to the corpus of ME *nomina*—IG, AScand, and CG. Without this foundation, the later research directed to the social and cultural expression of *nomina* could not have been achieved. In the act of our writing, we honor the work of Thorvald Forssner and Olof von Feilitzen.

---

[97]For these questions in the context of "cultural consumption" see John Storey, *Cultural Consumption and Everyday Life* (London, 1999), esp. pp. 36–60.

[98]For this issue now, Peter McClure, "The Interpretation of Hypocoristic Forms of Middle English Baptismal Names," *Nomina* 21 (1998), 101–32, which also considers the syntactical processes in the formation of hypocorisms, but not the social and cultural processes considered by Storey, *Cultural Consumption*.

[99]"Rolls of the Collectors in the West Riding of the Lay Subsidy (Poll Tax) 2 Richard II," *Yorkshire Archaeological Journal* 6 (1880), 2–8.

That tradition is continued in its best possible manner by Gillian Fellows Jensen and John Insley, who combine the accuracy and learning of those early pioneers of the linguistic analysis of *nomina* with a wide appreciation of the social and cultural contexts of naming processes. Since the studies in this volume largely concern the English later Middle Ages, perhaps the names of these erudite scholars occur less frequently than they should. No neglect is intended here, but we simply reveal our own deficiencies and thank them for their erudition.

THE *NOMEN*: A BRIEF EXCURSUS

In this short section, the intention is simply to indicate the broad contours of the *nomen* in the English High and later Middle Ages as a context for the studies printed and reprinted here. In pre-Conquest England, the origins of the *nomen* were multiple. The earliest IG personal names had been imported from West Germany with the English invasion. Similar name forms had migrated from West Germany into Scandinavia; these were then introduced into England by the Anglo-Scandinavians with the Viking incursions. The difference between these two corpora of West Germanic names is, to a non-linguist (like myself), problematic, but it has been suggested by linguists that there are phonemic differences between similar forms in the two corpora.[100] To complicate matters further, name forms from the Scandinavian stock migrated into Normandy, whence they were introduced into England with the Norman invasion. How to differentiate these name forms from the earlier AScand stock is yet another conundrum. The traditional method is to resort to Jean Adigard des Gautries's compendium of Norman Scandinavian names, but Insley has ingeniously suggested recently that there may also be differences in whether name forms are syncopated (elided) or not.[101]

We are then confronted with the importation of the other new name forms in the late eleventh century, the post-Conquest introductions. These

---

[100] A more precise elucidation is contained in Clark, "English Personal Names ca. 650–1300: Some Prosopographical Bearings," *MP* 8/1 (Spring 1987), 31–60 (repr. above, pp. 7–28).

[101] Jean Adigard des Gautries, *Les noms de personnes scandinaves en Normandie de 911 à 1066* (Lund, 1954); John Insley, *Scandinavian Personal Names in Norfolk: A Survey Based on Medieval Records and Place-Names*, Acta Academiae Regiae Gustavi Adolphi 62 (Uppsala, 1994), p. xxviii.

forms were predominantly CG forms, largely recognizable in such names as *William* and *Robert*. Although not completely absent from England before the Conquest, the influx of these name forms was predominantly post-Conquest. Alongside CG *nomina*, however, arrived Breton and Flemish ones, for the new aristocracy was not uniformly Norman. The distribution of lands to these non-Norman lords might be a matter of interest in investigations of the influencing of regional patterns of the *nomen*. Finally, the twelfth century witnessed the introduction of Christian *nomina*, that is, saints' and biblical names, and their rate of adoption is another matter of considerable interest.

What seems clear is that the *nomen* was the real name. Whilst bynames, as elucidated by Gösta Tengvik, had existed in an OE context, they seemingly remained unusual, except amongst the highest levels of the Norman aristocracy, amongst whom bynames (unstable, second qualifying names—the *cognomen*) and surnames (hereditary, family second qualifying names) had already been adopted.[102] What happened in the twelfth century and later is a complicated process, but for some time the *nomen* should be considered as *the* name.[103] Even in the late thirteenth and indeed the fourteenth centuries, some of the peasantry holding *nomina* less usual in their *local* circumstances might be identified in written records by *nomina* without byname or surname, so sufficient were their *nomina* to identify them. Thus in the Rutland lay subsidy of 1296–97, eight male taxpayers were identified without bynames: Alexander (Oakham); Alwin (Langham); Aubrey (Ketton); Bartholomew (Whitwell); Gervase (Wardley); Hamund (Oakham); Remund (Greetham); and Wolewin (Essendine). These *nomina* were not generally exceptional, but they were unusual within their local context at that time, so that it was still, if unusually, possible to identify these taxpayers simply by their *nomina* without the necessity for qualifying names.[104] Perhaps it is even more surprising that several taxpayers in the poll tax of 1379 in the West

---

[102]Gösta Tengvik, *Old English Bynames*, NG 4 (Uppsala, 1938); James C. Holt, *What's in a Name? Family Nomenclature and the Norman Conquest*, Stenton Lecture 1981 (Reading, 1982).

[103]What, for example, are we to make of the large number of peasant tenantry on the Bury St. Edmunds estate in 1065x1098 who were attributed bynames? See Postles, "Cultures of Peasant Naming," p. 45.

[104]Postles, "Notions of the Family," p. 182.

Riding of Yorkshire were recorded without byname or surname, by *nomen* only: Arnulph (Rythir); Gervase and Ingram (Hirst); Christopher (Farnley, a smith contributing at the higher level of 6d.); Denis (Aldfield); Maurice (Hunsingore); Hanse (presumably a hypocorism of *Johannes*) (Ribstan); Marmeduke (Garsington, a servant); Patrick (Marton); Amary (Silsden); and Matthew (Acomb *cum* Holgate).[105] This abstraction, however, hardly does justice to the complexity of the adoption of bynames and surnames.

BIBLIOGRAPHICAL NOTE

Not claiming to be comprehensive, this note lists some of the works on the Middle English *nomen* cited in this volume. Only discrete works on the *nomen* are included; for example, although J. Ambrose Raftis and Ann Reiber DeWindt and Edwin DeWindt (of the "Toronto School") have discussed peasants' personal naming in their studies of the Ramsey Abbey estate, it would not be practical to give references to their work here. Peter McClure, too, has constantly introduced some interesting insights into personal naming, but most frequently within articles dealing mostly with bynames. It might also be contended that Judith M. Bennett (once of the "Toronto School") also stimulated research into the gendered aspects of peasant forenames in her *Women in the Medieval English Countryside: Gender and Household in Brigstock before the Plague* (Oxford, 1987), p. 69. For early modern England we now have the benefit of Scott Smith-Bannister, *Names and Naming Patterns in England, 1538–1700* (Oxford, 1997).

Clark, Cecily. "People and Languages in Post-Conquest Canterbury." *Journal of Medieval History* 2 (1976), 1–33. Reprinted in *Words, Names and History: Selected Writings of Cecily Clark*, edited by Peter Jackson, pp. 179–206. Cambridge: D. S. Brewer, 1995.

———. "Women's Names in Post-Conquest England: Observations and Speculations." *Speculum* 53 (1978), 223–51. Reprinted in *Words, Names and History: Selected Writings of Cecily Clark*, edited by Peter Jackson, pp. 117–43. Cambridge: D. S. Brewer, 1995. Also reprinted below (pp. 65–102).

———. "Battle c.1110: An Anthroponymist Looks at an Anglo-Norman New Town." In *Proceedings of the Battle Conference on Anglo-Norman Studies II,*

---

[105]"Rolls of the Collectors in the West Riding," *Yorkshire Archaeological Journal* 6:133, 143, 327, 332, 333, 338; 7:149, 157, 160.

1979, edited by R. Allen Brown, pp. 21–41 and 168–72. Woodbridge: Boydell Press, 1980. Reprinted in *Words, Names and History: Selected Writings of Cecily Clark*, edited by Peter Jackson, pp. 221–40. Cambridge: D. S. Brewer, 1995.

————. "The Early Personal Names of King's Lynn: An Essay in Socio-Cultural History. Part I—Baptismal Names." *Nomina* 6 (1982), 51–71. Reprinted in *Words, Names and History: Selected Writings of Cecily Clark*, edited by Peter Jackson, pp. 241–57. Cambridge: D. S. Brewer, 1995.

————. "English Personal Names ca. 650–1300: Some Prosopographical Bearings." *MP* 8/1 (Spring 1987), 31–60. Reprinted above (pp. 7–28).

————. "*Willelmus rex? vel alius Willelmus?*" *Nomina* 11 (1987), 7–33. Reprinted in *Words, Names and History: Selected Writings of Cecily Clark*, edited by Peter Jackson, pp. 280–98. Cambridge: D. S. Brewer, 1995.

————. "Anthroponymy." In *The Cambridge History of the English Language*. Vol. 2, *1066–1476*, edited by Norman Blake, pp. 551–86. Cambridge: Cambridge University Press, 1992.

————. "Socio-Economic Status and Individual Identity: Essential Factors in the Analysis of Middle English Personal-Naming." In *Words, Names and History: Selected Writings of Cecily Clark*, edited by Peter Jackson, pp. 100–13. Cambridge: D. S. Brewer, 1995.

————. *Words, Names and History: Selected Writings of Cecily Clark*. Edited by Peter Jackson. Cambridge: D. S. Brewer, 1995.

Dodgson, John M. "Some Domesday Personal Names, Mainly Post-Conquest." *Nomina* 6 (1985), 41–52.

Feilitzen, Olof von. *The Pre-Conquest Personal Names of Domesday Book*. NG 3. Uppsala: Almqvist and Wiksells boktryckeri-a.-b., 1937.

————. "Notes on Some Scandinavian Personal Names in English 12th-Century Records." *Anthroponymica Suecana* 6 (1965), 52–68.

————. "The Personal Names of the Winton Domesday." In *Winchester in the Early Middle Ages, an Edition and Discussion of the Winton Domesday*, edited by Martin Biddle and Frank Barlow, pp. 143–229. Winchester Studies 1. Oxford: Clarendon Press, 1976.

Fellows Jensen, Gillian. *Scandinavian Personal Names in Lincolnshire and Yorkshire*. Navnestudier 7. Copenhagen: Academisk Forlag, 1968.

————. "The Names of the Lincolnshire Tenants of the Bishop of Lincoln c.1225." In *Otium et Negotium: Studies in Onamatology and Library Science Presented to Olof von Feilitzen*, edited by Folke Sandgren, pp. 86–95. Acta Bibliothecae Regiae Stockholmiensis 16. Stockholm: P. A. Norstedt and Söner, 1973.

―――. "On the Identification of Domesday Tenants in Lincolnshire." *Nomina* 9 (1985), 31–40.

Forssner, Thorvald. *Continental-Germanic Personal Names in England in Old and Middle English Times*. Uppsala: K. W. Appelbergs boktryckeri, 1916.

Franklin, Peter. "Normans, Saints and Politics: Forename-Choice among Fourteenth-Century Gloucestershire Peasants." *LPS* 36 (1986), 19–26. Reprinted below (pp. 177–88).

Haas, Louis. "Social Connections between Parents and Godparents in Late Medieval Yorkshire." *MP* 10/1 (Spring 1989), 1–21. Reprinted below (pp. 159–75).

Insley, John. "Regional Variation in Scandinavian Personal Nomenclature in England." *Nomina* 3 (1979), 52–60.

―――. "The Names of the Tenants of the Bishop of Ely in 1251: A Conflict of Onomastic Systems." *Ortnamnssällskapets i Uppsala Årsskrift* (1985), 58–78.

―――. "Some Scandinavian Personal Names in South-West England from Post-Conquest Records." *Studia Anthroponymica Scandinavica* 3 (1985), 23–58.

―――. "Some Aspects of Regional Variation in Early Middle English Personal Nomenclature." In *Studies in Honour of Kenneth Cameron*, edited by Thorlac Turville-Petre and Margaret Gelling, pp. 183–99. Leeds Studies in English, n.s. 18. Leeds: School of English, University of Leeds, 1987. Reprinted below (pp. 191–209).

―――. *Scandinavian Personal Names in Norfolk: A Survey Based on Medieval Records and Place-Names*. Acta Academiae Regiae Gustavi Adolphi 62. Uppsala: Royal Gustavus Adolphus Academy, 1994.

Morgan, G. "Naming Welsh Women." *Nomina* 18 (1995), 119–39.

Niles, Philip. "Baptism and the Naming of Children in Late Medieval England." *MP* 3/1 (Spring 1982), 95–107. Reprinted below (pp. 147–57).

Postles, D[avid] A. "Personal Naming Patterns of Peasants and Burgesses in Late Medieval England." *MP* 12/1 (Spring 1991), 29–56.

―――. "The Baptismal Name in Thirteenth-Century England: Processes and Patterns." *MP* 13/2 (Spring 1992), 1–52.

―――. "The Distinction of Gender? Women's Names in the Thirteenth Century." *Nomina* 19 (1996), 79–89.

————. "Cultures of Peasant Naming in Twelfth-Century England." *MP* 18 (1997), 25–54.

Rumble, Alexander R. "The Personal Name Material." In *Survey of Medieval Winchester*, edited by Derek J. Keene, pp. 1405–11. Winchester Studies 2/2. Oxford: Clarendon Press, 1985.

Seltén, Bo. *The Anglo-Saxon Heritage in Middle English Personal Names: East Anglia 1100–1399*. 2 vols., Lund Studies in English 43, 73. Lund: Gleerup, 1972–79.

PART II—SOCIAL GROUPS

WOMEN'S NAMES
IN POST-CONQUEST ENGLAND:
OBSERVATIONS AND SPECULATIONS

[†]*Cecily Clark*

"Sed unus homo Wihenoc amauit quandam feminam in illa terra & duxit eam & postea tenuit ille istam terram . . .": so, with a rare romantic touch, Domesday Book on a tenant at South Pickenham in Norfolk.[1] There is, however, nothing at all romantic in a modern wish to know more about the Norman settlers' marriages, on which must have hung so much of the transmission of language and of culture in the post-Conquest period. By the mid-twelfth century not only did many of the aristocracy know some

---

It is a pleasure to record how much this paper owes to Professor Giles Constable, who not only offered the hypothesis on which it is based but also gave great help with the marshaling of the evidence. Without his prompting it would never have been begun, and only his own generosity prevents his name from appearing at its head.

This essay, originally published in *Speculum* 53 (April 1978), 223–51, and reprinted in *Words, Names and History: Selected Writings of Cecily Clark*, ed. Peter Jackson (Cambridge: D. S. Brewer, 1995), pp. 117–43, is reprinted here with the permission of The Medieval Academy of America, G. R. Anderson, and Peter Jackson. Minor changes have been made to the original text.

[1]*Domesday Book seu liber censualis Willelmi Primi Regis Angliae, &c.*, 4 vols. (London, 1783–1816), 2:fol. 232. Cf. the conflicting interpretations in *VCH Norfolk* 2:3, 16: as "unus homo Wihenoc" can hardly denote Wihenoc himself, a major landholder in the district before the Breton forfeiture, it seems best to take *Wihenoc* as an uninflected genitive and translate "a certain man of Wihenoc's." The estate is assessed at three shillings.

English,[2] but a few of them were even beginning to identify with the AS past.[3] So far, however, the background and the mechanism of this cultural shift remain little known: was it connected with the settlers' patterns of marriage?

Mixed marriages certainly took place. For instance, several of the twelfth-century Anglo-Latin chroniclers—to name one group involved in recording culture if not in transmitting it—evidently sprang from such unions. William of Malmesbury makes his origins clear when he protests that in matters of national rivalry he is impartial, "quia utriusque gentis sanguinem traho."[4] So, too, Henry of Huntingdon's father, a clerk at Lincoln called Nicholas, was probably an immigrant.[5] Most interesting of all is Orderic Vitalis. Born in 1075 in Shropshire as the eldest son of Odelerius of Orléans, a clerk to the Montgomerys, and of an unidentified mother, not only was he, unlike his two brothers, baptized with an AS name, that of the officiating priest—a name which, "quod Normannis absonum censebatur," was later replaced by *Vitalis*—but also he seems to have reached the age of ten without learning his father's tongue, for when sent at that age to Saint-Evroul "exul in Normanniam veni," he tells us, ". . . Linguam, ut Joseph in Ægypto,

---

[2]See especially William Rothwell, "The Role of French in Thirteenth-Century England," *Bulletin of the John Rylands Library* 58 (1975–76), 445–66, esp. 448–49, 455, and the still-valuable paper by G. E. Woodbine, "The Language of English Law," *Speculum* 18 (1943), 395–436. See also Albert C. Baugh, *A History of the English Language*, 2nd ed. (London, 1959), chs. 5 and 6, esp. pp. 133–35, 141–46; and for some specialist points of view: Percy van Dyke Shelly, *English and French in England 1066–1100* (Philadelphia, 1921); M. D. Legge, "Anglo-Norman and the Historian," *History*, n.s. 26 (1941), 163–75; eadem, *The Significance of Anglo-Norman*, Inaugural Lecture (Edinburgh, 1968); R. M. Wilson, "English and French in England 1100–1300," *History*, n.s. 28 (1943), 37–60. The contribution by R. Berndt, "The Linguistic Situation in England from the Norman Conquest to the Loss of Normandy," *Philologica Pragensia* 8 (1965), 145–63, is thin and unilluminating.

[3]See Ralph Davis, *The Normans and Their Myth* (London, 1976), pp. 122–32, and also Richard Southern, "England's First Entry into Europe," in *Medieval Humanism and Other Studies* (Oxford, 1970), pp. 154–55. Both point to Gaimar's *L'estorie des Engles*, written in French for AN patrons but based on the *Anglo-Saxon Chronicle* and telling of the Conquest from an English point of view.

[4]*Willelmi Malmesbiriensis monachi De gestis regum Anglorum libri quinque*, ed. William Stubbs, 2 vols., Rolls Series (London, 1887–89), 2:283.

[5]*Henrici archidiaconi Huntendunensis Historia Anglorum*, ed. Thomas Arnold, Rolls Series (London, 1879), pp. 237–38 (recording Nicholas's death s.a. 1110), cf. pp. xxxi–xxxiii.

quod non noveram audivi," and that unknown language can hardly have been Latin as for the last five years he had been studying "letters, psalms, and hymns" with Siward, an English priest in Shrewsbury. Throughout his life he remained aware that Normandy was not his first home, repeatedly calling himself "Angligena," "advena," "barbarus et ignotus advena."[6] Everything, and especially young Orderic's evident ignorance of French, implies that the unknown wife of Odelerius of Orléans was English. Later in the twelfth century descent from a mixed marriage—perhaps even from a tradition of mixed marriages—may underlie the way the satirist Nigel ("Wireker," "Wetekre," or "Longchamp"), probably a son of a knightly family settled in Kent, distinguishes between two languages. Warning a "parvus libellus" of his to mind its manners when greeting the bishop of Ely (probably his kinsman), he commands it to speak as with the "paternal tongue":

> Lingua tamen caveas ne sit materna, sed illa
> Quam dedit et docuit lingua paterna tibi.[7]

As the bishop, William Longchamp, was notoriously a monoglot French-man,[8] choice between the vernaculars would matter; but it is interesting that Nigel should fear an uncouth lapse into the "mother tongue," presumably the English which the bishop did not know (conceivably, the "mother tongue" might be French and the second language "learnt from the father" Latin; but that seems less likely than that the two vernaculars are in question).

---

[6]*The Ecclesiastical History of Orderic Vitalis*, ed. and trans. Marjorie Chibnall (Oxford, 1969–in progress [completed 1980]), 2:xii–xiv, 262, and 3:6–8, 142–50; *Orderici Vitalis: Historiae ecclesiasticae libri tredecim*, ed. Auguste le Prévost, 5 vols., Société de l'Histoire de France (Paris, 1838–55), 5:133–35. For Odelerius, see also Chibnall, "Ecclesiastical Patronage and the Growth of Feudal Estates at the Time of the Norman Conquest," *Annales de Normandie* 8 (1958), 103–18, esp. 114, and J. F. A. Mason, "The Officers and Clerks of the Norman Earls of Shropshire," *Transactions of the Shropshire Archaeological Society* 56 (1957–60), 244–57, esp. 253.

[7]*Satirical Poets and Epigrammatists of the Twelfth Century*, ed. Thomas Wright, 2 vols., Rolls Series (London, 1872), 1:151. For further information about Nigel, see J. H. Mozley, "Nigel Wireker or Wetekre?" *Modern Language Review* 27 (1932), 314–17; Nigel de Long-champs, *Speculum Stultorum*, ed. J. H. Mozley and R. H. Raymo (Berkeley, CA, 1960), pp. 1–2, 123–25; William Urry, *Canterbury under the Angevin Kings* (London, 1967), pp. 153–54.

[8]See *Chronica magistri Rogeri de Houedene*, ed. William Stubbs, 3, Rolls Series (London, 1870), p. 146, also 142–43; the tale is perhaps a shade highly colored.

Both William of Malmesbury and Orderic assure us that intermarriage was common. William puts it generally, as one aspect of the Normans' characteristic affability and lack of prejudice: "matrimonia quoque cum subditis jungunt." Orderic is more specific: "Ciuiliter Angli cum Normannis cohabitabant . . . , conubiis alteri alteros sibi coniungentes."[9] So common would it seem to have been that by the late 1170s *Dialogus de Scaccario* could declare the two "nations" to have merged, at least above peasant level: "Iam cohabitantibus Anglicis et Normannis et alterutrum uxores ducentibus uel nubentibus, sic permixte sunt nationes ut uix decerni possit hodie, de liberis loquor, quis Anglicus quis Normannus sit genere."[10] This assertion occurs, however, in a complex context, that of the *murdrum* fine exacted from the local community whenever a victim of a secret slaying could not be proved to be English "ex parte patris."[11] This fine, the text explains, was now payable for all victims of unsolved murder "exceptis hiis de quibus certa sunt . . . seruilis conditionis indicia," which on the face of it implies that all free-born English people had come to be esteemed "honorary Normans." Perhaps, since the *murdrum* fine was not abolished until 1340 and as "Presentment of Englishry" meanwhile continued as a device for avoiding the corporate fine for unsolved murder, the situation might best be interpreted, as sometimes it was by contemporaries, in fiscal rather than in racial terms.[12] Be that as it may, the general statement may remain valid, that widespread intermarriage had blurred awareness of national origins.

Writers so far quoted do not distinguish between marriages of immigrant men with English women, such as were contracted by "Wihenoc's man" and evidently by Odelerius of Orléans, and those of English men with

---

[9]*De gestis regum* 2:306; *Orderic Vitalis*, ed. Chibnall, 2:256.

[10]*Dialogus de Scaccario*, ed. and trans. Charles Johnson, Nelson's Medieval Texts (London, 1950), p. 53.

[11]See *Leges Henrici Primi*, ed. Leslie John Downer (Oxford, 1972), pp. 284–92, also 234–36, 332, 417–22. See also F. C. Hamil, "Presentment of Englishry and the Murder Fine," *Speculum* 12 (1937), 285–98; N. Hurnard, "The Jury of Presentment and the Assize of Clarendon," *EHR* 56 (1941), 374–410, esp. 385–90; *Anglo-Saxon Writs*, ed. Florence Harmer (Manchester, 1952), p. 85.

[12]See *The Life and Miracles of St. William of Norwich*, ed. and trans. Augustus Jessopp and Montague Rhodes James (Cambridge, 1896), p. 25: "Cumque murdri sermo circumcirca percrebuerit, non dubium est quin regie justicie exactores ad lucrandum voluntarii ambiciosas aures falso facile adhibeant rumore."

women of Continental origin. Undoubtedly alliances of the latter sort took place (although the "turba" of female relatives whom William Longchamp was in the late twelfth century accused of importing were destined for "noble" bridegrooms, not for specifically "English" ones).[13] After all, quite apart from diplomatic and dynastic unions, occasional marriages of such kind had taken place even in pre-Conquest times, one probable case being the mid-eleventh-century marriage between the thane "Ælfgeardus" and "Edgithe venerande regine camerariam, Mahtildam nomine."[14] After the Conquest such families of Insular descent as contrived to retain some standing naturally allied themselves with the new rulers. In the late eleventh century the London magnate Deorman named one of his sons "Tierry" (a specifically French form of *Theodric*) and had him married to a Maud connected, perhaps illegitimately, with the FitzGilbert ("Clare") family.[15] In the 1150s the second FitzHarding lord of Berkeley, of AS descent as the

---

[13]See *Chronicles of the Reigns of Stephen, Henry II, and Richard II*, ed. Richard Howlett, 1, Rolls Series (London, 1884), p. 335.

[14]*Hemingi Chartularium Ecclesiae Wigorniensis*, ed. Thomas Hearne, 2 vols. (Oxford, 1723), 1:253. See also R. L. G. Ritchie, *The Normans in England before Edward the Confessor*, Inaugural Lecture (Exeter, 1948), pp. 15, 20 n. 5, and Henry Loyn, *The Norman Conquest*, 2nd ed. (London, 1967), p. 50 (both taking the queen to be, not the Confessor's Eadgyð, but Emma-Ælfgifu); Frank Barlow, *Edward the Confessor* (London, 1970), pp. 166, 192. The name *Ælfgeard*, although rare (see William George Searle, *Onomasticon Anglo-Saxonicum* [Cambridge, 1897], p. 9), is acceptably English (see Olof von Feilitzen, *The Pre-Conquest Personal Names of Domesday Book*, NG 3 [Uppsala, 1937], pp. 146, 259); *Mahtilda* (-*dis*) is a CG form (see Thorvald Forssner, *Continental-Germanic Personal Names in England in Old and Middle English Times* [Uppsala, 1916], pp. 181–82, and von Feilitzen, *Pre-Conquest Personal Names*, p. 323).

[15]David Douglas, ed., *The Domesday Monachorum of Christ Church, Canterbury* (London, 1944), pp. 62–63. The Pipe Roll for 31 Henry I lists "Tierrico fil. Dermanni" under London (*Magnum rotulum scaccarii . . . de anno trecesimo-primo regni Henrici Primi*, ed. Joseph Hunter [London, 1833; re-issued Pipe Roll Society, 1929], p. 148). See also Christopher Brooke and Gillian Keir, *London 800–1216: The Shaping of a City* (London, 1975), pp. 218–19, 344, 372.

For the change from *Theodric* to *Tierri*, see Mildred Pope, *From Latin to Modern French, &c.* (Manchester, 1934), p. 140. No firm evidence in any event exists for *Theodric* as a native English name: see Forssner, *Continental-Germanic Personal Names*, pp. 231–33, and von Feilitzen, *Pre-Conquest Personal Names*, p. 323 (but cf. Eilert Ekwall, *Early London Personal Names*, Acta Regiae Societatis Humaniorum Litterarum Lundensis 43 [Lund, 1947], pp. 2, 66, 115).

patronymic implies, married a daughter of the Norman family just dispossessed of that lordship.[16] From the north, where the Insular aristocracy survived most strongly, several such marriages are noted: thus, the founder of the "Birkin" family, the Domesday Book tenant Assolf (an ANorse name), married his son Peter to Emma de Lascelles, and Peter's son Adam was in his turn married to the Norman Maud de Caux;[17] in the first half of the twelfth century Peter son of Gamel son of Ketel son of Norman, founder of the junior branch of the "Meaux" family, married Beatrix daughter of Robert son of Radbod, and in the next generation his nephew Robert, from the senior line, married Maud daughter of Hugh Camin, each of them acquiring further estates thereby;[18] in the mid-twelfth century an heiress with Lacy connections was the bride of the William son of Godric who founded the FitzWilliams "of Emley and Sprotborough";[19] and in the 1220s Robert son of Meldred of Raby, himself probably the offspring of an alliance with an Estouteville lady, married an AN heiress whose surname he adopted, thus founding the Nevilles "of Raby."[20]

---

[16]*Complete Peerage* 2:124–26; the family is probably descended from the Eadnoth the Staller of the Confessor's time.

[17]*Early Yorkshire Charters*, ed. William Farrer and Charles Clay, 12 vols. (Edinburgh, later Wakefield, 1914–65), 3:357–61, 365–67, 371; also *The Registrum Antiquissimum of the Cathedral Church of Lincoln*, 7, ed. Kathleen Major, Lincoln Record Society 46 (Hereford, 1953), pp. 209–17. For the name *Assolf* see von Feilitzen, *Pre-Conquest Personal Names*, p. 169, and Gillian Fellows Jensen, *Scandinavian Personal Names in Lincolnshire and Yorkshire* (Copenhagen, 1968), p. 35; the Gallo-Norse equivalent was *Osulf*: see Jean Adigard des Gautries, *Les noms de personnes scandinaves en Normandie de 911 à 1066*, NG 11 (Lund, 1954), pp. 302–03.

[18]*Early Yorkshire Charters* 9:140 and 11:261–64, 345 ff.; Charles Clay, "The Family of Meaux," *Yorkshire Archaeological Journal* 43 (1971), 99–111. For the typically ANorse names *Gamel* and *Ketel*, see Fellows Jensen, *Scandinavian Personal Names*, pp. 89– 95, 166–70; for *Norðmann*, see von Feilitzen, *Pre-Conquest Personal Names*, pp. 331–32 (but cf. below, n. 79).

[19]*Early Yorkshire Charters* 3:335–36.

[20]*Complete Peerage* 9:491–94; John Horace Round, "The Origin of the Nevilles," in *Feudal England* (London, 1895; repr. 1964), pp. 370–72; *Early Yorkshire Charters* 9:24, 26, and 10:xii; C. T. Clay, "A Note on a Neville Ancestry," *Antiquaries' Journal* 31 (1951), 201–04; also Lewis Loyd et al., *The Origins of Some Anglo-Norman Families* (Leeds, 1951), pp. 72– 73. See also F. M. Stenton, "English Families and the Norman Conquest," repr. in *Preparatory to Anglo-Saxon England, Being the Collected Papers of Frank Merry Stenton*, ed.

A priori, however, we might expect the commoner case to be, as at South Pickenham, that of the English heiress married for her lands, or perhaps her father's (or late husband's) business connections, by a foreign adventurer (had a pre-Conquest match of such kind provided the apparently mixed parentage of the first William Malet?).[21] Unattached English girls may not have been far to seek, for, apart from the men killed not only in the three battles of 1066 but also in the various later rebellions, many others had emigrated to Malcolm of Scotland's court or to Byzantium, presumably leaving their sisters behind.[22] So Geoffrey "de Wirce," "de Wirchia" (probably from La Guerche near Rennes), may have got some of his wide estates through his wife "Alveva" (that is, *Ælfgifu*), named in his charter to the priory of Monks Kirby, which he founded in 1077.[23] William Pecche, a minor magnate in the eastern counties, had a first wife, still living in 1088, called "Alffwen" (that is, *Ælfwynn* or *Ælfwēn*).[24] In London Otho "aurifaber," ancestor of the hereditary diesinkers to the Mint, who although his name may look German certainly had Norman connections, not only got lands through his marriage with a rich citizen's widow but also frustrated the late husband's intention of ultimately bequeathing those lands to St. Paul's.[25] "There

---

Doris Mary Stenton (Oxford, 1970), pp. 325–34, esp. 333, and idem, *The First Century of English Feudalism, 1066–1166*, 2nd ed. (Oxford, 1961), p. 110 n. 3.

[21]See Edward Freeman, *The History of the Norman Conquest of England*, 2nd ed., 4 vols. (Oxford, 1870–76), 3:776–81; also *The Carmen de Hastingae Proelio of Guy Bishop of Amiens*, ed. Catherine Morton and Hope Muntz, Oxford Medieval Texts (Oxford, 1972), p. 38, lines 587–88 and the note there.

[22]For noble maidens and widows unprotected, see *Orderic Vitalis*, ed. Chibnall, 2:268; also *Eadmeri Historia Novorum in Anglia*, ed. Martin Rule, Rolls Series (London, 1884), p. 57.

[23]William Dugdale, *Monasticon Anglicanum*, ed. John Caley et al., 6 vols. in 8 (London, 1817–30; repr. 1970), 6/2:996. See also A. S. Ellis, "Biographical Notes on the Yorkshire Tenants Named in Domesday Book: XVIII Goisfridus de la Wirce," *Yorkshire Archæological and Topographical Journal* 4 (1877), 223–26; *VCH Northants.*, 1:292; F. M. Stenton, "English Families," p. 329, and idem, *English Feudalism*, p. 10 n. 2.

[24]*Cartularium monasterii de Rameseia*, ed. William Henry Hart and Ponsonby A. Lyons, 3 vols., Rolls Series (London, 1884–93), 1:121; *Complete Peerage* 10:331.

[25]See J. H. Round, "An Early Reference to Domesday," in *Domesday Studies*, ed. Patrick Edward Dove, 2 vols. (London, 1888–91), 2:539–59, esp. 555–57. Some records call the wife "Leveva" (*Leofgifu*; e.g., *Feudal Documents from the Abbey of Bury St. Edmunds*, ed. David Douglas [London, 1932], pp. cxxxix–cxli, 61–62, 109, 127–28), others "Eideva," "Eadgiva" (*Eadgifu*; e.g., *Early Charters of the Cathedral Church of St Paul, London*, ed. Marion Gibbs,

was at least a medieval tradition," Sir Frank Stenton tells us, "that Robert d'Oilly, the first castellan of Oxford, married a daughter of King Edward's kinsman Wigot of Wallingford"; and, as for the second Robert d'Oilly (nephew of the first), about 1130 a charter of his is attested by his wife, "ipsa domina Edit" (that is, *Eadgyð*), who can be shown to have been a former mistress of Henry I.[26] By the early twelfth century Muriel, a daughter of the

---

Camden 3rd ser., 58 [1939], pp. 136 n. 1, and 280). Otho was a minor tenant-in-chief in several counties, mainly Essex and Suffolk; for him and his descendants as moneyers, see George Cyril Brooke, *A Catalogue of English Coins in the British Museum: The Norman Kings*, 2 vols. (London, 1916), 1:cxxxiii ff., and Derek Fortrose Allen, *A Catalogue of English Coins in the British Museum: The Cross-and-Crosslets ("Tealby") Type of Henry II* (London, 1951), pp. cxii–cxiii. He certainly had Norman connections (either he or a son of the same name made the Conqueror's jeweled shrine at Caen—see *Orderic Vitalis*, ed. Chibnall, 4:110–11), although his name suggests that, like others engaged in the London jewelry trade at this time, he may have been of German origin (see Forssner, *Continental-Germanic Personal Names*, pp. 198–99, and cf. Brooke and Keir, *London 800–1216*, pp. 266–68).

[26](i) See Stenton, "English Families," p. 329; if the spurious foundation charters of St. George's, Oxford, are to be trusted, the wife's name was "Alditha" (*Ealdgyð*; *Cartulary of Oseney Abbey*, ed. Herbert Edward Salter, 6 vols., Oxford Historical Society 89, 90, 91, 97, 98, and 101 [Oxford, 1929–36], 4:1, 2, 4). For the supposed link with Wigot, see Freeman, *Norman Conquest* 4:728–34 (note C), and Ivor Sanders, *English Baronies: A Study of Their Origin and Descent 1086–1327* (Oxford, 1960), p. 93 n. 2; and for Wigot as the Confessor's "dear kinsman," see *Anglo-Saxon Writs*, ed. Harmer, no. 104—with Wigot's ancestry unknown and with his name among the Norse forms current in Normandy as well as in England (see Adigard des Gautries, *Les noms de personnes scandinaves*, pp. 238–39, and cf. Fellows Jensen, *Scandinavian Personal Names*, pp. 335–36), it is in any case not clear how "English" the family was. (ii) *Cartulary of Oseney Abbey* 4:11, 19, 266, and 5:61, 206, 207, 208, 209; see also *Complete Peerage* 9:708–09, and Stenton, *English Feudalism*, p. 281, cf. p. 189; also below, p. 75.

Traditions more dubious surround "Lucy," wife of Ivo Taillebois, *dapifer* to Rufus and a sheriff of Lincoln (either she herself or a daughter of the same name later married, first, Roger FitzGerold, so becoming the mother of William of Roumare, and, then, Rannulf le Meschin of Chester, so becoming the mother of Rannulf II of Chester: see *Complete Peerage* 3:166–67 and 7:677–80, 743–46). Although some fourteenth-century sources call her a daughter of Earl Ælfgar of Mercia (*Monasticon Anglicanum* 3:215), more probably she was a daughter of Turold, a post-Conquest sheriff of Lincoln, himself probably Norman (*Turold*, although possibly ANorse, is among the commonest of all Gallo-Norse names: see Adigard des Gautries, *Les noms de personnes scandinaves*, pp. 171–73, 342–47), and of a woman of the Malet family. See H. A. Cronne, "Ranulf de Gernons, Earl of Chester, 1129– 53," *Transactions of the Royal Historical Society*, 4th ser., 20 (1937), 103–34, esp. 104–06, and James W. F. [Sir Francis] Hill, *Medieval Lincoln* (Cambridge, 1948), pp. 91–98.

post-Conquest Lincoln magnate Colsuein, usually believed to have been an ANorse quisling, had been married to the Norman Robert de la Haye ("de Haia"), constable of Lincoln Castle.[27] The first lay steward of the abbey of Bury St. Edmund's, Ralph, installed in Abbot Baldwin's time (that is, before 1098), had a wife "Editha";[28] his successor Maurice of Windsor (from the family later to produce Gerald of Wales), installed before 1119, also had a wife variously called "Edit(ha)" or "Edgidia."[29] In the mid-twelfth century Reginald, one of Henry I's illegitimate children by the AN Sybil Corbet, married a Cornish heiress related to a family of English descent which had furnished two of his father's scribes, and was then created earl of Cornwall.[30] Towards the end of the century Christiana, granddaughter of Swan Magnusson, a landholder in Lincolnshire, became the bride of Roger de Neville.[31] Nor, as mentioning Henry I has reminded us, must we forget the less regular alliances, any children of which might have been especially likely to follow their mother's traditions. Rannulf Flambard, later bishop of Durham, had a large family by Alveva, an aunt of Christina of Markyate's and from a respectable English bourgeois line (subsequently she was married off to a burgess of Huntingdon).[32] In the mid-twelfth century one scion of the gentry, Thomas son of Richard, lord of Cuckney in Nottinghamshire,

---

[27]See Hill, *Medieval Lincoln*, pp. 48–50, 87–88, 95, 133 ff., and John Le Patourel, *Normandy and England 1066–1144*, Stenton Lecture 1970 (Reading, 1971), pp. 34–35; and for the de la Haye family, Loyd, *Origins*, p. 51. The Norse name *Colsuein* was current in England (see Fellows Jensen, *Scandinavian Personal Names*, pp. 179–80) but not, apparently, in Normandy (see Adigard des Gautries, *Les noms de personnes scandinaves*).

[28]See B. Dodwell, "Some Charters Relating to the Honour of Bacton," in *A Medieval Miscellany for Doris Mary Stenton*, ed. P. M. Barnes and C. F. Slade, Pipe Roll Society, n.s. 36 (London, 1962), pp. 147–65, esp. 149, 160; also Douglas, *Feudal Documents*, pp. cxxxviii n. 5, and 60.

[29]See Dodwell, "Bacton," pp. 149 n. 5 and 161–62, 165; for tenurial reasons Miss Dodwell suggests identifying the two Ediths and, further, that despite the apparent difference of name Maurice's wife is the "Eadiva" (that is, *Eadgifu*, not *Eadgyð*) whose brothers were the minor Essex landholders Walter Maskerel and Alexander of Wix (see ibid., pp. 150, 152, 154–55 n. 3, and 164; also L. Landon, "The Barony of Little Easton and the Family of Hastings," *Transactions of the Essex Archæological Society*, n.s. 19 [1930], 174–79).

[30]Southern, *Medieval Humanism*, p. 229, also 225 ff.

[31]F. M. Stenton, *The Free Peasantry of the Northern Danelaw* (Oxford, 1969), p. 55.

[32]*The Life of Christina of Markyate*, ed. and trans. Charles Holwell Talbot (Oxford, 1959), p. 40; see also Southern, "Ranulf Flambard," in *Medieval Humanism*, pp. 183–205.

can be seen providing for a mistress from the villein class when he grants "to Ailiua [that is, *Æðelgifu*] and her younger daughter by me the land of her father which he held for the service of one bovate, and Reginald, her own brother, with his land which he also held for the service of one bovate."[33] In general, however, the only alliances well documented are those of high politics, such as that of Earl Waltheof with the Conqueror's niece Judith and that of Henry I with Edith-Matilda of Scotland.[34] Even among "the upper ranks of feudal society, the barons and their mesne tenants," Professor Painter complains, ". . . one cannot regularly discover who men's wives were and hence it is impossible to know all family connections."[35] For settlers of more modest condition, those most perhaps involved in passing on languages and traditions, information is even more sparse and sporadic: it survives for the tenant of South Pickenham only because luckily (for us as well as for him) his love alighted where land was, and because the Norfolk survey is preserved in the "Little" Domesday Book which was less drastically sub-edited than the main volume. How many of the Norman men who settled in England did arrive alone and then marry English women?[36]

Nor is it only wives and mistresses that are in question. We began from the premise that it is usually women who are instrumental in transmitting language, and other traditions, from generation to generation; and that process does not involve mothers only, nor indeed, except in the humblest families, mothers principally. If indeed the Norman settlers brought with them comparatively few women of their own kind, then not only would some of the men have married English women but also, *a fortiori*, many children, some of purely Continental parentage as well as those of mixed blood, would

---

[33]Doris Mary Stenton, *The English Woman in History* (London, 1957), pp. 47–48, citing an unpublished charter.

[34]A projected alliance which, had it taken place and produced offspring, might also have come in this category was to have been between Gunnilda, Harold Godwinesson's daughter, and Count Alan the Red of Richmond, who abducted her from Wilton but died before he could marry her, as did his brother, Count Alan the Black, after him; see *S. Anselmi Cantuariensis opera omnia*, ed. F. S. Schmitt, 4 (Edinburgh, 1949), pp. 45–50 (Epp. 168, 169), and Richard Southern, *St. Anselm and His Biographer* (Cambridge, 1963), pp. 185 ff.

[35]Sidney Painter, "The Family and the Feudal System in Twelfth-Century England," *Speculum* 35 (1960), 1–16, esp. 2.

[36]Cf. Shelly, *English and French in England*, pp. 62 ff., and Frank Barlow, "The Effects of the Norman Conquest," in Dorothy Whitelock et al., *The Norman Conquest: Its Setting and Impact* (London, 1966), pp. 123–61, esp. 137.

have been cared for by English nurses, maids, and other servants. Not many references to children's nurses in post-Conquest England come readily to mind. A girl called "Brichtiva" (that is, *Beorhtgifu*) was employed by a priest Odo to look after his children, apparently in the late eleventh century, when a name like "Odo" might well indicate Continental origin.[37] And a story told by Gerald of Wales (whether or not it is literally true hardly matters) may imply that waiting women in general, even those of the highest nobility, were expected to be English-speaking. One of Henry I's mistresses, a "puella nobilis," had a devoted "matrona magistra," who, when a prayer on the lady's behalf—"Rorate celi desuper"—went unanswered, rounded in English on the priest responsible—"lingua materna, anglice scilicet, . . . 'Rorie se þe rorie, ne wrthe nan!' " ("Roar who will, it's useless!").[38] Admittedly, two of Henry I's recorded mistresses were English: that is, the Edith afterwards married to Robert II d'Oilly, a daughter of the Cumbrian magnate Forne of Greystoke,[39] and another Edith, the mother of the countess of Perche;[40] and these might naturally have had maids of their own nation.[41] Gerald does not, however, put forward any such explanation,

---

[37] *Memorials of St. Edmund's Abbey*, ed. Thomas Arnold, 1, Rolls Series (London, 1890), p. 164; although no date is specified, the context suggests Baldwin's abbacy, that is, ante 1098. For *Odo*, see Forssner, *Continental-Germanic Personal Names*, pp. 198–99, and von Feilitzen, *Pre-Conquest Personal Names*, p. 334.

[38] *Giraldi Cambrensis opera*, ed. John Sherren Brewer, 2, Rolls Series (London, 1862), p. 128 (the printed text has been checked with a photograph supplied by the courtesy of the Lambeth Palace Librarian, Mr. E. G. W. Bill). Although the unique manuscript of *Gemma ecclesiastica*, the thirteenth-century Lambeth MS 236, is described as a careful copy (see E. A. Williams, "A Bibliography of Giraldus Cambrensis, c. 1147–c. 1223," *National Library of Wales Journal* 12 [1961–62], 97–140, esp. 116), the English phrase is patently garbled (I am deeply grateful to Prof. Dorothy Whitelock for discussing with me some of the grammatical problems it raises); Gerald's own translation is free: "In uanum cotidie roras tantum, oras et ploras, nosque ieiunandi tam male afficis et affligis, quia quod tantopere petis proculdubio non obtinebis." Tentatively, one might reconstruct the Old English equivalent (that is, classical tenth-century forms, not twelfth-century ones) as: **Rārige sē þe rārige, ne weorð[eð] nān þing* ("Let him roar who will, nothing happens").

[39] See *Complete Peerage* 9:105–21, esp. 108–09; cf. above p. 72. For the ANorse name *Forne*, see Fellows Jensen, *Scandinavian Personal Names*, pp. 84–85.

[40] See *Complete Peerage* 9:122–13.

[41] As the bilingual pun requires a southerly dialect in which OE $\bar{a} > \bar{o}$ by the early twelfth century, the "matrona" could hardly have been Cumbrian like Edith daughter of Forne; but

apparently assuming that any waiting woman of any AN "puella nobilis" might speak like that. Now, although the role of such "matronae," waiting women and nurses, in educating the children of the Norman settlers may be hidden from us, nevertheless they may well have been the agency by which, in little more than a century, the language of the conquered people became familiar to some at least of the ruling class.[42]

Is there, then, any evidence for a small proportion of women—as wives, and, *a fortiori*, as waiting women and nursemaids—among the Norman settlers? Orderic's evidence is inconsistent, ranging from, on the one hand, the well-known comedy of the Norman wives afraid not only of warfare but even more of the Channel crossing—"Non enim ad maritos suos propter inusitatam sibi adhuc nauigationem transfretare audebant"—to the arrival in England of the Conqueror's Matilda with a train of "noble ladies."[43] Women are far from easy to trace in most kinds of early record, and after the Conquest they become even less so than before. Except for the greatest ladies, they rarely witness charters, not even those recording grants in favor of nunneries.[44] Even as party to a transaction a woman might be specified only as a man's nameless wife, widow, mother, sister, daughter, aunt, or niece. Moreover, by contrast with AS custom the women of AN times had reduced rights to hold land or to make wills.[45] Tenancies by knight service would

---

perhaps one should not press any tale of Gerald's too far.

[42]Cf. above nn. 2 and 3. See also Shelly, *English and French*, pp. 86–87; Legge, *Significance*, p. 3; Einar Haugen, *The Ecology of Language* (Stanford, 1972), p. 68; Frank Barlow, *The Feudal Kingdom of England 1042–1216*, 2nd ed. (London, 1961), p. 134.

[43]*Orderic Vitalis*, ed. Chibnall, 2:218–20, 214.

[44]See, for instance, *Cartulary of St. Mary, Clerkenwell*, ed. William Owen Hassall, Camden 3rd ser., 71 (London, 1949). For some exceptional cases of charters witnessed by women other than the grantor's wife, all as it happens from the former Danelaw, see *Documents Illustrative of the Social and Economic History of the Danelaw*, ed. F. M. Stenton (London, 1920), pp. 116, 121–22, 148, 285–86, 288; D. M. Stenton, *The English Woman*, pp. 36–37; and two both from the same Yorkshire milieu, (a) in Charles Frost, *Notices Relative to the Early History of the Town and Port of Hull, &c.* (London, 1827), pl. between pp. 8–9, cf. pp. 7–8, and (b) in *Early Yorkshire Charters* 11:348.

[45]See D. M. Stenton, *The English Woman*, pp. 29–34, and, for a wider view, Eileen Power, *Medieval Women*, ed. M. M. Postan (Cambridge, 1975), pp. 38–40; for thirteenth- and fourteenth-century statistics of women as landholders, see Josiah Russell, *British Medieval Population* (Albuquerque, 1948), pp. 62–63. For the more liberal AS practice, cf. D. M.

not be initially granted to women and, if inherited, would normally be vested in a husband.[46] Customary tenancies were seldom in women's names, except for a few widows,[47] and those sometimes under pressure to remarry so as to have a man to drive the plow.[48] Consequently, source after source proves virtually silent about the women living in England in the late eleventh and early twelfth centuries.

Direct evidence will no doubt always elude us; but, as several examples already cited may have suggested, perhaps a faint sidelight on the proportions of men and of women involved in the post-Conquest settlement may be thrown by patterns of nomenclature.[49] Name patterns might hardly seem significant enough to support such an argument, were it not that some contemporaries did see meaning in choice of name. For instance,

---

Stenton, *The English Woman*, pp. 5–6, 9, 23, 25–27, and the fuller account by F. M. Stenton, "The Historical Bearing of Place-Name Studies: The Place of Women in Anglo-Saxon Society," in *Collected Papers*, pp. 314–24. From the twelfth century on the common law increasingly limited the proprietary and testamentary rights of married women; see M. M. Sheehan, "The Influence of Canon Law on the Property Rights of Married Women in England," *Mediaeval Studies* 25 (1963), 109–24. Some link the legal changes with general social climate: see B. Bandel, "The English Chroniclers' Attitude toward Women," *Journal of the History of Ideas* 16 (1955), 113–18.

[46]Exceptionally, an heiress or a widow might hold on such tenure in her own right: see, for instance, *Liber Henrici de Soliaco Abbatis Glaston.*, ed. John Edward Jackson, Roxburghe Club (London, 1882), p. 6, and *St. Benet of Holme 1020–1210*, ed. James Rowland West, 2 vols., Norfolk Record Society 2 and 3 (1932), vol. 1, item 66, cf. 2:243–44.

[47]The only status allowing an Englishwoman of this date much independence, for which see: D. M. Stenton, *The English Woman*, pp. 34–35, 76 ff., 84; James Ambrose Raftis, *Tenure and Mobility: Studies in the Social History of the Mediaeval English Village*, Pontifical Institute of Mediaeval Studies, Studies and Texts 8 (Toronto, 1964), pp. 36–42; Power, *Medieval Women*, pp. 38, 55–57; cf. above n. 45. Russell, *British Medieval Population*, pp. 64–65, suggested that often widows might be moved into landless cottages.

[48]For at least one lord, the abbot of Ramsey, compelling widowed tenants to remarry, see D. M. Stenton, *The English Woman*, pp. 83–84.

[49]The analogous question how many women took part in the Viking settlement of Normandy is discussed in an onomastic context by Adigard des Gautries, *Les noms de personnes scandinaves*, pp. 251–53 (cf. Davis, *The Normans and Their Myth*, pp. 26–27, on the regular intermarriage between the ducal house and the Frankish aristocracy). As for Scandinavian women's names in England, I myself hope shortly to carry out a study comparable with this present one (cf. F. M. Stenton, "The Danes in England," in *Collected Papers*, pp. 136–65, esp. 154–55).

certain partisans of Robert Curthose, as William of Malmesbury reports, mocked Henry I for his political marriage with Edith of Scotland, "Godri- cum eum, et comparem Godgivam, appellantes," with an insulting intent emphasized in the context.[50] Nor must we forget how the young Orderic's name was changed because Norman ears found it "inharmonious."[51] So, with styles of name drastically altered in post-Conquest England,[52] perhaps the patterns which the innovations followed may justifiably be interpreted in social terms.

The Anglo-Saxons, sharing as they did a common Germanic tradition with Franks, Flemings, and other Continental peoples, had mainly used names of the typical Germanic types, with dithematic forms, such as *Æþel- gifu* and *Wulf-stan*, predominating over monothematic ones, such as *Offa*

---

[50]*De gestis regum* 2:471.

[51]See above, p. 66.

[52]"Post-Conquest" puts it too crudely, as, not only during the Confessor's reign but at least from the time of his mother's marriage to Æthelred II, military, ecclesiastical, and courtly infiltration from the Continent had been familiarizing many English milieux with foreign fashions. See Round, "The Normans under Edward the Confessor," in *Feudal England*, pp. 247–57; Ritchie, *The Normans in England before Edward the Confessor*; E.-J. Arnould, "Deux siècles de contacts culturels franco-anglais (871–1066)," *Annales de Normandie* 8 (1958), 71–85 (over-reliant on secondary sources); Loyn, *The Norman Conquest*, pp. 50–59; M. W. Campbell, "A Pre-Conquest Norman Occupation of England?" *Speculum* 46 (1971), 21–31. For the specifically onomastic consequences of these contacts, see Forssner, *Con- tinental-Germanic Personal Names in England*, esp. pp. lx–lxi; von Feilitzen, *Pre-Conquest Personal Names*, pp. 26–29, and idem, "Some Continental-Germanic Personal Names in England," in *Early English and Norse Studies Presented to Hugh Smith*, ed. Arthur Brown and Peter Foote (London, 1963), pp. 46–61; also sporadic instances among moneyers' names collected by V. J. Smart, "Moneyers of the Late Anglo-Saxon Coinage, 973–1016," in *Com- mentationes de nummis saeculorum ix–xi in Suecia repertis II*, Kungl. Vitterhets Historie och Antikvitets Akademiens Handlingar: Antikvariska Serien 19 (Stockholm, 1968), pp. 191–276, and by O. von Feilitzen and C. Blunt, "Personal Names on the Coinage of Edgar," in *England before the Conquest: Studies in Primary Sources Presented to Dorothy Whitelock*, ed. Peter Clemoes and Kathleen Hughes (Cambridge, 1971), pp. 183–214. The *TRE* landholders listed in the Winchester survey of ca. 1110 (see also below, p. 94) already show some 15% of "Continental" names: see O. von Feilitzen, "Personal Names," in Martin Biddle et al., eds., *Winchester in the Early Middle Ages: An Edition and Discussion of the Winton Domesday*, Winchester Studies 1 (Oxford, 1976), pp. 145–91, esp. 185 (I am deeply grateful to the late Dr. von Feilitzen for allowing me to see this important study before its official publication).

and *Gode* (often hypocoristic). Common though the tradition was, each Germanic people had its own preferred range of names and name elements, and the Anglo-Saxons had theirs.[53] From time to time during the AS period CG forms do appear in English records,[54] and throughout the Danelaw Norse names were from the tenth century onwards widely adopted alongside native ones;[55] but such additions only variegated the Insular pattern without superseding it. Then, between the Conquest and the end of the twelfth century, almost all the distinctively Insular names were rapidly discarded, by peasants almost as fast as by burgesses, in favor of those current among the Norman settlers.[56] These "Continental" names were of several kinds. There

---

[53]See Searle, *Onomasticon Anglo-Saxonicum* (obsolescent); von Feilitzen, *Pre-Conquest Personal Names*; idem, "Some Unrecorded Old and Middle English Personal Names," *Namn och Bygd* 33 (1945), 69–98; idem, "Some Old English Uncompounded Personal Names and By-names," *Studia Neophilologica* 40 (1968), 5–16; P. H. Reaney, "Notes on the Survival of Old English Personal Names in Middle English," *Studier i Modern Språkvetenskap* 18 (1953), 84–112; Mats Redin, *Studies on Uncompounded Personal Names in Old English* (Uppsala, 1919). Owing to the nature of the sources available, many studies listed here and in later notes offer only scanty information about women's names, exceptions being von Feilitzen's paper in *NoB* 33 and Reaney's in *SMS* 18; see especially Maria Boehler, *Die altenglischen Frauennamen*, Germanische Studien 98 (Berlin, 1930), and also H. B. Woolf, "The Naming of Women in Old English Times," *Modern Philology* 36 (1938–39), 113–20.

[54]See above, n. 52.

[55]See Erik Björkman, *Nordische Personennamen in England in alt- und frühmittelenglischer Zeit*, Studien zur englischen Philologie 37 (Halle, 1910), and idem, *Zur englischen Namenkunde*, Studien zur englischen Philologie 47 (Halle, 1912); cf. the review article by R. E. Zachrisson, "Notes on Early English Personal Names," *Studier i Modern Språkvetenskap* 6 (1917), 269–98 (still interesting although now dated); D. Whitelock, "Scandinavian Personal Names in the Liber Vitae of Thorney Abbey," *Saga-Book of the Viking Society* 12 (1937–45), 127–53; von Feilitzen, *Pre-Conquest Personal Names*, pp. 18–26, and idem, "Notes on Some Scandinavian Personal Names in English 12th-Century Records," in *Personnamnstudier 1964 tillägnade minnet av Ivar Modéer (1904–1960)* = *Anthroponymica Suecana* 6 (1965), 52–68; Fellows Jensen, *Scandinavian Personal Names.* For some complex international interactions, see O. von Friesen, "Personal Names of the Type *Bótolfr*," *Studia Neophilologica* 14 (1941–42), 357–65.

[56]Thus, in the admissions lists of Hyde Abbey names of Continental type begin to appear regularly, especially for "pueri," from about the 1170s on (*Liber Vitae: Register and Martyrology of New Minster and Hyde Abbey, Winchester*, ed. Walter de Gray Birch, Hampshire Record Society [London, 1892], esp. pp. 36–37). See also: Ekwall, *Early London Personal*

were CG names, of the same general types as the Insular ones, but permutating a different stock of name elements: these were now mainly adopted in gallicized form, thus *Raulf* for *Radulf*, *Gilbert* for *Giselber(h)t*, and so on (of course, the spoken forms are often partly disguised by scribal latinizations).[57] There were Gallo-Norse names stemming from the Norse settle-

---

Names, pp. xii, 87, 90–96, 98–100; P. H. Reaney, "Pedigrees of Villeins and Freemen," *Notes and Queries* 197 (1952), 222–25, and idem, *The Origin of English Surnames* (London, 1967), pp. 129–52; G. Fellows Jensen, "The Names of the Lincolnshire Tenants of the Bishop of Lincoln, c. 1225," in *Otium et Negotium: Studies in Onomatology and Library Science Presented to Olof von Feilitzen*, Acta Bibliothecae Regiae Stockholmiensis 16 (Stockholm, 1973), 86–95 (Mrs. Dorothy Owen points out to me that the true date of the document studied is 1258); von Feilitzen, "Personal Names," in *The Winton Domesday*, esp. pp. 183–91.

Many studies have concentrated on the AS elements surviving in post-Conquest nomenclature: as well as Ekwall's monograph on London names, see also Reaney, "Survival," and Bo Seltén, *The Anglo-Saxon Heritage in Middle English Personal Names: East Anglia 1100–1399*, Lund Studies in English 45 (Lund, 1972).

[57]For the present purpose the most useful compilation is: Marie-Thérèse Morlet, *Les noms de personne sur le territoire de l'ancienne Gaule du VIe au XIIe siècle*, 2 vols. (Paris, 1968–73), 1 (*Les noms issus du germanique continental et les créations gallo-germaniques*); for some shortcomings of this see, however, the review by C. Wells in *Medium Ævum* 39 (1970), 358–64. Most studies of French names have been narrowly localized and concentrated on periods rather later than ours, thus: Harry Jacobsson, *Études d'anthroponymie lorraine: Les bans de tréfonds de Metz (1267–1298)* (Göteborg, 1955); M. le Pesant, "Les noms de personne à Evreux du XIIe au XIVe siècles," *Annales de Normandie* 6 (1956), 47–74; Marie-Thérèse Morlet, "Les noms de personne à Eu du XIIIe au XVe siècle," *Revue internationale d'onomastique* 11 (1959), 131–48, 174–82, and ibid. 12 (1960), 62–70, 137–48, 205–19; *Le nécrologe de la confrérie des jongleurs et des bourgeois d'Arras (1194–1361)*, ed. Roger Berger, 2 vols., Mémoires de la Commission départementale des Monuments Historiques du Pas-de-Calais 11 (pt. 2) and 13 (pt. 2) (Arras, 1963–70); Marie-Thérèse Morlet, *Étude d'anthroponymie picarde: Les noms de personne en Haute Picardie aux XIIIe, XIVe, XVe siècles*, Collection de la Société de linguistique picarde 6 (Amiens, 1967); G. T. Beech, "Les noms de personne poitevins du 9e au 12e siècles," *Revue internationale d'onomastique* 26 (1974), 81–100.

For West Germanic name traditions other than Frankish/French, see Henry Bosley Woolf, *The Old Germanic Principles of Name-Giving* (Baltimore, 1939); Ernst Förstemann, *Altdeutsches Namenbuch*, 3 vols., rev. ed. (Bonn, 1900–16), 1 (*Personennamen*), and *Ergänzungsband*, ed. Henning Kaufmann (Munich, 1968); Wilhelm Schlaug, *Studien zu den altsächsischen Personennamen des 11. und 12. Jahrhunderts*, Lunder Germanistische Forschungen 30 (Lund, 1955); idem, *Die altsächsischen Personennamen vor dem Jahre 1000*, Lunder Germanistische Forschungen 34 (Lund, 1962); Joseph Mansion, *Oud-Gentsche Naamkunde: Bijdrage tot de kennis van het oud-nederlandsch* (The Hague, 1924); C. Tavernier-

ment of Normandy,[58] sometimes hard to tell from the corresponding ANorse forms,[59] and sometimes also open to confusion with Frankish forms.[60] And there was a comparatively new range of names which at this time was fast gaining ground on the Continent, that is, the specifically "Christian" names, the Hebrew, Greek, and Latin names of biblical characters and of saints.[61] For names of all these kinds there was also a great stock of hypocoristic forms, both shortenings and elaborate diminutives. By the end of the twelfth century nearly all Englishmen, in all districts and of all ranks, were bearing names drawn from this new "Continental" stock. Thus, although—as we

---

Vereecken, *Gentse Naamkunde van ca. 1000 tot 1253: Een Bijdrage tot de kennis van het oudste Middelnederlands*, Bouwstoffen en Studien voor de Geschiedenis en de Lexicografie van het Nederlands 11 (Brussels, 1968); O. Leys, "De oudste Vrouwennamen in Zuid-Nederland," in *Onomastica Neerlandica: Anthroponymica* 10 (Louvain, 1959), 5–28.

[58] See Adigard des Gautries, *Les noms de personnes scandinaves*; also idem, "Les noms de personnes scandinaves dans les obituaires de Jumièges," in *Jumièges: Congrès scientifique du XIIIe centenaire* (Rouen, 1955), pp. 57–67.

[59] See Fellows Jensen, *Scandinavian Personal Names,* pp. lxi, lxiii, and passim; also Ekwall, *Early London Personal Names*, pp. 73–74, 87, 88, and Reaney, *Origin*, pp. 125–27. This is the most trying source of ambiguity in our material. Ritchie, *The Normans in England before Edward the Confessor*, suggested that the Scandinavian element in Norman culture may have been recognized and welcomed in the English Danelaw. Further complications arise from possible ANorse influence on the original settlement of Normandy; see L. Musset, "Pour l'étude des relations entre les colonies scandinaves d'Angleterre et de Normandie," *Mélanges de linguistique et de philologie Fernand Mossé in memoriam* (Paris, 1959), pp. 330–39, and idem, "Pour l'étude comparative de deux fondations politiques des Vikings: Le royaume de York et le duché de Rouen," in *Essays in Honour of John Le Patourel = Northern History* 10 (1975), 40–54, esp. 47–51.

[60] See Adigard des Gautries, *Les noms de personnes scandinaves*, pp. 26–29; also Zachrisson, "Notes on Early English Personal Names," pp. 280–84.

[61] See Morlet, *Les noms de personne sur le territoire de l'ancienne Gaule*, 2: *Les noms latins ou transmis par le latin*; H. Carrez, "Noms de personne féminins dans la région dijonnaise du XIIe au XVe siècle," *Annales de Bourgogne* 14 (1942), 85–129, esp. 109 ff.; Jacobsson, *Études d'anthroponymie*, pp. 28–29; le Pesant, "Les noms de personne à Evreux," pp. 50–51; Morlet, "Les noms de personne à Eu," 11:135; eadem, *Étude d'anthroponymie picarde*, pp. 17, 23; Berger, ed., *Le nécrologe* 2:305–08; Beech, "Les noms de personne poitevins," passim. For Flemish Flanders, see O. Leys, "La substitution des noms chrétiens aux noms pré-chrétiens en Flandre occidentale avant 1225," in *Cinquième congrès international de toponymie et d'anthroponymie: Actes et mémoires = Acta Salmanticensia (Filosofía y Letras)* 11 (1958), 2 pts. independently paginated, 1:403–12.

have ventured to suggest in several instances already quoted—the "nationality" of a name may for the first generation after the Conquest be a fair though not infallible guide to its bearer's origins, after that fashion comes to play a larger and larger part. With the trend as it was, use of the unfashionable Insular names, insofar as it persisted, must have implied not only parentage at least partly Insular—Norman settlers would have been unlikely to adopt forms which some at least of them mocked at for supposed uncouthness—but also some family attachment to English traditions.

Now, until the end of the twelfth century at least, the Insular strain remains far commoner in women's names than in men's. This has several times been remarked: by Reaney, for instance, for the names of late twelfth-century peasants,[62] and by Cameron for the 1177 survey from Newark;[63] but as yet no adequate investigation of the discrepancy seems to have been attempted.[64] And yet it is a very marked discrepancy: the late twelfth-century pedigrees of near-villein families analyzed by Reaney show that, whereas by that time and in that class Insular forms accounted for less than 30% of men's names, among women's they amounted to almost half (Thomas of Cuckney's Ailiva, we may recall, had a brother "Reginald").

For this discrepancy the easiest explanation would be "fashion." Certainly fashion could work differentially on women's names and men's. In France itself, when between the tenth and the fifteenth centuries the specifically "Christian" names, the biblical names and saints' names, came to displace the Germanic ones originally favored, this change affected women's names faster than men's.[65] Yet this analogy is poor, as fashion was working

---

[62]Reaney, "Pedigrees," pp. 224–25; idem, *Origin*, p. 106.

[63]Kenneth Cameron in *Documents Relating to the Manor and Soke of Newark-on-Trent*, ed. Maurice Willmore Barley et al., Thoroton Society Record Series 16 (Nottingham, 1956), p. xii, cf. pp. xiii–xiv.

It may or may not chime with these observations that when Gillian Fellows Jensen instances "return to Scandinavian nomenclature after a break of one generation" the examples she cites involve a high proportion of women's names (*Scandinavian Personal Names*, p. lxiii).

[64]Thus, Seltén, *The Anglo-Saxon Heritage*, attempts no comparison between masculine and feminine name patterns.

[65]See le Pesant, "Les noms de personne à Evreux," pp. 50–51, 63, and Morlet, *Étude d'anthroponymie picarde*, p. 23; likewise, Berger's statistics of the most popular names for both sexes seem to imply that in Arras also "Christian" names were adopted faster for women

in exactly opposite ways on the two sides of the Channel, with women's names leading the fashion in France but in England remaining Germanic, Insular, and archaic. What makes this conservatism of English women's names all the more noteworthy is the narrowness of the Insular name stock in common use. Some factor must have been at work other than simple modishness.

A hypothesis might be put forward. In some districts at least the Continental names first to be adopted by the peasantry were identifiably those of the local gentry and magnates.[66] If, then, a fair number of the post-Conquest male immigrants had, like Geoffrey of La Guerche, like William Pecche, like that "man of Wihenoc's," married English women instead of bringing wives of their own nation with them, then the early patterns of upper-class naming offered to fashion-conscious people of English stock would have included fewer women's names than men's. If, moreover, some of these hypothetical mixed couples had named more of their daughters than of their sons according to the maternal traditions, then imbalance in the name stock would have persisted (unhappily, the rarity of records naming entire families makes this last point unverifiable). Such practices would indeed explain the discrepancy between the rate at which Continental men's names were being adopted by English families and that for women's; and they would have implications going far beyond mere name patterns.

Before indulging in interpretation, we must, however, be sure that the discrepancy is genuine and not a mere random quirk in the limited materials from which it has so far been reported. And, before further materials are analyzed, we must face several problems. That some name forms are ambiguous we have already noted: with many Norse names scribal forms like *Turchetillus* and *Turmodus* conceal whether the spoken reality was Gallo- or Anglo-Norse;[67] and again, with name forms represented both in AS and

---

than for men (*Le nécrologe* 2:306). New fashions often affect women's names more drastically than men's (for an observation of this in a milieu very different from ours, northern Sweden in recent times, see *Anthroponymica Suecana* 6:291). In Flanders development was complex, as there "Christian" names seem to have been adopted later for women than for men but, once adopted, then to have spread faster; see Leys, "La substitution des noms chrétiens," p. 411, and idem, "De oudste Vrouwennamen," p. 17 (his explanation by differences in male and female psychology is irrelevant, as it assumes that individuals choose their own names).

[66]See below, p. 87 and n. 80.

[67]See Adigard des Gautries, *Les noms de personnes scandinaves*, pp. 163–67, 322–26,

in CG, scribal forms like *Osbertus*, *Wibertus*, even *Wlfricus*, might with equal plausibility be referred to either origin.[68] Common sense suggests that a theoretically ambiguous form may often be safely assigned to the same nationality as its bearer. Truly ambiguous forms are best left right out of the reckoning; luckily, they are seldom so numerous as gravely to affect the statistics. Other problems arise from the kinds of document available and their form. Often, when the same name recurs several times, it may be impossible to determine how many distinct individuals were involved. And, as we have already noted, documents concerned with property holding refer almost exclusively to adult males, and mainly to the upper classes. Such women as are named are often specified as widows, and so might well be a generation or more older than some of the men listed alongside them—an age gap which, unless compensated for, would falsify our whole analysis. For all these reasons, only gross discrepancies between the name patterns of the sexes will be relevant; citing percentages to several decimal places (easy though these are to calculate mechanically) would only lend a spurious precision to what can at best never be more than a shadow of the truth. Even the grossest discrepancies will not deserve much weight unless they occur consistently in a wide range of unrelated documents from many parts of the country. The imbalance between the totals of men's and women's names recorded does, moreover, make it impractical to apply one of the subtler measures of foreign influence by counting how many different foreign names were in use rather than how great a percentage of the recorded population bore them.

Indeed, the silence of so many records at times raises doubts whether any investigation at all will be possible. Domesday Book and its satellites deal with feudal tenancies of kinds only exceptionally held by women; so too the early twelfth-century surveys from Abingdon, Lindsey, and Lei-

---

429–31, and Fellows Jensen, *Scandinavian Personal Names*, pp. 309–11; also von Feilitzen, *Pre-Conquest Personal Names*, pp. 394–95, idem, in *The Winton Domesday*, p. 174, and Ekwall, *Early London Personal Names*, p. 83. Pronunciation must, of course, have differed; cf. modern English surnames such as *Thurkell*, *Thurkettle*, with Norman place names such as *Torqueville, Tourmanville*. See also above, nn. 59, 60.

[68]See Forssner, *Continental-Germanic Personal Names*, p. 252; von Feilitzen, *Pre-Conquest Personal Names*, pp. 338, 413, 423–24; idem, in *The Winton Domesday*, pp. 167, 177, 178; Schlaug, *Die altsächsischen Personennamen des 11. und 12. Jahrhunderts*, pp. 160–61, 167; Tavernier-Vereecken, *Gentse Naamkunde*, pp. 78, 106; Morlet, *Les noms . . . gallo-germaniques*, cols. 46a, 223a, 231a.

cestershire.[69] The survey of the Peterborough estates made in the 1120s names few of the customary tenants and scarcely a woman at all, of any rank.[70] The cartulary of St. Benet of Holme offers only a dozen women's names datable between 1066 and 1150.[71] The fascinating series of legal memoranda entered in the Exeter Book likewise offers too few women's names for any statistical comparison, especially as the men's names here represent no one social class but range from those of magnates to those of manumitted serfs.[72] The two Burton Abbey surveys, dating respectively from about 1115 and about 1126, offer only twenty-two women's names all told—too few to make effective evidence either way, at least these do not contradict our pattern, for, whereas the men's names here show 18% to 24% of Continental forms, all the women's names look Insular except for two instances of *Avelina*, both probably referring to the same individual.[73]

Several manorial surveys do, however, more amply illustrate the differential fashion we are studying, but only late in the twelfth century. The Glastonbury survey made by Henry of Sully in 1189 shows the contrast clearly: among men's names Insular forms amount to under a quarter, but among women's to almost a half.[74] The other side of the country is rep-

---

[69]D. C. Douglas, "Some Early Surveys from the Abbey of Abingdon," *EHR* 44 (1929), 618–25; *The Lincolnshire Domesday and the Lindsey Survey*, ed. Charles Wilmer Foster et al., Lincoln Record Society 19 (Horncastle, 1924); *The Leicestershire Survey c. A.D. 1130*, ed. Cecil Frederick Slade, University of Leicester Department of English Local History: Occasional Papers 7 (Leicester, 1956).

[70]*Chronicon Petroburgense*, ed. Thomas Stapleton, Camden Society (London, 1849), pp. 157–82. The only woman named seems to be *Johanna* (Wake), p. 181.

[71]*St. Benet of Holme*, ed. West.

[72]*The Exeter Book of Old English Poetry* (facsimile), ed. Raymond Wilson Chambers et al. (London, 1933), fols. 3v–7v; see also M. Förster, "The Preliminary Matter," ibid., pp. 44–54.

[73]C. G. O. Bridgeman, ed., "The Burton Abbey Twelfth-Century Surveys," *Collections for a History of Staffordshire Edited by The William Salt Archaeological Society 1916* (London, 1918), pp. 209–310, esp. 212–47; see also J. H. Round, "The Burton Abbey Surveys," ibid., n.s. 9 (London, 1906), pp. 271–89. For *Avelina*, see Morlet, *Les noms . . . gallo-germaniques*, col. 48a.

[74]*Liber Henrici de Soliaco*, ed. Jackson, pp. 21–142. Unfortunately, no comparably significant pattern seems discernible in the patronymics and metronymics, not in any case very common here.

resented by two documents. One of these is complex, a Ramsey survey usually dated in the 1160s and incorporating sporadic comparison with "the time of the older King Henry," apparently the 1130s; it offers about a thousand names, mainly of peasants, less than a tenth being women's names.[75] Over 55% of such women's names as there are show Insular forms, against an average of under 30% for the corresponding men's names. Predictably, most of the women named are widows, and fortunately the chronological complexity of the survey allows their names to be compared with those of the current men's fathers or other antecessors (insofar as these are given); even these earlier men's names show Insular forms already amounting to much less than half the total. Rather later than the Ramsey survey is the one in the Kalendar of Abbot Samson of Bury St. Edmunds, dating from between 1186 and 1191: not, unfortunately, the handiest document to use, for, as well as being highly repetitive, it does not consistently note the status of the various tenants.[76] Nevertheless, it emphatically exemplifies our patterns of name giving: whereas only 25% of the names of the current male tenants show Insular forms, about 60% of those of the current female tenants (amounting as usual to less than a tenth of the total and mainly widows) show such forms; and, whereas men of the preceding generations (fathers, former landholders) show under 50% of Insular names, women in the same categories show well over 70%. So women's names here—even more so than at Ramsey—are more conservative than those of the previous generation of men.

The famous Bury survey of about a century earlier, that in the Feudal Book of Abbot Baldwin,[77] does, however, prove frustrating from our point of view. Not surprisingly at a date when most tenants must have been born before the Conquest, about 95% of men's names are still Insular, with some ANorse cast. The women's names, much in the minority (less than forty out

---

[75]*Cartularium monasterii de Rameseia*, ed. Hart and Lyons, 3:218–315; see also James Ambrose Raftis, *The Estates of Ramsey Abbey*, Pontifical Institute of Mediaeval Studies, Studies and Texts 3 (Toronto, 1957), pp. 305–06. One section also refers to "King John" (p. 292). The figures cited are averages, as the balance of Insular names to Continental ones varies markedly from section to section.

[76]*The Kalendar of Abbot Samson of Bury St. Edmunds and Related Documents*, ed. Ralph Davis, Camden 3rd ser., 84 (London, 1954), pp. 3–72.

[77]*Feudal Documents from the Abbey of Bury St. Edmunds*, ed. Douglas, pp. 25–44; for the date, see ibid., p. xlix, but cf. V. H. Galbraith, "The Making of Domesday Book," *EHR* 57 (1942), 161–77, esp. 168 n. 1, where he suggests "the early part of Henry I's reign."

of some seven hundred) and as usual mainly those of widows, show no certain Continental forms at all.[78] We might have guessed as much about the peasantry of the 1090s; and where evidence would have been most welcome it fails entirely. The abbey's "feudati homines," that is, those holding by knight service, are duly listed, and their names (not one unambiguously Insular)[79] neatly suggest how *Durandus, Fulcerius, Guarinus, Hubertus, Ricardus, Walterus,* and so on were introduced into the local name stock for the English peasants to copy;[80] but of these enfeoffed knights' wives, not one word.

Yet one record about Bury does move the imagination. "In uilla ubi quiescit humatus Scs Eadmundus" there were, Domesday Book tells us, "xxxiiii milites int*er* fr*ancos* & anglic*os*."[81] As the "feudati homines" included several magnates far too grand to attend personally upon an abbot, these knights resident at the abbey gates were presumably stipendiaries who performed the actual military duties. Now, with such a mixed band of Frenchmen and Englishmen, there might have been little to hinder the in-

---

[78]Many of the names here have been discussed in the papers by von Feilitzen and by Reaney listed in nn. 52, 53, and 55 above. The feminine *Æilgild*, for which a Continental etymology has been proposed, is a ghost form, the true reading being *Æilgid* (that is, *Æþelgyð*); see Cambridge University Library MS Mm. iv. 19, fol. 138(2)v, and cf. *Feudal Documents*, p. 33.

[79]Two forms might be Insular, that is, *Normannus* (*Feudal Documents*, p. 24) and *Wlwardus* (ibid., p. 17), but the equivalent Continental forms were widespread: see Forssner, *Continental-Germanic Personal Names*, p. 260; von Feilitzen, *Pre-Conquest Personal Names*, pp. 31–32, and idem, in *The Winton Domesday*, p. 178; Ekwall, *Early London Personal Names*, pp. 55–56, 72; Schlaug, *Die altsächsischen Personennamen des 11. und 12. Jahrhunderts*, p. 166; Tavernier-Vereecken, *Gentse Naamkunde*, p. 35; Morlet, *Les noms . . . gallo-germaniques*, cols. 174a–b, 231a.

[80]I hope to publish a paper demonstrating this in more detail. For aping the upper classes as a general practice see O. Leys, "Socio-Linguistic Aspects of Name-Giving Patterns," *Onoma* 18 (1974), 448–55, esp. 452, cf. 453–54. In Normandy the names most popular were those associated with the ducal house and with local families of magnates (see le Pesant, "Les noms de personne à Evreux," p. 55, and Morlet, "Les noms de personne à Eu," 11:138), and in Flanders the countesses' foreign names were widely copied (see J. Lindemans, "Over de Infloed van enige Vorstinnennamen op. de Naamgeving in de Middeleeuwen," *Verslagen en Mededelingen der Koninklijke Vlaamse Academie voor Taal- en Letterkunde* [1950], pp. 99–106).

[81]*Domesday Book* 2:fol. 372r. See also Douglas, *Feudal Documents*, pp. cvi–cviii, and S. Harvey, "The Knight and the Knight's Fee in England," *PP* 49 (November 1970), 3–43, esp. 12–13.

comers from marrying the sisters, or daughters, or widows of their English comrades. Indeed, if the suggestion is true that small tenants by knight service barely differed in financial or social standing from free farmers,[82] then throughout the country there might have been little barrier, other than language, to marriage between the humbler French "knights" and the sisters, daughters, or widows of the more prosperous of their peasant neighbors. In this context we may think of the anonymous "Francigenae" scattered in twos and threes, or even singly, across the manors belonging to the abbey of St. Albans and across several counties in the Welsh Marches, regularly listed in Domesday Book alongside the villeins and borders.[83] How often such intermarriages may in fact have taken place remains, unfortunately, mere speculation.

And consideration of those thirty-four knights living in the "villa" of Bury opens a further line of thought. Perhaps clues to the merging of the two peoples might better be sought from town records than from rural ones. To begin with, women might well be more adequately represented in town records; for, whereas physical incapacity barred them from tenure (except by proxy) based either on military service or on driving a plow team, town life and trade afforded them more scope for independence and so for having their names recorded. At least this was so by the thirteenth century in such a town as Battle, where not only widows but also unmarried daughters often inherited property and held it in their own right.[84] For another thing, whereas in the country the two "nations" often enjoyed different types of tenure and so to some extent occupied different social ranks, in many towns French burgesses were living alongside English ones on more or less equal terms. Some English towns encouraged French settlers by granting them specific fiscal privileges.[85] Apart from the mixed band of knights at Bury St. Edmunds,

---

[82]See F. M. Stenton, *English Feudalism*, pp. 142–45, and Harvey, "The Knight," passim; but cf. the literary evidence for strong class feeling in France itself adduced by P. Noble, "Attitudes to Social Class as Revealed by Some of the Older Chansons de Geste," *Romania* 94 (1973), 359–85.

[83]*Domesday Book* 1:fols. 135v–136v, 138r–138v, 139v, 173r–173v, 174v–177r, 179v–180r, 181r–183r, 252v–253r, 254v–255v, 256v, 258v–259r, 260r.

[84]See Eleanor Searle, *Lordship and Community: Battle Abbey and Its Banlieu, 1066–1538*, Pontifical Institute of Mediaeval Studies, Studies and Texts 26 (Toronto, 1974), pp. 118–20; also Power, *Medieval Women*, pp. 10, 57 ff.

[85]See, for instance, Loyn, *The Norman Conquest*, pp. 173, 177, 179.

Domesday Book notes sixty-five Frenchmen at Southampton, a hundred and forty-five at York, forty-three at Shrewsbury, twenty-four at Dunwich, twenty-two at Wallingford, four at Stanstead and four at St. Albans, three at Cambridge, at Hereford a number unspecified but evidently considerable, and at Norwich forty-one "in nouo Burgo" and apparently also eighty-three other "burgenses franci."[86] Even though some so-called "burgenses" were absentee landlords, such towns may nonetheless have had many French residents—Shrewsbury, for instance, where forty-three burgages out of some hundred and fifty were in French hands. Such an admixture must necessarily, one might think, have affected the language and the customs of the towns that experienced it; populous places full of the to-ing and fro-ing of trade ought, after all, to see languages and traditions more briskly and more thoroughly mixed than they would be in a sparsely peopled countryside. When Orderic spoke of the two nations living side by side and inter-marrying, it was in such an urban context: "Ciuiliter Angli cum Normannis cohabitabant, in burgis, castris et urbibus, conubiis alteri alteros mutuo sibi coniungentes...."[87]

Matters were not, however, so simple, for the two groups did not always live in the closest harmony. At Norwich thirty-six Frenchmen at first shared their "new town" with six English neighbors, but by 1086 the Englishmen had been ousted by five more Frenchmen; where the other eighty-three Frenchmen lived is not clear.[88] At Southampton some demarcation between the two groups is implied by a "French street" running parallel to the main "English street."[89] At Shrewsbury the English burgesses openly resented the tax exemptions granted to the foreigners.[90] Were Englishmen so hostile or Frenchmen so aloof as to hinder the former from marrying their daughters to the more privileged incomers?

All too often the surviving documents again fail to reply. The earliest extensive burgess list extant, that of the king's burgesses in Colchester at

---

[86]*Domesday Book* 1:fols. 52r, 56r, 179r, 189r, 252r, 298r, and 2:fol. 118r. Northampton and Nottingham also each comprise a "novus burgus" as well as the old, but without any note on the origin of the residents (ibid. 1:fols. 219r, 280r).

[87]*Orderic Vitalis*, ed. Chibnall, 2:256.

[88]*Domesday Book* 2:fol. 118r.

[89]Colin Platt, *Medieval Southampton: The Port and Trading Community, A.D. 1000–1600* (London, 1973), pp. 6–7.

[90]*Domesday Book* 1:fol. 252r.

the time of the Domesday survey, contains about two hundred and seventy names.[91] Not one of the few women's names here—less than thirty—seems Continental.[92] Men's names include a few Continental forms—not surprisingly, for the list includes tenants-in-chief (including our old friend William Pecche) who happened to hold burgages as well as rural estates. So all this shows is that in a town with only a tiny (and probably non-resident) foreign minority the independent widows flourishing one generation after the Conquest were all of unquestionably native stock.

One town whose residents certainly included some French people was Battle. Here, on a dry upland previously uninhabited, all were incomers and some specifically from overseas, "ex transmarinis etiam partibus nonnulli."[93] A rental of about 1110 incorporated in the late twelfth-century chronicle of the abbey lists well over a hundred burgage tenants, including nine women.[94] Unexpectedly, baptismal names show similar proportions of Continental forms for both sexes: about 40%. A few of the men have bynames plainly indicating foreign origins, like "Gilberti *extranei*" and "Rotberti *de Cirisi*."[95]

---

[91]*Domesday Book* 2:fols. 104r–106r. Not surprisingly for the date, the comments by J. H. Round in *The Antiquary* 6 (1882), 5–6, and in *VCH Essex* 1:414–24, cf. 574–76, are of little use for name study; some individual forms are discussed by von Feilitzen in "Some Unrecorded Old and Middle English Personal Names." See also the next note.

The other lists of citizens' names in *Domesday Book*—e.g., that for Oxford (1:fol. 154r), which shows Insular forms as normal for both sexes—are all too brief to be representative.

[92]The gender of some names is uncertain, as final -*a* might mark either a Continental feminine name or an OE feminine latinized or else an OE weak masculine; see von Feilitzen, *Pre-Conquest Personal Names*, pp. 127–28, and idem, in *The Winton Domesday*, pp. 224, 227. For *Berda* as masculine, see idem, "Some Unrecorded Old and Middle English Personal Names," p. 74, and for *Dela* likewise, see Redin, *Studies on Uncompounded Personal Names*, p. 75.

[93]*Chronicon monasterii de Bello*, [ed. J. S. Brewer], Anglia Christiana Society (London, 1846), pp. 12, 28.

[94]*Chronicon*, pp. 11–16; the text has been checked with the manuscript, London, British Library, Cotton MS Domitian A II, fols. 15v–18r. See also H. W. C. Davis, "The Chronicle of Battle Abbey," *EHR* 29 (1914), 426–34, and especially Searle, *Battle Abbey*, pp. 69–78 and App. 12, pp. 465–66, for comments on the distribution of population through the several districts of the town.

[95]Northern France offers several place names of possible form; see Auguste Longnon, *Les noms de lieu de la France: Leur origine, leur signification, leurs transformations* (Paris, 1920–29), p. 625, item 6949, and, with a different etymology proposed, Albert Dauzat and

Among the other bearers of "Continental" baptismal names[96] an unknowable number must, of course, have been of at least partly English stock, like "Rotberti *filii Siflet*" (a metronymic formed with the English *Sigeflǣd*). The women's names offer no notes of parentage, of origin, or even of widowhood. The pattern is unusual but, with numbers so small, random events might easily have affected the balance of the list. In any event, a new town like Battle, where wives as well as husbands had all to be incomers, might well have had an untypical structure of population.

One of the documents we noted earlier as already known to show a discrepancy between the name patterns of the sexes was the 1177 survey of Newark-on-Trent.[97] Here over 40% of the women's names remain Insular, beside only some 20% of the men's. As usual, the women amount to only about an eighth of the total (some forty instances) and are mostly specified as widows, thus once again carrying the risk of an age gap between them and the men.

Fortunately, as was to some extent the case with the Ramsey and Bury surveys we already examined, some sets of urban records do enable us to allow for any generation gap. The archives of Christ Church Priory in Canterbury contain several substantial rentals, ranging in date from just

---

Charles Rostaing, *Dictionnaire étymologique des noms de lieux en France* (Paris, 1963), col. 162. For Cerisy-la-Forêt (*dép.* Manche), some early eleventh-century charters of the abbey show *Cirisiacus* as an alternative to the commoner *Cerisiacus* (e.g., *Recueil des actes des ducs de Normandie de 911 à 1066*, ed. Marie Fauroux, Mémoires de la Société des Antiquaires de Normandie 36 [Caen, 1961], p. 194; cf. *Monasticon Anglicanum* 6/2:1073). (I am grateful to Mr. Fairclough and the staff of the Map Room of Cambridge University Library for kind assistance with this problem.)

[96]The form *Herod'* (fol. 17r) is difficult, as the biblical name hardly seems acceptable (and is not, for instance, listed by Morlet in *Les noms latins ou transmis par le latin*); it can, however, be paralleled elsewhere in twelfth-century England (e.g., *Kalendar of Abbot Samson*, p. 37). Perhaps it was a "pageant" nickname (for this category, see Reaney, *Origin*, pp. 170–71), or else it may represent a form of *Herold*, to be derived either from CG *Her(i)wald* or from Norse *Haraldr* (see Förstemann, *Personennamen*, col. 780, cf. col. 813, also Kaufmann, *Ergänzungsbuch*, p. 183; von Feilitzen, *Pre-Conquest Personal Names*, pp. 284–86; Schlaug, *Die altsächsischen Personennamen des 11. und 12. Jahrhunderts*, p. 111; idem, *Die altsächsischen Personennamen vor dem Jahre 1000*, p. 106; Fellows Jensen, *Scandinavian Personal Names*, pp. 132–34; Morlet, *Les noms . . . gallo-germaniques*, col. 127a).

[97]See above, n. 63.

after the middle of the twelfth century to the opening of the thirteenth.[98] Here too women's names are far fewer than men's and mainly those of widows. Within each rental the proportions of Insular to Continental names conform to the pattern already noted elsewhere. In Rental B, dating from the mid-1160s, Insular forms still predominate among women's names, amounting to over 55% (some fifty-one individuals, with some thirty bearing Insular names), whereas for men's names Insular forms amount to less than 25%. The roughly contemporary list of "brothers and sisters" of the Gild of St. Ansclm offers higher proportions of Insular names but a similar balance between the sexes, with some 35% of men's names Insular beside over 60% of women's (again a small sample, as many women members are nameless wives or daughters).[99] Perhaps the members of the Gild were on average older than the Christ Church tenants, or perhaps they belonged to more rural milieux. Around the turn of the century Rentals D, E, F, and G still show over 40% of women's names as Insular (some sixty-seven individuals, with some twenty-eight bearing Insular names), as against only 10% of all names taken together. Of these figures some corroboration comes from the cartulary of a minor religious house in Canterbury, St. Gregory's Priory; here, about a score of women's names datable in the last quarter of the twelfth century (some certainly from rural milieux) prove to be fairly equally divided between Insular and Continental forms.[100] If, then, the women's names recorded in the rentals from about the turn of the century are set beside men's of the mid-1160s—surely a more than generous allowance for any age gap—there is still a discrepancy, with over 40% of the later women's names remaining Insular beside less than 25% of the earlier men's. On the other hand, a list intermediate in date, Rental C, dated about 1180, shows only some 25% of women's names as Insular; but the sample is tiny (less than a dozen names) and, as this rental lists not rents received but payments made to overlords, may in any case be weighted towards the gentry.

These Canterbury rentals, dating from a century to about a century and a half after the Conquest, presumably refer to individuals born and baptized

---

[98]Urry, *Canterbury under the Angevin Kings*, pp. 221–382 (I am deeply grateful to my friend Mrs. Dorothy Owen for a very long-term loan of this basic text).

[99]William Urry, "Saint Anselm and His Cult at Canterbury," *Spicilegium Beccense* 1 (1959), 571–93, esp. 585.

[100]*Cartulary of the Priory of St. Gregory, Canterbury*, ed. Audrey Woodcock, Camden 3rd ser., 88 (London, 1956).

from about 1110 to 1175; but where those individuals had been born or of what parentage they do not say, except for the few bearing foreign territorial surnames or specified as *Flandrensis* or *Mansel*.[101] What they illustrate so amply are twelfth-century fashions in names and the underlying cultural attitudes these imply. The names may indeed reflect some cultural groupings. In no list is the number of women whose fathers' names are given large enough for analysis; but (deceased) husbands' names conform to a clear pattern. Although in the 1160s Insular forms generally amount to under 25% of men's names, over 40% of the husbands of women with Insular names have Insular names themselves (nine beside twelve Continental): conversely, among husbands of women with Continental names less than 15% bear Insular names (two beside thirteen Continental). Forty years later, in Rentals D and F, some 35% of the names of husbands of women with Insular names still show Insular forms (four beside seven Continental), beside only 10% as the average for all names taken together, whereas for husbands of women with Continental names the proportion is about average (one Insular beside ten Continental). Admittedly, the numbers are so small as hardly to make a scientific sample; but the regularity of the pattern is striking. It seems as though—in spite of the insistence in *Dialogus de Scaccario* that French and English had merged—some social or cultural division, not rigid or watertight yet nonetheless real, must have been persisting between those families of Canterbury townspeople by now using Continental names almost exclusively and those others still keeping partly to Insular forms, most markedly with women's names but to some extent with men's as well.

As for the cities *par excellence* of eleventh-century England, London and Winchester, these were, notoriously, omitted from Domesday Book.[102] For Winchester, which, although smaller not only than London but also than York, Lincoln, or Norwich, was in many ways the premier city, the omission is more than made good by the successive surveys dating from about

---

[101]Possibly an adjective "from Le Mans" (see Morlet, *Étude d'anthroponymie picarde*, p. 77; but Robert, *Dictionnaire alphabétique et analogique de la langue française* 4:col. 406a, notes *manceau* as first recorded in the seventeenth century, cf. Godefroy, *Dictionnaire de l'ancienne langue française* 5:154–55, where the medieval form is given as *mansois*, so also Tobler-Lommatzsch, *Altfranzösisches Wörterbuch*); alternatively, from a diminutive of CG *Manzo* (cf. *Manselinus* noted by von Feilitzen, in *Smith Festschrift*, p. 55; see also Förstemann, *Personennamen*, cols. 1093–94, and Kaufmann, *Ergänzungsbuch*, p. 248).

[102]Brooke and Keir, *London 800–1216*, pp. 149, 156, suggest it was the very size and complexity of these two cities which defeated the Domesday clerks.

1110 and again about 1148.[103] Even in the Confessor's reign Continental influence had been at work here: some 15% of the names of property holders *TRE* included in the 1110 survey already show Continental forms. After the Conquest Norman magnates became familiar figures, if not all as residents, certainly as landlords; and they included some women, as witness, for instance, the names in both surveys of "Emma de Perci" and of "Adeliz soror Henrici de Port."[104] With potential foreign influence thus at a maximum, the "national" balance in personal names here ought to be significant. Rich though they are, these surveys are not, however, ideal for our study: all too often women property holders are specified only by a relationship or even more vaguely as "quedam vidua," "quedam lauandaria," so that the women's names mentioned, amounting to no more than some 5% of the totals, scarcely make a fair sample. For what such scanty samples may be worth, they do emphatically conform to our pattern.[105] Already in 1110 the men's names—including, admittedly, a good few belonging to Norman magnates—show Insular forms reduced to under 30%: the corresponding women's names—also including some belonging to members of Norman families—show Insular forms still amounting to some 65% (ten out of fifteen). These figures are remarkable, being almost as advanced as those we have noted fifty years later in Canterbury, a city by no means sheltered from foreign influences. In the survey of 1148 Insular forms amount to less than 20% of the men's names recorded but still to 40% of the women's—a higher proportion than in the men's names of over a generation earlier. Coupled with the maintenance of native street names,[106] the comparative con-

---

[103]Republished in *The Winton Domesday*, ed. Biddle et al. (see above n. 52); see also *Domesday Book*, 4 (*Additamenta*):531–42, 542–62, and Martin Biddle, "The Winton Domesday: Two Surveys of an Early Capital," in *Die Stadt in der europäischen Geschichte: Festschrift Edith Ennen*, ed. Werner Besch et al. (Bonn, 1972), pp. 36–48.

[104]*The Winton Domesday*, pp. 45 etc., 63 etc., also pp. 40 (n. 39.2), 147, 155.

[105]Von Feilitzen gives very full statistics in *The Winton Domesday*, pp. 183–87, 190. Although for the present purpose these figures need some adjustment, in the event our estimates do not much differ from his; the main difficulty arises from the cultural ambiguity of names of Norse origin (see above nn. 59, 67, and von Feilitzen, ibid., p. 191).

[106]See *The Winton Domesday*, pp. 231–39, and cf. the maintenance of English names for streets and other topographical features in twelfth-century Canterbury (Cecily Clark, "People and Languages in Post-Conquest Canterbury," *Journal of Medieval History* 2 [1976], 1–33, esp. 22–23).

servatism of the women's names recorded suggests that even here, in probably the most gallicized of all English towns, foreign influences may not have gone very deep. Certainly the men's names recorded in these surveys can scarcely have been typical of those of the local population as a whole.

A few names from these surveys appear also in the *Liber Vitae* of Hyde Abbey, Winchester.[107] At first glance, this looks promising for our study, as it offers women's names, not indeed in equal proportions with men's, but as about two fifths of the total, and as it sometimes names both spouses (more rarely, whole families) together. Admittedly, those enjoying confraternity with an abbey do not reliably represent either a social class or a geographical location: not all need have lived in Hampshire, or even in England, let alone in Winchester itself. That a few did live there, and at dates relevant to our study, is guaranteed by the recurrence of their names in the surveys. But even more than most records this *Liber Vitae* needs careful interpretation, as from the mid-eleventh century on names are entered without apparent system, according as spaces presented themselves.[108] Therefore, to rely overmuch on the simplified printed versions of the name lists would be unwise. For what it may be worth, analysis of some of these, apparently ranging in date from the mid-eleventh century well into the twelfth and perhaps later,[109] suggests a name pattern not unlike that of the 1148 survey, with Insular forms amounting to only some 20% to 25% of men's names but to some 40% or 45% or even more of women's. Especially relevant to our study—although not invariably supporting our hypothesis—are some of the names of married couples. In the later strata, dating from the mid-eleventh century on, a good few entries show couples one of whom bears an Insular name and the other a Continental one. Sometimes, as we

---

[107]British Library MS Stowe 944; *Liber Vitae*, ed. Birch (see above n. 56). For description of the manuscript, see Birch, *Liber Vitae*, pp. i–ii, lii–liv and footnotes to the relevant pages of text, and also Neil Ker, *Catalogue of Manuscripts Containing Anglo-Saxon* (Oxford, 1957), pp. 338–40.

A striking example of a name shared is *Godwine Greatseod* "big purse," *Liber Vitae*, fol. 29r (p. 74), beside *Godwinus Gretsud*, in *The Winton Domesday*, p. 64 (*TRE*), see also ibid., p. 212.

[108]The benefactors' names are entered on fols. 20r, 24v, 25r, 25v, 28v, 29r, 54v, and 55r. The complex stratification invites a study far more detailed than the present context allows; for an analogous case, see Giles Constable, "The *Liber Memorialis* of Remiremont," *Speculum* 47 (1972), 261–77.

[109]Pp. 64–70 (top) and 123–47 of the printed text: over 1,300 names.

have already observed at Canterbury, a man with an Insular name might have a wife with a Continental one (for one thing, "national" origins and social class apart, men often choose wives younger than themselves, even by as much as a whole generation). Of such matches the Hyde *Liber Vitae* offers perhaps half a dozen clear examples: "Eaduuinus" and "Oriald," "Eaduuardus" and "Matildis," "Godricus" and "Sufficia," "Æaduuinus uenator" and "Odelma," and also "Godwinus" the priest and "Erenburch," who gave their son the culturally ambiguous Norse name "Stigandus."[110] In accordance with the general trend, the reverse pattern seems about twice as common, perhaps a dozen husbands with Continental names having wives with Insular ones: for instance, "Hermannus" and "Coleruna," "Rodulf" and "Ælfgyfu," "Regnoldus" and his "Gyðe" with her ANorse name, "Odo" and "Oreguen," "Waerinus" and the Norse-named "Ingrith," "Gotselin" and "Ealdgið," "Egnulfus" and "Æilíuu," "Ansketillus" and "Eadgyfu," and also "Anscetillus" and "Eadgiþa," "Ricardus Palmarius" and "Brihgiua."[111] There is seldom any way of knowing which, if any, of the people with Continental names may have been of foreign stock: "Walter scot," husband of "Leofyue," was evidently not;[112] for "Teotselinus laicus," husband of "Ealdgida," his father's name "Folcuuinus" does suggest Continental origins, at all events if this is the same "Teotselinus" as attests a document of the 1080s.[113] Another possible clue is that spellings like *Ælfgyfu, Eadgyfu*, suggest early dates, perhaps before Continental names had been much adopted by the English even for men.

---

[110]Fols. 20r (p. 30), 24v (p. 51), 28v (p. 67). For the women's names, see Morlet, *Les noms de personne sur le territoire de l'ancienne Gaule* 1:cols. 46b, 79b, 166b, 176b, and 2:cols. 108b–109a; for *Stigandus*, see Adigard des Gautries, *Les noms de personnes scandinaves*, pp. 138–39, and Fellows Jensen, *Scandinavian Personal Names*, p. 266.

[111]Fols. 20r (p. 30), 28v (p. 64), 29r (p. 71), 29r (p. 72), 29r (p. 73), 54v (p. 124), 54v (p. 125), 55r (p. 136), 55r (p. 138); a number of less clear examples have been omitted. For *Coleruna*, see von Feilitzen, in *The Winton Domesday*, p. 153, and for *Oreguen* (probably *Ordwynn*), see idem, "Some Unrecorded Old and Middle English Personal Names," p. 86; for *Gyðe* and *Ingrith*, see Fellows Jensen, *Scandinavian Personal Names*, pp. 119–20, 151.

[112]Fol. 29r (p. 72); cf. p. 164, where he appears as witness to a charter dated 1080–87.

[113]Fol. 29r (p. 74); cf. p. 164, where he appears as witness to a charter dated 1080–87. For *Folcwine*, see von Feilitzen, in *Smith Festschrift*, p. 52, and Morlet, *Les noms . . . gallo-germaniques*, cols. 95b–96a; for *Teotselinus*, see Forssner, *Continental-Germanic Personal Names*, p. 229, and Morlet, *Les noms . . . gallo-germaniques*, col. 71b.

As for London, this is far less well represented than Winchester by the extant documents. No adequate survey exists; but then, if modern estimates of its eleventh-century population are anywhere near the mark,[114] to be adequate a survey of London would need to be many times larger than any extant for anywhere in post-Conquest England. Such material as does survive is in fact small in scale: for instance, a list of tenants holding from St. Paul's about 1130 offers less than a hundred names all told[115] (whereas hardly more than 40% of men's names remain Insular here, the grand total of eight women's names includes only one, *Eua*, that is certainly Continental, plus one, *Ragenild*, that is ambiguous).[116] Information is excellent about a few special groups, such as the canons of St. Paul's, "the best documented chapter of the twelfth century in Christendom" (although even in the first decades of the century Continental names predominate among them, some English element persists until a good deal later);[117] but these of their very nature contain no names of women. To tantalize us further, that vast

---

[114]Brooke and Keir, *London 800–1216,* pp. 70 n. 3, and 100, emphasize the unreliability of all such estimates, e.g., Russell's guess of over 17,000, based on an inflated notion of parish size (*British Medieval Population*, pp. 51, 286–87, cf. Brooke and Keir, *London 800–1216*, pp. 122–48).

[115]H. W. C. Davis, "London Lands and Liberties of St. Paul's, 1066–1135," in *Essays in Medieval History Presented to Thomas Frederick Tout*, ed. A. G. Little and F. M. Powicke (Manchester, 1925), pp. 45–59, esp. 55–59 (cf. Brooke and Keir, *London 800–1216*, pp. 86, 163 n. 2); see also Ekwall, *Early London Personal Names*, pp. 111–17.

[116]For *Eua*, see Morlet, *Les noms latins . . .* , col. 49a; for *Ragenild*, either Norse or CG, see von Feilitzen, *Pre-Conquest Personal Names*, p. 347, Ekwall, *Early London Personal Names*, pp. 80, 104, 112, Morlet, *Les noms . . . gallo-germaniques*, col. 185a, and Fellows Jensen, *Scandinavian Personal Names*, pp. 213–15 (Viking influence in London had been far from negligible; see Ekwall, *Early London Personal Names*, pp. 73–85, 86–87, and Brooke and Keir, *London 800–1216*, pp. 141–42, 178, 261–65). The other names are: *Alueva, Edild, Godid, Liuiua* (only in a metronymic), *Wakerild,* and *Bugia*. This last Ekwall, *Early London Personal Names*, p. 112, tentatively identified as a French nickname "candle," but a better source seems to be *Bucge*, an OE hypocoristic form for names in *Burg-* or *-burg* (see Redin, *Studies in Uncompounded Names*, p. 115, Boehler, *Die altenglischen Frauennamen*, pp. 213–14, and also F. M. Stenton, in *Collected Papers*, p. 317).

[117]See C. N. L. Brooke, "The Composition of the Chapter of St. Paul's, 1086–1163," *Cambridge Historical Journal* 10 (1950–52), 111–32, esp. 121–22, and Brooke and Keir, *London 800–1216*, pp. 341–47; cf. Ekwall, *Early London Personal Names*, pp. 105–07 (too easily assuming, here and elsewhere, that even in the early twelfth century a Continental name still means Continental blood).

population embodied a deep paradox: long since involved in trade with all
northwestern Europe (laws of Æthelred II give special mention to merchants
from the Low Countries and from Rouen),[118] London might well have become the most cosmopolitan of cities,[119] yet modern authority after modern
authority, each concentrating on a different aspect of affairs, witnesses to
the irreducible "Englishness" not only of its populace but of its patriciate
as well.[120] Plainly, no immigration, let alone the passing contacts of trade,
could do more than season so vast a population.

Yet, "English" though London remained, it saw immigrants enough in
the upper ranks of society: men of property, traders and craftsmen such as
had already so long been frequenting the city, and senior churchmen (who,
with the persistence of clerical marriage,[121] would by no means lie outside
the scope of our study, but for the dearth of information about their wives).[122]

---

[118]*Die Gesetze der Angelsachsen,* ed. Felix Liebermann, 1 (Halle, 1903), p. 232. By the Confessor's time men from Ghent and from Rouen had each their own wharf: see F. M. Stenton,
"Norman London," in *Collected Papers,* pp. 23–47, esp. 41–42.

[119]See Brooke and Keir, *London 800–1216,* pp. 29, 178–79, 258–76.

[120]Thus: Ekwall, *Early London Personal Names,* pp. 1, 173; Stenton, "Norman London,"
pp. 35–37; Susan Reynolds, "The Rulers of London in the Twelfth Century," *History* 57
(1972), 337–57, esp. 339; Brooke and Keir, *London 800–1216,* pp. 13–14, 29, 31–32, 86,
96 ff., 142, 246–47. In the London section of the Pipe Roll for 31 Henry I, Insular names are
not uncommon (Hunter, *Magnum rotulum,* pp. 143–50).

[121]See C. N. L. Brooke, "Gregorian Reform in Action: Clerical Marriage in England,
1050–1200," *Cambridge Historical Journal* 12 (1956), 1–21, also 187–88. Among the early
twelfth-century canons of St. Paul's not only marriage but also inheritance of prebends were
common; see idem, "The Chapter of St. Paul's," pp. 121, 125, and cf. Ekwall, *Early London
Personal Names,* pp. 106–07.

[122]The name of one canon's wife has been preserved in the Durham *Liber vitae:* "Raulf filius
Algoti . . . et Mahald socia eius . . . et mater Raulfi Leouerun" (*Liber vitae ecclesiae
Dunelmensis: A Collotype Facsimile . . . &c.* [ed. A. H. Thompson], Surtees Society 136
[Durham, 1923], fol. 42 (+)r, and see also Brooke, "The Chapter of St. Paul's," p. 123 n. 66);
although the couple both have French names of CG origin, the man's mother has an Insular
name (*Lēofrūn;* see von Feilitzen, *Pre-Conquest Personal Names,* p. 315) and his father an
ambiguous one, probably ANorse but possibly CG (see von Feilitzen, *Pre-Conquest Personal
Names,* p. 146, Ekwall, *Early London Personal Names,* pp. 74–75, and Morlet, *Les noms . . .
gallo-germaniques,* col. 16a).
   An earlier couple seems purely Continental: Canon Ansger (from Bayeux) and his wife
Popelina, the parents of Audouen bishop of Evreux and of Thurstan archbishop of York (see
Brooke, "The Chapter of St. Paul's," p. 124 and n. 71, and Donald Nicholl, *Thurstan, Arch-*

Some of these incomers did, of course, bring wives with them, among these the father of St. Thomas of Canterbury, Gilbert Becket, a merchant from Rouen with a wife from Caen, and in London prominent enough to become a sheriff.[123] What percentage of the settlers may thus have brought wives with them it would be idle to enquire, for the evidence is not there, having survived for the Becket couple only because their son became a saint. Other incomers certainly married in London. Otho the goldsmith we have already met, with his well-dowered widow and the estates she brought him.[124] Another well-known example, brought to light by Round over eighty years ago as illustrating "the close amalgamation of the Normans and the English," is that of the "Cornhill" family.[125] The titular founder of this family was Edward "Upcornhille," "de Cornhella,"[126] who flourished in the early twelfth century; he and his wife "Godeleva," daughter of another prominent citizen, Edward "de Suthwerke,"[127] gave their daughter the fashionable name "Agnes" and married her to Gervase, son of the one-time sheriff of London, Roger Hubert's nephew, and of Ingenolda daughter of Herlewin—a se-

---

bishop of York (1114–1140) [York, 1964], pp. 5, 7–8).

[123]*Materials for the History of Thomas Becket, &c.*, ed. James Craigie Robertson and J. B. Sheppard, 7 vols., Rolls Series (London, 1875–85), 3:14 "Mahalt," 4:3 "Machildis," and 81 "Roesam, natione Cadomensem" (for this name, see Forssner, *Continental-Germanic Personal Names*, p. 220, also Morlet, *Les noms . . . gallo-germaniques*, col. 138a). See also R. Foreville, "Les origines normandes de la famille Becket et le culte de saint Thomas en Normandie," in *Mélanges Andrieu-Guitrancourt = L'année canonique* 18 (1973), 433–80, esp. 439–48. For Gilbert as sheriff, see Brooke and Keir, *London 800–1216*, pp. 33, 210, 212–13, 353, 372.

[124]See above, p. 71 and n. 25.

[125]John Horace Round, *Geoffrey de Mandeville: A Study of the Anarchy* (London, 1892), App. K, pp. 304–12; see also idem, *The Commune of London, &c.* (London, 1899), p. 107, and Brooke and Keir, *London 800–1216*, pp. 206–11; also the Pipe Roll for 31 Henry I, Hunter, *Magnum rotulum*, pp. 147, 148.

[126][H. C. Maxwell-Lyte], *Ninth Report of the Royal Commission on Historical Manuscripts* (London, 1883), pt. 1, pp. 1–72 (*Report on the Manuscripts of the Dean and Chapter of St. Paul's*), esp. col. 61b; *Calendar of the Letter-Books . . . of the City of London . . . : Letter-Book C*, ed. Reginald Robinson Sharpe (London, 1901), p. 219. See also Ekwall, *Early London Personal Names*, p. 31.

[127]*Letter-Book C*, p. 220. For *Godeleva* (*Godleofu*; not included in von Feilitzen, *Pre-Conquest Personal Names*, or in *The Winton Domesday*), see Ekwall, *Early London Personal Names*, pp. 39–40.

quence of names such as at this early date seems likely to mean a family whose male lines at least were Continental.[128] This Gervase took his father-in-law's surname, "of Cornhill," and throve exceedingly, becoming in his turn a City sheriff and surviving into the 1180s.[129] A probable uncle of Gervase's, Ralph son of Herlewin, also at one time a sheriff of London, married Mary, who was herself the child of a mixed marriage between a Baldwin of Arras and an unnamed daughter of Algar (probably, that is, *Ælfgar*) son of Cole, the hereditary incumbent of St. Michael "le Querne"; Algar's son Nicholas was in old age to make the church over to his great-nephew Robert, a son of Ralph and Mary.[130]

Confined as it has been to the tiny oligarchy of "shrieval" families, our London material has so far been anything but representative. Moreover, such analysis as we can carry out rests to a dangerous degree on the name forms themselves, with all the uncertainties these inescapably entail once the post-Conquest generations enter the records. Thus, the "Geroldus de Stratford" who around 1115 had a wife "Godeva"[131] may or may not have been of immigrant stock. Yet sometimes patterns of naming do seem to imply mixed marriages in the background, even though the names of the wives and mothers themselves have not been recorded. A London goldsmith of the early twelfth century was called "Leofstan son of Witso";[132] as he already

---

[128]Round, *Commune*, p. 107, notes an early thirteenth-century tradition that this family hailed from Caen. Of their names only *Roger* and *Herlewin* are recorded by von Feilitzen, *Pre-Conquest Personal Names*, pp. 248, 350, both as rare and alien; see also Forssner, *Continental-Germanic Personal Names*, pp. 74, 79–80, 110–11, 156, 217–18, and Morlet, *Les noms de personne sur le territoire de l'ancienne Gaule* 1:cols. 81b–82a, 136b, 140a, 146b, 2:col. 57a.

[129]See Reynolds, "Rulers of London," pp. 346–47, also 354; and Brooke and Keir, *London 800–1216*, pp. 210–11.

[130]See *Report* 1:col. 20a: "Nicolaus sacerdos Sancti Micaelis filius Algari Colessune . . . Roberto filio Radulfi filii Herlewini filio nepte mee, scilicet Marie filie Baldwini de Araz"; see also Round, *Geoffrey de Mandeville*, pp. 309 ff., and Ekwall, *Early London Personal Names*, p. 103. As a base for the English patronymic *Colessune*, Ekwall, *Early London Personal Names*, pp. 78–79, prefers Norse *Kolr* or *Koli* (see von Feilitzen, *Pre-Conquest Personal Names*, p. 307, and Fellows Jensen, *Scandinavian Personal Names*, pp. 176–77) to English *Cola* (see von Feilitzen, *Pre-Conquest Personal Names*, pp. 217–18).

[131]*Report*, 1:col. 61b. For Geroldus, see Forssner, *Continental-Germanic Personal Names*, pp. 103–04, and Morlet, *Les noms . . . gallo-germaniques*, col. 100b.

[132]"Levestano filio Withsonis, Withsone filio ejus": *Chronicon abbatiæ Rameseiensis, &c.*,

at this time had a grown son, his own father "Witso" can hardly have been born, at latest, much after 1055, a date at which such a name seems likely to mean Continental birth, so that Leofstan's own English name may mean he had an English mother; in spite of the strong tendency for London patricians to adopt Continental names, Leofstan himself kept up the bi-cultural tradition by naming his own sons "Witso" and "Edward."[133] A more questionable case is that of the alderman in office about 1130, "Eilwardus fil. Wizeli";[134] not only might his father "Wizelo" (a diminutive of *Witso*) have been born and named after the Conquest but his own name "Eil-wardus," although most probably representing English *Æþelweard*, might possibly stand for the Continental *Agilward*.[135]

Clear records of mixed marriages are rare. Nor, in any event, was it invariably the wife who was the English one. Tierry son of Deorman and his Clare bride we have already met.[136] And early twelfth-century London records offer some more speculative possibilities of such marriages, such as the reference to "Sinodus [that is, *Sigenoð*] scutarius gener Radulfi (?aurifabri)."[137] Records are, however, far too sparse to allow even a guess at the relative frequency of the two kinds of intermarriage. And, as for material allowing statistical analysis of naming patterns, nothing at all of such kind seems to have survived from early post-Conquest London.

At the end of the day our picture remains ill-focused: the few identi-fiable individuals resist reduction to statistical trends, and what background we have of statistics concerns fashion only, reflecting the origins of the names themselves rather than of the people bearing them. Yet the view may

---

ed. William Dunn Macray, Rolls Series (London, 1886), p. 245; also "Witso fil. Leuestani" in the Pipe Roll for 31 Henry I, Hunter, *Magnum rotulum*, p. 145. For *Witso*, see Forssner, *Continental-Germanic Personal Names*, p. 259, and Morlet, *Les noms . . . gallo-germaniques*, col. 222b.

[133]*Report* 1:col. 63b; Pipe Roll for 31 Henry I, Hunter, *Magnum rotulum*, p. 145; see also preceding note. See Ekwall, *Early London Personal Names*, p. 97.

[134]E.g., Davis, "London Lands and Liberties," p. 57. For *Wicelo*, see Morlet, *Les noms . . . gallo-germaniques*, col. 222b.

[135]See Ekwall, *Early London Personal Names*, p. 16 (but cf. pp. 97, 101), and Morlet, *Les noms . . . gallo-germaniques*, col. 24a.

[136]See above, p. 69 and n. 15.

[137]*Report* 1:col. 61b; see also Ekwall, *Early London Personal Names*, p. 103 (for some even more speculative possibilities of similar matches, see ibid., p. 104).

have cleared a little. In twelfth-century England women's names did lag oddly behind the fashion which was so drastically changing those given to men. That time lag could be explained by a paucity of women, and so of feminine name models, among the post-Conquest French settlers, and, if not so explained, would imply among twelfth-century English parents some otherwise unrecorded feeling that daughters were, in a way that sons were not, vessels of the native tradition. A paucity of women among the in-comers, although far from demonstrable statistically, is at least compatible with such patterns of marriage as can be traced among magnates and pa-tricians. It is compatible also with the interpretation of the satirist Nigel's distinction between "mother's" and "father's" tongues as referring respec-tively to English and to French;[138] but, quite apart from its uncertain inter-pretation, that statement is too personal and individual to form any base for generalization. Yet, if our guess is right, that Norman women did play but little part in the post-Conquest settlement of England, it would have been no wonder that the AN gentry of Nigel's sort, with some English mothers and many English maids and nurses, should soon show some acquaintance with the English language, uncourtly though they felt it to be.[139] Perhaps such considerations ought to move us, not necessarily to reject entirely, but at all events somewhat to qualify certain recent pronouncements about Norman attitudes in twelfth-century England: thus, "The Normans were Normans through all these years. Normandy was their home country. . . ."[140] Did those nameless, humble "Frenchmen" scattered in ones and twos across the Welsh Marches marry their sons only to one another's daughters? Did the Cornhills of London wholly reject the language and the traditions of the line of City burgesses from whom their ancestress Agnes was descended? Did "Wihenoc's man" and his modest Norfolk heiress disdain employing local maids for their children? High politics tells one tale, and tells it in a clear and dominating voice; but the story being quietly lived out in towns and in manor houses had a different theme as well as a different style.

---

[138]See above, p. 68 and n. 7.

[139]See above, pp. 65–66 and nn. 2 and 3.

[140]Le Patourel, *Normandy and England 1066–1144*, p. 29. The argument here rests partly on literary evidence which a more recent study has adjudged to be politically inspired rhet-oric (Davis, *The Normans and Their Myth*, passim and esp. pp. 66–67).

THE POPULARITY OF LATE MEDIEVAL
PERSONAL NAMES AS REFLECTED
IN ENGLISH ORDINATION LISTS, 1350–1540

Virginia Davis

Names and naming practices have increasingly attracted the attention of historians for the light they can shed on cultural history. Work on onomastics in recent years has highlighted the influences which lay behind the process of choosing a name for a son or daughter in medieval England. This work has also stressed the relatively narrow stock of personal fore-names from which children's names were usually chosen in late medieval England. While the Norman Conquest expanded and changed the stock of forenames in common use within England, introducing substantial numbers of new CG names which came to replace Insular personal names,[1] subsequent centuries were to see a gradual narrowing of the range of forenames in popular use. This was a development particularly of the thirteenth and fourteenth centuries, although the precise timing and nature of this development has not yet been established.[2]

---

[1]Cecily Clark, *"Willelmus Rex? vel alius Willelmus?" Nomina* 11 (1987), 7–33; eadem, "English Personal Names ca. 650–1300: Some Prosopographical Bearings," *MP* 8/1 (Spring 1987), 31–60 and above (pp. 7–28).

[2]D. A. Postles, "Personal Naming Patterns of Peasants and Burgesses in Late Medieval England," *MP* 12/1 (Spring 1991), 29–56; idem, "The Baptismal Name in Thirteenth-Century England: Processes and Patterns," *MP* 13/2 (Autumn 1992), 1–52; idem, "The

Recent historiographical debate has centered on the complexities of how individuals' names were chosen, the role of godparents, and the way in which the transmission of forenames may have reflected spiritual kinship or a family's desire to make statements about lineage.[3] This paper will not address these issues. Instead it examines the trends in popularity of male forenames in England during the period 1350–1540, using a database of over eight thousand names drawn from surviving English clerical ordination lists.[4] The naming of every individual was clearly open to a range of family, local, and social pressures;[5] this substantial database enables broad trends to be identified and examined. In particular, changes in the popular name stock over this period—both additions and deletions—can be identified.

The late medieval English name stock was dominated by a handful of names. These were followed by a larger group of names which were fairly popular, and then there was a very long "tail" of names that occur only once or twice in the time period. These names—such as *Joachim*, *Lancelot*, *Marmaduke*, *Nigel*, and *Valentine*—may reflect particular family concerns

---

Changing Pattern of Male Forenames in Medieval Leicestershire and Rutland to c.1350," *LPS* 51 (1993), 54–61; idem, "Notions of the Family, Lordship and the Evolution of Naming Processes in Medieval English Rural Society: A Regional Example," *Continuity and Change* 10/2 (1995), 169–98.

[3] Louis Haas, "Social Connections between Parents and Godparents in Late Medieval York-shire," *MP* 10/1 (Spring 1989), 1–21 and below (pp. 159–75); Philip Niles, "Baptism and the Naming of Children in Late Medieval England," *MP* 3/1 (Spring 1982), 95–107 and below (pp. 147–57); Michael J. Bennett, "Spiritual Kinship and the Baptismal Name in Tra-ditional European Society," in *Principalities, Powers and Estates*, ed. L. O. Frappell (Ade-laide, 1979), pp. 1–14 and below (pp. 115–46). The debate is briefly summarized in Postles, "Personal Naming Patterns."

[4] The database project which has provided these names is discussed in Virginia Davis, "Late Medieval English Clergy Database," *History and Computing* 2 (1990), 75–87. Since men do not appear to have changed their names when they entered the secular church as priest, unlike the practice in some religious orders, these names should therefore reflect the general popularity of these names amongst a very wide section of the population at large including across social classes, since ordinands ranged from men from fairly humble backgrounds to high-flyers who would become members of the episcopate.

[5] Dave Postles has shown the dominance of particular local concerns in the case of the Leicestershire manor of Kibworth Harcourt, where the names *Ivo* and *Hugh* are unusually prominent, reflecting local memories of the post-Conquest founders of the honor of Harcourt ("The Baptismal Name," pp. 16–19).

or preoccupations relating to individuals, but they reveal little of the general patterns of personal name choice in this period.

There is no doubt as to which were the most popular names in late medieval England, and these remained popular well into the early modern period.[6] *John*, *William*, and *Thomas* dominate, followed by *Richard* and *Robert*. The consistency and dominance of this small group of names are impressive. Amongst them, these five names account for about three quarters of all names in the database. The overwhelming popularity of *John* in particular is little short of astonishing; the appearance of this name as a dominant one by the mid-thirteenth century has not been fully explained.[7] It was not a name widespread in use amongst the invaders of 1066, as can be seen from its rarity in Domesday Book, but the twelfth century saw the gradual appearance of the name as a popular one, especially amongst men entering the church. *John* accounts for more than one third of all names in the later fourteenth century and for a quarter of all names in the later fifteenth and early sixteenth centuries. *William* and *Thomas* likewise held their places consistently throughout the period, with *William* accounting for 16–17% of named ordinands and *Thomas* between 11% and 15%.

Below the top level, names which are quite high in the popularity chart were in fact given to relatively few people. By the time the names in positions in the upper teens are reached in the lists, numbers are down to single figures, despite the size of the database. For example, in the fifty-year period 1350–99, where there are over twenty-eight hundred people in the database, *Philip*, which is in nineteenth place, has only eleven entries and *Reginald*, which is twentieth, has only eight. Below this level the numbers are so small that a handful of idiosyncratic choices is in danger of assuming undue significance.

---

[6] Scott Smith-Bannister, *Names and Naming Patterns in England, 1538–1700* (Oxford, 1997).

[7] Postles has suggested in "The Baptismal Name in Thirteenth-Century England," pp. 12–13, that *John* may have been favored due to the sacrosanct approach towards using the names of members of the Holy Family in the period; John, as Jesus' cousin, provided the next available name. Also, baptism in itself was an act that brought to mind the image of John the Baptist.

ANALYSIS OF THE MOST POPULAR NAMES BY PERIODS IN THE LATE MIDDLE AGES[8]

Each column gives the position in the popularity lists for each name in the period concerned, followed by the percentage of individuals given the name. Names that occur outside the top twenty for the period are given in square brackets. Percentages are used rather than absolute numbers because there are some variations in sample sizes amongst the periods.

Name	1350–99	1400–49	1450–99	1500–40
John	1 (38.00%)	1 (35.00%)	1 (26.00%)	1 (25.00%)
William	2 (16.00%)	2 (16.00%)	2 (17.00%)	2 (16.00%)
Thomas	3 (11.00%)	3 (14.00%)	3 (15.50%)	3 (13.00%)
Richard	4 (7.00%)	4 (8.00%)	5 (8.50%)	5 (7.50%)
Robert	5 (6.00%)	5 (7.60%)	4 (9.50%)	4 (8.50%)
Henry	6 (2.50%)	6 (2.40%)	6 (2.40%)	6 (2.80%)
Nicholas	7 (2.20%)	7 (1.75%)	7 (2.14%)	9 (1.80%)
Walter	8 (2.15%)	8 (1.70%)	9 (1.50%)	17 (0.77%)
Roger	9 (1.90%)	9 (1.20%)	12 (1.10%)	12 (1.40%)
Simon	10 (1.20%)	10 (0.90%)	[26]	18 (0.60%)
Hugh	11 (1.15%)	14 (0.70%)	10 (1.20%)	16 (0.90%)
Stephen	12 (0.90%)	15 (0.50%)	18 (0.50%)	19 (0.50%)
Adam	12 (0.90%)	15 (0.50%)	[26]	[25]
Peter	14 (0.75%)	10 (0.90%)	15 (0.80%)	14 (1.00%)

[8]In assigning the ordinands to time periods, the assumption has been made that the priests were being ordained at the canonical age of twenty-four. Twenty-four has therefore been subtracted from the year of ordination as priest in order to obtain an estimate of the decade in which each was born and named.

Name	1350–99	1400–49	1450–99	1500–40
Ralph	14 (0.75%)	12 (0.90%)	20 (0.30%)	14 (1.00%)
Edmund	16 (0.60%)	15 (0.50%)	15 (0.80%)	10 (1.70%)
David	16 (0.60%)	13 (0.80%)	15 (0.80%)	[23]
Geoffrey	16 (0.60%)	15 (0.50%)	18 (0.80%)	[38]
Philip	19 (0.40%)	15 (0.50%)	[26]	[28]
Reginald	20 (0.25%)	28 (0.20%)	20 (0.30%)	[25]
Andrew	20 (0.25%)	30 (0.10%)	[26]	[28]
Jacob	20 (0.25%)	21 (0.25%)	10 (1.20%)	11 (1.60%)
George	[31 (0.10%)]	20 (0.25%)	13 (0.90%)	8 (2.00%)
Christopher	No entries	[35 (0.10%)]	13 (0.90%)	13 (1.25%)
Alexander	[23]	[21]	20 (0.30%)	19 (0.50%)
Lewis	[21]	[39]	20 (0.30%)	[37]
Michael	[31]	[21]	20 (0.30%)	19 (0.50%)
Oliver	[31]	1 example	20 (0.30%)	[37]
Edward	[31]	[24]	8 (1.80%)	7 (2.50%)

As indicated above, for the period as a whole *John, William, Thomas, Richard, Robert, Henry,* and *Nicholas* are consistently the top seven names, although *Henry* and *Nicholas* trail well behind the top five in terms of numerical distribution. Below these consistent performers some striking winners and losers can be identified, which sheds some light on the cultural influences that lie behind individual name choices.

Two names stand out strikingly as new appearances in the fifteenth century—*Christopher* and *George.* Both were to retain their popularity into

the early modern period.[9] There are no entries for *Christopher* in the fourteenth-century ordination lists, and only three in the first half of the fifteenth
century (out of 2,915 entries); however, the name is thirteenth in the level
of popularity for the period 1450–1540. A closer analysis of decades aids
exploration of this trend: only after the 1450s does the name begin to occur
regularly in each decade. How can this soaring growth in popularity be
explained? Saint Christopher was a popular saint throughout England in the
Middle Ages; he was patron of travelers but also was invoked against sud-
den death, water, tempest, and plague. His legend was disseminated in the
Golden Legend, and he was frequently represented in English church wall
paintings, carrying the Christ Child. Given this long-standing devotion to
the saint throughout the whole period, why was it only in the fifteenth century that the name became popular as a Christian name? An explanation
may lie in the devotion which grew up in the late Middle Ages to the cult
of the Holy Name of Jesus.[10] This devotional concentration on the actual
name of Christ may have helped to erode an earlier feeling that it might not
be appropriate to name one's child after Christ. At the same time as the *IHS*
monogram became increasingly displayed both on religious objects and on
more secular ones such as pottery, *Christopher* appears to have gained
ground as a forename.

The second personal name which makes a striking appearance in late
medieval name lists, *George*, was also well-known to an English audience.
The rapidly growing popularity of this name can be seen in the late fifteenth
and early sixteenth centuries. In the late fourteenth century it was extremely
infrequent. *George* just makes it to twentieth place in the first half of the
fifteenth century, but it is eighth in the lists by the early sixteenth century.
George is a name which might be described as the success story of the later
fifteenth century, a continuing success since it was in the top ten by the
1540s. Parents and godparents naming their children in the fifteenth century
were clearly influenced by the growing cult of St. George, which reached
its apogee in the late Middle Ages. A number of countries regarded him as

---

[9]In Smith-Bannister's lists for the period 1538–49, *George* is ninth in the list and *Christopher* is fourteenth.

[10]On the cult of the Holy Name of Jesus see R. W. Pfaff, *New Liturgical Feasts in Later
Medieval England* (Oxford, 1970), and more recently, E. A. New, "The Fraternity of the
Holy Name of Jesus in St Paul's Cathedral, c.1450–1550," unpub. Ph.D. thesis (University
of London, 1999).

their patron, and he was viewed as the personification of the ideals of Christian chivalry. Early in the century, shortly after the battle of Agincourt, Archbishop Chichele had the feast of St. George raised in rank to that of one of the principal feasts of the religious year. The execution of George duke of Clarence in the late 1470s does not seem to have had a negative impact on the popularity of the name. Parents opting for this name are likely to have been influenced by a combination of national sentiment and the continuing flowering of chivalric culture, in literature if not in practice.

National fervor may also be reflected in the renewed popularity of *Edward* as a name that shot into the top ten in the period from 1450 onwards, perhaps stimulated by the advent of the Yorkist monarchy. Another royal name, albeit an AS one, *Edmund*, rose from sixteenth to tenth place in the same period, more than tripling its "market share" from only 0.5% to over 1.5%. This may have been the result of Tudor propaganda encouraging support for royal saints.

If some names gained in popularity as the Middle Ages drew to a close, others declined. Several names in the top ten in the later fourteenth century more or less disappear in the early Tudor period. *Roger* dropped from ninth to twelfth position, which still left it as the name of choice for over 1% of the population; *Walter* dropped more significantly, from eighth place (which meant it was chosen for 2% of the male population) in the late fourteenth century to seventeenth position, with less than 1%, in the early sixteenth century. *Simon* dropped more rapidly, from tenth place in the late fourteenth century to twenty-sixth a century later. Some names were clearly conceived of as old-fashioned by this period—*Adam* dropped out of the top twenty altogether, as did *Geoffrey*, *Philip*, and *Reginald*.

Many parents choosing names for their sons in the later Middle Ages stuck to a limited range, which contributed to the continuing dominance of a few very popular names. Closer examination of selected names below these top few suggests that the name stock in later medieval England was far from being entirely static: new names joined the common corpus, while names popular in earlier periods declined in popularity.

APPENDIX

POPULAR NAMES AND TRENDS IN THEIR USE IN ENGLAND, 1350–1540

This appendix considers the fluctuations of some of the more popular names in use during the later Middle Ages. Since the most popular names—*John, William, Thomas, Richard*, and *Robert*—did *not* fluctuate in popularity but always remained the top five choices, we have not considered them here; we trace the rise and fall of usage for names only from Number 6 on the list.[11]

Henry   In the fourteenth and fifteenth centuries this name normally accounted for around 2–2.5% of given names. *Henry* became significantly more popular in the first thirty years of the fifteenth century, even before the evident success of Henry V in France may have encouraged parents to name their children after him. In the period 1400–09 its popularity peaked when it accounted for nearly 4% of the male population. By 1500 it had returned to close to this level, doubtless inspired by Henry Tudor.

Nicholas   Consistently popular, but more so in the first half of the fourteenth century when it represented between 2% and 3% of names, *Nicholas* dropped to under 2% in the early fifteenth century. Reaching almost 4% in the 1440s and 1450s, it then reverted to the early-fifteenth-century level of 1–1.5%. The name *Nicholas* was in use in England from AS times; the iconography of the saint's life cycle is found depicted on fonts, in stained glass, and in paintings. He has been described as the "most frequently-represented saintly bishop," and he was also a popular figure in medieval drama.

Walter   This Germanic name, which had gained in popularity in England after the Norman Conquest, was in decline by the period of the Black Death. It was still popular in the early fourteenth century (just under 5% in the 1320s); normally it ran at 1.5–2% but was at its lowest ebb by 1400–10.

Roger   *Roger*, which was amongst the most popular of names introduced into England after the Norman Conquest, was declining in popu-

---

[11]References to the mid-sixteenth-century lists are drawn from the work of Smith-Bannister, who prints lists based on baptismal registers for 1538–49.

larity by the later Middle Ages although it still remained just within the overall top ten, but beginning to lose its popularity. It was most popular in the early fourteenth century—3.5% in 1320, 2.25% in the 1330s—but it declined after the Black Death to less than 2% for the remainder of the period. There are clear regional variations in the popularity of this name. *Roger* was rare in northern England by the late Middle Ages; its continued position in the lists is due to its popularity south of the Humber.

Hugh   The model of the twelfth-century Carthusian bishop of Lincoln, St. Hugh, was influential throughout the later Middle Ages in ensuring that his name was given to children, especially in eastern England, although the name was widespread throughout England.[12] The name *Hugh* fluctuated between 0.5% and 2% throughout the period, without any clear trends until the very end of the period. Although still popular in the final decades of the fifteenth century, it rapidly disappeared from the popular name stock in the first half of the sixteenth century, and it did not appear in the top twenty-five in the lists of the mid-sixteenth century.

Peter   *Peter*, the name of the leader of the Apostles and the first pope at Rome, was relatively uncommon as a Christian name in the fourteenth and early fifteenth centuries, hovering at under 1% of names. A brief rise in popularity can be seen in the first half of the fifteenth century: it reached 1.5% in the 1420s, 1.8% in the 1430s, and 2.5% in the 1440s. Subsequently it began to decline slowly in popularity, hovering at around 1%. It had dropped out of the top twenty names by the mid-sixteenth century.

Simon   *Simon*, another Apostolic name, had already begun to decline in popularity by the mid-fourteenth century. Its position as twelfth overall in the late medieval popularity lists was due to its fourteenth-century strength. By the second half of the fifteenth century this rather old-fashioned name had dropped out of the top twenty, although it briefly scraped back again in the early sixteenth century before disappearing from the mid-sixteenth-century lists.

---

[12]Postles in "The Baptismal Name," p. 14, comments on the high incidence of the name *Hugh* amongst the male tenants of the bishop of Lincoln in the thirteenth century.

Ralph

Ralph, common among post-Conquest landholders, fluctuated in popularity in England throughout the later Middle Ages without any clear pattern emerging. *Ralph* was rarely found in Wales or the Marcher counties but was clearly widely popular elsewhere, in both northern and southern England. It had disappeared from the top names by the mid-sixteenth century.

Edmund

An East Anglian royal saint's name, *Edmund* (from the AS Edmund who was martyred by the Vikings in 869) was consistently popular in England. Saint Edmund's cult was encouraged by the Normans, and the idea of a royal saint was fostered by successive kings of England. Edmund and Edward the Confessor were represented as the two royal patrons of England in the late-fourteenth-century panel painting the Wilton Diptych, where they can be seen presenting Richard II to the Virgin and Child. In the late Middle Ages nationally, *Edmund* usually represented less than 1% of the name stock but had a marked increase in popularity between the 1470s and 1500. It retained its popularity post-Reformation, perhaps due to its royal connections, and is eleventh on Smith-Bannister's 1538–49 list. This name was widely popular, but as it came from an East Anglian saint it is not surprising to find that the name was particularly in use in the dioceses of Ely and Norwich.

Edward

That *Edward* was (surprisingly enough) not noticeably popular in the fourteenth century suggests that people were not drawn to name children after monarchs during this period. In the 1340s, for example, despite the popularity of Edward III (with his successes in the Hundred Years' War), only 0.1% of children were given this name. Neither is it a name often found in the first half of the fifteenth century, perhaps because of its identification with the Plantagenet rather than the new Lancastrian dynasty. In the second half of the fifteenth century a change can be seen—in the 1450s its use rose to 1.8%; in the 1460s, 2.4%; 1470s, 3.3%; 1480s, 1.6%; 1490s, 2.0%. This does suggest a change in attitude by the fifteenth century. A comparison with the situation in the late thirteenth and the fourteenth centuries suggests that there had been a change in the culture, and that by the later Middle Ages it had become more acceptable, and indeed popular, to name children after a reigning monarch.

Stephen

Consistently at around 0.5% of given names from 1400 onwards with relatively few fluctuations, the name was slightly more popular in the fourteenth century. As the name of the first Christian martyr, *Stephen* remained popular into the post-Reformation period.

David Saint David was regarded from the twelfth century onwards as patron of Wales, and *David* is primarily a Welsh name that was rarely found outside Wales and the Welsh Marches. Within the lists of names drawn from the Welsh clergy alone, *David* occurs in second place to *John*, outstripping *William* and *Thomas*. The links between this name and Wales are so close that it is likely that anyone bearing this name in the later Middle Ages would have had some Welsh connection.

James *James* (or Latin *Jacobus*) was relatively uncommon until the mid-fifteenth century, just scraping into the top twenty in the late fourteenth century. This was despite the popularity of pilgrimages to the shrine of St. James at Compostella in northern Spain—over four hundred churches were dedicated to him in England. From the last decades of the fifteenth century the name appears to have become increasingly popular, and it remained so, reaching the top ten names by the mid-sixteenth century, although the reason for this continued rise in popularity is unclear.

Adam *Adam*, like *Walter* and *Simon*, was clearly in decline by the later period. *Adam* was most popular in the early- to mid-fourteenth century (1–1.5% in the 1330s, 1340s, 1350s) but then it dropped down to less than 0.5% in the 1370s and 1380s. The fifteenth century saw a continued decline in the popularity of this name, which was clearly conceived of as old-fashioned.

George *George* had little popularity before the mid-fifteenth century but it then began rapidly to gain popularity. See the text above for discussion of this trend.

Geoffrey This name saw steady if very limited popularity, rather like *Reginald*, another post-Conquest French personal name.

Philip An Apostolic name, *Philip* was more popular between 1350 and 1450 than later, when it drops out of the tables, although it returns by the mid-sixteenth century. It was, however, always restricted to a small number of men.

Christopher	Uncommon overall because it does not appear until the fifteenth century, *Christopher* then rapidly became popular (2% in the 1460s; 0.9% in the 1470s; 1.25% in the 1480s; 1.5% in the 1490s). See the text above for discussion.
Reginald	This personal name of French origin occurs steadily at a fairly low level of popularity, accounting for about 0.25% throughout the period, perhaps largely used by older gentry families.
Alexander	Rarish but visibly very much more popular by the later fifteenth century than in the fourteenth when it was given to fewer than 0.25% of men, *Alexander* had about doubled in use by the early fifteenth century, and from 1470 onwards it occurs more frequently, perhaps encouraged by growing lay literacy and interest in the Alexander story.

SPIRITUAL KINSHIP
AND THE BAPTISMAL NAME
IN TRADITIONAL EUROPEAN SOCIETY

Michael Bennett

The history of spiritual kinship in pre-industrial Europe is a virtually uncharted field.[1] In view of its importance in many contemporary southern European and Latin American communities, it has been assumed that its role in western society in earlier times was even more significant. Unfortunately the bonds established at baptism (between godchild and godparent, between godparent and natural parent, and between godchild and certain other participants) brought no property rights and entailed no legally enforceable obligations, and accordingly were seldom recorded. In this paper it is proposed to assemble such documentation as has been found on spir-

---

This essay, originally published in *Principalities, Powers and Estates: Studies in Medieval and Early Modern Government and Society*, ed. L. O. Frappell (Adelaide, 1979), pp. 1–13, is reprinted here with the permission of Michael Bennett. The original text has been copyedited towards the style of the present book; some typographical errors have been corrected, some bibliographic information in the notes has been revised.

[1]The only general survey of spiritual kinship with a historical dimension is S. W. Mintz and E. R. Wolf, "An Analysis of Ritual Co-parenthood (Compadrazgo)," *Southwestern Journal of Anthropology* 6 (1950), 341–68. See also G. M. Foster, "Cofradia and Compadrazgo in Spain and Spanish America," *Southwestern Journal of Anthropology* 9 (1953), 1–28, and J. Pitt-Rivers, "Ritual Kinship in Spain," *Transactions of the New York Academy of Sciences*, series 2, 20 (1957–58), 424–31.

itual kinship in western Europe between the fifth and the eighteenth centuries. More specifically, it is intended to draw attention to some late medieval English evidence linking spiritual kinship with patterns of personal nomenclature, which might well prove valuable to an understanding both of this interesting institution and of other aspects of traditional European society.

I

The first section of the paper attempts to sketch in general terms the emergent characteristics of the institution of spiritual kinship in western Europe. Given the meager and diffuse nature of the documentation, this survey is necessarily extremely tentative. S. W. Mintz and E. R. Wolf have traced the notion of spiritual kinship back to earlier forms of ritual sponsorship evident in the Roman world, many of which were in their turn derived from the practices of far older civilizations.[2] Indeed in religious cults the world over the initiation of a new member usually involves the presence of a senior initiate to act as sponsor. The early Christian sects, which especially in periods of persecution needed to be certain of the good faith of their new members, were no exception in their demand for a number of ritual sponsors or *fidei iussores*. Since initiation into the mysteries of the Christian religion was regarded as being a spiritual rebirth, it was possible to view the sponsor as a spiritual parent, and to view the sacrament of baptism as bringing into existence a whole new network of ritual kin relations. It is unclear whether Christian communities were entirely original in this conception, but assuredly they took the idea further than other sects by gradually extending to spiritual kinship the restrictions on marriage which applied to blood relationships. If up until the fifth century a child's sponsors had often enough been his or her own parents, in the following centuries this practice came to be regarded as highly problematical. It was felt that participation in the sacrament of baptism rendered the relationship between husband and wife ambivalent and incestuous by the creation of the new spiritual bond. At first sight this curious attitude can be viewed as the product of the inexorable progress of a powerful metaphor; on closer investigation it can be related to the various demographic, economic, and political pressures which en-

---

[2]Mintz and Wolf, "Ritual Co-parenthood," pp. 343–47.

couraged the widening of exogamic circles in late Roman society. A consideration of the complex factors involved in the remarkable process by which the incest taboo was extended to larger and larger sections of the population is beyond the scope of this paper, but it is assuredly a problem to challenge even the most sophisticated theories of social change.

Beginning apparently in the Greek-speaking provinces of the Roman Empire, where the institution seems to have taken its most elaborate form,[3] the notion of spiritual kinship gradually filtered through to the barbarian West. Whilst there is evidence that the Germanic peoples had their own traditions of fictive kinship, which undoubtedly helped to give institutional shape to spiritual kin relations in western Europe, there is very little documentation from which a clear picture of this process can be derived. It must be assumed that there would have been little uniformity in custom either across space or across time, but that with the re-emergence of larger-scale political and ecclesiastical organizations in the eighth century a convergence between disparate practice and inchoate theory could begin to take place. The testimony of St. Boniface (680–755) is instructive regarding this latter development. A native of southwest England, he was bewildered by the association made between spiritual relations and blood relations in late Merovingian Gaul. Around 735 he wrote three letters to colleagues in which he remarked on the curious intelligence that the Romans and the Franks held it to be a capital crime and a mortal sin for a man to marry the widowed mother of his godchild, and asked for further guidance on the matter. Feeling that all Christians became through baptism "sons and daughters of Christ and the church, and thereby brothers and sisters," he saw the problems inherent in the logic of a doctrine which brought spiritual relations within the prohibited degrees.[4] In this matter the pragmatic Anglo-Saxon was out of touch with the assumptions of the Frankish world. By the ninth century Frankish church councils were stating explicitly that natural parents could not act as baptismal sponsors to their own children, and that spiritual kinship was an insurmountable impediment to marriage.[5] In the heartland

---

[3]See P. Brown, "The Rise and Function of the Holy Man in Late Antiquity," *Journal of Roman Studies* 61 (1971), 95, and now E. Patlagean, "Christianisation et parentés rituelles: Le domaine de Byzance," *Annales ESC* 33 (1978), 625–36.

[4]Edward Kylie, ed. and trans., *The English Correspondence of Saint Boniface* (New York, 1966), pp. 72–77.

[5]Mintz and Wolf, "Ritual Co-parenthood," p. 344.

of Latin Christendom in the ninth and tenth centuries spiritual kin relations were taking institutional shape.

It is rather ironical that St. Boniface should have shown himself so naive regarding spiritual kinship, because it is from his own generation and his home province of Wessex that the first western reference to godparenthood in a specifically secular context is to be found. The laws of King Ine (d. 726), in whose service Boniface had earlier worked, suggest a close correspondence between the institutions of godparenthood and lordship:

> Chapter 76. If anyone kills the godson or godfather of another, the compensation for the relationship is to be the same as that to the lord: the compensation is to increase in proportion to the wergild. . . . If, however, it is the king's godson, his wergild is to be paid to the king the same as to the kindred.[6]

The virtual equation drawn between spiritual kin and lord-follower relations is instructive: it suggests that the spiritual bond had material import. There are several other early references which indicate that the godfather was regarded as a protector and benefactor. A number of the estates granted to the abbey of Cluny in the late tenth century were described as *filiolagia or filiolatus,* that is, properties originally obtained by the grantors as gifts from their godparents.[7] The *chansons de geste*, although assuming written form in the twelfth century and later, attest the significance of godparenthood in this heroic age. In *Guibert d'Andrenas*, for example, the hero's father is shown planning to disinherit his son in favor of his godson.[8] Evidence of a more substantial sort can be obtained from various chronicles compiled in the twelfth century. The histories of the counts of Guînes and the counts of Nevers both relate how benevolent godfathers were instrumental in helping the founders of the dynasties to establish their fortunes. The first count of Guînes was Ardolph, the bastard son of Sifrid, a Scandinavian adventurer at the turn of the ninth and tenth centuries. His godfather was Arnold, count of Flanders, who not only granted him a vast estate as his *filiolagium* but

---

[6]Dorothy Whitelock, ed., *English Historical Documents*, 1: *c. 500–1042* (London, 1955), p. 372.

[7]Auguste Bernard and Alexandre Bruel, eds., *Recueil des chartes de l'abbaye de Cluny*, 6 vols. (Paris, 1876–1903), vol. 1, no. 322, and vol. 2, no. 924.

[8]W. O. Farnsworth, *Uncle and Nephew in the Old French Chansons de Geste: A Study in the Survival of Matriarchy* (New York, 1913), p. 22.

was also responsible for his appointment as count.[9] In the history of the counts of Nevers there is an even more dramatic episode, which is worth quoting in its entirety:

> Landricus, having taken a wife of Angevin stock, had by her a son by the name of Bodo, whom Bodo de Montibus lifted from the holy font. The boy, when he had grown up, sought something in the way of a gift from his godfather. "What would you like to be given, godson?" he said. "I wish," he replied, "that you would grant me as much land as the shadow of this mountain here ranges over in the course of one day." This request having been granted, the young man rose up on summer mornings at the break of day, and took his own boundary-markers and placed them around the land as the shadow turned with the shifting sun. And here he built a castle which he called Moncellis.[10]

Later it is suggested that these episodes might merely represent twelfth-century attempts to legitimize usurpations of the tenth century. Whether apocryphal or not, such stories illustrate the sorts of godfather men of the time dreamed about.

Spiritual kinship in western Europe did not only, or even principally, involve the godparent and the godchild. The relationship which caused St. Boniface concern was the bond between the godparent and the natural parent: in Latin *compaternitas*, in modern Spanish *compadrazgo*, and in the terminology of American anthropologists ritual co-parenthood. From the eighth century onwards there is evidence that the relationship had social as well as ritual importance. When Pope Hadrian I acted as baptismal sponsor of Charlemagne's sons, the two men entered into a *pactum compaternitatis*. What this spiritual bond implied at the time is unclear, but it assuredly entailed reciprocal obligations of protection and support between the two leaders of western Christendom.[11] The life of St. Heribert of Cologne illustrates some of the connotations of ritual co-parenthood in the Rhineland at the beginning of the eleventh century. The episode of most interest is the chapter in which the author extols the archbishop's outstanding humility. It concerns a pauper of Cologne, whose infant child no priest in the city was willing to baptize. Hearing the poor man's laments, the archbishop hurried

---

[9]*Historia comitum Ghisnenium*, MGH Scriptores 24 (Hanover, 1879), pp. 568–69.

[10]R. B. C. Huygens, ed., "Brève histoire des premiers comtes de Nevers," in *Monumenta Vizeliacensia*, Corpus Christianorum, continuatio medievalis 42 (Turnhout, 1976), p. 237.

[11]Robert Folz, *The Coronation of Charlemagne, 25 December 800*, trans J. E. Anderson (London, 1974), pp. 111–12.

to offer to perform the sacrament himself. The pauper, doubtless trusting to his newly found good fortune, put a further request to the archbishop: "Then you also raise him from the holy font, and deign to be my *compater*." Heribert willingly accepted this invitation, putting to shame the uncharitable and probably simoniacal priests who had previously refused to administer the sacrament. Nor was this the end of the matter: a new relationship had been born at the baptismal font. The hagiographer proceeds to relate how some time later Heribert was riding past an old hovel, when out rushed the self-same pauper, reminding the churchman of the bond between them. To the surprise of his retinue, the good archbishop dismounted his horse and was welcomed into his *compater*'s hut to partake of his humble fare. Whilst this episode suggests that a bond between a magnate and a pauper was somewhat remarkable, even at this stage an easy familiarity and a close reciprocity seem to have been the hallmarks of the relationship between *compatres*.[12]

From the twelfth century onwards references to spiritual kinship become more plentiful, even if no more amenable to systematic analysis. The universality of the institution across Christian Europe, and its survival over the generations, provide masses of detail but no coherent picture. In essence it can be said that the requirement that each child should have a number of baptismal sponsors provided parents with a useful opportunity to extend, reinforce, or sanctify their relationships with other members of the community. Given that spiritual kin relations involved no property rights, and positively impeded future matrimonial entanglements, such bonds were regarded as far less problematical than the regular ties of blood and marriage. Indeed many communities found the arrangement so useful that the concept of spiritual kinship was progressively extended not only to include the officiating priest and the relatives of the godparents, but also to embrace persons acting as sponsors on other sacramental and ritual occasions. Similarly ambitious individuals sought the services of an increasing number of godparents at the font, and from the thirteenth century church councils struggled in vain to restrict the number of sponsors to a canonical two or three.[13] Obviously the institution of spiritual kinship was far from monolithic, subject as it was to variation and modification from region to region and from

---

[12]"Vita S. Heriberti," in PL, ed. J.-P. Migne, 170 (Paris, 1854), cols. 412–13.

[13]J. Bossy, "Blood and Baptism: Kinship, Community and Christianity in Western Europe from the Fourteenth to the Seventeenth Centuries," in *Sanctity and Secularity: The Church and the World*, ed. Derek Baker, Studies in Church History 10 (Oxford, 1973), p. 133.

generation to generation. Nevertheless, in the complex of relationships which spiritual kinship might involve two coalitions assume pivotal importance: the vertical bond between godparent and godchild, and the horizontal bond between godparent and natural parent.

At first sight the relationship between the godparent and the godchild might appear the more fundamental. The idea of the indulgent godfather or godmother, whose moral support and material aid were freely bestowed on the child, certainly become rapidly ingrained in the collective unconscious of western civilization. The popular belief that godparents ought not to deny their godchildren any reasonable request has been evidenced by anthropologists in contemporary European communities, revealing a remarkable continuity of tradition from the age when the counts of Nevers first ascribed their family fortunes to the generosity of Bodo de Montibus. Not surprisingly, it became the aim of many families to secure the services of the rich and powerful as sponsors of their children, though how consistently godparents lived up to the more material expectations of their role is difficult to ascertain. There were assuredly no legally enforceable obligations, and a great deal must have always depended on the godfather's own means, his affection for the particular child, and the nature of his prior relationship with the child's parents. Tradition demanded that the sponsors brought presents to the christening, and men and women customarily remembered their godchildren in their wills, but for the most part such gifts were made in the spirit of piety rather than indulgence. There were even some parents in the Middle Ages who felt it was wrong to select godparents for material reasons. In the late fourteenth century a pious Tuscan father reacted against what he regarded as "a bad custom," and sought only men and women of humble station to serve as sponsors for his fourteen children. He informed his close friend, Francesco di Marco Datini, the affluent merchant of Prato, that he would only accept his candidature if he promised not to come to the christening laden with gifts, "but like a poor pilgrim; and thus will I respectfully take you as my *compare,* and in no other manner."[14] In the strict sense such an attitude was more appropriate to a spiritual relationship, and from the start it was felt that a godchild was the heir to the spirit just as the child was the heir to the body. The thirteenth-century poem *Meier Helmbrecht,* for example, gives expression to the related idea, apparently commonplace

---

[14]Iris Origo, *The Merchant of Prato, Francesco di Marco Datini*, rev. ed. (Harmondsworth, 1963), p. 212.

in German folklore, that a person inherited his moral character from his godparents. Thus Helmbrecht, the ambitious peasant youth, justified his social pretensions in the following way:

> The Roman law says, and it's true:
> A child will, in his early days
> Take on his sponsor's virtuous ways.
> A noble knight once sponsored me,
> And blessed may he ever be
> Through him I am a noble kind,
> And have a proud and knightly mind![15]

A similar set of attitudes has been observed by Juliet Du Boulay in some twentieth-century Greek communities, where at their funerals persons who have acted as godparents are distinguished by their attire from persons who have failed to "pass on to others the kingdom of the spirit . . . to do in spiritual terms what (they) should also do in the flesh, and that is to have children."[16]

Whilst the relationship between godparent and godchild was of manifest importance, it would seem that from the earliest times until the Reformation it was the horizontal bond of *compaternitas* that had the greater social significance. After all the bond of spiritual kinship was first established when a parent asked another person to act as sponsor to his child, and often the baptism must be regarded as a sanctification of an old, rather than an initiation of a new, relationship. Evidence from the ages of Charlemagne and St. Heribert suggests that from the very beginnings the relationship between the two *compatres* was ideally one of equality and balanced reciprocity. The *pactum compaternitatis* could represent at one level the sacred alliance between the spiritual and temporal leaders of Christendom, and at another level the ready hospitality and easy familiarity of "gossips." Later references to ritual co-parenthood can be plotted on a broad spectrum, ranging from the historically significant to the historically inconsequential; but what is interesting is that the main features of the institution remain constant, and can still be evidenced in many contemporary southern European and Latin American communities. Furthermore, given that *compaternitas*

---

[15]Clair Hayden Bell, ed. and trans., *Peasant Life in Old German Epics: "Meier Helmbrecht" and "Der Arme Heinrich,"* new ed. (New York, 1968), lines 480–86.

[16]J. Du Boulay, *Portrait of a Greek Mountain Village* (Oxford, 1974), pp. 163–64.

could bring into formal association two individuals of different backgrounds, its social importance might be considerable. At times ritual co-parenthood merely overlaid existing bonds of kinship, affinity, neighborhood, and community, but at other times it served to extend the network of personal relations in such a way as to transcend social boundaries. In the village or larger community it was a means of bringing into ritual relationship two feuding, or potentially hostile, factions. There was certainly less risk involved in making an alliance through baptism than through marriage, and Bossy has argued convincingly that spiritual kinship played a vital role in counteracting the rivalries and tensions of village life from the fourteenth to the sixteenth centuries.[17] At a higher level of political activity it was a means of establishing coalitions between the greater men of the realm. In the early fifteenth century a canny abbot in war-torn France petitioned the pope to be absolved from the ruling that monks could not act as godparents, "seeing that the favour of nobles and other powerful folk is most necessary . . . and seeing also that, in these parts, close relationships are contracted between those who stand as godparents and the parents of the children," and to be granted permission to establish *compater* relations with some forty local noblemen.[18] Obviously in societies in which the population was divided into a number of virtually endogamous communities, spiritual kinship could assume immense structural significance. In his study of the village of Montaillou at the end of the thirteenth century, E. Le Roy Ladurie has shown the importance of spiritual relations not only within the settled community but also as a means of linking the villagers with the pastoralists who passed through the neighborhood on their transhumance routes twice each year. The affable shepherd, Pierre Maury, is depicted as having collected godchildren, *comperes* and *commeres*, and presumably free board and lodging in every village on his path.[19] A similar symbiosis between agriculturalists and pastoralists, associated through ritual kinship, has been noted by contemporary anthropologists in their studies of Greek, Serbian, and even Turkish communities.[20] Even more striking is the possible role of

---

[17]Bossy, "Blood and Baptism," pp. 132–35.

[18]Quoted in Mintz and Wolf, "Ritual Co-parenthood," p. 348.

[19]Emmanuel Le Roy Ladurie, *Montaillou, village occitan de 1294 à 1324* ([Paris], 1975), p. 184.

[20]J. K. Campbell, *Honour, Family and Patronage: A Study of Institutions and Moral Values in a Greek Mountain Community* (Oxford, 1964), p. 223; E. A. Hammel, *Alternative Social*

baptismal sponsorship in helping to bind together distinct ethnic or religious groups, especially when intermarriage appeared problematical. Innumerable *pacta compaternitatis* must have served to bring into formal relationship pagan Scandinavians and their reluctant Christian hosts in northwest Europe in the ninth and tenth centuries. The nineteenth-century historian E. Freeman claimed, with some plausibility but apparently without documentary evidence, that it was through baptismal sponsorship that Anglo-Saxons and Normans were brought into close personal relationship.[21]

Even more powerful testimony to the structural significance of spiritual kinship in traditional European society is the fact that it was not unknown for members of different sects and religions to exchange sponsorship duties. Despite attempts to prohibit the practice, in some parts of southern Europe the social advantages of entering into ritual kin relations with heretics and Moslems could more than compensate for the dubious spiritual predicament it entailed.[22]

From the foregoing evidence it is clear that spiritual kin relations could assume considerable importance in pre-industrial Europe. Obviously the institution of spiritual kinship can never be as copiously documented for the past as it is for the present, but there is scarcely an important facet of godparenthood or *compaternitas* which has been noted by modern anthropologists which cannot also be observed in European society before the Reformation. Without wishing to go over too much of the ground already covered by Mintz and Wolf, a tentative analysis of some of the functions of spiritual kinship in the Middle Ages is perhaps appropriate. Most basically, the institution provided each child, at the time of his or her initiation into the Christian community, with a number of sponsors, who were regarded quite literally as additional parents. Sometimes the spiritual bond seems to have carried more emotional charge than the relationship of blood. This is the scenario depicted in *Guibert d'Andrenas*, and again in *Meier Helmbrecht*, where the hero, who felt no compunction at forsaking his own parents, took

---

Structures and Ritual Relations in the Balkans (Englewood Cliffs, NJ, 1968), passim; P. J. Magnarella and O. Yurkdogan, "Descent, Affinity and Ritual Relations in Eastern Turkey," *American Anthropologist* 75 (1973), 1626–33.

[21] Edward A. Freeman, *The History of the Norman Conquest of England, Its Causes and Its Results*, 5 vols., 2nd ed. (Oxford, 1870–76), 5:559–61.

[22] Mintz and Wolf, "Ritual Co-parenthood," pp. 349–50; Hammel, *Alternative Social Structures*, p. 88.

it upon himself to avenge an insult to his godfather. Where the godparent was in addition an uncle, an aunt, or a grandparent, the sentimental attachment was even stronger, and in such cases spiritual kinship can be seen as a means of reinforcing kin solidarity by neutralizing possible intra-familial and inter-generational jealousies.[23] With the growing emphasis on the patri-lineage in the eleventh and twelfth centuries, it was doubtless an especially useful way of either reinforcing the connection with paternal grandfather, or providing surrogate sons for married uncles, or redefining the increasingly problematical status of maternal kinsmen. At the same time, the need to find sponsors for the baptism of the child provided the parent with an additional way of expanding the network of social relations. Since consanguinity and affinity too often involved competition over property, men needed other means of effecting alliances; and spiritual kinship, which was irrevocable, involved no rights of inheritance and positively precluded the possibility of both marital entanglement and sexual liaison, was the ideal medium. As has been noted earlier, godparenthood and *compaternitas* were particularly useful mechanisms for forging alliances between individuals and groups for whom intermarriage was either inconceivable or undesirable. Accordingly spiritual kinship in the Middle Ages can be seen transcending such important social boundaries as were erected by considerations of age, lineage, affinity, neighborhood, occupation, rank, race, and so on, and binding together with sacramental bonds the various components of an increasingly differentiated society. The ties of godparenthood and *compaternitas* served as the warp and weft of the social fabric, and would seem to have played a vital historic role in the integration of the expanding moral community of Latin Christendom.

Obviously the social significance of spiritual kinship in European society in earlier centuries completely transcended its particular import in the lives of individual godparents, gossips, and godchildren. A role of historical importance has been attributed to the institution, and a preliminary and extremely tentative survey of the claims would be in order. In the first place it needs to be noted that fictive kin relations are by no means unique to the Christian world. The Teutonic invaders of the Roman Empire in the fifth and

---

[23]See J. Pitt-Rivers's comments on this facet of godparenthood in modern Andalusia: "the guardianship of the individuality of the child, his 'Christian-self,' that which will grow up and destroy the parental unit, is transferred to *padrinos* who have no concern in the structural destiny of the family": Pitt-Rivers, "Ritual Kinship in Spain," pp. 429–30.

sixth centuries, like their Scandinavian cousins several centuries later, brought with them well-articulated concepts of blood brotherhood, the avunculate, and fosterage, which would seem to have blended with ideas of Christian sponsorship to form the distinctive spiritual kin institutions of medieval and modern Europe. The vital importance of the relationship between mother's brother and sister's son in the old Germanic world is well enough attested in the early epics, the *chansons de geste*, and the sagas,[24] and in some respects it can be seen to prefigure the relationship between godfather and godson, which is evidenced increasingly in the literature from the twelfth century onwards. Since fictive kin relations can be viewed as essentially a means of extending kinship categories to non-kin, so at an even more abstract level it is possible to regard them as an intermediary form between kinship proper and wider-based notions of community. In practical terms the Germanic and Scandinavian peoples found in spiritual kinship a convenient means of securing a place for themselves in the more complex societies in which they settled.[25] Pagan invaders adopted Christianity at the time of their settlement; local dignitaries served as their sponsors at baptism; and later generations rationalized the usurpations of Scandinavian pirates as *filiolagia*. Furthermore, spiritual kinship provided the newcomers with the conceptual apparatus necessary to come to terms with more complex forms of social organization. Fictive kin relations doubtless played an important role in enabling individuals to conceptualize patronage as well as parentage, community as well as sibling solidarity. The proliferation of more sophisticated institutions in western Europe in the eleventh and twelfth centuries probably owed as much to the mentalities bred of spiritual kinship as to classical models. It is symptomatic that Charlemagne found it impossible to conceptualize his relationship with the pope other than as a *pactum compaternitatis*.[26]

Similarly, it is no coincidence that so many of the new solidarities and corporations which emerged from the late tenth century onwards regarded themselves as confraternities, as spiritual brotherhoods. Even as late as the

---

[24]See Farnsworth, *Uncle and Nephew in the Old French Chansons de Geste*, and Clair Hayden Bell, *The Sister's Son in the Medieval German Epic: A Study in the Survival of Matriliny* (Berkeley, 1922).

[25]Note also the importance of spiritual kinship in linking the Byzantines with their Slav and Bulgar neighbors: Patlagean, "Christianisation et parentés rituelles," pp. 631–32.

[26]Folz, *Coronation of Charlemagne*, pp. 111–12.

sixteenth century confraternities in Champagne tended to be associations of spiritual kin as well as guilds devoted to saints.[27] At the same time, the terminology of spiritual kinship infused other developing institutions in medieval society. The senior knight who supervised the training and sponsored the initiation of a young squire into the order of chivalry was regarded as a sort of godfather; so was the saint who showed particular favor to a suppliant; so was the bureaucrat who expedited a poor suitor's business; so in modern times are the Latin American "fixer" and the Italian mafia boss. In a fairly literal as well as a figurative sense, the godfather can be seen in the ninth and tenth centuries acting as a sponsor for the new social order, facilitating the emergence of the distinctive civilization of Latin Christendom.

II

In the discussion so far it has been attempted to depict in general terms the forms and functions of spiritual kinship in traditional European society. Building upon the available documentation and utilizing the insights provided by anthropological studies of contemporary Christian communities, it has been argued that in a number of respects spiritual kinship played an important role not only in the organization of particular communities but also in the development of western European society as a whole. Obviously the more grandiose claims made on behalf of spiritual kinship cannot be established until a great deal more research has been undertaken into the functioning of the institution in particular places at particular times. Such basic questions as whether spiritual kin relations were used primarily to intensify or to extend pre-existing kin relations would seem to be readily amenable to statistical analysis, and accordingly demand some solution. Unfortunately, as has been mentioned earlier, spiritual kin relations were seldom recorded, and research on the institution will entail the laborious collation of very occasional references in narrative sources, and perhaps in ecclesiastical archives. Nevertheless, it is hoped that for certain favored regions quantifiable data will be available, and will ultimately provide surer foundations for a general analysis of the institution in western Europe during

---

[27] A. N. Galpern, *The Religions of the People in Sixteenth-Century Champagne* (Cambridge, MA, 1976), pp. 43–45.

the Middle Ages and beyond. In the following section it is intended to make a modest start by reviewing some of the possibilities for research into spiritual kinship in late medieval England.

Among the public records of England there is one class of records which fortunately makes regular reference to godparenthood: the "inquisitions of proof of age."[28] As their name suggests, these inquests were undertaken by the escheator to determine whether wards of the crown seeking seisin of their estates had actually reached their majority. The procedure was to empanel a number of local jurors, who were to attest the age of the ward and to state their reasons for remembering his or her year of birth. Not unnaturally there were a great many references to the child's baptism in the testimonials, and among the jurors there was usually someone who mentioned the names of godparents, or who acted as a sponsor himself. Rather regrettably for the social historian, some doubt has been cast on the authenticity of much of the interesting, corroborative detail included in the inquisitions of proof of age.[29] Despite the "common form" apparent in many of the testimonials, and despite the fact that a fair amount of the supporting evidence was concocted by witnesses, it is felt that the references made to godparents can be taken as authentic. In the first place, even if all the evidential detail were specious, there can be no doubt that in the escheator's mind a number of basic facts were well-established: there was a named ward, the child of a named feudal tenant, who had then come of age. Where a specific individual is named as having been the godparent, especially where the godparent was a man of some note in the community, it is reasonable to accept this information as forming part of the kernel of truth. Secondly, even if the testimonies regarding the baptismal ceremonies can be shown to have been fabricated, it is fair to assume that the fabrications would actually reflect the customs of the time. Indeed, since the evidence would have had to appear credible to contemporaries, it would perhaps be of even greater value to the historian of the mores of late medieval England.

The picture of godparenthood provided by the inquisitions of proof of age is for the most part unexceptionable. Most of the evidence relates to the

---

[28]The "inquisitions of proof of age" are classified with the "inquisitions post mortem" at The National Archives, Kew, and have been calendared in *Calendar of Inquisitions Post Mortem* (HMSO, in progress).

[29]See the articles entitled "Legal Proofs of Age" by R. C. Fowler, M. T. Martin, and A. E. Stamp in *EHR* 22 (1907), 101–03 and 526–27; and 29 (1914), 323–24.

christening ceremony itself, and the role of the godparents at the font can be reconstructed in some detail. Immediately after the birth of the child, the father and the mother seem to have chosen three godparents, two of the same sex as the child, and either asked them personally or sent messengers to ask their consent. On the whole the prospective sponsors would seem to have considered it an honor to be invited. There are several references to godfathers contesting precedence, and to their pique at having their office usurped by others.[30] Whether acting as godparent involved great material expense is difficult to estimate. Probably the baptismal sponsors were expected to bring gifts. Only the very rich could give silver; but christenings were an occasion for ostentatious generosity, and the more lavish gifts were recalled in the inquisitions of proof of age.[31] Godparents also seem to have had to bear a part of the costs of the christening ceremony, but their contribution, like the value of their gift, would have been proportionate to their economic status. The most common recollections regarding the godparents, of course, involved their ritual duties at the font. The various sponsors are remembered as having held a lighted taper or the chrism cloth, or most important, as having raised the child from the font and given it its Christian name. Indeed it is the performance of the latter two functions which tends to identify the main godparent both at the ceremony and in the records. When a magnate was not able to attend in person to act as godparent, he sometimes sent deputies specifically to lift the child from the font and give it its name. In the inquisitions of proof of age and other sources the words "he raised from the holy font" (*suscepit de sacro fonte*) are synonymous with the words "he was the godfather."

Nor is the utility of the inquisitions of proof of age limited to an elucidation of the duties of the godparents at the font. Since the records in print provide the names of over three hundred groups of godparents, gossips, and godchildren from fourteenth-century England, the prospect emerges of placing the study of spiritual kinship on a far more solid foundation. The nature of the pre-existing relationship between the parent and the godparent is an obvious point of interest. Insofar as any definite structural patterns influencing the selection of spiritual kin can be discerned, it will be possible to make useful inferences regarding the social functions of the institution.

---

[30]*CIPM* 5:63–64; 7:339–40; 10:229–31.

[31]*CIPM* 10:285–87; 11:296–97; 12:77; 14:289–90.

Obviously a vast program of research is called for to establish from the local angle the family connections and the socio-economic status of the various individuals mentioned in the inquisitions of proof of age. Even as regards the most basic question, whether spiritual kinship functioned to intensify or to extend kinship relations, it is difficult to come to any definite conclusion. From the evidence it is unlikely that more than a small minority asked paternal kinsmen to act as godparents. Less than one in ten heirs and heiresses in the inquisitions of proof of age had godparents with the same surname as themselves; and examples of two or more paternal kinsmen acting as sponsors are very uncommon. Sir William Gramary and Thomas Gramary serving as godfathers to William son of John Gramary is a rare example of keeping spiritual kinship within the patrilineage, whilst the decision of Edmund of Woodstock, earl of Kent, to ask his son and daughter to act as sponsors to their younger brother appears positively incestuous.[32] Unfortunately there is no easy means of identifying relatives on the distaff side. Occasionally such a connection is recorded, as when Marmaduke Tweng and Gavin Tweng, the godfathers of Marmaduke son of Robert Lumley, are identified as maternal kinsmen.[33] A similar inference can perhaps be made in some of the other cases where parents seem to have invited a number of members of the same family to act as godparents. The evidence that Thomas Hildeyerd and his wife selected as the sponsors of their two daughters four members of the Colville family and two members of the Ligard family suggests that the three families were closely related.[34] The question of whether parents tended to seek godparents of higher socio-economic status is even harder to answer categorically. There can be no doubt that, all things being equal, a baptismal sponsor of wealth, rank, and influence was desirable. There are several examples of Edward II acting as godfather to the sons of gentlemen, and a number of queens and princesses appear in the list of godmothers recorded in the inquisitions of proof of age.[35] Peers of the realm and their wives also made prestigious gossips for the country gentry, as did influential churchmen. On the other hand, members of the aristocracy did not disdain to ask trusted retainers to act as godparents to their children,

[32]*CIPM* 10:239–40; 9:455–56.

[33]*CIPM* 7:482–83.

[34]*CIPM* 7:385–86; 8:90–91.

[35]*CIPM* 8:30–31 and 150–51; 3:327–28; 7:296–97.

and the majority of parents of all ranks would have had to be content with gossips drawn from amongst their equals or even their social inferiors. The results of a sample study of the thirteen Cheshire inquisitions of proof of age which record spiritual kin relations are instructive on this point.[36] Eight out of thirteen fathers would seem to have chosen men of the same or marginally lower status, whilst five selected men who might have been in a position to act as patrons. Three relationships are worth noting: Thomas Beeston, Roger Venables, and William Chauntrell, respectively, chose as their gossips Sir William Bagot, the influential knight who later attained notoriety as a minister of Richard II; Sir Hugh Holes, a justice of Chester, soon to be promoted to the King's Bench; and Sir John Stanley, the wealthiest and most powerful magnate in northwest England.

Obviously a fuller appreciation of the role of godparenthood and *compaternitas* in late medieval England must await many more detailed local studies. It can at least be demonstrated that spiritual kinship was used both to intensify and to extend the kinship network. Furthermore, unless maternal kinsfolk served as sponsors with far greater regularity than relatives on the father's side, it would seem that "extension" was a more important function than "intensification."[37] At another level it is evident that men were reciprocating duties as godparents both with their peers and with individuals of different socio-economic status. Whilst the dream was doubtless to find a wealthy benefactor and powerful patron, the majority would seem to have had to settle for a gossip of roughly equivalent rank. The analogy with matrimonial alliances is perhaps apposite, but its use must not be allowed to obscure the fact that most people had more godparents than fathers-in-law, and more gossips than they could count. Whether sponsorship at the

---

[36] George Ormerod, *The History of the County Palatine and City of Chester*, 3 vols., 2nd ed. (London, 1882), 1:570; 2:270, 497, 667, 704, 765, 774; 3:39, 102, 307, 384, 394, and 657.

[37] In seventeenth-century England there seems to be a growing tendency for godparents, especially for the eldest children, to be chosen from amongst close relatives. The twenty-seven sponsors of the children of Richard Fogg, born between 1639 and 1656, included three Foggs and at least nine other kinsmen: T. G. Faussett, ed., "Family Chronicle of Richard Fogge of Danes Court, in Tilmanstone," *Archaeologia Cantiana* 5 (1863), 112–13. Of the twenty-two named sponsors of John Evelyn's children, born between 1652 and 1669, eight had the surname *Evelyn*, and ten others were described as close relatives of the father or mother: *The Diary of John Evelyn*, ed. E. S. De Beer, 6 vols. (Oxford, 1955), 3:75, 89, 147, 194, 368, 421, 495, and 528.

font served on occasion as a means of ritually settling feuds in late medieval England remains an interesting hypothesis. Significantly the jurors often mention "love-days" (*dies amoris*) between feuding parties as having taken place at the church on the day of the christening, but there is no evidence that the same men were involved in the two ceremonies.[38] Nor can the inquisitions of proof of age, alluding only to the beginning of the relationship, provide solutions to other important problems regarding spiritual kinship. A number of jurors identified themselves as the godfathers of the young person in question, which must demonstrate some sort of continuing interest in the relationship. Even more significant is the testimony of a Hampshire gentleman that his father had been the godfather of Thomas son of Sir William Overton, and that he recalled being told on a number of occasions that he was his *confrater*.[39] For further insights into the subsequent roles of the godparent, godchild, and gossip it is necessary to turn again to other, less satisfactory sources. Ecclesiastical records show that godparents had to remain mindful of their spiritual kin, if for no other reason than that intermarriage was canonically illicit. A study of fifteenth-century English wills reveals that many men and women did remember their godchildren, although the bequests tended to be rather small.[40] This is the sort of field in which contemporary literature ought to be helpful, but is rather silent, perhaps ominously silent. There are occasional references which suggest that godparenthood might be viewed as a form of patronage. In the Cely letters a young tradesman could write to George Cely asking him to expedite some business, and praying him to be his "gud godfader in the mater," without making it clear whether he is alluding to a relationship or using a metaphor.[41] A similar development took place with the concept of *compaternitas*. The original AS *God-sib*, meaning quite literally a "kinsman in God," was shifting its ground semantically to the more generalized term *gossip*. When William Shakespeare refers to Elizabeth Woodville and her allies at the court of Edward IV as "mighty gossips" within the realm, it is difficult

---

[38]E.g., Ormerod, *Hist. Cheshire* 2:667 and 774.

[39]*CIPM* 11:412–13.

[40]E.g., see Samuel Tymms, ed., *Wills and Inventories from the Registers of the Commissary of Bury St Edmund's and the Archdeacon of Sudbury*, Camden Society 49 (1850), pp. 5, 10, 13, 45, 83, 86, 97, 98, 104, 125, 127, 129, 132–34, 138–39, 143, 146, 151–52, 173, and 194.

[41]Alison Hanham, ed., *The Cely Letters, 1472–1488*, EETS 273 (1975), no. 152.

to know whether he is making a specific reference to spiritual kinship along with his general allusion to "petticoat" government.[42]

The marked shift in the semantic fields represented by spiritual kinship terms is testimony both to the former importance and the subsequent dissolution of the institution in England. It would be ironic indeed if the region with the best set of records for the study of godparenthood in the later Middle Ages should also prove to be the part of Christendom in which it first lost its social significance. Without wishing to prejudge the issue, it must be said that there is little in the inquisitions of proof of age or other contemporary evidence to suggest that spiritual kinship had anything like the social significance in late medieval England that it has in some contemporary rural communities in southern Europe and Latin America. Given that there were no clear structural patterns influencing the selection of spiritual kin, it is unlikely that their social obligations were at all clearly defined. The bond of *compaternitas* doubtless tended to imply the reinforcement and sanctification of a pre-existing relationship, rather than the creation of a whole new set of reciprocal rights and obligations. Godparenthood was probably coming to be whatever individuals wished to make of it. In England spiritual kinship, like kinship proper, was developing as a far more flexible institution, and was beginning to assume the amorphous contours of contemporary godparenthood. It needs to be stressed, of course, that historical sources tend to record the ideals and practice of the literate elite. It is probable that spiritual kinship held its ground much longer amongst the English rural peasantry, who had far greater need of their kinsfolk, whether of blood or baptism. Yet it is significant that the reforming churchmen of sixteenth-century England, unlike either their Protestant or Catholic counterparts on the Continent, did not feel the need to legislate against abuses arising from the social functions of baptismal sponsorship. In the seventeenth century some Puritans questioned the need for godparents, whilst others salved their consciences by calling them *susceptores,* but by this stage godparenthood had long ceased to be a pivotal institution in English society. Obviously a full consideration of the factors involved in the decline of spiritual kinship in England cannot be attempted in this paper, and immense though such a study would have to be, it would be best treated as merely one chapter in a far larger discussion of the apparent precociousness of

---

[42]William Shakespeare, *King Richard the Third*, Act I, sc. 1, line 83.

English society in the pre-industrial period. If Alan Macfarlane's study of the rise of individualism in England is any guide, it would be necessary to trace its roots back to the thirteenth century and beyond.[43] Yet the continued vitality of godparenthood and *compaternitas* in parts of the contemporary world must provide some clues as to the sorts of variables involved in sustaining and undermining such institutions. Perhaps one conclusion would be that spiritual kinship tends to be at its most functional in societies characterized by low levels of integration. In heavily stratified or segmented social systems, where godparenthood and *compaternitas* relations provided a fibrous undergrowth binding communities together, spiritual kinship could assume considerable structural importance. It can be no coincidence that the institution has gained a new lease of life, possibly even grown in strength, in contemporary southern European and Latin American communities which are divided into relatively simple and relatively sophisticated sectors, in which peasant families confront increasingly complex bureaucracies. If these suppositions have any validity, spiritual kinship performed its most valuable role in the formative period of western European civilization, when new elites were being established and new solidarities forged in the first and second feudal ages.

III

In the preceding sections a preliminary attempt has been made to outline the main features of spiritual kinship in traditional European society, and to draw attention to a class of records from late medieval England which ought to prove valuable in more detailed and localized studies of the institution. It is hoped that enough has been said at least to stimulate further research in the field, and doubtless other sources will be found in Continental archives, which might prove to have even more potential than the inquisitions of proof of age. As more detailed regional studies from different countries and different periods become available, it is possible that the observable variations in spiritual kin institutions might in their turn provide interesting insights into other aspects of the societies under consid-

---

[43] Alan Macfarlane, *The Origins of English Individualism: The Family, Property and Social Transition* (Oxford, 1978).

eration. The strength of spiritual kinship in European societies might be used as a rough index of levels of integration, whilst the variable emphasis on the vertical bonds of godparenthood or the horizontal bonds of *compaternitas* might be correlated with particular forms of social organization. Obviously a great deal of work needs to be done at both an empirical and theoretical level before this sort of potential is realized, but as a modest example of the possibilities arising from a knowledge of the functions of spiritual kinship it is appropriate to turn again to the evidence of the inquisitions of proof of age. Even though the general conclusion was that spiritual kinship was declining in importance in late medieval English society, in one sphere at least the godparent left an indelible mark on the life of the godchild. Whilst it is common knowledge that it was the responsibility of the principal godparent to name the child at the font, what has not been so far recognized is that in late medieval England it was the norm for the chief gossip to give the child his or her own name. It is this feature of godparenthood in England which would seem to have most potential as a research tool for the social historian. As a growing number of studies on the *anthroponymie* of early European societies amply testify, a knowledge of how personal names were transmitted from generation to generation has interesting possibilities in a whole range of studies.

As was noted earlier, the inquisitions of proof of age provide the names of several hundred godparents and godchildren from fourteenth-century England. If only the records providing the names of one or both godparents of the same sex as the child are counted, a sample of 313 spiritual kin relationships can be obtained for analysis. In 248 of the cases it can be seen that the godchild has the same Christian name as at least one of the godparents. In a further thirty-nine cases there is reference to only one godparent of the relevant sex, leaving the possibility that the child was named after the unmentioned godparent. In only twenty-six of the cases is there categorical evidence that the child was not given the name of either of his godfathers or her godmothers. After adding in a percentage of the christenings at which there is incomplete evidence, it is reasonable to infer that as many as 90% of the nobility and gentry of fourteenth-century England shared the same Christian name as one of their godparents.

Far from being merely a statistical regularity, there is every reason to believe that this system of name giving was the established norm. It is significant that in five out of the twenty-six exceptional cases, the jurors felt obliged to offer some explanation for the apparent aberration from custom.

At the christening of William son of William Deyncourt, for example, there was evidently a quarrel between the two godfathers over precedence, and as a sort of compromise it was decided to name him William because most of his ancestors were so named.[44] On three other occasions there was talk amongst the parishioners as to how the child came to have a name other than that of the godparents, and it was explained that the child was named after a particularly honored saint.[45] In another instance, the baptism of John son of Thomas Aylesbury, an inquisitive villager asked the same question of one of the godfathers, Sir Ralph Basset, who gave him a cuff round the neck for his pains.[46] In many of the other exceptional christenings it is possible to advance other factors which might account for the departure from custom. Three such cases involve aristocratic families whose backgrounds were only marginally English: the earls of Desmond, Athol, and March.[47] In three other instances there is evidence of a strong, and fairly idiosyncratic, family tradition of nomenclature: Ralph son of Ralph Basset; Reynold son of Reynold Cobham; and Arnold son of Arnold Savage.[48] Indeed, given the importance attached to names in some lineages, it is possible that parents sometimes chose gossips for the sake of their Christian names. In the inquisition of proof of age of Joan, daughter of John de Eglesfield, it is suggested that the father deliberately selected as godmothers two of his friends' wives who were named Joan.[49] The frequency of this sort of arrangement, which might also have involved the reciprocation of sponsorship duties between lineages using the same stock of names, is further suggested by the large number of occasions when two godparents are found to have had the same Christian name. The two godfathers of Simon son of Simon Pakeman in 1306 were Simon Mayel and Simon Osbern; the sponsors of William son of William de Stoppeham in 1307 were William de Sothill and William Fairfax; and the godparents of Robert son of Robert Bertram in 1308 were Robert de la Vale and Robert de Mora.[50] Another well-contrived occasion

---

[44]*CIPM* 15:63–64.

[45]*CIPM* 3:327–28; 5:84–85; and 8:90–91.

[46]*CIPM* 10:229–31.

[47]*CIPM* 10:325–26; 7:235–36; 13:261–62.

[48]*CIPM* 10:236; 12:374–75; 15:118–19.

[49]*CIPM* 13:50–51.

[50]*CIPM* 7:83–84, 137, and 132–33.

was the christening of Bartholomew Redham, at which Bartholomew de Castre served as godfather, on St. Bartholomew's Day 1305.[51]

The evidence of the inquisitions of proof of age so far considered relates almost entirely to the nobility and gentry of fourteenth-century England, but occasional references from other sources suggest that this particular system of name giving was far more widespread. Even members of the royal family do not seem to have been immune from the custom. According to a contemporary chronicler, Richard II owed his name to Richard, king of Armenia, who by a curious set of circumstances raised him from the font at Bordeaux.[52] Moving down the social scale, the wills of tradespeople suggest that the custom was as prevalent in an urban milieu as it was in landed society. In her will Agnes Stubbard of Bury St. Edmunds rather interestingly made a distinction between the god-daughters who had and had not been named after her, making bequests of twice the value to the girls called Agnes.[53] Nor did the tradition of naming children after the principal godparent die out with the Reformation. Whilst members of the royal family and leading magnates doubtless did not always feel constrained by this practice, and whilst the Puritans introduced a new fashion of biblical nomenclature, the custom proved extremely tenacious.[54] At the end of the seventeenth century it would still appear to have been the norm amongst most classes of society, and it seems to have been the mechanism by which many surnames were introduced as forenames in this period. An interesting notice of a christening in 1693 records how the two godfathers, a Mr. Bamfield and a Major Moore, contested precedence. A coin was tossed; the former gentleman won, and the child was christened Bamfield Moore Carew.[55]

---

[51] *CIPM* 7:80–81.

[52] J. de Trokelowe et al., *Chronica et annales, regnantibus Henrico tertio, Edwardo primo, Edwardo secundo, Ricardo secundo, et Henrico quarto*, ed. H. T. Riley, Rolls Series (1866), pp. 237–38.

[53] Tymms, *Wills and Inventories*, p. 5.

[54] Eight out of nine children of Richard Fogg, and six out of eight children of John Evelyn, appear to have been named after their godparents: see n. 37.

[55] B. M. Carew, *The Life and Adventures of Bampfylde-Moore Carew, the noted Devonshire stroller and dog-stealer, as related by himself, during his passage to the plantations of America* (Exeter, 1745), p. 2.

It is perhaps testimony to the relative remoteness of the pre-industrial past in England that recollection of this tradition of name giving has been all but effaced from the memories of the present generation. Significantly enough, the nineteenth-century historians Thomas Carlyle and Edward Freeman show an awareness of the custom, though not of its potential as a tool for further research.[56] Scholars on the Continent have generally shown themselves to be in closer touch with the traditions of their forefathers. Marc Bloch in his discussion of name giving in the ninth and tenth centuries noted in passing that the custom of naming children after godparents had not then arisen.[57] Perhaps this latter was the practice he remembered from his own youth, for a recent study of spiritual kinship by Françoise Zonabend noted the survival of this custom into the second half of the nineteenth century in northern Burgundy.[58] Tracing the institution backwards in time, she has further shown that homonymy between the child and the godparent, typically a grandparent, was the norm as early as the beginning of the eighteenth century. Assuming some sort of correspondence with the English situation, it seems inconceivable that the custom was not already some centuries old. In his discussion of popular religion in sixteenth-century Champagne, A. N. Galpern has observed that in both Catholic and Huguenot families children were typically named after their godparents.[59] Going even further back, into the later Middle Ages, a number of isolated references suggest that this custom was as prevalent in France under the Valois as it was in England under the Plantagenets. It is noteworthy, for instance, that seven out of the ten recorded godparents of Jeanne d'Arc were named Jean, Jeanne, or Jeannette.[60] If the transmission of Christian names in England and France in the late medieval and early modern periods was from godparent to godchild, it is pertinent to enquire at what stage the custom established itself in northwestern Europe. Over the past few decades an enormous amount of research has been done on the personal names of the

---

[56]Thomas Carlyle, *History of Friedrich II. of Prussia, Called Frederick the Great*, 10 vols., rev. ed. (London, 1872–73), 1:20; Freeman, *Hist. Norman Conquest* 5:559–61.

[57]Marc Bloch, *Feudal Society*, trans. L. A. Manyon, 2 vols. (London, 1965), 1:45.

[58]F. Zonabend, "La parenté baptismale à Minot (Côte-d'Or)," *Annales ESC* 33 (1978), 656–76.

[59]Galpern, *Religions of People in Sixteenth-Century Champagne*, pp. 111–12.

[60]V[ictoria] Sackville-West, *Saint Joan of Arc* (London, 1936), pp. 34–35.

French and German aristocracies in the late Carolingian and Ottonian periods, and it has been possible to discern a distinctive pattern of nomenclature, in which names were passed from grandparent to grandchild.[61] This apparently well-attested custom has proved of considerable value in the reconstruction of genealogies, and in the provision of data on the vexed problem of continuity amongst the Frankish aristocracy in the period following the dissolution of the Carolingian Empire. Unfortunately, as an approach to the study of feudal society it has been shown to have definite chronological limitations. In a growing number of regional studies historians have noted a remarkable shift in patterns of nomenclature taking place in the eleventh and twelfth centuries. In his magisterial study of the Mâconnais nobility Georges Duby observed how scores of the traditional Germanic names in evidence in 1000 went out of circulation in the following century, to be replaced by a smaller stock of popular Christian names.[62] Studies of personal names in regions as diverse as Normandy and Latium have revealed a similar transformation in the eleventh and twelfth centuries,[63] a transformation which approaches in scale and suddenness the dramatic, but more readily explicable, shift in patterns of naming in England after the Norman Conquest. In a recent discussion of Capetian genealogies Bernard Guenée, remarking again on this *bouleversement onomastique*, asked rhetorically whether the transformation might not be attributable to the growing importance of godparenthood in this field.[64] Quite clearly, if a watershed between the two systems of name giving in evidence in pre-industrial Europe is to be postulated, there are strong *prima facie* grounds for viewing the eleventh and twelfth centuries as the critical period.

The fragmentary sources available for the study of godparenthood in the tenth, eleventh, and twelfth centuries provide a measure of support for this

---

[61]See the observations of J. Martindale, "The French Aristocracy in the Early Middle Ages: A Reappraisal," *PP* 75 (1977), esp. 9–10 and 383–39.

[62]G. Duby, "Lignage, noblesse et chevalerie au XIIe siècle dans la région Mâconnaise. Une revision," *Annales ESC* 27 (1972), esp. 805–06.

[63]M. Le Pesant, "Notes d'anthroponymie normande. Les noms de personne à Evreux du XIIe au XIVe siècles," *Annales de Normandie* 6 (1956), 47–74; Pierre Toubert, *Les structures du Latium médiéval. Le Latium méridional et la Sabine du IXe siècle à la fin du XIIe siècle*, 2 vols. (Rome, 1973), pp. 699–700.

[64]B. Guenée, "Les généalogies entre l'histoire et la politique: La fierté . . . d'être Capétien, en France, au moyen âge," *Annales ESC* 33 (1978), 457.

hypothesis. Chronicles from this period occasionally record the conversion to Christianity of Scandinavian chieftains, describing their baptism and their adoption of a new name. After his defeat at Edington in 878 the Danish King Guthrum was baptized under the AS name of *Athelstan*. One of his godfathers was Alfred the Great, but the identity of the second was unfortunately not recorded.[65] The baptism of Rollo "the sea-ganger" in 912 is more illuminating in this respect. Robert, duke of Paris, raised him from the baptismal font, and the new duke of Normandy was henceforward known by his godfather's name.[66] Another early tenth-century example was Bodo, the ancestor of the counts of Nevers, whose sponsor was alleged to have been Bodo de Montibus.[67] Turning to the testimony of hagiographers, it is evident that at least three eleventh-century saints were named after their godfathers: St. Hugh of Cluny after Hugh, bishop of Auxerre; St. Godfrey of Amiens after Godfrey, abbot of Mont-Saint-Quentin; and St. Arnulf of Soissons after Arnulf of Oudenarde.[68] Indeed the episode regarding the christening of the latter saint is very interesting in this context. Like all good holy men, his birth had been presaged by an angel, who specifically informed his mother that he should be named Christopher. The worthy matron took the message seriously; but not so his godfather, Arnulf of Oudenarde, who "from a too great love for his kin and from an ostentatious pride, did not permit him to be named Christopher, but had him given the self-same name, Arnulf." Even in the middle of the eleventh century the right of the godfather to name the child was so well-entrenched that even the wishes of the mother and the angels in heaven were of little avail.

It would be pointless to attempt to chronicle with any exactitude the introduction of the new system of name giving in western Europe. From the fragmentary evidence available it is likely that the new fashion spread

[65]W. H. Stevenson, ed., *Asser's Life of Alfred: Together with the Annals of Saint Neots, Erroneously Ascribed to Asser*, new ed. (Oxford, 1959), pp. 46–47 and 140.

[66]William of Jumièges, "Historia Northmannorum," PL 149 (Paris, 1853), col. 801.

[67]Huygens, "Brève histoire," p. 237. Note also that in the early eleventh century Robert the Pious, king of France, christened and gave his name to a bell at a church in Orléans: Helgaud de Fleury, *Vie de Robert le Pieux, Epitoma vitae Regis Rotberti Pii*, ed. and trans. R. H. Bautier and Gillette Labory (Paris, 1965), p. 112.

[68]Noreen Hunt, *Cluny under Saint Hugh, 1049–1109* (Notre Dame, IN, 1968), p. 27; "Vita S. Godefridi," in *Acta Sanctorum*, November III (1910), pp. 907–08; "Vita S. Arnulfi," PL 174 (Paris, 1854), cols. 1377–78.

outwards from the Frankish heartland, the source of so many new cultural influences in this period, but its diffusion across the countryside and through the various strata of society must have been extremely uneven. For a number of generations the two main systems of nomenclature doubtless competed for the allegiance of the people. Nor were the two modes entirely incompatible. Where grandparents also acted as godparents, there would be no break in the transmission of names through the lineage. As has already been mentioned, this was the practice in northern Burgundy in the eighteenth century, and it was the option of a significant number of families in late medieval England. Nevertheless, only by postulating a reasonably sharp break with custom in the eleventh and twelfth centuries is it possible to account for the dramatic shift in naming habits in western Europe at this time. Given the considerable population growth evidenced in Latin Christendom from the eleventh century onwards, the problem of the disappearance of so many of the old Germanic names, and their replacement by a more limited stock of fashionable names, is even more perplexing. As Duby has demonstrated, whereas there were few homonyms amongst his relatively small sample of the Mâconnais nobility in 1000, a hundred years later over half of a much larger sample of nobles share five names: *Hugh, Geoffrey, Josseran, Bernard,* and *Humphrey*. It is reasonable to infer that the popularity of the names is associated with the local eminence of Hugh the Great, abbot of Cluny, Geoffrey, count of Mâcon, and a number of castellans named *Josseran, Bernard,* and *Humphrey*.[69] In a similar manner it can be no coincidence that the two most common names in Normandy in the twelfth and thirteenth centuries were the two names most associated with the ducal house. According to Michel le Pesant more than one in five men living in Évreux between 1100 and the Black Death were named either *William* or *Robert*.[70] Identical observations could be made with regard to twelfth-century England, where the names of the Norman rulers made dramatic progress at the expense of AS nomenclature. The problem arising from this information is that of identifying the processes by which the more eminent men were passing their names on to a disproportionate number of men in the following generations. It has been generally assumed that it was simply a matter of the lower orders adopting the prestigious names of their

---

[69]Duby, "Lignage, noblesse et chevalerie," pp. 805–06.

[70]Le Pesant, "Notes d'anthroponymie normande," pp. 47–49.

social superiors, and recently Cecily Clark has advanced some interesting evidence in support of this thesis.[71] In her analysis of personal nomenclature in twelfth-century England, she noted the far greater resilience of women's names to Continental influence. Given that the Norman settlement of England was very largely a male enterprise, she suggested that AS women's names survived better because there were far fewer Norman name models available to the female population. This is not a completely satisfactory argument, since if it were purely a matter of fashion there would be nothing to prevent what feminine name models there were sweeping through the countryside like an epidemic. In actuality, her data fits better the hypothesis that the diffusion of Christian names depended on specific personal relationships rather than generalized cultural emulation, and that the agent of diffusion was the godparent. As long ago as the late nineteenth century Edward Freeman, in bewailing the rapid disappearance of Germanic names after the Norman Conquest, laid the blame on the AS practice of calling upon their new overlords to act as godparents to their children.[72] Although he offered no corroborative evidence, it is beginning to appear that he was substantially correct.[73]

It is clear that a knowledge of how men and women acquired their names in traditional European society is of enormous utility to the historian. At a most obvious level it can help to explain a number of curious trends in the history of nomenclature. Since men of rank, wealth, and power doubtless acted as godparents to a much larger number of children than did the average person, over the generations, by a process of natural selection, a limited number of names would become dominant. This process would be accelerated to the extent that parents came to feel the need to choose godparents with the same name. Accordingly over the centuries there ought to be a diminution in the number of personal names, and a corresponding increase in the number of homonyms. As the researches of Duby and others

---

[71]Cecily Clark, "Women's Names in Post-Conquest England: Observations and Speculations," *Speculum* 53 (1978), 223–51 and repr. above (pp. 7–28).

[72]Freeman, *Hist. Norman Conquest*, 5:559–61.

[73]There is some evidence for this practice amongst the Normans: Orderic Vitalis was baptized, and probably sponsored, by Orderic, priest of Atcham, whilst William Clito seems to have owed his name to William Bonne-Ame, archbishop of Rouen, rather than to his grandfather, William the Conqueror: *The Ecclesiastical History of Orderic Vitalis*, ed. and trans. Marjorie Chibnall, 3 (Oxford, 1972), p. 7; vol. 5 (Oxford, 1975), p. 301.

have revealed, this is exactly what seems to have happened amongst the nobility in the eleventh and twelfth centuries. With the continued growth in population, and with the gradual diffusion through the population of the new system of name giving, the problem of homonyms must have escalated in the late twelfth, thirteenth, and early fourteenth centuries. Nor was the trend reversed in the period of demographic contraction following the Black Death. Using Le Pesant's figures for Évreux it is possible to show that the proportion of men sharing the three most popular names—*William*, *Robert*, and *John*—rose from 30% in the period 1100–1249 to 42% in the period 1250–1349, and to 45% in the period 1350–99.[74] A similar pattern can be discerned in England from the data provided by J. A. Raftis for the village of Warboys in Huntingdonshire.[75] In the first half of the fourteenth century 965 men shared thirty-eight names; in the second half of the fourteenth century 448 men shared twenty-nine names; and in the first half of the fifteenth century 337 men shared seventeen names. Whilst in the period before the Black Death the proportion of the male inhabitants named either *John* or *Thomas* was 23%, in the period after 1400 it had risen to a remarkable 63%. Logically enough, the confusion caused by the spread of homonyms gave a stimulus to the development of surnames. It can be no coincidence that at just the time the French aristocracy began to have its children named after their godparents, the use of the surname rapidly developed to reassert the link with the patrilineage and to facilitate identification. In the following centuries other classes in society seem to have been forced to follow suit, and possibly regional correlations might be made between the rising number of homonyms and the adoption of surnames at particular times.

Since the problem of homonyms is implicit in a system of name giving based on godparenthood, it is interesting to note the expedients to which communities turned in later periods of demographic expansion. At all times it was an option, although never a particularly favored one in late medieval England, to name children after saints, or even to bring in new names from religious or secular literature. As has been already noted, in the late sixteenth and early seventeenth centuries many Puritans turned to the Scriptures for a whole new series of Christian names. What is interesting, in view of the rapid growth of the population in this period and again in the eighteenth

---

[74] Le Pesant, "Notes d'anthroponymie normande," pp. 47–49.

[75] J. A. Raftis, *Warboys: Two Hundred Years in the Life of an English Mediaeval Village* (Toronto, 1974), pp. 64–66.

century, is the fact that the Puritan experiment was so ephemeral and the traditional fashion so resilient. Beginning at the end of the sixteenth century in England, and gaining momentum for at least a century and a half, there appear two singularly adaptive variations on the old theme. In the first place, godparents started to give godchildren their surname as a Christian name, and secondly the two godfathers or godmothers increasingly succeeded in having their godchildren given two personal names.

Above all, an understanding of the system of name giving in operation in western Europe between around the twelfth and the eighteenth centuries provides a valuable tool for further research in a variety of fields. Most basically, the assumption of homonymy between godchildren and godparents will make possible the elucidation of many more spiritual kin relationships. With this sort of supposition in mind, it is relevant to enquire whether Edward Balliol was the godson of Edward I, whether Lewis Chaucer was the godson of Sir Lewis Clifford, and whether John Paston was the godson of Sir John Fastolf. It might even be possible to compile spiritual genealogies: an interesting one might link Horatio Nelson at the beginning of the nineteenth century with some sixteenth-century humanist by way of a succession of men named Horace in the Walpole and associated families.[76] Obviously, many of the connections made by this method would remain purely hypothetical, but it ought to be capable of providing some new insights into the functioning of spiritual kinship. It should reveal, for example, the existence of lineages which regularly reciprocated sponsorship functions, and aristocratic dynasties like the Sydneys and the Stanleys, whose personal names mirrored at one generation's remove the nomenclature of the royal family.[77] Since an invitation to act as a godparent must

---

[76]Horatio, the first Lord Walpole, brother of the prime minister, was godfather to Horace Walpole, the man of letters, and Horace Mann, one of the latter's correspondents, as well as Horatio Nelson: W. S. Lewis et al., eds., Yale Edition of Horace Walpole's Correspondence, vol. 13: *Horace Walpole's Correspondence with Thomas Gray, Richard West, and Thomas Ashton* (New Haven, CT, 1948), p. 3; and vol. 17: *Horace Walpole's Correspondence with Sir Horace Mann* (1954), p. xxx; and Robert Southey, *Life of Nelson,* new ed. (London, 1906), p. 1. Possibly the name was introduced into the country by Horatio Palavicino: Lawrence Stone, *An Elizabethan: Sir Horatio Palavicino* (Oxford, 1956).

[77]Members of the royal family were godparents to three generations of the Sydneys: Henry VIII to Sir Henry Sydney; Philip II of Spain to Sir Philip Sydney; and Queen Elizabeth to Elizabeth Sydney: M. W. Wallace, *The Life of Sir Philip Sydney* (Cambridge, 1915), pp. 5, 12, and 22. Amongst the Stanleys, earls of Derby, note Henry, fourth earl (b. 1531),

have almost always implied a relationship of some sort, a study of personal names can be used to help to monitor the informal coalitions operating at various levels in society. In northwest England in the early fifteenth century the steady rise to regional hegemony of the Stanley family can be seen reflected in the increasing popularity of the name *John* for the firstborn of a number of key gentry families.[78] Quite clearly, the rarer the Christian name is, the more fruitful such investigations can become. A name like *Simon*, for example, was extremely unusual in England before the thirteenth century. It was doubtless popularized by the godsons of Simon de Montfort, and its diffusion across the countryside could be mapped from the various tax returns of the fourteenth century. In this fashion it ought to be possible to discover a great deal more not only about the connections of particular magnates in England and France, but also about the social geography of western Europe and the diffusion of cultural patterns from class to class, and from region to region.

IV

In this paper it was intended to open up new fields of investigation, rather than to offer definitive answers. Given the meagerness of the available documentation and the complexity of the methodological problems involved, the study of spiritual kinship must necessarily be a collaborative enterprise. It is hoped at least that this paper, by revealing something of the interest and importance of godparenthood and *compaternitas* in early European society, will stimulate historians in their various fields to take spiritual kin institutions more seriously. The role of the godparent in the transmission of names, in particular, deserves to be better known. Amongst other things, it could make *anthroponymie* an enormously valuable auxiliary discipline in the study of history. If some of the claims made on behalf of spiritual kinship and systems of name giving in this paper appear unduly

---

James, seventh earl (b. 1607), and Charles, eighth earl (b. 1628): G. E. Cockayne, *The Complete Peerage*, vol. IV (London, 1916), pp. 211, 214, and 215. There is definite evidence that Charles gave his name to one member of the family: Phyllis Cunnington and Catherine Lucas, *Costume for Births, Marriages and Deaths* (London, 1972), p. 54.

[78]M. J. Bennett, *Community, Class and Careerism. Cheshire and Lancashire Society in the Age of 'Sir Gawain and the Green Knight'* (Cambridge, 1983), p. 220.

extravagant, in mitigation it must be pleaded that hitherto the institutions have been scandalously neglected. It is time that godparents, gossips, and godchildren found more effective sponsorship, and that the study of personal names in England was graced with a name.

BAPTISM AND THE NAMING OF CHILDREN
IN LATE MEDIEVAL ENGLAND

Philip Niles

I would like to question an assumption medievalists have made about Christian names because I have some evidence which places in doubt a well-recognized practice: the use of Christian names to confirm a suspected family relationship. Medievalists have too readily assumed, I believe, that families maintained Christian names to identify lineage and dynasty. George Beech recently stated the assumption quite succinctly. A common name does "not in itself prove the existence of a family relationship" but it does "establish the possibility and, more often, the probability of one. . . ."[1] I will argue that in England Christian names indicate little about family relationships because parents usually did not select the names of their children. Godparents did.

Medievalists have not been concerned with the naming of children by godparents.[2] Genealogists have observed the practice in the sixteenth cen-

---

This article, originally published in *MP* 3/1 (Spring 1982), 95–107, is reprinted with permission of the author and the publisher, with minor revisions.

[1]George Beech, "Prosopography," in *Medieval Studies, An Introduction*, ed. James M. Powell (Syracuse, 1976), p. 163. See also A. R. Wagner, *English Genealogy*, 2nd ed. (Oxford, 1972), p. 411.

[2]Michael Bennett of the University of Tasmania and I independently and almost simultaneously discovered the Proofs of Age contained evidence about the naming of children in the fourteenth century. In "Spiritual Kinship and the Baptismal Name in Traditional Euro-

tury.[3] In the fourteenth century William Langland knew; he warned god-parents that they were responsible for much more than the naming of their godchildren.[4] Occasionally a medieval romance or biography mentions the practice.[5] In the Salisbury *Manual*, where the order of baptism is set out, the godparents name the child after the priest has recited the opening prayer. The rubric is incomplete and terse: "Hic patrini et matrinae nominent puerum."[6]

The evidence I will discuss comes from the Proofs of Age contained among the Inquisitions *post mortem* in the Public Record Office. The proof of age was a legal procedure and established the age of an heir in the Middle Ages. It was held in pursuance of a writ *de etate probanda*, issued at the request of the heir and addressed to the king's escheator in the county where the heir was born and baptized. The escheator was instructed to collect knowledgeable men.[7]

A jury gathered and each juror was asked in turn where and when the child was born and then how he remembered after so long a time. To give credence to testimony jurors recalled what had happened to mark permanently the date upon the mind. They remembered a pilgrimage, a death, a marriage, a house fire, or a court case. Or they may recall having seen the baby; they did not see the birth, of course, because jurors were men. If they remembered the birth, they had not seen it; they heard it from a discreet distance from the garden, the court, or the hall beside the chamber where

---

pean Society," in *Principalities, Powers and Estates: Studies in Medieval and Early Modern Government and Society*, ed. L. O. Frappell (Adelaide, 1979), pp. 1–13 [and repr. above (pp. 115–46)], he discusses the Proofs of Age that have been printed. My examination extends the study into the fifteenth-century sources which are available only in manuscript.

[3]E. Chitty, "Naming after Godparents," *Genealogists Magazine* 16 (1969), 47–49. D. J. Steel, *National Index of Parish Registers*, 1: *General Sources of Births, Marriages and Deaths before 1837* (London, 1976), pp. 112–13.

[4]William Langland, *Piers Plowman: The B Version*, ed. George Kane and E. Talbot Donaldson (London, 1975), pp. 396–97.

[5]*The Romance of William of Palerne*, ed. W. W. Skeat, EETS, e.s. 1 (1867), p. 131. Reginald of Durham, *Libellus de vita et miraculis S. Godrici, heremitae de Finchale*, ed. Joseph Stevenson, Surtees Society 20 (1847), p. 28.

[6]*Manuale ad usum percelebris ecclesie Sarisburiensis*, ed. A. J. Collins, Henry Bradshaw Society 91 (1960), p. 26.

[7]S. S. Walker, "Proof of Age of Feudal Heirs in Medieval England," *Mediaeval Studies* 35 (1973), 306–23.

the mother called out in pain or asked the help of the Blessed Virgin. They had a better chance of seeing the child at the baptism.

Before I discuss their contents, I will say something about the numbers and qualities of the Proofs of Age. Let me explain first, the Proofs of Age used in this study number 956. The series begins in 1272 and ends in 1509. Two sections of the series have been published in the *Calendar of Inquisitions Post Mortem*: the first from 1292 through 1392 and the second from 1485 to 1509. The fifteenth-century Proofs of Age are available only in the Public Record Office.[8] Now the problems.

The first is that these Proofs of Age do not present a representative cross-section of English society because they are for the heirs of tenants-in-chief. The tenants-in-chief included all the peers of the realm, the most important knights and gentry, and some rather insignificant people; but as a group they are especially wealthy and powerful. They were, moreover, usually men because of primogeniture; women inherited only when there was no male heir. The second problem is more substantial: the reliability of these proofs has often been questioned. Some have been found incorrect in detail and a few contain testimonies copied from other inquisitions.[9] There was, of course, good reason to misrepresent an age. The decision affected the incomes of two people, the heir and his guardian. If the jury confirmed the majority, the inheritance passed from the guardian to the heir. Therefore a guardian may have tried to retard the process while his ward may have tried to speed it up. Jurors to accommodate one interest or another sometimes perjured themselves.

However, these are problems more for biographers than for social historians. Even when jurors reported the heir's age incorrectly, the detail about the baptismal service, about godfathers, and about the naming of children must be believable if not correct. They must have said what contemporaries expected to be told because incorrect detail, insignificant to the purpose of the Proof of Age, would only discredit testimony on the important issue, the age of the heir. There is no reason therefore to disbelieve

---

[8]*Calendar of Inquisitions Post Mortem and Other Analogous Documents Preserved in the Public Record Office*, 16 vols. (London, 1904–55). *CIPM,* 2nd ser., Henry VII, 3 vols. (London, 1898–1955).

[9]R. F. Hunnisett, "The Reliability of Inquisitions as Historical Evidence," in *The Study of Medieval Records: Essays in Honour of Kathleen Major*, ed. D. A. Bullough and R. L. Storey (Oxford, 1971), pp. 206–07.

the Proofs of Age on the naming of children. Particularly not because they so often say the same thing. Godparents did it. For example, John de Bassiburn named John, son and heir of John Chamberlayn: "Levavit ipsum eodem tempore de sacro fonte et imposuit ei nominem Johannis."[10] Jurors recalled that a godparent gave (*dedit*) the infant a name, or called (*vocavit*) him John or Thomas, or named (*nominavit*) him John or Thomas. In thirty-three Proofs of Age godparents are said to have named the child.

Jurors tell too about the names godparents gave. Sometimes children were named for saints. Eleanor, Henry III's queen, was a godmother to Mary de Mohun whom, a juror said, the queen "lifted from the font and named her Mary because she was born on the eve of the Conception of the Blessed Mary."[11] Or a child could be named for a member of his family, a son after his father or a daughter after her mother or perhaps after a grandparent. Laurence Parely, for example, was so named because his father wished that he should bear the name of the grandfather.[12] But saints' names and family names were exceptions rather than the rule. The usual practice was clear to the jurors. The child's name was that of one of his godparents because one of the godparents named the child after himself. Jurors explained, for example, that John de Clynham named after himself John, son of John de Norton,[13] and Alice Boson named the daughter of John de Oxford: "vocavit eam nomine sua Alicia."[14] I can find no contemporary who explains why children should be named for godparents. But it is suggested by two distinct meanings of a Latin verb, *filiolare*. *Filiolare* was a cognate of *filiolus*, the usual word for *godson*. *Filiolare* meant both "to christen" and "to name after."[15] That the practice was prevalent is suggested by an oblique reference in Robert of Gloucester. Robert wanted to explain the origin of the name of the Lateran in Rome, and he fancied that the word *Lateran* was derived from the word *rana* meaning "frog." His explanation

[10]*CIPM* 5:68, PRO, C 134 6/6.

[11]*CIPM* 3:430.

[12]*CIPM* 9:124.

[13]*CIPM* 12:268.

[14]*CIPM* 12:261, PRO, C 134/204 (8).

[15]*Revised Medieval Latin Word-List from British and Irish Sources*, ed. R. E. Latham (London, 1965), p. 191.

is contorted but interesting because the frog, *rana*, became the godfather of the Lateran. This is the story. The emperor Nero compelled his physicians to implant him with a child. At length he gave birth to a frog, whom Nero pampered and let rear a noble court at one end of Rome which was called Lateran after the frog. Now let me emphasize something: the area of Rome was named after the frog: the frog did not name it. Nevertheless, Robert concludes, "Feble was the godfather after whom the name was."[16]

Despite infrequent comment, the practice was very common. A boy almost always had the name of one of his two godfathers while girls shared names with one of their two godmothers. In the Proofs of Age 302 sets of godparents are reported. Of these, 261 (86%) of these godchildren bear the name of one of their godparents. Only forty-one or 14% did not. So important was the rule that failing to observe it could be a matter for discussion among the onlookers at a baptism. We learn, for example, about such a discussion from a juror at the proof of age of Catherine Hildegaard. Catherine, it seems, was named by a Beatrice and by a Christiana and the juror recalled: "There was a question amongst those in the church how she could be called Catherine as neither of her godmothers was so called, and to this it was replied for the love of St. Catherine she was so named."[17] The practice was more than a rule; it was a matter of importance; and a godfather without a namesake could, when questioned, be brought to anger. Ralph Basset was. He and Warin Latimer sponsored John Aylsbury. A juror remembered the occasion well because he asked Ralph after the baptism how a John could have been sponsored by a Ralph and a Warin. The juror remembered having asked "how it was the boy was called John whereas none of the godfathers was so named; whereupon the said Ralph got angry and hit him in the neck."[18]

Naming children after godparents survives into the sixteenth century when parish registers were first kept. At Banbury in Oxfordshire, for example, of fifty-nine baptisms recorded in 1558–59, fifty-one (86%) of the

---

[16]*The Metrical Chronicle of Robert of Gloucester*, ed. W. A. Wright, 2 vols., Rolls Series 86 (1887).

[17]*CIPM* 8:142.

[18]*CIPM* 10:262, PRO, C 134/132/4: "Et rogavit predicto Radu qualiter demodo nullus compater eorum nominabatur hoc nomine Johannis propterea quod idem Radus irascebatur et procecidit praedictum Racardum in colle."

children were named after a godparent,[19] which is interestingly enough the percentage found among the Proofs of Age of the fourteenth and fifteenth centuries. The modern practice is clearly to prefer family names even though the modern Episcopal prayer book retains a command that godparents name the child. Modern godparents usually repeat a family name rather than their own. Nearly three quarters of all children are named for paternal relatives in middle-class American families.[20]

Naming children with family names was unusual in the fourteenth and fifteenth centuries. Even first sons, which most heirs were because of primogeniture, did not often share a name with a father. This can be established rather precisely from the writs and the Proofs of Age because both often mention the fathers' names. In 246 Proofs of Age of men, the fathers' names are known. Only seventy-two (or 29%) share a name with a son.

Even fewer heirs had paternal grandfathers' names. Finding grandfathers' names is a bit more difficult since grandfathers are usually not mentioned in the Proofs, and families must be traced. I selected fifty families and in only thirteen (26%) of them do paternal grandfathers and grandsons share a name, fifteen (30%) share a name with a father. Dynastic names were clearly not in favor; only five men had a name common in three generations. Therefore of these fifty, only twenty-three (46%) had a name of a father, a grandfather, or both. On the other hand, forty-three (86%), nearly double, shared a name with a godfather. Plainly they preferred to name children after godfathers.

Women's names are more difficult because mothers cannot be easily identified. Forty-nine of the heirs were women. Of these, we know the mother's names of twenty. Only two had their mothers' names while of the forty-nine, forty-one (84%) had the name of a godmother.

A common Christian name marked dynasties like that of the three Edwards or of the Lancastrian Henrys. In each, father, son, and grandson all carried a name. Continuity may reveal family pride but it need not have. We need not assume that Henry VI was Henry at the font because his father and his grandfather were. He may have been Henry because one of his godfathers was Henry Beauford.[21] Now I do not know that Henry VI was

---

[19]Chitty, "Naming after Godparents," pp. 47–49.

[20]Alice S. Rossi, "Naming Children in Middle-Class Families," *American Sociological Review* 30 (1965), 510.

[21]*CIPM* 3:214.

named for his godfather rather than for his father and his grandfather, but contemporaries could know that a Henry, son of Henry, was not named for the father. Henry son of Henry Percy was known to bear the name of his godfather, not his father.[22] And a Henry could be named for a grandfather because the grandfather was the godfather. That seems to have been the case of Henry Conan, the grandson of Henry Conan for whom the younger Henry was named. The grandfather refused the messenger dispatched to fetch him to serve as godfather at the baptism, "from infirmity he could not go but [he] commanded that they should give the heir his name whether male or female."[23] I have one final example about family Christian names, one that makes a point: a family name may not reveal dynastic pride as much as godparents' whim. William Deyncourt was named after his father when his godfathers, a Thomas and a Roger, disagreed about which had named the child first. The father's name was accepted by both as a compromise.[24]

There was one very good reason why medieval baptisms could not be controlled by parents: the importance of haste. Priests were instructed to baptize the child within eight days of birth. In fact, few baptisms were so long delayed. Almost always baptisms were on the day of birth.[25] The father had little time to prepare the infant and to alert the godparents who could presumably have been invited beforehand, but we hear often in the Proofs of Age about plans that went awry. A godparent fails to appear and an onlooker is pressed into service.[26] Or someone standing by interferes and prevents the person invited by the parents from sponsoring the child. A bystander therefore becomes the godparent.[27] And we hear of baptisms so hastily

---

[22]*CIPM* 3:623.

[23]*CIPM* 15:159.

[24]While most Proofs of Age mention the baptism, jurors do not always date it because age was determined by birth, but sometimes the day of baptism is indicated. I began with the Proofs of Age of 22 Edward III (25 January 1348) and collected the next fifty for which the date of the baptism is given. Of these only one baptism was delayed; it occurred two days after birth. One hundred years later the practice may already be showing some sign of change. I began with the first Proof for 27 Henry VI (1 September 1448) and collected through 19 Edward IV (3 March 1480). Four baptisms were delayed: three by one day, one child waited ten days.

[25]*CIPM* 5:151.

[26]*CIPM* 7:477.

[27]*CIPM* 11:379.

arranged that godparents are selected at the church from among the people already there.[28] In short, baptisms were hasty, sometimes spontaneous.

Hastily chosen godparents at the church were not necessarily disinterested because the baptism brought together allies and retainers of families. The birth of a child was not just a matter of family concern. Indeed, very few (only 8%) of godparents have the godchild's surname. Neighbors and friends gathered for a baptism and they celebrated it. We read often in the Proofs of Age about men who helped to carry bread and wine from the father's house to the church for a celebration after the ceremony.

Such people could well have fit the contemporary term for godparents. The usual English word was *gossib*. The word could be applied either to one's godparent or to the godparent of one's children. It had another important application. It was used for one's best friend. Alice, Chaucer's Wife of Bath, describes in some detail her relationship with her *gossib*, to whom Alice would more freely tell her private thoughts than she would her priest.

Close friends and retainers named the child, and the family may have been unwilling to interfere with their decision. Godparents could be very independent, as John Bulkley and William Cosen were. They agreed before the service that William would name the child because William bought the privilege from John:

> The godfathers disputed which of them should give the child his own name, and William Cosen to have the naming agreed to give the said John Bulkley a gallon of wine, which he paid; and because there was no wine in Wiltshire, Richard Couchyn rode a black horse to Amesbury to fetch it, was thrown on his way back, and a jug full, or nigh half a gallon, was spilt.[29]

Measuring the alliance between parents and godparents is difficult because strong alliances and long-lasting friendship could easily go unrecorded. Occasionally, however, it is possible to trace an alliance of some duration. For example, Queen Isabella, Edward II's queen, responded to a call in the middle of January of 1317 to sponsor the daughter of Elizabeth, the recent widow of Theobold Verdon. The queen's interest in the Verdon child was natural enough. The mother was a Clare, the daughter of Gilbert de Clare and by her first husband, John de Burgo, mother of the earl of

---

[28]*CIPM*, 2nd ser., Henry VII, 1:919.

[29]*Calendar of the Patent Rolls*, 1307–1313, p. 568. *CIPM* 7:395.

Ulster. Her second husband, the girl's father, had been justiciar in Ireland. So close was the mother to the king that he visited her while she recovered in bed. Doubtless the queen agreed to sponsor the child because the parents were close to the royal family. And probably the mother invited the queen to sponsor because she would ably protect her goddaughter, who became Queen Isabella's ward.[30]

We read too about *gossibs* who were family retainers. William le Marshall, for example, an heir to extensive East Anglian holdings, was named by William de Beauchamp, steward to the heir's mother. John le Chamberlain was named by his father's esquire as was Giles de Badelsmere, while Fulm Rucote's godfather was his father's steward's son.[31]

Godparents must have been especially interested in the family if they assumed the responsibilities listed for them by contemporary preachers. Godparents were to protect the child against natural disaster: from water, fire, horse's foot, and hound's tooth. And they were to have the infant confirmed when the bishop was next within seven miles. They were also to teach the godchild his belief: the Pater Noster, the Ave Maria, and the Credo.[32]

The relationship established at baptism was described as a spiritual consanguinity and called *godsibrede*. A juror could speak to the age of an heir because they were spiritual brothers. The juror's father had often reminded him of his spiritual brotherhood with the father's godson.[33] Baptism joined the priest, the godfather, the godmother, and spouses of the godparents, and the parents and all of their children in a spiritual consanguinity among whom there was no intermarriage.[34] This spiritual incest taboo was taken so seriously that men and women refused to become godparents because they might want to marry within the *godsibrede* that the baptism would establish. Richard Argym remembered, for example, having refused to sponsor William Kele's son on the basis of prohibited marriage. His bluntness is

---

[30]*CIPM* 2:471; 3:483; 5:68; 6:123; 7:691.

[31]*English Fragments from Latin Medieval Service-Books*, ed. Henry Littlehales, EETS, e.s. 90 (1903), p. 5.

[32]*The Lay Folks Mass Book*, ed. T. F. Simmons, EETS 71 (1879), p. 66.

[33]"Sibi narravit multetiens quod ipse Thomas filius et heredes Williami fuit confrater suus." PRO, C 134 179/14.

[34]John Myrc, *Instructions for Parish Priests*, ed. Edward Peacock, EETS 31 (1868), p. 6. R. J. Kearney, *Sponsors at Baptism According to the Code of Canon Law*, Catholic University of America, Canon Law Studies 30 (Washington, DC, 1925), pp. 104–09.

shocking. He said no because "it was possible for him to survive the said William and afterwards to marry his wife."[35]

I would like to now return to my initial question. Did parents or godparents name children? The answer is clearly that godparents did. They sometimes did so quite independently; they sometimes did it in fulfillment of the wishes of the parents. To distinguish sharply between the interests of parents and godparents as I have done is to impose an anachronistic distinction upon the medieval family. We are much more inclined to do that than they were. We tend to distinguish inside from outside the family, to divide us of the family who belong together from them. How little it was done in the Middle Ages is shown by their language. The classical Latin word *amicus* could in medieval England be used in the classical sense for a friend. An *amicus* could also be a kinsman. So could the Middle English words *frend* and *allie*.[36] And the word *sib*, which in the modern tongue is applied to siblings, was then extended to kin and even close friends. Moreover, there was no word to describe the nuclear family. *Family* itself entered the language in the seventeenth century when it was diverted from its medieval sense and adapted from Latin. In the Middle Ages that *familia* was a household, a *famulus* a servant, and *familiars* the people of the same household. From our point of view they confused their kith and their kin.

The point is that friendship was much more important to them than it is to us. They felt more strongly about friends and allies than we do; and they may have been less concerned about their mothers, their fathers, and their children than we are. Barbara Hanawalt has recently suggested that homicide statistics measure some of the power in the ties outside the family. In the fourteenth and fifteenth centuries, she found "fatal attack tended to be with fellow villagers and friends rather than family members." Since homicide is seldom random and most often occurs between people who know each other well, she concludes, "It is possible that the strong ties were with the outside rather than with members of the immediate household."[37]

---

[35]PRO, C 134 204/10. "William Kele pater predicti pueri rogabat eum ut esset compater eiusdem Johanni qui totaliter reesabat eo quo possibile ei esset predictum William Kele superviviare et postea uxorem eius maritare."

[36]*Middle English Dictionary*, ed. Hans Kurath et al. (Ann Arbor, MI, 1952–), 1:202–03, 3:884–86.

[37]B. A. Hanawalt, "Childrearing among the Lower Classes of Late Medieval England," *Journal of Interdisciplinary History* 8 (1977), 22.

Baptism publicly expressed these ties, the *godsibrede* defined them, and children's names reminded everyone about who the *gossibe* was and why.

The statistics on naming, like the statistics on homicide, support the general description of the medieval family written by Lawrence Stone:

> The most striking characteristic of the late medieval and early sixteenth-century family, at all social levels, was the degree to which it was open to external influences, a porosity that is in contrast to the more sealed-off and private nuclear family type that was to develop in the seventeenth and eighteenth centuries.[38]

Lawrence Stone's description has been criticized by Alan Macfarlane, who believes that late medieval England was already highly individualized and dominated by the nuclear family.[39] On that disagreement, I have taken Lawrence Stone's side.

I think that naming practices changed as the family did, as it became, in Lawrence Stone's words, "more sealed-off and private." The sealing-off is reflected in the later history of the word *gossib*. Modern English has lost the two important medieval meanings. We would no longer call godparents or best friends *gossibs*. The word *gossib* is reserved for light and trifling talk and for the person who delights in it. *Gossip* we take to be rumor, often groundless and frequently malicious; and when we call people gossips, we do not speak highly of their wisdom, their knowledge, or their characters. The connotations of the word reveal the solidarity and the isolation of the modern family. To the modern family, close friendships and strong alliances are suspicious and even threatening. For us gossips are idle, even mendacious and treacherous, while in the Middle Ages *gossibs* were best friends who sponsored and named children.

---

[38]Lawrence Stone, *The Family, Sex and Marriage in England, 1500–1800* (New York, 1979), p. 69.

[39]Alan Macfarlane, *The Origins of English Individualism: The Family, Property, and Social Transition* (Cambridge, 1979).

SOCIAL CONNECTIONS
BETWEEN PARENTS AND GODPARENTS
IN LATE MEDIEVAL YORKSHIRE

Louis Haas

One can imagine the thrill, the excitement, the sense of expectation. A child was to be born into a noble household in late medieval Yorkshire. Both mother and father, like most parents anywhere and anytime, were pleased with the prospect. And they undoubtedly had many plans for the child particular to their time and place: maybe the child would be the surviving heir, maybe this child would secure an excellent marriage alliance for the family, maybe the child would rise to power within the religious hierarchy. At any rate, this child would certainly advance the honor and status of the family. Or so the parents hoped. Birth, such a common biological process, carries with it so much social and ritual import. Many things then needed to be done in preparation: arrange for a midwife; prepare for the mother's lying-in; arrange for clothing and furniture for the child; prepare a celebration; prepare for the baptism; choose the child's sponsors. This last task, this choice, was not lightly made. Husband and wife would confer, debate, decide; then they would send letters and messengers to notify their choices, or they would ask them in person.[1]

This article, originally published in *MP* 10/1 (Spring 1989), pp. 1–21, is reprinted with the permission of the author and publisher, with minor revisions.

[1]Much work has come out recently on the history of the medieval family. See, for instance, David Herlihy, *Medieval Households* (Cambridge, MA, 1985) and Frances and Joseph Gies,

The baptism occurred—sometimes just hours after the birth. Around the font gathered the participants: father, sponsors, priest, infant, and the mother—in spirit only (since birth was rigorous, she needed rest, and she had not yet been purified). Using the rite prescribed in *The York Manual*, the priest asked if the child renounced Satan, believed in God and the Creed, and wished to be baptized. The sponsors answered for the child with a clear, decisive "Yes." Then, while the sponsors held or touched the child, the priest performed triple immersion (or aspersion if he felt the need), baptizing the child into the church.[2] But something much more than the introduction of someone into the Christian community had just occurred here. All the participants except the priest had just entered into the relationship known as baptismal kinship.[3]

The term *baptismal kinship* refers to the voluntary religious and social network created by the Christian rite of baptism. Baptismal kinship has existed in most Christian cultures, but its specific form has varied according to time, place, and sect. For the rest of their lives, the individuals entwined

---

Marriage and the Family in the Middle Ages (New York, 1987). On the medieval English family in particular, see Ralph A. Houlbrooke, *The English Family, 1450–1700* (London, 1984); Nicholas Orme, *From Childhood to Chivalry: The Education of the English Kings and Aristocracy, 1066–1530* (London, 1984); Barbara A. Hanawalt, *The Ties That Bound: Peasant Families in Medieval England* (New York, 1986); Alan Macfarlane, *Marriage and Love in England: Modes of Reproduction, 1300–1840* (New York, 1986); and Kate Mertes, *The English Noble Household, 1250–1600: Good Governance and Politic Rule* (Oxford, 1988). These works have supplanted the standard work on the premodern and modern English family, which did touch briefly but inaccurately on the nature and character of the English medieval family; see Lawrence Stone, *The Family, Sex, and Marriage in England, 1500–1800* (New York, 1977). For a summary and amplification of the massive criticism directed against Stone's work, see Linda Pollock, *Forgotten Children: Parent-Child Relations from 1500 to 1900* (Cambridge, 1983).

[2]On baptism in late medieval Yorkshire see Louis Haas, "Baptism and Spiritual Kinship in the North of England, 1250–1450," M. A. thesis (The Ohio State University, 1982), 54–97; Houlbrooke, *The English Family*, pp. 130–33; Orme, *From Childhood to Chivalry*, pp. 1–3, 8–11.

[3]Charles J. Erasmus, "Current Theories of Incest Prohibition in the Light of Ceremonial Kinship," Kroeber Anthropological Papers 2 (1950), 42–50; and Joseph H. Lynch, "Spiritual Kinship and Sexual Prohibitions in Early Medieval Europe," in *Proceedings of the Sixth International Congress of Medieval Canon Law* (Berkeley, CA, August, 1980), Monumenta iuris canonici, Series C: Subsidia, vol. 7 (Vatican City, 1985), pp. 271–88.

by this rite maintain certain responsibilities toward each other that either the church or society or both prescribe. For instance, baptismal kin, while cultivating a heightened degree of friendship and mutual aid, should not engage in sexual relations with one another. Anthropologists who have studied baptismal kinship have concluded that this sexual taboo is universal to all forms of baptismal kinship regardless of time, place, or sect.[4]

Anthropologists have long known the significance of baptismal kinship for people in premodern and modern Latin America, where the practice performs many functions. It socializes children, creates or reinforces friendship and political ties, and provides opportunities for economic aid.[5] Only recently, however, have anthropologists and historians investigated baptismal kinship in premodern Europe. The work of scholars such as John Bossy, Michael Bennett, Philip Niles, Christiane Klapisch-Zuber, and Joseph Lynch indicates that premodern European baptismal kinship performed many of the same functions found in Latin American baptismal kinship.[6]

---

[4]Julian Pitt-Rivers, "Pseudo Kinship," *International Encyclopedia of the Social Sciences*, 8 (New York, 1968), pp. 408–13. For the anthropologists' theory of the universality of the sexual taboo inherent to baptismal kinship, see Erasmus, "Current Theories." This taboo was very apparent in early medieval Europe (see Lynch, "Spiritual Kinship and Sexual Prohibitions").

[5]Stephen Gudeman, "Spiritual Relations and Selecting a Godparent," *Man* 10 (1975), 223. The anthropologist George Foster claims that rural Latin American society would collapse without the baptismal kinship network; see Foster, "Godparents and Social Networks in TzinTzunTzan," *Southwestern Journal of Anthropology* 25 (1969), 262–63. The anthropological literature dealing with baptismal kinship is legion. For the most up-to-date accounting, see the bibliographies and bibliographical essays in Hugo Nutini and Betty Bell, *Ritual Kinship: The Structure and Historical Development of the Compadrazgo System in Rural Tlaxcala*, 1 (Princeton, 1980), and Hugo Nutini, *Ritual Kinship: Ideological and Structural Integration of the Compadrazgo System in Rural Tlaxcala*, 2 (Princeton, 1984).

[6]John Bossy, "Blood and Baptism: Kinship, Community and Christianity in Western Europe, 14th–17th Centuries," in *Sanctity and Secularity: The Church and the World*, ed. Derek Baker, Studies in Church History 10 (Oxford, 1973), pp. 13–35; idem, "Padrini e madrini: Un istituzione sociale del christianesimo popolare in Occidente," *Quaderni storici* 14 (1979), 440–49; idem, "Godparenthood: The Fortunes of a Social Institution in Early Modern Christianity," in *Religion and Society in Early Modern Europe, 1500–1800*, ed. Kaspar von Greyerz (London, 1984), pp. 194–201; Michael Bennett, "Spiritual Kinship and the Baptismal Name in Traditional Society," in *Principalities, Powers and Estates: Studies in Medieval and Early Modern Government and Society*, ed. L. O. Frappell (Adelaide, 1979),

Since baptismal kinship in the Middle Ages did form a voluntary religious and social network of individuals maintaining responsibilities toward each other, parents would have had certain goals in mind when they chose godparents for their children. Self-interest certainly was a major factor in this decision. Whom could the parents choose who would be most effective in aiding them and their child? Another factor in the decision was the sexual taboo, which made marriage within the godparenthood or co-parenthood nexus spiritual incest—an idea which was codified as early as the Justinian Code.[7] By the thirteenth century, canon law held that godparents were spiritually related to their godchildren and their godchildren's parents. Godchildren, in like manner, were even spiritually related to their godparents' children. None of these individuals could marry one another.[8] Whom could the parents choose who would not interfere with their children's future marital strategies? Children in medieval Europe commonly had more than one godparent. The late medieval church prescribed at most three, two of the same sex as the child and one of the opposite sex. People, however, broke this rule often in favor of more godparents.[9] Parents, therefore, could

---

pp. 1–13 and repr. above (pp. 115–46); Philip Niles, "Baptism and the Naming of Children in Late Medieval England," *Medieval Prosopography* 3/1 (Spring 1982), 95–107 and repr. above (pp. 147–57); Christiane Klapisch-Zuber, "Compérage et clientélisme à Florence (1360–1520)," *Richerche storiche* 15 (1985), 61–76, and *Women, Family, and Ritual in Renaissance Italy* (Chicago, 1985); Joseph H. Lynch, "Baptismal Sponsorship and Monks and Nuns 500–1000," *American Benedictine Review* 31 (1980), 108–29; idem, "Hugh of Cluny's Sponsorship of Henry IV: Its Context and Consequences," *Speculum* 60 (1985), 800–26; idem, *Godparents and Kinship in Early Medieval Europe* (Princeton, 1986).

[7] Code 5.4.26.2, dated 530; and see James A. Brundage, *Law, Sex, and Christian Society in Medieval Europe* (Chicago, 1987), p. 193.

[8] Gudeman, "Spiritual Relations and Selecting a Godparent," pp. 230–32. The Council of Trent (1545–63) narrowed the number of spiritually related people in the baptismal kinship nexus, but the Catholic Church today still recognized a spiritual impediment prohibiting godparents from marrying their godchildren. English bishops in the thirteenth century always enumerated the degrees of spiritual incest in their diocesan states. See *Councils and Synods with other Documents Relating to the English Church*, ed. F. M. Powicke and C. R. Cheney, 1 (Oxford, 1964), pp. 88, 190, 234, 636.

[9] Powicke and Cheney, *Councils and Synods* 1:31, 69, 183, 233, 269, 440, 453, 590, 635. People in medieval Europe could and did have swarms of godparents. Joan of Arc (b. 1412 or 1413), for instance, had seven godmothers and four godfathers; see Edward Lucie-Smith, *Joan of Arc* (New York, 1976), p. 8.

choose to pursue a number of social strategies in their choices of godparents for their children (and co-parents for themselves).[10]

The reasons for these choices and social relationships between medieval parents and godparents are obscure.[11] Was baptismal kinship used to intensify the kinship network—that is, did parents choose godparents who were blood or affinal kin? Or was baptismal kinship used to extend the kinship network—that is, did parents choose godparents who were not blood or affinal kin, thereby allowing new people into their kinship network? Did parents make horizontal connections, choosing godparents from the same status group as themselves? Or did parents make vertical connections, choosing godparents from a different status group than their own?[12]

Answering these questions is difficult since historians of medieval societies, unlike cultural anthropologists, cannot directly question their sources. Then, too, much evidence concerning medieval baptismal kinship was never

---

[10]*Godparent* and *co-parent* are terms for the same person in the baptismal kinship nexus, though they denote different types of relationships. *Godparenthood* is the tie between the child and the sponsor(s); *co-parenthood* is the tie between the child's parents and the sponsor(s). I use the terms here interchangeably, which should emphasize some of the complexity of baptismal kinship since the sponsor fulfills a dual role. On the terminology see Lynch, *Godparents and Kinship*, pp. 5–7. On the social strategies that parents can employ in selecting godparents, see both Gudeman, "Spiritual Relations and Selecting a Godparent," and Foster, "Godparents and Social Networks." Klapisch-Zuber discusses these social strategies for Renaissance Florentines in *Women, Family, and Ritual*, pp. 89–92.

[11]Niles puts it bluntly: "Measuring the alliance between parents and godparents is difficult because strong alliances and long-lasting friendship could easily go unrecorded" ("Baptism and the Naming of Children," p. 102).

[12]These terms, *intensify, extend, horizontal*, and *vertical*, are common to the anthropological literature on godparenthood and, unfortunately, seem unavoidable. I hope the use of this jargon does not alienate readers; in fact, I think these terms do aid in conceptualizing the social flexibility and utility of baptismal kinship. What I mean by *status group* (or "social status"), unfortunately, is a bit more vague. *Status group* means much more than just social class; it threads together the strands of power, position, wealth, friendship, and family—actual and perceived—an amorphous concept to an outsider, but one which an insider understands and recognizes implicitly. Trying to define status groups in present-day societies is difficult, but for the past it is almost impossible (at least it leads to a lot of questions and debate). On the difficulty of identifying and analyzing social structure in the past, see Thomas A. Brady, Jr., *Ruling Class, Regime, and Reformation at Strasbourg, 1520–1555* (Leiden, 1978), pp. 19–41.

written down—the commonplace and daily rarely are.[13] English baptisms, for instance, were not formally recorded until the sixteenth century. Yet there is one set of medieval English records dating from the thirteenth and extending through the sixteenth centuries that inadvertently provides us with evidence about baptism and baptismal kinship: the Feudal Proofs of Age in the *Calendar of Inquisitions Post Mortem*.[14]

These records contain edited translations of inquests into the king's feudal rights such as relief, wardship, or escheat. These inquests were conducted upon the death of one of the king's tenants-in-chief, whereupon the escheator of the county assembled a jury to determine such things as the extent and worth of the tenant's lands, the lands pertaining to the king, and the existence of an heir. If an heir existed and was underage, the crown took him and his lands (or her and her lands) into wardship. A Proof was later made by authority of the writ *de etate probanda* to determine whether or not the heir had gained legal age.[15] The escheator again assembled a jury. In their testimony jurors usually tried to link the birth of the heir with some event significant to them, to the heir, the heir's father, the town, the county, or even to England as a whole. In essence, reporting either first- or second-hand about the baptism constituted solid evidence that a juror knew an heir's age.[16]

In a Yorkshire Proof of Age from 1354 for Mauger Vavasour, the son of Thomas Vavasour, a juror declared that

> the said Mauger was born at Denton Co. York, on Saturday before St. Barnabas, 6 Edward III, and baptized in the chapel of Denton within the parish of Ottele, that Robert de Crumbewelbothum, chaplain, lifted the said Mauger from the sacred font, and Mauger Vavasour, knight, and Thomas Lascy were his godfathers.[17]

The Proofs of Age thus furnish us with the names of the heir, his father, and his godparents. Sometimes the Proofs detail additional information about the godparents, indicating their social status. Since the heirs and their

---

[13]Lynch, "Hugh of Cluny's Sponsorship," pp. 814–15.

[14]*CIPM*, vols. 1–16 (London, 1904–74).

[15]The legal age for males was twenty-one years; for married females, fourteen; for unmarried females, sixteen (Orme, *From Childhood to Chivalry*, p. 78).

[16]On the Proofs in general see Sue Sheridan Walker, "Proofs of Age of Feudal Heirs in Medieval England," *Mediaeval Studies* 35 (1973), 306–23.

[17]*CIPM* 10:120.

fathers were tenants-in-chief of the king, a significant body of feudal lords that included the most powerful peers of the realm, they possessed a definite and high social status in medieval England. Information from the Proofs of Age, therefore, provides us with the basis for a study illuminating the social relations between medieval English tenants-in-chief and the godparents they chose for their children. Additional information on the social status of these parents and godparents comes from other records such as the *Calendar of Close Rolls* and the *Calendar of Patent Rolls*, both of which list letters from the king to individuals or groups, and *Feudal Aids*, which lists landholders in thirteenth-, fourteenth-, and fifteenth-century England.[18]

To make this study manageable, I have investigated only the individuals mentioned in the Yorkshire Proofs of Age from the late thirteenth to the mid-fourteenth centuries.[19] These thirty-eight Proofs provide us with the names of ninety-one godparents: sixty-nine men and twenty-two women.[20] Whom, then, did the feudal nobility of late medieval Yorkshire choose as co-parents and as godparents for their children?

Since the evidence from most anthropological studies of baptismal kinship indicates that people primarily choose godparents from the group of individuals with whom they already have some form of association, the most logical social relationship to investigate concerning these Yorkshire tenants-in-chief and their co-parents is that of blood or affinal kinship. In other words, did these tenants-in-chief use baptismal kinship to intensify their kinship network? In ten of the thirty-eight Proofs from Yorkshire, one or both of the godparents of the same sex as the heir had the same surname as that heir.[21] These individuals were in all likelihood paternal relatives. It is more

---

[18]*Calendar of Close Rolls, 1272–1279 to 1377–1381; Calendar of the Fine Rolls*, vols. 1–9; *Calendar of the Patent Rolls, 1272–1281 to 1377–1381*; G. E. Cokayne, *The Complete Peerage* (London, 1910–59), 1–13; *Feudal Aids*, ed. J. V. Lyle, 6 (London, 1920); Jerome V. Peel, Jr., *Index to Biographies of Englishmen 1000–1485 Found in Dissertations and Theses* (Westport, CT, 1975); William Shaw, *The Knights of England*, 1–3 (London, 1906); *VCH: Yorkshire*, 1–3, ed. William Page (London, 1907–13), *Yorkshire North Riding*, 1–2, ed. William Page (London, 1914–23), *The City of York*, ed. P. M. Tillot (London, 1961), *York East Riding*, 3, ed. K. J. Allison (Oxford, 1976).

[19]This study formed the core of ch. 4 of my "Baptism and Spiritual Kinship."

[20]Thirty-eight Proofs should, theoretically, give us the names of at least 114 godparents. Jurors, however, failed at times to remember the names of all the godparents.

[21]*CIPM* 3:139; 7:339; 10:116, 120, 239; 11:413; 14:295.

difficult to detect the presence of any maternal relatives as baptismal kin, but these ties did exist. A Lucy de Tueng's godparents, for instance, included a paternal uncle, a paternal grandmother, and a maternal great-aunt.[22] In the four Proofs in which I could determine the exact familial relationships, at least one of the related godparents in each Proof was the child's grandparent.[23] Grandparents, therefore, seem to have been a popular choice as godparents whenever individuals chose godparents from within the family.

Overall, the Yorkshire Proofs of Age denote ten paternally related godparents and four maternally related godparents, showing that some 15% of the godparents for heirs of these Yorkshire tenants-in-chief were relatives.[24] While blood or affinal kinship may have been a criterion for the choice of godparents, it was not a major one.

According to the anthropologist Stephen Gudeman, whenever parents and godparents possess different social statuses the godparents usually have a higher social status than do the parents.[25] In other words, people use baptismal kinship to make upwardly vertical social connections. In late medieval Yorkshire, however, just the opposite occurred. The majority of godparents chosen by Yorkshire tenants-in-chief were not themselves tenants-in-chief. In fact, many of these godparents do not appear anywhere else in medieval English records; this strongly implies that they were neither tenants-in-chief nor significant landholders. Of the ninety-one godparents listed in the Yorkshire Proofs of Age, twenty-three belong to this anonymous group. Forty-one godparents include certain family members and women (for whom determining a social status level is difficult if not impossible), and clerics, whom I shall examine in a different context below. But, of the twenty-seven

---

[22]*CIPM* 3:139, and Cokayne, *Complete Peerage* 12:738–39.

[23]In one proof the paternal grandfather could not fulfill his role as godfather because of illness (*CIPM* 3:499).

[24]Niles found for the whole of England that only 8% of the godparents listed in the Proofs of Age (both edited and manuscript) had the same surname as did the heir ("Baptism and the Naming of Children," p. 101). My findings for Yorkshire show a bit higher percentage but not significantly higher.

[25]Gudeman, "Spiritual Relations and Selecting a Godparent," p. 235. Some historians have identified this same phenomenon among the aristocracy in medieval and early modern England; see Judith Schneid Lewis, *In the Family Way: Childbearing in the British Aristocracy, 1760–1860* (New Brunswick, NJ, 1986), p. 203; Houlbrooke, *The English Family*, p. 131; Mertes, *The English Noble Household*, pp. 154–55.

godparents for whom I could determine a definite social status level, eight had social status inferior to their co-fathers, fifteen had roughly similar social status, and four had superior social status.[26]

In 1301 John Hothum and Henry Lyndale became godfathers to Henry Percy, the son of Baron Percy. Hothum was only a knight, and Lyndale fails to appear anywhere else in the records.[27] In a Proof for Thomas Verdon, Thomas Bosevyle claimed that "he was present [at the baptism] with Thomas de Furnyvaus, then his lord, and lifted the aforesaid Thomas [Verdon] from the sacred font." Thus, Thomas Bosevyle, in service to someone else, became a co-father with a tenant-in-chief, someone much higher than himself on the social scale. Thomas Verdon's other godfather, Thomas de Furnyvaus, was a knight, but his father, John, was not yet a knight.[28] John Verdon, therefore, made vertical social connections in both directions at the same time with his choice of godfathers. William Greystoke chose Ralph Neville and Henry Scrope as godfathers for his son William in 1354. All three men were tenants-in-chief and barons.[29]

What, then, may be said about the function of social status in the selection of godparents? No set requirement seems to have existed, since superior, similar, and inferior social relations existed between parents and godparents. Nevertheless, the tendency for a Yorkshire tenant-in-chief to choose a godparent who possessed lower social status in relation to himself seems definite, especially when the anonymous individuals are taken into consideration. Out of fifty Yorkshire godfathers to the children of tenants-in-chief, thirty-one or 62% had social status inferior to that of the father, fifteen or 30% had social status roughly similar to that of the father, and only four or 8% had superior social status when compared to that of the father.[30]

---

[26]*CIPM* 1:162; 3:139, 498; 5:3; 7:27, 54, 192, 294, 345; 9:135, 452; 10:120, 239; 12:70; 14:180; Page, *VCH Yorkshire North Riding* 1:447–47; 2:232, 383–84, 450–51; Cokayne, *Complete Peerage* 5:272–73; 7:452, 469–70; 12:738–40, 743; Lyle, *Feudal Aids*, pp. 117, 138, 162, 164, 167, 174, 207, 208, 218, 228, 232, 550; Shaw, *Knights of England* 1:121.

[27]*CIPM* 5:312; 6:64; Cokayne, *Complete Peerage* 10:456–60; Page, *VCH Yorks.* 3:403; Shaw, *Knights of England* 1:125.

[28]*CIPM* 3:336; Cokayne, *Complete Peerage* 1:192–93, 499–501.

[29]*CIPM* 14:66; Cokayne, *Complete Peerage* 5:580–81, 12:250–52.

[30]These findings parallel Bennett's for Cheshire; see Bennett, "Spiritual Kinship and the Baptismal Name," p. 6.

Some of these lower-status godparents did come from the tenant-in-chief's household or retinue. John Hay, a servant, became godfather to his lord's son.[31] Servants and retainers also appeared in the baptismal procession. According to Kate Mertes, having these people appear in the procession was one way to bind the different generations of the family to its entourage.[32] Making them godparents would serve the same purpose and would also allow a tenant-in-chief to confer honor and approval on selected members of his entourage.[33]

Considering that the English landed aristocracy in the late Middle Ages still used the practices of homage, fealty, vassalage, and lordship to define political, military, economic, and social relationships among themselves, it would only be reasonable to assume that these feudal relationships played a part in the selection of godparents. This was not the case, though, in Yorkshire.

As noted above, one of the tasks of an inquisition *post mortem* was to ascertain the lands held by a tenant-in-chief to determine which pertained to the king and which pertained to others. The inquests list what lands the tenant-in-chief held, from whom, and what lands he subinfeudated. Of the thirty-eight Proofs of Age from Yorkshire which I am using here, the inquisition *post mortem* for the heir's father is not listed for eight. Of the seventy-seven godparents listed in the thirty Proofs where the existence of a feudal relationship between the father and the godparent can be determined, only five had any sort of feudal relationship with their co-fathers. These five show godparents as both vassals and lords. John Mowbry was the lord of his son's two godfathers, John Barton and John Foxholes, prior of Newburgh. John Barton held land in Yorkshire valued at one and three-quarters knight's fee from John Mowbry. Fourteen of John Mowbry's manors were "held by the said prior and convent to their own use of the gift of the said ancestors." At Ulverton in Yorkshire there was "a quarter of a knight's fee held by the prior of Newburgh" from John Mowbry. Ralph Greystoke's godfathers, Ralph Neville and Henry Scrope, were feudal superiors to his father, William.[34]

---

[31]*CIPM* 7:345.

[32]Mertes, *The English Noble Household*, pp. 154–55.

[33]My thanks to Joel Rosenthal for suggesting this point.

[34]While these co-fathers were feudal superiors to William, I would argue that because all three were barons their social status was approximately equal.

According to Ralph Neville's inquisition *post mortem*, William had from Ralph "3 carucates of land held . . . by knight's service whereof 6 carucates make one knight's fee." William's inquisition *post mortem* states that there was a manor at Moreton "held of Henry Lescrop, knight, by knight's service and service of rendering 16s, 6d yearly."[35]

These examples, while interesting, are few. Overall, these Yorkshire tenants-in-chief chose only 6.5% of their co-parents from the people with whom they had feudal ties. Feudal connections, then, had little influence if any in the decision to create baptismal kinship ties.

About 23% of the godfathers chosen by Yorkshire tenants-in-chief were secular or regular clergy: chaplains, vicars, parsons, rectors, or priors.[36] This is puzzling since only about 2% of the English population in the fourteenth century possessed any sort of clerical designation.[37] Furthermore, *The York Manual*, which set the liturgical form standard in Yorkshire during the fourteenth century, forbade monks or nuns from becoming godparents.[38] Nevertheless, the ban was honored in the breach, for John Foxholes, John Mowbry's godfather, was a monk. Secular clergy, however, were allowed to sponsor; and in Yorkshire, as we can see, they often did.

Of these sixteen clerical godfathers, six were not attached to the parish where the baptismal ceremony took place. Eleven of these churchmen did hold office in an area where the family of the godchild also held land.[39] And two of these clerical godfathers had feudal ties with the father of the godchild. Therefore, these Yorkshire tenants-in-chief seem to have been well acquainted with the clergymen who became their co-fathers.

The testimony from the Proofs of Age does not explain why clerics seem to have been a popular choice for godparents. The jurors do not even

---

[35] *CIPM* 7:14, 54–55; 12:137; 14:30.

[36] *CIPM* 3:499; 7:192, 339; 9:116, 321; 11:127, 295; 12:159, 242, 248; 14:293; Cokayne, *Complete Peerage* 12:743.

[37] And Denys Hay considers 2% a high figure for a European country in the Middle Ages (*Europe in the Fourteenth and Fifteenth Centuries* [New York, 1966], pp. 58–59).

[38] "Nulli religiosi debent admitti in patrinos; quod de monialibus vero similiter observandum est" (*Manuale et processionale ad usum insignis ecclesiae Eboracensis*, ed. W. G. Henderson, Surtees Society 63 [1875], p. 21). This prohibition had a long tradition; see Lynch, "Baptismal Sponsorship."

[39] *CIPM* 3:499; 6:91; 7:192; 8:237–38; 10:116; 11:295, 413; 12:159, 248; 14:293.

make a special note of the fact, except to identify the cleric as such. I can offer a couple of hypotheses, however. Expediency may have been one reason why tenants-in-chief chose clerics as co-fathers. Perhaps on the day of the baptism, which usually occurred on the first day after birth and rarely later than the third day, the person originally chosen as godfather could not be found or was late—an event that did occur in this society which lacked precise, popular instruments for measuring time. Here was a problem which interfered with social, ritual, and religious goals. With the infant mortality rate so high, and considering their concern for the child's soul, the parents would be anxious to baptize their child as quickly as possible. They would also certainly want to perform their Christian (and social) duty of introducing a new member to the community as soon as possible. More pressing yet, the other godparents, relatives, and guests would have already gathered for the baptism. They, the community, and God's servants would all be waiting for the ritual to begin. What was a tenant-in-chief to do at such an embarrassing moment? Simple: the personnel surrounding a parish church could provide someone to stand in for the missing godparent during the ceremony. The testimony from Henry Kelkefield's Proof supports this hypothesis:

> Henry, son of Conan, his grandfather, was dwelling at Leverton, 5 leagues from Leysingby, at the time of the heir's birth, and there came messengers announcing the birth and praying him to come to the baptism, which from infirmity he could not do, but commanded that they should give the heir his name whether male or female. He [the heir] was baptized at Sokeburn in the parish church, the chaplain was named Gilbert, and godparents were William, parson of the church, Thomas his clerk and one Elizabeth, lady of the same town.[40]

Another reason why Yorkshire tenants-in-chief may have chosen clerics as godparents for their children is more deliberate and may be tied to their tendency to choose godparents from a lower social status or from the immediate family. Because of the marital taboos associated with baptismal kinship, choosing godparents narrowed the pool of available marriage partners for the godchildren. And spiritual incest was a real concern. Of some 557

---

[40]*CIPM* 3:499. Niles, perhaps, overemphasized the hastiness of baptism and the mishaps that could occur along the way ("Baptism and the Naming of Children," pp. 100–01). Despite the need for speed, these ceremonies seem very well planned, with letters and messengers sent, personnel gathered, and parties planned.

papal dispensations to England between 1305 and 1447 for all manner of marital impediments, forty-six or 8% involved spiritual kinship.[41] While this number may not be large, it was significant for those who petitioned for dispensation, especially when some couples noted that they had been living apart for years. At Lincoln in 1389 a dispensation was granted

> to Thomas Seymour and Joan, daughter of the late John Creme, who married in ignorance that John was Thomas's godfather which impediment came to their knowledge after two years and more of cohabitation, whereupon they ceased to cohabit for ten years and more and still cease.[42]

Moreover, some petitions were not approved:

> 1347, Oct. 5. Commission to Mr. John de Craven, official of the archdeacon of Richmond, William de Balderston, vicar of St. Michael's on Wyre, and William Ballard, dean of Amunderness, to absolve Adam de Brokhole and Matilda, widow of Laurence Travers, from excommunication for marrying. Adam de Bury, father of Matilda, was Brokhole's godfather. They are to be divorced.[43]

Baptismal kinship could be a powerful double-edged social sword.

For tenants-in-chief, their high social status, combined with the standard marital taboos stemming from blood and affinal kinship, meant that the pool of potential godparents was already constricted. It did not need any more pressure on it. To avoid shrinking this already limited pool, tenants-in-chief could simply choose godparents from people with whom they never would have contemplated marital alliances for their children—the celibate, the related, the socially insignificant.[44]

---

[41] *Calendar of the Papal Registers* (hereafter *CPapR*), 2–8 (London, 1895–1909).

[42] *CPapR* 4:340.

[43] *Testamenta eboracensia*, 4, ed. James Raine, Jr., Surtees Society 53 (1868), p. 339.

[44] John of Gaunt's marriage to his mistress Katherine Swynford was that much more notorious because they were co-parents (in their petition to the pope they wrote that they feared "grave scandal would arise" if the impediment made their marriage illegitimate). In a letter of 1396 the pope told the bishop of Lincoln to dispense the impediments and confirm the marriage (*CPapR* 7:545). On how significant (and troublesome) this spiritual impediment was in the early medieval world, see Lynch, *Godparents and Kinship*, pp. 16, 47, 144, 160–62, 194, 203, 219–81. In the fifteenth and sixteenth centuries spiritual kinship was the most frequently discussed of the marital impediments at the episcopal court at Constance (Thomas

According to Niles and Bennett, medieval English godparents tradi-tionally selected the names of their godchildren and usually gave them their own names.[45] In a Proof from Northumberland "Thomas Turpyn . . . says that he lifted Thomas from the font that day and named him with his own name."[46] Niles saw this custom as proof that medieval English parents had little control in selecting the names for their children.[47]

In some cases, however, the godparents did not name their godchildren with their own names. That this was against accepted custom is evident from bystanders' shocked reactions. In a Proof for Katherine Hildeyerd, William Whitik testified that her godparents were Alan Ligard, Beatrice Coleville, and Christina Ligard, "and there was a question amongst those in the church how she could be called Katherine, as neither of her god-mothers was so called, and to this it was replied that for the love of St. Katherine she was so named."[48]

Parents could, therefore, decide the names selected for their children either by forcing the godparent to give the child the name they preferred—we have evidence that this did occur—or, better, by choosing a godparent who had a desired name. In other words, if parents wished their daughter to be named Joan, they would choose godmothers for her whose names were Joan. A Cumberland Proof gives an instance: "Gilbert de Suthaik says that John sent a servant of his to his house to ask specifically to send his wife, because her name was Joan, to the church of Castelcayrok to be a god-mother to John's daughter."[49] Thus English parents craftily manipulated baptismal kinship customs to get the particular first names they wanted for their children.

Max Safley, *Let No Man Put Asunder: The Control of Marriage in the German Southwest: A Comparative Study, 1550–1600* [Kirksville, MO, 1984], p. 22).

[45]Bennett, "Spiritual Kinship and the Baptismal Name," p. 9; Niles,"Baptism and the Naming of Children," pp. 99–100, 103–04.

[46]*CIPM* 13:47.

[47]"I will argue that in England Christian names indicate little about family relationships because parents usually did not select the names of their children. Godparents did" (Niles, "Baptism and the Naming of Children," p. 95).

[48]*CIPM* 8:90.

[49]*CIPM* 13:50.

Of the thirty-eight children listed in the Yorkshire Proofs of Age, thirty-three had the same first name as did one or more of their godparents. These thirty-three form four distinct groups. Seven children had the same first name as did both of their same-sex godparents and their same-sex parent, while two children had the same first name as did one of their same-sex godparents and their same-sex parent. These nine instances suggest rather strongly that the parents chose these godparents to guarantee a set first name for the children—the parent's own. Eight children had the same first name as did both of their same-sex godparents, but it was not the name of their same-sex parent. Yet, these eight instances suggest again that Yorkshire tenants-in-chief chose godparents to guarantee a set name for their children. Regardless of which godparent would actually name the child, the parents could be assured that it would in all likelihood be the name that they had chosen—the one both godparents possessed. Two of these eight children, interestingly enough, did have paternal grandfathers with the same first name as they received. Finally, sixteen of these children from the Yorkshire Proofs of Age have the same first name as did one of their same-sex godparents. Since custom dictated that only one godparent would have the honor of naming the child, these sixteen instances suggest, albeit less strongly than the others, that the parents picked these godparents specifically to guarantee a set name for their child. Overall it would seem that 86% of the baptisms from Yorkshire show evidence that parents chose godparents at least partially for their names. In 44% of these baptisms in which the godchild had the same name as the same-sex godparent or a same-sex godparent and same-sex parent, this conclusion is much stronger. A first name certainly was a strong consideration in choosing a godparent.[50]

After the baptismal ceremony had ended, the participants proceeded outdoors. Members of the community had had a good look at the party coming to the church, standing outside the church, clustering around the

---

[50]Bennett, "Spiritual Kinship and the Baptismal Name," p. 8. Niles found for England as a whole that 86% of the children of tenants-in-chief had the same first name as at least one of their godparents ("Baptism and the Naming of Children," pp. 98–100). These numbers indicate to me that somebody within the family had planned for this to happen—it was not random.

On the Continent, however, the naming function of godparents was not as significant. In fact, in late medieval Florence godparents rarely chose the names of their own godchildren, that being an honor reserved to and jealously guarded by the father (Christiane Klapisch-Zuber, "Parrains et Filleuls. Une Approche Comparée de la France, l'Angleterre et l'Italie Médiévales," *MP* 6/2 (1985), 51–77; and eadem, *Women, Family, and Ritual*, pp. 283–309.

font. Now they saw them leaving the church, heading home. They would probably see these baptismal kin together again, at the heir's home, at the party to celebrate both birth and baptism. Among other things, these public displays indicated and fixed for the participants and the community just who was bound to whom by baptismal kinship. And they would remember.[51] At this point, some in the community were probably wondering just who, exactly, the co-parents of these tenants-in-chief were and what prompted the choices. But, as members and participants of the culture, they had immediate clues and patterns to answer this, at least in a general way, rather quickly. We, alien intruders into the past, need much more time and thought to answer these two questions—who? and why?

In conclusion, the evidence indicates that late medieval Yorkshire tenants-in-chief used baptismal kinship to extend their kinship networks. The majority of their social connections were vertical, and for the most part these were "downward" connections made with people from a lower social status. Medieval Yorkshire tenants-in-chief overwhelmingly chose to ignore the political, economic, social, and psychological benefits of obtaining same- or higher-status godparents because these benefits tended to impinge on other, apparently more significant, goals such as suitable marital alliances and family naming practices. The unexpectedly large percentage of clergymen as godfathers, the tendency of the tenants-in-chief to choose lower-status co-parents, and their choice of blood and affinal kin as co-parents all may

---

[51]That a juror in the Proofs of Age would remember the birth and baptism of a godchild after so many years indicates how significant were the event, ritual, and responsibility of baptismal kinship for people in medieval England. Even nonparticipants would remember someone's birth and baptism and testify about it in a Proof of Age.

A Proof of Age was not the only legal process whereby a godparent could testify to benefit a godchild. The city of York could and did require certification of English birth for people accused of being Scottish. Godfathers and godmothers figure prominently in these records as witnesses proving English birth (*A Volume of English Miscellanies Illustrating the History and Language of the Northern Counties of England*, ed. James Raine, Surtees Society 85 [1890], pp. 35–52). And the baptismal kinship bond lasted even till death. People left bequests for their godchildren or co-parents in their wills. Of 1,488 wills which I surveyed from the late fifteenth to the mid-sixteenth century, 202 or 13.5% had bequests to baptismal kin (*Wills and Inventories*, ed. James Raine, Surtees Society 2 [1835]; *Wills and Inventories from the Registry at Durham Part II*, ed. William Greenwell, Surtees Society 38 [1960]; *North Country Wills*, 1–2, ed. J. W. Clay, Surtees Society 116 and 121 [1908–12]; *Testamenta Leodiensia*, 1–4, ed. George Denison Lumb, Thoresby Society 9, 11, 19, 27 [1899, 1904, 1913, 1930]).

represent a social strategy to prevent their children's future marital alliances with people of their own or higher status from being restricted by the marital taboos associated with baptismal kinship. Additionally, the similarity in first names among baptismal kin shows a social strategy aimed at perpetuating certain names. The heir of a late medieval Yorkshire tenant-in-chief, therefore, most likely had one or two same-sex godparents with the same name as he or she possessed, and was unrelated to his or her godparents. The heir possessed social status superior to his or her godparents, and a good chance existed that one or more of these godparents was of the secular clergy.

These last two observations suggest something interesting, a possible byproduct, surely unintended, of a tenant-in-chief's choice of godparents. Medieval and early modern England were very fortunate in relation to the Continent in that England never saw heresy and popular rebellion to the extent (in terms of longevity, danger, and severity) that the Continent did. Perhaps because the English nobility had such significant ties through baptismal kinship with the clergy (albeit parish clergy for the most part), heresy never found real favor among them to the degree it did in Bohemia (the Hussites) and in southern France (the Albigensians). After all, one of the duties of a godparent was to teach the fundamentals of Christianity to one's godchild, and who was better qualified to teach this than a clergyman? Perhaps because the English landed elite had such significant ties through baptismal kinship with the common people, the peasantry in particular, popular rebellion never flared up in England to the extent it did in France (the Jacquerie), in Florence (the Ciompi), and in Germany (the 1525 Peasants' Revolt). Baptismal kinship, with all its social customs for friendly behavior, could have muted some of the harshness of premodern economic relations.[52] As they stand, these are only suggestions. To find out more, medievalists need to pursue further research, especially comparative, into the dynamics of baptismal kinship and its social functions both throughout England and on the Continent.

---

[52] I do not wish to minimize the impact in England of the 1381 Peasants' Revolt or the activities of the Lollards, including their abortive 1414 revolt. But it is well known that few noblemen or knights supported Lollardy and that after 1414, despite some flare-ups, Lollardy went underground. The 1381 revolt and subsequent scattered revolts do not seem as vicious in their start and finish as the Jacquerie or as widespread and ideological as the revolts in late medieval Germany culminating in the 1525 Peasants' Revolt.

NORMANS, SAINTS, AND POLITICS: FORENAME CHOICE AMONG FOURTEENTH-CENTURY GLOUCESTERSHIRE PEASANTS

Peter Franklin

The later Middle Ages are of great interest as the time when surnames were becoming fixed and hereditary in England and when the local records through which their evolution and behavior can be traced become abundant. The *forenames* of this period have attracted much less attention, perhaps because many of those in use are familiar. The forenames used and the popularity of particular names and kinds of names can, however, constitute a subject of considerable interest; a local study of the present kind shows the effects of the wider trends in nomenclature recorded in works such as E. G. Withycombe's dictionary,[1] to which repeated references will be made, and raises questions about the religious and political attitudes of the name givers.

This article examines the forenames used in a small and well-documented part of Gloucestershire (the large lay estate of Thornbury[2]) by

---

This article was originally published in *LPS* 36 (1986), 19–26. We reprint it with permission of the publisher, with minor revisions and style adjustments.

[1] Elizabeth G. Withycombe, *The Oxford Dictionary of English Christian Names*, 3rd ed. (Oxford, 1977) (hereafter, Withycombe).

[2] Peter A. Franklin, "Thornbury Manor in the Age of the Black Death," unpub. Ph.D. thesis (University of Birmingham, 1982) (hereafter, Thesis).

peasants active in and around the second quarter of the fourteenth century. It makes use of three separate sources—a manorial extent, a tax assessment, and a series of manorial court rolls—and compares their scope and comprehensiveness for this work. Ideally I would have used records of the same years, but such were not available: the three sources were, however, close together in time and there was probably little change in the use of names in the intervening periods, save perhaps in a few special cases discussed below.

I will begin by describing the three sources and the kinds of people who appear in them. The 1322 Extent of Thornbury Manor forms part of the unprinted document known as the "Contrariants' Survey," which gives detailed accounts of the confiscated estates of those who took part in Thomas of Lancaster's rebellion.[3] The extent divides Thornbury tenants into freemen, villeins, and cottars, and lists separately the lords and tenants of two little sub-manors at Cowhill and Thieves' Hope: altogether there are 121 names of rich, middling, and poor tenants,[4] but as it is a tenant list few women appear, and no one who did not hold directly of the lord of the manor or the lords of the sub-manors. Unfortunately it covers only part of the estate because Thornbury was considered to be held jointly by the lord and his wife, and her half was not confiscated. (This legal nicety did not affect its ordinary day-to-day working.) A few non-residents are included, but do not significantly affect the study.

The Gloucestershire Subsidy Roll of 1327 records the individuals assessed to pay that year's subsidy of one twentieth from both towns and country. I used the printed edition of the document.[5] People assessed are listed in short sections, each covering one or two settlements and arranged by hundreds. Thornbury Hundred is covered in sixteen sections, of which the first deals with Thornbury Borough, the second to ninth inclusive Thornbury Manor, and the remaining seven other estates within the hundred. The eight manorial sections yield 122 names, again including a few non-residents; the whole estate is covered, but as it is a tax document many people too poor to be assessed are omitted. (A few rich peasants also seem to have escaped the taxman's net.) Again it is an incomplete tenant list with few women appearing, but nevertheless a useful source.

---

[3]London, Public Record Office (PRO), Ancient Extents, E142/24.

[4]Three names were not given or have been lost through damage to the manuscript.

[5]Sir Thomas Phillipps, *Gloucestershire Subsidy Roll, 1 Edward III. A.D. 1327* (Middle Hill, 1856).

The best evidence comes from the third source, the series of unprinted Thornbury manorial court rolls. This article draws upon the earliest surviving rolls, from October 1328 to June 1352.[6] We cannot simply go through these collecting names as they appear because some peasants used a number of distinct surnames, and because many names of outsiders who had business with the court were recorded.[7] This brings us up against the problem of "individual identification," and to produce lists of *individual* peasants I collected references to events which could only happen once to each person.[8] There could be only one record of death for each man and woman, and only one record of paying *merchet*—the fine for permission to contract a first marriage—for each villein woman, so records of deaths and merchets produced lists of individually identified local peasants. I omitted freemen who formed a small part of the population, did not pay merchet, and whose deaths often went unrecorded,[9] and was left with 352 villeins who died[10] and 154 women who paid merchet. Both samples cover the whole manor. The dead include tenants of all sizes and many peasants who held no land directly of the lord (103 of 265 men, 49 of 87 women)—subtenants and landless people who owed heriot on their deaths by local custom.

The bias to men is still present, but the record of merchets does much to redress it. The latter undoubtedly includes most local villein women and may be almost comprehensive if, as has been suggested,[11] women in English peasant society nearly always married.

The sources give forenames in Latin, for example *Robertus* for *Robert* and *Johanna* for *Joan*, and they are often abbreviated, but translation was usually simple and debatable names were referred to C. T. Martin's list.[12]

---

[6]Stafford Record Office (hereafter, SRO), D641/1/4C/1(i)–(iii), /2.

[7]Thesis, pp. 53–56.

[8]Thesis, pp. 67–77; Zvi Razi, "The Toronto School's Reconstitution of Medieval Peasant Society: A Critical View," *PP* 85 (1979), 141–57.

[9]Thesis, pp. 72–74.

[10]Excluding three who had lived outside Thornbury.

[11]John Hajnal, "European Marriage Patterns in Perspective," in *Population in History: Essays in Historical Demography*, ed. D. V. Glass and D. E. C. Eversley (Chicago, 1965), pp. 101–43.

[12]Charles Trice Martin, *The Record Interpreter: A Collection of Abbreviations, Latin Words*

Unusual names not found there were generally left as they appeared in the sources. The use of some names by both sexes posed no serious problems: all *Thomas*es appear to have been men, and *Nicholas* was used by only one woman (Latinized as *Nichola*).[13] Problems arose only in cases of *Margaret* (*Margareta*) and *Margery* (*Margeria*), both of which were commonly abbreviated to "Marg." by Thornbury scribes, but it is clear from the subsidy roll that *Margery* was the more common in this part of the county, and there appear to have been only two *Margaret*s in the combined sources.

The total 749 names from the three sources are set out in Tables 1 and 2. Most will be familiar, but their use was by no means devoid of interesting features and two are quite striking—the limited range of names in use for each sex and the great popularity of small groups of names. The court rolls give twenty men's names, and although their samples are much smaller the subsidy roll gives twenty-one and the extent twenty-two. There were twenty-seven distinct male forenames in the three sources, so each omits some rare ones.

TABLE 1. THORNBURY MEN'S FORENAMES

	1322 Extent	1327 Subsidy Roll	1328–52 Court Rolls (Deaths)
Adam	2	5	5
Aubrey	0	1	0
Bartholemew	2	2	3
Bernard	1	0	0
David	1	1	1
Denis	0	0	1
Edward	4	4	7

and Names Used in English Historical Manuscripts and Records, 2nd ed. (London, 1910), pp. 451–64.

[13]Withycombe, p. 228.

	1322 Extent	1327 Subsidy Roll	1328–52 Court Rolls (Deaths)
Ellis	1	1	0
Geoffrey	1	0	1
Gilbert	2	3	3
Henry	2	2	2
Hugh	1	0	3
Isaac	1	0	0
John	17	19	62
Nicholas	5	2	5
Note	1	1	0
Philip	0	0	2
Rhys	0	1	0
Richard	12	10	24
Robert	6	11	40
Roger	2	1	3
Sebert	2	1	1
Simon	2	1	3
Stephen	0	1	0
Thomas	9	10	21
Walter	9	11	32
William	19	12	46
Totals	102	100	265

TABLE 2. THORNBURY WOMEN'S FORENAMES

	1322 Extent	1327 Subsidy Roll	1328–52 Court Rolls	
			Deaths	Merchets
Agnes	4	3	13	30
Alice	3	2	6	24
Amice	0	0	1	0
Aubrida	0	0	0	1
Beatrice	0	0	1	0
Christine	0	0	0	3
Clarice	1	0	0	0
Edith	2	5	15	27
Ella	0	0	0	2
Ellen	0	1	4	6
Emma	0	0	1	1
Felise	1	1	0	0
Gunnell	0	1	1	0
Isabel	1	2	8	6
Joan	0	0	5	17
Julian	0	2	4	6
Lettice	0	0	2	1
Margaret	1	0	0	1
Margery	0	1	2	1
Matilda	5	4	24	25
Nichola	0	0	0	1
Sarah	0	0	0	1
Symonda	1	0	0	1
Totals	19	22	87	154

The court rolls reveal a distinct group of six very common men's names—*John, William, Robert, Walter, Richard,* and *Thomas,* in order of descending popularity. Each accounted for at least 8% of men's names, and *John* for 23.5%. Together they covered 84.9% of male villein deaths, and the least popular of them appeared *three times as often* as the name (*Edward*) which headed the less popular group. I have called the six very popular names "Group A" and the others "Group B." The subsidy roll reveals the same pattern and similar detailed results: Group A names emerged clearly and each accounted for at least 10% of men's names. They covered 73% of the male population, and the least common of them appeared twice as often as the leading Group B name (now *Adam*).

The extent's partial coverage of the manor now becomes apparent. Although its sample is slightly larger than the subsidy roll's, the clear division between Groups A and B has disappeared. The six most popular names are the same, but *William* is now the greatest favorite. Each accounts only for at least 5.9% of men, but the proportion of the male population they cover has only fallen to 70.6%.

Court rolls' merchets reveal a very similar pattern for women's names. A distinct Group A of five names emerges—*Agnes, Edith, Matilda, Alice,* and *Joan,* in order of descending popularity. Each accounted for at least 11% of women, and *Agnes* for 19.5%. Group A names covered 79.9% of women, and the least popular of them appeared *nearly three times as often* as the names—*Ellen, Isabel,* and *Julian*—which jointly headed Group B. The small sample sizes in the extent, subsidy roll, and court rolls' record of deaths considerably restrict their usefulness as sources for women's names. Although they formed a significant proportion of Thornbury tenants—at least one in seven[14]—only a tiny proportion of the female population were tenants. Some deaths were recorded of villein women who held no land of the lord, apparently a mixed group of unmarried girls and subtenants, but it is unlikely that more than one third of actual women's deaths were recorded. Court rolls' merchets give eighteen women's names, deaths recorded there fourteen, the subsidy roll ten, and the extent only nine. The sources give a total twenty-three distinct names, of which sizeable proportions are missing from each. This usually affects rare names, but leading merchets Group B names like *Ellen* and *Julian* were rare in the subsidy roll and

---

[14]Thesis, p. 127.

absent from the extent, and the Group A name *Joan* does not appear in either of the earlier sources. The clear division between Groups A and B does not appear in the smaller samples, and even in the recorded deaths it has become blurred.

This general pattern of forename use is well known and marks the end of a period of development which concentrated forename choice. Many names were in use in late twelfth- and early thirteenth-century England but numbers decreased rapidly in later years. Even at the end of the twelfth century there were small groups of extremely popular names, and these increased in importance as the range in use narrowed. *Henry*, *John*, *Richard*, *Robert*, and *William* together accounted for 38% of recorded men's names in the twelfth century, 57% in the thirteenth, and 64% in the fourteenth.[15] They accounted for 65.7% of recorded male deaths in Thornbury, although *Henry* was rare. I compared Thornbury names with those published for Holywell-cum-Needingworth and Warboys, Huntingdonshire, and with national figures for men's names.[16] A distinct Group A emerged for Holywell men and women (six names each, covering 75.9% and 64.0% of the population) and for Warboys women (eight names covering 78.3% of the population), but not for Warboys men. Thornbury men's Group A names were the six most popular at Holywell and Warboys (though the order differed), except that *Walter* was replaced by *Nicholas*. Most Thornbury women's Group A names were popular in Huntingdonshire, but *Joan* was rare at Warboys and *Edith* not used on either manor. Thornbury men's names were closer to national trends than those of the other manors, but the popularity of *Robert* was an interesting local feature (see Table 3, below).

The names in Table 1 reflect the enormous influence of the Conquest on nomenclature. Nearly all those used in Thornbury were Norman introductions or had in earlier times been restricted to occasional monks or priests, such as *John*, *Nicholas*, and *Thomas*.[17] A few, for example *Denis*,

---

[15]Withycombe, pp. xxvii–xxviii.

[16]Edwin Brezette DeWindt, *Land and People in Holywell-cum-Needingworth: Structures of Tenure and Patterns of Social Organization in an East Midlands Village, 1252–1457* (Toronto, 1972), pp. 184–85 n. 63; J. Ambrose Raftis, *Warboys: Two Hundred Years in the Life of an English Mediaeval Village* (Toronto, 1974), pp. 64–65. (Peasants were not identified in either work, so results can only be approximate.) Withycombe, p. xxvi.

[17]Withycombe, pp. 178, 227, 279.

were brought in late in the twelfth century.[18] AS forenames had almost been eclipsed, and only *Edward* had survived and retained a little popularity without being bolstered by a Norman form. The only Welsh name used was *Rhys* ("Rees") and it was rare, reflecting the limited Welsh influence on the estate. *Note* is of interest as a form of *Cnut*, which Withycombe records was in use until the thirteenth century.[19] *Isaac* was rare before the Reformation except among Jews; it was also a local surname.

TABLE 3. POPULAR MEN'S NAMES

	England End C12	England End C13	Thornbury 1328–52 (Deaths)	Holywell C13–C15	Warboys 1290–1347
	%	%	%	%	%
John	2.0	25.0	23.4[a]	20.9[a]	19.9
Nicholas	—[b]	—	1.9	6.2[a]	4.7
Richard	8.0	10.0	9.1[a]	8.0[a]	11.7
Robert	11.0	11.0	15.1[a]	8.9[a]	9.4
Thomas	—	—	7.9[a]	6.2[a]	5.9
Walter	—	—	12.1[a]	1.2	0.6
William	15.0	14.0	17.4[a]	25.8[a]	17.2
Sample	—	—	266	664	865

[a] Group A
[b] Figure not known

---

[18]Withycombe, p. 81.

[19]Withycombe, p. 189.

TABLE 4. POPULAR WOMEN'S NAMES

	Thornbury 1328–52 (Merchets)	Holywell C13–C15	Warboys 1290–1347
	%	%	%
Agnes	19.5[a]	10.0[a]	14.6[a]
Alice	15.6[a]	13.3[a]	18.7[a]
Beatrice	0.0	2.4	6.4[a]
Christine	1.9	3.8	7.1[a]
Edith	17.5[a]	0.0	0.0
Ellen	3.9	9.5[a]	1.5
Emma	0.6	3.8	9.7[a]
Joan	11.0[a]	12.8[a]	1.9
Julian	3.9	2.4	6.4[a]
Margaret	0.6	10.0[a]	7.1[a]
Matilda	16.2[a]	8.5[a]	8.2[a]
Sample	154	211	267

[a] Group A

The women's names in Table 2 show a similar pattern, most having been introduced after the Conquest or—like *Agnes* and *Joan*—during the twelfth century.[20] Again, only one AS forename (*Edith*) had remained popular. One local woman bore the ON name *Gunnell* ("Gonilda").

The post-Conquest revolution in names was to a great extent a change to church names, but examination of particular names suggests a restricted picture of local peasant piety. The parish church was dedicated to the Virgin Mary, and there were separate chapels to Sts. Arild and Mildburh. Churches in parishes bordering Thornbury were dedicated to the Virgin and to Sts.

---

[20]Withycombe, p. xxvii.

Andrew, Helen, James, John the Evangelist, Leonard, Mary of Malmesbury, Michael, and Oswald. By custom the Virgin's name was not used,[21] but of the nine available only *John* and *Helen* (= *Ellen*) were used by local people. The name of St. Arild, traditionally martyred in Thornbury parish,[22] was not used. Five Apostles' names were used, but only *John* and *Thomas* were common and these probably owed their national popularity to the Baptist and to Becket.[23] St. Thomas was quite a rare dedication in this county.[24] The popularity of church names followed national trends: attitudes to the local church were probably ambivalent, and are reflected in peasants' failure to pay one chaplain's wages and to call for the dismissal of another.[25]

Royal names and those of lords and ladies of the manor show similar trends. Of names borne by post-Conquest kings, *William*, *Richard*, and *John* were Group A names, but *Henry* was rare and *Stephen* almost unknown. The last may reflect the county's memories of Stephen's war with the empress, and the popularity of *Robert* might reflect support for Robert of Gloucester. *Edward*'s limited popularity at this time reflects the alienation of the peasantry in the reign of Edward II rather than the popularity of his shrine in St. Peter's Abbey, Gloucester.[26] Many years of rule by Gilbert Clares (earls of Gloucester and Hertford) produced few local ones, and Hugh Audley (lord from 1317 to 1347) is known to have been unpopular from evidence of a peasant movement.[27] Some queens' and ladies' names were popular—*Edith* and *Matilda*, *Alice* and *Joan*—but these were common in England as a whole. The fact that *Joan* does not occur in the earliest docu-

---

[21]Withycombe, p. 211.

[22]Samuel Rudder, *A New History of Gloucestershire* (Cirencester, 1779; repr., Gloucester, 1977), p. 756.

[23]Withycombe, pp. 178–79, 279–80.

[24]Irvine E. Gray and Elizabeth Ralph, eds., *Guide to the Parish Records of the City of Bristol and the County of Gloucester*, Records Section, Bristol and Gloucestershire Archaeological Society (1963).

[25]SRO, D641/1/4C/1(iii) court sessions 22 October 1338, 2 January 1339, 25 February 1339, 22 March 1339; SRO, D641/1/4C/2 court session 5 February 1347.

[26]John R. Maddicott, *Thomas of Lancaster, 1307–1322: A Study in the Reign of Edward II* (Oxford, 1970), p. 107; William H. Hart, ed., *Historia et Cartularium Monasterii Sancti Petri Gloucestriae*, 3 vols., Rolls Series 33 (London, 1863–67), 1:46.

[27]Thesis, pp. 191–226.

ments may suggest, though the samples are small, that it was unpopular while Joan of Acre's time as lady of the manor (from 1290 to 1307) was remembered and later recovered. Opposition to Edward II might have meant support for Queen Isabel—Withycombe suggests the name's spread may have been partly due to her[28]—but her name was little more popular than her husband's.

This survey of peasant nomenclature has shown that manorial extents, subsidy rolls, and manorial court rolls are valuable sources for men's names. Extents and subsidy rolls are poor sources for women's names because of their restricted coverage, though the latter *may* accurately reflect nomenclature over wider areas, such as whole counties. Thornbury forenames provide excellent illustrations of the chief features of forename choice in the period when the most fundamental change in the history of English forenames had been accomplished. Names introduced or popularized by the Normans had, with some more recent importations, swept nearly all before them; few AS names were still used and few derived from ON. Ranges of names in use had narrowed over the previous century and small groups had become extremely common. At least 98% of these men and 90% of women in a medieval rural parish had names familiar to us, and most of the common names English men and women would bear for the next 650 years were already established among them.

This study has raised questions about how forename choice may reflect peasants' religious and political views, but the lack of hard evidence for these makes proof difficult. They commonly gave their children saintly and royal names, but those of local saints, lords and ladies, and recent monarchs enjoyed little popularity. Withycombe's view that royal use made names popular or kept them in use must be questioned. The study has also drawn attention to regional variations in the use of names which seem to have affected women's names more than men's. These call for examination and explanation: sources are not lacking.

See now Peter Franklin, ed., *The Taxpayers of Medieval Gloucestershire: An Analysis of the 1327 Lay Subsidy Roll with a New Edition of its Text* (Stroud, 1993).

---

[28]Withycombe, p. 164.

PART III—LOCAL SOCIETIES

SOME ASPECTS OF REGIONAL VARIATION IN EARLY MIDDLE ENGLISH PERSONAL NOMENCLATURE

John Insley

Towards the end of the OE period, a certain *Gospatrik*, lord of Allerdale and Dalston in Cumberland, issued a writ, now preserved only in an imperfect thirteenth-century copy,[1] declaring that one *Thorfynn mac Thore* should be free in respect of all things that were Gospatrik's in Allerdale and that the men who dwelt with the same Thorfynn at Cardew and Cumdivock in Dalston should be free. The writ went on to forbid that the peace granted to any man should be broken and to issue certain geld exemptions, as well as to grant Thorfynn financial and legal rights over land in Cardew and Cumdivock. The personal nomenclature contained in this record is an exact reflection of the heterogeneous nature of settlement patterns in this northern borderland of AS England. This area was occupied by Anglian settlers from Northumbria during the latter part of the seventh century, but was subject to renewed British penetration from Strathclyde from the beginning of the

This article was originally published in *Studies in Honour of Kenneth Cameron*, ed. Thorlac Turville-Petre and Margaret Gelling, Leeds Studies in English, n.s. 18 (1987), pp. 183–99. We reprint it with minor changes, with permission of the publisher.

[1]For the text of this writ, see *Anglo-Saxon Writs*, ed. F. E. Harmer (Manchester, 1952), pp. 423–24 (no. 121); and A. M. Armstrong, A. Mawer, F. M. Stenton, and Bruce Dickins, *The Place-Names of Cumberland*, English Place-Name Society 20–22 (1950–52), pt. 3, pp. xxvii–xxx.

tenth century onwards.[2] In addition, it was subject to Gaelic-Scandinavian settlement, which was formerly thought to have come from the Hiberno-Norse colonies in Ireland, but which has been recently suggested by Gillian Fellows Jensen to have been the result of the influx of Vikings who had previously lived in mixed Gaelic-Scandinavian communities in Galloway or the Western Isles.[3]

Gospatrik's own name is a reflex of a British *Gwaspatric, and he can be identified either with the person of this name (probably the third son of Earl Uhtred of Northumbria) who was murdered at the court of the Confessor on 28 December 1064,[4] or with Gospatric, son of Maldred, a member of the old Northumbrian comital dynasty, who held the Northumbrian earldom for a short time after the Norman Conquest and later received the estate of Dunbar and other extensive properties in Berwickshire and East Lothian from Malcolm III of Scotland.[5] Gospatric, son of Maldred, was the founder of the Scottish comital family of Dunbar, and the name was borne in the twelfth century by two of the earls of this house.[6] The popularity of the name *Gospatric* in the old Northumbrian comital family was an obvious factor contributing to its ubiquity throughout the North. Scottish examples additional to those found in the comital house of Dunbar include *Gospatric* son of *Uhtred* son of *Ulfkil*, sheriff of Roxburgh in the early twelfth century,[7] and, on a more humble level, two jurors in a perambulation of boundaries at Strobo, west of Peebles, from ca. 1200.[8] Turning to the southwestern corner of the old Northumbrian linguistic area, we find several examples of the name in Lancashire. Note the following forms: *Thoma filio Gospatricii* (witness) 1184–1202 (17c) Cockersand, p. 368 (for abbreviations see end

[2]See Kenneth Jackson, "Angles and Britons in Northumbria and Cumbria," in *Angles and Britons*, O'Donnell Lectures (Cardiff, 1963), 60–84, at pp. 71–73.

[3]Gillian Fellows Jensen, *Scandinavian Settlement Names in the North-West*, Navnestudier 25 (Copenhagen, 1985), pp. 319–21.

[4]See Harmer, *Anglo-Saxon Writs*, p. 562.

[5]See Archibald A. M. Duncan, *Scotland: The Making of the Kingdom* (Edinburgh, 1975), pp. 98–99; and G. W. S. Barrow, *Kingship and Unity: Scotland, 1000–1306* (London, 1981), p. 7.

[6]For the twelfth-century earls of Dunbar, see Duncan, *Scotland*, pp. 374–75.

[7]Barrow, *Kingship and Unity*, p. 7.

[8]G. W. S. Barrow, *The Anglo-Norman Era in Scottish History* (Oxford, 1980), pp. 34–35.

of article, p. 209); *Gospatricius* 1194–1219 (1268) Cockersand, p. 943 (Whittington); *Gospatricius de Chorlton* 1200–23 (1268) Cockersand, p. 707 (Beswick in Chorlton-upon-Medlock); *Cospatricio albo* (witness) 1200–27 (1412) Furness II, p. 274; *Gospatricius filius Willelmi de Fel* 1200–40 (1268) Cockersand, p. 823 (Lancaster). Going a step further, we can also ascribe the ubiquity of ME reflexes of OE *Ēadwulf*, OE *Ōsulf* < *Ōswulf*, OE *Ūhtrēd*, and AScand *Wælþēof* < ON *Valþjófr* in the north of England and southern Scotland to the influence of the naming practices found within the old Northumbrian comital family.[9]

Turning now to Thorfynn mac Thore, we find that his name belongs to a West Scandinavian-Gaelic onomastic region. *Thorfynn* reflects ON *Þorfinnr*, a name which is well represented in Norwegian and Icelandic sources,[10] but which is apparently absent from the onomasticon of the East Scandinavian area.[11] In England, ON *Þorfinnr* is frequently attested in independent use in Yorkshire from the late eleventh to the early thirteenth century.[12] It is also contained in the place names Thorpen Lees and Thorfinsty in Lancashire;[13] in the lost Cumberland names *Briggethorfin* and *Aynthorfin*, noted in documents of ca. 1260;[14] and in the place name Corstorphine in Midlothian.[15] An example of the name in independent use in Lancashire is contained in the form *Jurdanus filius Torphini de Gairstang* 1246 (1268) Cockersand, p. 276 (Garstang). A Scottish example occurs in the form *Gillepatric mac Torphin* (perambulator of bounds at St. Monance and Pitten-

---

[9]With especial reference to Lancashire, see the remarks of John Insley, "Lancashire Surnames," *Nomina* 6 (1982), 93–98, esp. p. 96.

[10]E. H. Lind, *Norsk-isländska dopnamn ock fingerade namn från medeltiden* (Uppsala, 1905–15), cols. 1158–59; *Supplementband* (Oslo, 1931), cols. 846–51.

[11]It should be noted that *Thorfin* has been recorded in Denmark, but only in a folk tale borrowed from Norwegian. See *Danmarks Gamle Personnavne*, 1: *Fornavne*, ed. Gunnar Knudsen and Marius Kristensen with the collaboration of Rikard Hornby (Copenhagen, 1936–48), cols. 1382–83, for full details.

[12]Gillian Fellows Jensen, *Scandinavian Personal Names in Lincolnshire and Yorkshire*, Navnestudier 7 (Copenhagen, 1968), pp. 302–03.

[13]Eilert Ekwall, *The Place-Names of Lancashire* (Manchester, 1922), pp. 166, 200.

[14]Armstrong et al., *Place-Names of Cumberland* 2:360.

[15]W. F. H. Nicolaisen, *Scottish Place-Names: Their Study and Significance* (London, 1976), p. 115.

weem, Fife) 1153–62 (1189–99) RRS I, p. 215 (no. 168). *Thore*, the name of the father of the Thorfynn of Gospatric's writ, is a reflex of ON *Þórir*, ODan *Thori*, a common enough name in the eastern Danelaw.[16] The patronymic function, however, is indicated by the use of the Gaelic *mac*. Parallel forms of this type have been noted in medieval Scottish records. We have already mentioned the *Gillepatric mac Torphin* of a record of 1153–62. A further example, contained in the witness clause of a charter of 1153–59 from the mid-thirteenth-century part of the *Registrum* of Dunfermline Abbey, is *Alwyno mac Arkil* (ablative).[17] The name of this witness appears in various forms in the attestation clauses of Scottish royal charters from ca. 1128 to ca. 1155.[18] He was the Scottish king's *rannaire*, a Gaelic title with the sense "distributor of food."[19] His name (OE *Ælfwine*) and that of his father (ON *Arnkell*) belong to the AScand tradition of Northumbria, though his son and successor bore the Gaelic name *Gilleandrais*.[20]

Gospatric's writ stipulates that the men dwelling with Thorfynn at Cardew and Cumdivock should be free "swa Melmor 7 Thore 7 Sygoolf weoron on Eadread dagan." The *Thore* of this clause may be Thorfynn's father, though, as F. E. Harmer remarked,[21] the name is common. If this *Thore* was Thorfynn's father, then we can, for chronological reasons, take *Eadread* to be a mistake for *Ealdred* and to relate to the Northumbrian earl of that name who ruled from 1018 to 1039.[22] The form *Melmor* belongs to

---

[16]See Fellows Jensen, *Scandinavian Personal Names*, pp. 307–09.

[17]RRS I, p. 182 (no. 117). Cf. also: *Alfwin Mac arch'* (witness) ca. 1136–47, perhaps 1141–47 (14c, after 1316) RRS I, p. 151 (no. 29); *Alwino Macarkil* (witness) 1153–62 (13c, transcript of ca. 1840) RRS I, p. 189 (no. 125); *Ælwynus filius Arkil* (witness) 1154–59 (mid-13c, *temp.* Alex III) RRS I, p. 185 (no. 118); quam *Elwinus Renner 7 Eda uxor eius* . . . dederunt (confirmation by Malcolm IV to Dunfermline Abbey of the grant of the church of Kirknewton, Midlothian, made by Alfwin the *rannaire* and his wife Eda) 1153–62 (mid-13c, *temp.* Alex III) RRS I, p. 213 (no. 164).

[18]For further references to Alfwin mac Archill, see RRS I, p. 32 and nn. 4 and 5.

[19]The office of *rannaire* is fully discussed in RRS I, pp. 32–33.

[20]RRS I, p. 32 and n. 5. For English examples of Gaelic *Gilleandrais*, see Olof von Feilitzen, *The Pre-Conquest Personal Names of Domesday Book*, NG 3 (Uppsala, 1937), p. 261, and the works cited there.

[21]*Anglo-Saxon Writs*, p. 420.

[22]See Harmer, *Anglo-Saxon Writs*, p. 559, s.n. *Eadread*, and the references cited there.

the Gaelic personal name *Maelmuire*, while *Sygoolf* is a reflex of the rare ON *Sigólfr*.

Gospatric went on to grant the men of Cardew and Cumdivock exemption from geld "swa ic bȳ 7 swa Willann, Wallðeof 7 Wygande 7 Wyberth 7 Gamell 7 Kunyth 7 eallun mine kynling 7 wassenas." Of these names, *Wallðeof* and *Gamell* are unambiguous, reflecting AScand *Wælþēof* < ON *Valþjófr* and ON *Gamall*, respectively. *Wyberth* is perhaps best interpreted as a reflex of OE (Angl) *Wīgberht*,[23] though, on formal grounds, the Continental cognate, represented by OSax *Wīgber(h)t*, OHG *Wīpreht* etc., cannot be entirely excluded. *Wygande* is probably a Continental name corresponding to OHG *Wīgant*; alternatively, however, we may be concerned here with a Cumbric name corresponding to OBret *Uuicon*.[24] *Kunyth* has been explained by Max Förster as an ancestor of ModE *Kenneth* derived from Welsh *Cennydd*, the name of a sixth-century saint.[25] *Willann* is difficult. It may be a Continental name corresponding to MHG *Wielant*; for palaeographical reasons, we must reject Liebermann's reading of the form as *Willelmi*.[26]

---

[23]For the appearance of OE *Wīgbeorht* in the early-ninth-century part of the *Liber Vitae* of Durham, see Rudolf Müller, *Untersuchungen über die Namen des nordhumbrischen Liber Vitae*, Palaestra 9 (Berlin, 1901), p. 83, though it should be noted that he wrongly assigns the variant spelling *uicbercht* to an OE element *Wīc-*, an element which, it should be added, does not occur in the OE onomasticon.

[24]Cf. Ekwall's discussion of the Lancashire place name Wigan (*Place-Names of Lancashire*, p. 103).

[25]Harmer, *Anglo-Saxon Writs*, p. 564, s.n. *Kunyth*. Cf. also George F. Black, *The Surnames of Scotland: Their Origin, Meaning, and History* (New York, 1946), p. 393, s.n. *Kenneth*.

[26]"Drei nordhumbrische Urkunden um 1100," ed. F. Liebermann, *Archiv für das Studium der neueren Sprachen und Litteraturen* 111 (1903), 275–84, at p. 276 and n. 23 (p. 277). It should, however, be noted that Bruce Dickins, in his edition of the text contained in Armstrong et al., *Place-Names of Cumberland* (3:xxvii–xxx), interprets the form not as a personal name, but as a reflex of the OE verb *willan* "to be willing, wish, desire." He translates the passage in question as: "And let everyone abiding there be as free of (royal) taxation as I am and as Walltheof and Wygande and Wyberth and Gamell and Kunith may wish, and all my kindred and dependants" (ibid., p. xxix). Margaret Gelling has suggested to me that the absence of the Tironian sign between this form and *Wallðeof* is in favor of Dickins's interpretation. *Willann* would then represent the present subjunctive plural form of the verb, *willen*. This interpretation solves the problem of the obscure personal name, though it also throws up questions as to the position of Walltheof, Wygande, Wyberth, Gamell, and Kunith, in that it implies that they were practically of equal status with Gospatric himself. The general

Gospatric concluded the writ by granting Thorfynn sake and soke and toll and team over all the lands in Cardew and Cumdivock which had been granted to Thore "in the days of Moryn" (*on Moryn dagan*), this being granted free of the obligation of providing messengers and witnesses in the same place. From the context, it is clear that the Thore of this part of the text is Thorfynn's father. *Moryn* is otherwise unknown; it has been suggested that it is a reflex of either OIr *Morand* or OIr *Mórfind*.[27]

Gospatric's writ belongs to what can be best described as a "Northern onomastic zone." In this region, which stretched from the northern parts of Lancashire and Yorkshire to southern Scotland, we find that a Northumbrian onomasticon of Anglian and Sc origin meets, with varying degrees of intensity, a Gaelic onomasticon and, to a lesser extent, a Brittonic (Cumbric) onomasticon. After the Norman Conquest, of course, we have the additional factor of French personal names, often of West Frankish origin, throughout this region, as, indeed, in areas further south. The mixture of forms revealed in the language and orthography of this writ reflects the heterogeneous nature of settlement and of the patterns of political and cultural influence in the northwest between the tenth and the twelfth century. In this context, it is still relevant to quote the linguistic comments made by Alois Brandl over eighty years ago in Felix Liebermann's edition of the text:

> In keeping with the age of the original document, several genuine OE features, in particular, the retention of a full vowel in the endings *-as, (weor)on, (eall)un*, are preserved. In addition, the text retains the insular forms of *g* (apart from in the loanword *heyninga*), voiced *f* (instead of the later ME spelling *v*), and *w*, though in the case of the latter the insular letter was not always properly understood by the copyist. The Late West Saxon *Schriftsprache* is indicated by the appearance of *ea* resulting from fracture in the forms *ealle, weald* (alongside *ællun, Caldebek, Wallðeof*, however), the syncopated third person present indicative verb form *greot*, and probably also by *y* in *gegyfan* (cf., however, Bülbring, p. 155). On the other hand, there is a series of Southern forms of a type which first arose in the twelfth century, namely, the diphthongized spellings in *greot, weoron, þeo, þeor*, the development of *æ > e* in *he(o)bbe*, and the appearance of *byn* beside *beo*. As Northern dialect features, one should emphasize: the participle form in *-an(d)*;

---

context, however, would seem to make Harmer's translation somewhat more plausible, though the absence of comparable documents from this region means that the question must remain open.

[27]Harmer, *Anglo-Saxon Writs*, p. 568, s.n. *Moryn*.

d > *ð* in *mið, onðer, ðrenge* (for the dental change in *team* > *theam*, cf. Björkman, *Scand. Loanwords*, 1902, p. 223, and Stolze, *Ortsnamen im Domesday Book*, 1902, § 36 f.); *lêaf* > *leof frêols* > *freals* (if these are not merely antiquarian spellings of the type represented by *-read* < *-red* in *Eadread* < *Eadred*). The latest features, which can only be ascribed to an ill-trained thirteenth-century scribe, include such misreadings as *c* for *e* and *y* or *g* for *w,* the phonetically inexplicable doubling of *n* (*ann*), the use of *seo* as a neuter accusative, *h[w]ylkun* for *ilkan* or Southern *ilkon*, loss of the genitival ending (in *Eadread dagan, on Moryn dagan*), an accusative plural *eallun myne kynling*, and a genitive plural *(ænig) myne wassenas*. The mixture of forms gives the impression that our scribe was working from a considerably older copy with which he was not fully competent to deal. We also get the impression that this older copy was the work of a southern scribe, as has also been shown to be the case in the northern portions of *Domesday Book* (Stolze, p. 49), and, finally, that the West Saxon *Schriftsprache* was already present when our Cumberland record was originally drawn up. Amongst the loan elements, those from Old Norse are particularly conspicuous; these include the use of the present participle in *-and*, the words *dreng, bec, heyning,* and *gyrth,* and, of the personal names, certainly *Thore, Thorfynn,* and *Gamell.* One should probably regard the following as Norman scribal forms: *o* for *u* in *onðer, woonnan, Sigoolf; ch* for *c, k* in *brech; ey* instead of *i* in *freyth, geyld* (cf. Stolze, p. 23 f.). The Celtic element, as one would expect in Cumberland, is represented by many of the personal names. In addition, there is *mac (Thore),* and Stevenson has also linked the strange form *wassenas* with Welsh *gwassan* = followers (related to *vasallus*).[28]

Brandl's discussion shows its age in a number of errors, mainly of an etymological nature. For example, his reference to the form *Wallðeof* in the context of (or, in this case, absence of) fracture shows that he was unaware of the ultimate identity of this form with AScand *Wælþēof* < ON *Valþjófr* and regarded it as a reflex of some name in OE *W(e)ald-*. Brandl's identification of the form *Eadread* with the OE personal name *Ēadrǣd* may be a formal possibility, but it does not fit the historical context which suggests that the form may be plausibly interpreted as a mistake for the name of the Northumbrian earl Ealdred.[29] The second element of *Sigoolf* does not contain AN *o* as an inverted spelling for *u*, as suggested by Brandl, but reflects the ON variant *-ólfr*. One must, however, bear in mind that when Brandl wrote the above notes to Gospatric's will neither Lind's compendium of

---

[28]Liebermann, "Drei nordhumbrische Urkunden um 1100," pp. 277–78 (translated from the German by the present writer).

[29]Cf. above, p. 194 and n. 22.

West Scandinavian personal names[30] nor Björkman's works about Sc personal nomenclature in England[31] had yet appeared. Nevertheless, from a
methodological point of view, Brandl's commentary is remarkably modern.
Brandl separates the various orthographic, phonological, and morphological
layers within the extant text in order to arrive at its linguistic and textual
history. At the same time, the discussion is spatially differentiated through
its isolation of dialect features within the text and by its treatment of specific lexical and onomastic items (in this case, Scandinavian and Celtic
items) within the linguistic and regional contexts of the document.

Returning to our "Northern onomastic zone," we find that the onomastic
structure of this region can be typified by the history of a place name from
its northern approaches, Eddleston in Peeblesshire, which is documented by
twelfth-century charters contained in the *Registrum Episcopatus Glas-
guensis*.[32] Originally, this place had the Cumbric name *Penteiacob* "head,
end of James's house." This Cumbric name was then succeeded by *Gillemurestun*, "the *tūn* of Gillemuire," a name indicating the acquisition of the
property by a landowner with the Gaelic name *Gillemaire, -muire*. The use
of the specific *-tūn* indicates that the area was English-speaking, though the
replacement of Cumbric by English need not have been of any great antiquity.[33] *Gillemurestun* was acquired at farm by the Norman baron Richard
de Morville (ob. 1189), constable of the Scottish kings Malcolm IV and
William the Lion, from Bishop Ingram of Glasgow (1164–74). Richard de
Morville then turned the estate into a knight's fee for a Northumbrian named
Edulf, son of Uhtred, from whom the place acquired the name *Edulfestun*,
the modern *Eddleston*.

---

[30]For this work see above, n. 10.

[31]E. Björkman, *Nordische Personennamen in England in alt- und frühmittel-englischer Zeit*,
Studien zur englischen Philologie 37 (Halle, 1910); E. Björkman, *Zur englischen Namenkunde*, Studien zur englischen Philologie 47 (Halle, 1912).

[32]For the history of the place name Eddleston, see G. W. S. Barrow, *The Kingdom of the
Scots: Government, Church and Society from the Eleventh to the Fourteenth Century* (London, 1973), pp. 297–98; and Barrow, *Anglo-Norman Era*, p. 93 and n. 3.

[33]For the disappearance of the Cumbric language, see Jackson, "Angles and Britons,"
pp. 72–73; and Barrow, *Kingship and Unity*, pp. 11–12. Jackson (ibid., p. 78) suggests that
Penteiacob would have been the name in use in the eleventh century and goes on to point
out that it is a well-preserved three-element Cumbric name, whose very spelling suggests
a written document of Cumbric origin in the background.

As is indicated above, the Northumbrian "comital names" *Ēad(w)ulf,* *Gospatric,* *Ōs(w)ulf,* *Ūhtrǣd,* and *Wælþēof* (< ON *Valþjófr*) are characteristic of this "Northern onomastic zone." Occasionally we find striking examples of such names within the same family. Lancashire examples are represented by the following forms: *Ricardo filio Huctredi filii Osolf* (witness in a document dealing with land *iuxta Asseleieford* in Clifton in Salfordshire) 1195–1212 (17c) Cockersand, p. 725; *Walthef de Quitinton filius Hutredi* 1184–1210 (1268) Cockersand, p. 730 (Withington in Manchester). Coming, as they do, from south Lancashire, these forms, in fact, reflect the spread of a Northern onomasticon to the edge of the Midland area. It should not be forgotten that Lancashire is crossed by several important ME dialect isoglosses. Kristensson, on the basis of spellings in the subsidy rolls, regarded the area north of the Ribble as a separate southwestern division of the Northern dialects of ME and assigned the parts of the county south of this river to the Northwest Midland dialect of ME.[34] Long ago, Ekwall showed that the ME boundary between Northern *ā* and Southern/Midland *ǭ* (< OE, ON *ā*) followed the Ribble from its mouth to a little beyond Ribchester and then forked north to Longridge Fell, along which it ran east to the Hodder, turning down the latter to meet the Ribble again just east of Winckley Hall.[35] The Ribble has also been generally regarded as the northern boundary in ME of West Midland *u* for OE *y* (with the exception of OE *y* before *l*, for which ME spellings in <u> have also been noted in the north of the county).[36] One should, of course, bear in mind that such boundaries were not static and that their creation was the result of a long period of evolution.[37] This, however, does not detract from the significance of the Ribble as a phonological (and onomastic) boundary, though in such boundary areas

---

[34]Gillis Kristensson, *A Survey of Middle English Dialects, 1290–1350: The Six Northern Counties and Lincolnshire,* Lund Studies in English 35 (1967), pp. 241–43, 283 (map 17).

[35]Eilert Ekwall, "The Middle English ā/ō Boundary," *English Studies* 20 (1938), 147–68, at pp. 147, 149–50. Cf. also the remarks of Kristensson, *Survey of Middle English Dialects,* pp. 32–34.

[36]Kristensson, *Survey of Middle English Dialects,* pp. 116–20, 242, 291–95 (maps 25–29).

[37]Cf. the remarks of Jacek Fisiak, "Some Problems in Historical Dialectology," *Studia Anglica Posnaniensia* 16 (1983), 5–14. Note also Fisiak's interesting observations about the movement of dialect isoglosses in the fifteenth century in his article "English Dialects in the Fifteenth Century: Some Observations Concerning the Shift of Isoglosses," *Folia Linguistica Historica* 4/2 (1983), 195–217.

one must reckon with a certain degree of phonological and orthographic overlap.[38] Extending this argument, one can regard the examples of names typical of our "Northern onomastic zone" in records from the northern edge of the Midland area (as in the above-mentioned forms containing *Ōsulf*, *Ūhtrǣd*, and *Wælþēof* from the Manchester region) as representing a type of onomastic overlap. Of course, a certain amount of caution is necessary in dealing with this concept. Clearly, the appearance of such names as *Ōsulf* and *Ūhtrǣd* in the northern part of the Midland zone reflects Northern influence, and it is also clear that in the North the persistence and ubiquity of such names reflects their social prestige as "comital names" used by the pre-Conquest earls of Northumbria. This "comital" status does not apply when such names appear outside the North and its immediate environs. Whereas *Wælþēof* and *Gospatric* are almost entirely confined to this area, examples of *Ōsulf* have been found as far afield as Cornwall,[39] and *Ūhtrǣd* is not infrequent in East Anglian records of the ME period.[40] Despite these provisos, however, our anthroponymic boundaries can be defined with some clarity, though, here again, it would be wrong to regard them as static. It is, for example, probably significant that of the above examples of *Gospatric*, only one, *Gospatricius de Chorlton*,[41] is drawn from a locality south of the Ribble (Chorlton-upon-Medlock in Manchester). Similarly, if we examine the distribution pattern of ODan *Auti*, ME *Outi*, a name well attested in the East Midlands and Norfolk,[42] in medieval Lancashire, we find that there are no clear examples of its use north of the Ribble. The following forms have been noted: *Siwardo filio Avti et Ricardo fratre suo* (witnesses in a deed

---

[38]See the remarks of John Insley, "Lancashire Surnames," p. 97.

[39]For Cornish examples of OE *Ōs(w)ulf*, see John Insley, "Some Scandinavian Personal Names in South-West England from Post-Conquest Records," *Studia Anthroponymica Scandinavica* 3 (1985), 23–58, at pp. 26–27.

[40]See Bo Seltén, *The Anglo-Saxon Heritage in Middle English Personal Names*: *East Anglia 1100–1399*, 2, Acta Regiae Societatis Humaniorum Litterarum Lundensis 73 (Lund, 1979), p. 161.

[41]Above, pp. 192–93.

[42]The Domesday Book examples for 1066 are listed by von Feilitzen, *Pre-Conquest Personal Names*, p. 169. For post-Conquest examples from Lincolnshire, see Fellows Jensen, *Scandinavian Personal Names*, pp. 43–44. In Norfolk the name occurs in Lynn, for which see Cecily Clark, "The Early Personal Names of King's Lynn: An Essay in Socio-Cultural History. Part I – Baptismal Names," *Nomina* 6 (1982), 51–71, at p. 53.

concerning property at Elswick, Clayton-le-Woods, Whittle-le-Woods, Wheelton, Withnell, and Roddlesworth; in 1212 the Book of Fees recorded that in the previous generation Richard de Molyneux of Sefton had granted his sister in marriage to Siward, son of Outi, together with two carucates at Cuerden, just south of Preston [and, therefore, of the Ribble][43]) ca. 1160 Hoghton, no. 1 (facsimile in frontispiece); *Rogerus de Winstanisle filius Outi* 1190–1219 (1268) Cockersand, p. 654 (Winstanley); assartum *Outi* (in Upholland) 1190–1225 (1268) Cockersand, p. 610; *Alanus filius Outi* 1194 P NS 5, p. 124; sartum *Outi* (in Bury in Knowsley) 1199–1220 (1268) Cockersand, p. 606; *Rogerus filius Roberti filii Outi* 1200–20 (1268) Cockersand, p. 544 (Maghull). ODan *Auti*, ME *Outi* is characteristic of the AScand areas of eastern England; its appearance in south Lancashire must reflect penetration from an East Midland "onomastic zone." In this context, it is also significant that its distribution, insofar as our sources allow us to come to any conclusions, seems to have been confined to the parts of the county south of the Ribble.

It should be emphasized that regionally defined anthroponymic systems of the type described above overlap with a more generally valid onomastic system operative throughout the entire English-speaking area of the late OE and AN periods. This can be illustrated by again turning to the margins of our "Northern onomastic zone." In a charter of the period 1166–71 (probably of 1166),[44] King William the Lion of Scotland confirmed various properties granted by King Malcolm IV, the countess Ada (de Warenne, mother of King William), and Herbert the chamberlain to the Norman baron Hugh Giffard, lord of Yester in East Lothian. Among these properties, we find a part of Lethington in Haddington, East Lothian, *quam Edolf filius Gamel tenuit*, and a full toft in Linlithgow, West Lothian, *scilicet toftum quod Toke tenuit*. Whereas *Edolf* is a reflex of the typically Northumbrian "comital name" OE *Ēad(w)ulf*,[45] *Gamel* represents a Sc name, ON *Gamall* etc., which

---

[43] *The Book of Fees, Commonly Called "Testa de Nevill*," reformed from the earliest MSS by the Deputy Keeper of the Records, 3 vols. (London, 1920–31), 1:208.

[44] RRS II, pp. 154–55 (no. 48).

[45] Note, however, that in Domesday Book OE *Ēad(w)ulf* is attested in Devon, Herefordshire, Somerset, and Wiltshire, as well as in Yorkshire and Derbyshire (von Feilitzen, *Pre-Conquest Personal Names*, p. 240). Seltén, *Anglo-Saxon Heritage*, 2:74, has two East Anglian examples from documents of 1199 and 1209, respectively, and also records the appearance of the name as a surname in Norfolk in the subsidy roll of 1327.

has been noted throughout the areas of Sc settlement and influence in England,[46] and *Toke* is a characteristically East Scandinavian name, ODan *Tōki*, which is frequently attested in the Danelaw and occurs sporadically in other parts of England.[47] Somewhat earlier, in the period 1142–47 (probably 1143–47), Earl Henry of Northumberland, son of King David I of Scotland, issued a charter repeating and confirming his father's grants to the monks of Rievaulx Abbey at Melrose.[48] The charter includes two sets of witnesses, the first being witnesses to the later and fuller act of endowment and confirmation and the second being the witnesses to David I's original act of endowment of Melrose Abbey, which is to be dated to ca. 1136 and was probably limited to the properties of Melrose, Eildon, and Darnick, properties which are merely part of the items confirmed by Earl Henry. This second list of witnesses reads, "Preterea homines de Eadem terra. Gospatricio filio Gospatricij. Vlfchillo filio Ethelstan. Osolfo filio Huctredi. Macchus filio Vndwain. Huctredo filio Siot. Horm filio Eilaf. Osolfo filio Elstan. Roberto de Brus. Rad*ulfo* filio Turstani." The first of these witnesses is Earl Gospatric II of Dunbar, son of Gospatric Maldredsson and a descendant of the old Northumbrian comital house.[49] The newer Norman nobility is represented by Robert de Brus, lord of Annandale, whose family came from Brix in the Cotentin and who was an ancestor of King Robert I.[50] A further Norman witness is probably represented by *Radulfus filius Turstani*. His name is the normal Latin form of OFr *Ra(o)ul*; his father's name is probably an anglicized form of Norman *Turstinus* < ON *Þorsteinn* etc., rather than a latinized form of the corresponding AScand *Þurstān*.[51] The

---

[46]Cf. the Domesday Book forms collected by von Feilitzen, *Pre-Conquest Personal Names*, p. 257.

[47]For Lincolnshire and Yorkshire examples of ODan *Toki*, see Fellows Jensen, *Scandinavian Personal Names*, pp. 287–88. For the appearance of the name outside the Danelaw, see Insley, "Some Scandinavian Personal Names," p. 36, and the works cited there.

[48]RRS I, pp. 157–58 (no. 41).

[49]For the twelfth-century earls of Dunbar, see Duncan, *Scotland*, pp. 374–75.

[50]For the origins of the Bruce family in Normandy, see Barrow, *Kingdom of the Scots*, pp. 322–23.

[51]Cf. John Insley, "Field Names and the Scandinavian Settlement of England: A Comparative Study of the Evidence Provided by the English Place-Name Society's Survey of Northamptonshire," in *Giessener Flurnamen-Kolloquium 1. bis 4 Oktober 1984*, ed. Rudolf Schützeichel (Heidelberg, 1985), 113–28, at pp. 123–24.

other witnesses are all members of the local gentry of Roxburghshire and their names reflect the prevailing Northumbrian tradition. We have two witnesses with the "comital name" *Osolfus* < OE *Ōs(w)ulf*, the first of whom was the son of a man with the "comital name" *Ūhtrēd* and the second of whom was the son of one *Elstan* < OE *Ælfstān* or *Æðelstān*. The "comital name" *Ūhtrēd* is borne by a further witness; the name of his father, *Siot*, is best interpreted as a reflex of the CG *Sigot*. The witness *Vlfchillus* has a Sc name, ODan, OSwed (runic) *Ulfkil*, which is frequently attested in the northern Danelaw.[52] The form of his father's name, *Ethelstan* for OE *Æðel-stān*, is a "learned archaism" on the part of the scribe, since [ð] in the OE name element *Æðel-* had already been lost in the eleventh century with the result that *Ail-, Ayl-, Eil-, El-*, etc. are the normal ME reflexes of this element.[53] A further witness bearing a Sc name is *Horm*, son of *Eilaf. Horm* is ON *Ormr* etc., a name common throughout northern England, but rare south of the Humber.[54] The name of the father of this witness, ON *Eiláfr* etc., is sporadically attested throughout England in the early ME period.[55] The only Goidelic name in this list is *Macchus*, corresponding to Gaelic *Maccus*. The name of the father of this Macchus, *Vndwain*, is probably best interpreted as a corrupt form of an original byname based on the Sc appellative *hunda-sveinn* "dog-keeper," which has also been noted as the first element of the Cumberland place name Hunsonby.[56]

The examination of this Scottish witness list has shown that in our "Northern onomastic zone" we find personal names which have a more general distribution as well as names which appear to be peculiar to this particular region. The elements involved are Cumbrian, Gaelic, Anglian, Scandinavian, and French, a mixture characteristic of this northern region. It is obviously otherwise when one turns to the southeast. Here the OE system,

---

[52]For Lincolnshire and Yorkshire examples, see Fellows Jensen, *Scandinavian Personal Names*, pp. 325–27.

[53]Cf. Fran Colman, "The Name-Element *Æðel-* and Related Problems," *Notes and Queries* 28 (1981), 295–301.

[54]Cf. Fellows Jensen, *Scandinavian Personal Names*, pp. 204–06. For the use of the name in medieval Lancashire, see John Insley, "The Names of the Tenants of the Bishop of Ely in 1251: A Conflict of Onomastic Systems," *Ortnamnssällskapets i Uppsala Årsskrift* (1985), 58–78, at pp. 66–67.

[55]See Insley, "Some Scandinavian Personal Names," p. 28, and the works cited there.

[56]Armstrong et al., *Place-Names of Cumberland* 1:207–08.

with subsidiary Sc and Continental elements, defines the onomastic pattern of the latter part of the eleventh century. Celtic elements, with the exception of Breton names introduced after the Conquest by such men as Tihel of Helion Bumpstead (Essex),[57] are completely lacking. As an example of the anthroponymic situation in the Southeast at the end of the eleventh century, we can take the list of Colchester burgesses of 1086 recorded by Little Domesday.[58] The majority of the names in this list are OE dithematic names. In keeping with the general tendency of the late OE period, the number of different first elements is restricted. The following can be described as still productive: ME *Al-* < OE *Ælf-* or *Æðel-*; OE *Ælf-*; OE *Ēad-*; OE *God-*; OE *Gold-*; OE *Lēof-*; OE *Wulf-*. These first elements encompass the bulk of the OE first elements found in Colchester in 1086. In addition, we find the following:[59] OE *Æsc-*, in *Ascere* < OE *Æschere*; ME *Ail-* < OE *Æðel-*, in *Ailbriest* < OE *Æðelbeorht*; OE *Beohrt-*, late OE *Briht-*, in *Brictricus* (2x) < OE *Beorhtrīc* and *Brictuuinus* < OE *Beorhtwine*; OE *Blæc-*, in *Blacstan* (3x) < OE **Blæcstān*; OE *Brūn-* in *Brungarus* < OE *Brūngār*, *Brunloc* < OE **Brūnlocc*,[60] *Brumman* < OE *Brūnmann*, and *Brunuuinus* (2x) < OE *Brūnwine*; OE *Dēor-*, in *Deremanus* < OE *Dēormann*; OE *Here-*, in *Herstan* < OE *Herestān*; OE *Lēod-*, in *Ledmarus* < OE *Lēodmǣr*; OE *Man(n)-*, in *Manstan* (2x) < OE **Manstān*, *Mansune* (2x) < OE *Mansunu*,

---

[57]For Bretons in post-Conquest England, see Sir Frank Stenton, *The First Century of English Feudalism, 1066–1166*, 2nd ed. (Oxford, 1961), pp. 25–28. For Helion Bumpstead, see P. H. Reaney, *The Place-Names of Essex*, English Place-Name Society 12 (1935), pp. 508–09.

[58]DB II, fols. 104a–106a; *Domesday Book, 32: Essex*, ed. Alexander Rumble (Chichester, 1983), B3.

[59]The following OE dithematic personal names from the Colchester list have also been examined by Olof von Feilitzen, "Some Unrecorded Old and Middle English Personal Names," *Namn och Bygd* 33 (1945), 69–98: *Æschere*; **Blæcstān*; **Godflǣd*; **Goldhere*; **Goldrīc*; **Ordgēat*; **Stānburh*; **Tūnrīc*. In addition, the following have been dealt with by P. H. Reaney, "Notes on the Survival of Old English Personal Names in Middle English," *Studier i modern språkvetenskap* 18 (1953), 84–112: *Godsunu*; *Herestān*; *Lēofweald*; *Manwine*. Finally, see von Feilitzen, *Pre-Conquest Personal Names* for the following: **Brūnlocc*; *Goldstān*; **Mansunu*; **Sǣgār*.

[60]This name is morphologically identical with normal dithematic names in *Brūn-*. It is not, however, a true dithematic name of the traditional sort, but, as is shown by von Feilitzen, *Pre-Conquest Personal Names*, p. 210, it is an original byname formed from OE *brūn* "brown" and OE *locc* m. "hair, curl."

and *Manuuinus* (7x), *Manuinus* < OE *Manwine; OE *Ord-*, in *Orietus*[61] < OE *Ordgēat and *Orlaf* < OE *Ordlāf*; OE *Ōs-*, in *Osiet* < OE *Ōsgēat; OE *Sǣ-*, in *Sagarus* < OE *Sǣgār, *Salware* < OE *Sǣwaru* (fem.), *Sauuart* < OE *Sǣweard*, and *Saulf* < OE *Sǣwulf*; OE *Sige-*, in *Siricus* < OE *Sigerīc* and *Siuuardus* (2x) < OE *Sigeweard*;[62] OE *Stān-*, in *Stamburc* < OE *Stānburh (fem.)[63] and *Stanart*, *Stanhert* < OE *Stānheard*; OE *Tūn-*, in *Tunric* < OE *Tūnrīc; OE *Wine-*, in *Winemerus* < OE *Winemǣr*.[64]

The Colchester list shows the OE dithematic system to be largely intact, albeit in a process of strong concentration. As a corollary, we still find examples of OE monothematic personal names here. These are as follows:[65] *Berda* < OE *Bearda < OE *beard* m. "beard"; *Best*, an original byname belonging either to OE *bæst* m./n. "inner bark of trees, bast" or OE *bēost* m. "beestings, the first milk of a cow after calving";[66] *Chentinc* < OE *Centing, probably a late OE hypocoristic form of OE *Centwine*;[67] *Dela* < OE

---

[61]The MS form should be read as *Orietur*. This is quite clearly a mistake for *Orietus*, resulting from the scribe having mistakenly used the *-ur* contraction instead of the correct *-us* contraction.

[62]ODan *Sighwarth* is also theoretically possible as the etymon of *Siuuardus*. Cf. the discussion by von Feilitzen, *Pre-Conquest Personal Names*, pp. 361–63, esp. p. 363.

[63]Von Feilitzen's suggestion (*Pre-Conquest Personal Names*, p. 371 n. 4) that the Colchester form *Stamburc* may stand for ON *Steinbjǫrg* is unnecessary. Though he cites this reference in his article of 1945, it is there significant that he groups the form to the OE etymon without any further comment ("Some Unrecorded Old and Middle English Personal Names," p. 89).

[64]A possible alternative etymon is the CG personal name *Winemar*, for which see Thorvald Forssner, *Continental-Germanic Personal Names in England in Old and Middle English Times* (Uppsala, 1916), p. 258.

[65]The following OE monothematic personal names from the Colchester list are examined by von Feilitzen, "Some Unrecorded Old and Middle English Personal Names": *Bearda; *Centing; *Frēond; **Hnot(t)*; *Stūting. In addition, see Olof von Feilitzen, "Some Old English Uncompounded Personal Names and Bynames," *Studia Neophilologica* 40 (1968), 5–16, for the names *Best* and *Stan*. The Colchester examples of OE *Golding, *Sprot*, and *Wicga* are dealt with by von Feilitzen, *Pre-Conquest Personal Names*, pp. 273 (*Golding), 371 n. 1 (*Sprot*), 412 (*Wicga*).

[66]Von Feilitzen, "Some Old English Uncompounded Personal Names and Bynames," p. 7. *Domesday Book, 32: Essex*, B3a note, s.n. BEST, also includes the possibility that we may be concerned here with an early example of the ME surname *Best(e)* from OFr *beste* "beast."

[67]Von Feilitzen, "Some Unrecorded Old and Middle English Personal Names," p. 76, took OE *Centing to be an original byname "man of Kent."

Dealla, either an original byname belonging to OE *deall* "proud, exulting, bold, renowned" or a hypocoristic form of such a name as OE *Dealwine*;[68] *Frent* < OE **Frēond* < OE *frēond* m. "friend, relative"; *Goda* (5x) < OE *Goda*, a hypocoristic form of names in *God-*; *Godincus* (2x), *Godinc* < OE *Goding*, a late OE hypocoristic form of names in *God-*; *Goldinc* < OE **Golding,* a late OE hypocoristic form of names in *Gold-*; *Hunec* < OE **Hūnuc* or **Hunning*, hypocoristic forms of names in *Hūn-*;[69] *Not* < OE **Hnot(t)*, an original byname probably formed from OE *hnot,* ME *not* "short-haired, with closely cropped hair"; *Pic*, an original byname formed from OE *pīc* m. "point, pointed tool, pick, pickaxe," ME *pīk(e)* "spike, etc."; *Pote* < OE **Pota*, probably belonging to OE *potian*, ME *pōten* "to push something, to shove";[70] *Sprot* < OE *Sprot*, an original byname belonging to OE *sprott* m. "sprat" or OE *sprot(t)* n. "sprout, twig; peg"; *Stan* < OE **Stān*, a hypocoristic form of late OE names in *Stān-*;[71] *Stotinc* < OE **Stūting*, a diminutive in *-ing* of an original byname belonging to OE *stūt* m. "gnat";[72] *Tate* < OE *Tāta* (masc.) or OE *Tǣte* (fem.), hypocoristic forms of names in *Tāt-*; *Wicga* < OE *Wicga*, a name belonging to OE *wicg* n. "horse" rather than to OE *wicga* m. "insect, beetle."

As one would expect in a region bordering on an area of Sc settlement and influence like East Anglia, Sc personal names are not infrequent in Essex. This is fully borne out by the Colchester list, where we find the fol-

---

[68]See Mats Redin, *Studies on Uncompounded Personal Names in Old English* (Uppsala, 1919), p. 75; cf. also Olof von Feilitzen and Christopher Blunt, "Personal Names on the Coinage of Edgar," in *England before the Conquest: Studies in Primary Sources Presented to Dorothy Whitelock*, ed. Peter Clemoes and Kathleen Hughes (Cambridge, 1971), 183–214, at pp. 192–93.

[69]The editor of *Domesday Book, 32: Essex* interprets the form as reflecting **Hunning* (B3a note, s.n. *HUNNING*).

[70]See *Domesday Book, 32: Essex*, B3a note, s.n. *POTE.*

[71]For the theoretical possibility that this form might alternatively reflect an anglicized form of ODan *Stēn*, cf. von Feilitzen, "Some Old English Uncompounded Personal Names and Bynames," p. 11.

[72]Von Feilitzen, "Some Unrecorded Old and Middle English Personal Names," p. 89, suggested that this form might alternatively represent an OE **Stoting* from OE *stot* m. "a kind of horse."

lowing Sc names: *Cullinc* < ON *Kollungr*;[73] *Gothugo* < AScand **Gōdhugi*;[74] *Grimolf* < ON *Grímólfr*; *Hacon* < ON *Hákun, -kon*; *Osgot* < AScand *Ōsgot* < ON *Ásgautr*; *Sæuuele* < AScand **Sǣfugl*; *Sacrimus, Sagrim* < ON **Sǣgrímr*; *Sueno* < ON *Sveinn*; *Suertinc* < ON *Svertingr*; *Suertlincus* < AScand **Swertling*;[75] *Touius* < ODan *Tōvi*; *Turchillus* < ODan *Þurkil*; *Turstanus* < AScand *Þurstān* < ON *Þorsteinn*; *Westan* < ON *Vésteinn*.[76]

Although the Continental element was clearly visible at Colchester in 1086, it was still of far less importance than the native English element. In addition to the ubiquitous French personal names *Gau(l)tier* (OCFr) < (West) Frankish *Walthari(us)*, *Ra(o)ul* < (West) Frankish *Rādulf(us)*, *Roger* < (West) Frankish *(H)rôdgêr(us)*, and *Will(i)aume* (ONFr) < (West) Frankish *Willihelm(us)*, which are represented by the normalized scribal forms *Galt[erus]*, *Rad[ulfus]* (Pinel), *Rogerius*, and *Will[elmus]* (Peccatum), we find the following Continental names: *Ainolf*, corresponding to OSax *Einulf*; *Blancus*, an original byname formed from OFr *blanc* "white, fair";[77] *Colemanus,* corresponding to OHG *Col(o)man*; *Elebolt,* corresponding to (West) Frankish *Erlebold*;[78] *Filieman*, corresponding to (West) Frankish

---

[73]Note, however, that Gösta Tengvik, *Old English Bynames*, NG 4 (Uppsala, 1938), pp. 141–42, preferred to regard English forms in *Colling, Culling* as being of native rather than of Sc origin.

[74]*Gothugo* is wrongly interpreted by the editor of *Domesday Book, 32: Essex*, B3a note, s.n. *GOT HUGH*, as a patronymic formation in which ON *Gautr* is compounded with CG *Hugo* or Sc *Hughi*, the second component then having the function of a patronymic byname, hence "*Gautr* son of *Hugo/Hughi*." P. H. Reaney, *A Dictionary of British Surnames*, 2nd ed. with corrections and additions by R. M. Wilson (London, 1976), pp. 150–51, s.n. *Goodhew*, is nearer to the correct etymology with his interpretation of the form as belonging to an unrecorded Sc **Guð(h)ugi*. Reaney quite rightly interpreted the name as an original byname contrasting with the Sc *Ill(h)ugi* < **illhugi* "evil-minded." Reaney's forms, which include the one from Colchester, show quite clearly, however, that the first component of the name is *God-* < OE *gōd* "good, favorable, etc.," and the base is, therefore, an AScand hybrid **Gōdhugi*.

[75]Von Feilitzen, *Pre-Conquest Personal Names*, p. 379, gives the base as an unrecorded ON **Svartlingr* and, somewhat implausibly, adds that in some cases derivation from OE *swertling* "titlark?, warbler?" might perhaps also be considered.

[76]The editor of *Domesday Book, 32: Essex*, B3a note, s.n. *WIGSTAN*, wrongly interprets *Westan* as a reflex of OE *Wīgstān*.

[77]See Reaney, *Dictionary of British Surnames*, p. 37, s.n. *Blanc*.

[78]The editor of *Domesday Book, 32: Essex*, B3a note, s.n. *AETHELBALD*, wrongly assigns this form to OE *Æðelbeald*.

Filiman;[79] *Herdedunus* (scribal error for *Herdechinus*, reflecting MDu *Hardekin*);[80] *Rosellus*, an original byname formed from OFr *rossel* "red-faced, ruddy";[81] *Sunegot*, reflecting a West Frankish **Sunegaud(us)*; *Tescho*, corresponding to German *Thieziko*, a diminutive of names containing Germanic **Þeudō-* (OHG *Diot-*, OSax *Thiad-*, etc.) formed with the *-k* suffix; cf. such forms as *T(h)icekin*, *Thizelinus*, etc., noted in the Low Countries.[82]

The investigation of the regional distinctions in the English personal nomenclature of the late OE and early ME periods is still in its infancy. That is not to say that good regional studies do not exist—on the contrary, much of the best recent work has taken the form of regional investigations. What is lacking, however, is a systematic attempt to work out the different onomastic zones operative within the English-speaking area in the medieval period. Surveys of specific types of personal names found over the area of one or two counties provide us with an essential corpus of material, but they do not go far enough to create the systematic framework necessary for establishing regional criteria. Regional studies, whether based on the old county divisions of the period before the administrative reform of 1974 or on the region covered by a particular document, e.g., an assize roll or a monastic cartulary, must survey all the names within the region and not just those belonging to a specific type. In view of the wealth of material available, a certain setting of chronological limits is inevitable, though this should not be too narrow. Narrow chronological limits tend to give a deceptively static picture of an anthroponymic situation; they allow one to forget that anthroponymic systems are essentially dynamic and subject to continual change and innovation. The study of the regional aspects of anthroponymy must encompass the changes experienced within the onomastic system as

---

[79]See *Domesday Book, 32: Essex*, B3a note, s.n. *FILIMAN*.

[80]See *Domesday Book, 32: Essex*, B3a note, s.n. *HARDEKIN*. For a Flemish example of *Hardekin* from the first half of the thirteenth century, see C. Tavernier-Vereecken, *Gentse Naamkunde van ca. 1000 tot 1253* (Brussels, 1968), p. 17. Other English examples from Domesday Book are listed by von Feilitzen, *Pre-Conquest Personal Names*, p. 286.

[81]*Domesday Book, 32: Essex*, B3a note, s.n. ROSSELL.

[82]Ibid., s.n. *TESCO*. For eleventh- and twelfth-century examples of *Thiediko* from Westphalia, see Wilhelm Schlaug, *Studien zu den altsächsischen Personennamen des 11. und 12. Jahrhunderts*, Lunder Germanistische Forschungen 30 (Lund, 1955), p. 187. For Flemish examples of *T(h)icekin, Thizelinus*, etc., see Tavernier-Vereecken, *Gentse Naamkunde*, p. 140.

a whole. Obviously, this must also be linked to the study of the history of the language and be related to the development of dialect zones. Personal names cannot be viewed in sociological isolation; the historical background to onomastic change and the differences in the *modus* of such change in various social groupings must be analyzed in detail. It is only by using all the different types of evidence available that a comprehensive picture of the anthroponymic structure of England in this, or, for that matter, any other period, can be obtained.

ABBREVIATIONS

Angl	Anglian
Cockersand	*The Chartulary of Cockersand Abbey of the Premonstratensian Order*, ed. William Farrer, Chetham Society, n.s. 38–40, 43, 56–57, 64 (Manchester, 1898–1909); bracketed figures after the date of the entry indicate the date of the MS cited.
DB	*Domesday-Book, seu Liber Censualis Willelmi Primi Regis Angliæ*, ed. Abraham Farley and Henry Ellis, 4 vols. (London, 1783–1816).
Furness II	*The Coucher Book of Furness Abbey*, 2, ed. John Brownbill, Chetham Society, n.s. 74, 76, 78 (Manchester, 1915–19).
Hoghton	J. H. Lumby, *A Calendar of the Deeds and Papers in the Possession of Sir James de Hoghton, Bart., of Hoghton Tower, Lancashire*, Lancashire and Cheshire Record Society 88 (1936).
MHG	Middle High German
P NS	Pipe Roll Society, n.s. (London, 1925–).
RRS I	*Regesta Regum Scottorum*, 1: *The Acts of Malcolm IV, King of Scots, 1153–65*, ed. G. W. S. Barrow (Edinburgh, 1960).
RRS II	*Regesta Regum Scottorum*, 2: *The Acts of William I, King of Scots, 1165–1214*, ed. G. W. S. Barrow with the collaboration of W. W. Scott (Edinburgh, 1971).
s.n.	*sub nomine*

COMPARING HISTORIC NAME COMMUNITIES IN WALES: SOME APPROACHES AND CONSIDERATIONS

Heather Jones

1.0 INTRODUCTION

In any individual case, the choice of a name[1] for a child is done for particular and idiosyncratic reasons, but on the level of the community, name
choice and usage behave in systematic ways that can be measured, compared, and used as tools for examining other phenomena.[2] The social and
political conditions in Wales in the medieval and early modern periods provide a fertile ground for studying how naming practices and the available
name pool can shift in response to immigration, cultural influences, and

---

[1]For the sake of conciseness, *name* in this article should be understood to mean "given
name" or "forename," unless otherwise noted. The spellings of all actual names have been
normalized.

[2]See, e.g., Cecily Clark, "Women's Names in Post-Conquest England: Observations and
Speculations," *Speculum* 53 (1978), 223–51 (repr. above, pp. 65–102); Susan L. Norton,
"The Vital Question: Are Reconstituted Families Representative of the General Population,"
in *Genealogical Demography*, ed. Bennett Dyke and Warren T. Morrill (Academic Press,
1980), pp. 11–22; Kenneth M. Weiss, David L. Rossmann, Ranajit Chakraborty, and Susan
L. Norton, "Wherefore Art Thou, Romio? Name Frequency Patterns and Their Use in Automated Genealogy Assembly," in *Genealogical Demography*, pp. 41–61; Dave Postles, "The
Distinction of Gender? Women's Names in Thirteenth-Century England," *Nomina* 19
(1996), 79–89.

simple changes in fashion. The scarcity and frequently the small size of the available data-sets, however, can make it difficult to make more than anecdotal observations. For example, one will often encounter references to a drastic decrease in the size of the Welsh name pool (i.e., the number of different names in circulation) between the early medieval and early modern periods,[3] but this change can be hard to demonstrate in a rigorous, mathematical fashion. For example, how does one compare name frequency in a list of early saints, drawn from several centuries and the entirety of Wales, with that in a list of landholders in a particular village in a particular year?

In order to say useful things about overall changes or comparisons in naming practices, one must think like a statistician. However, many of the types of available data do not lend themselves well to strict statistical testing. Rather than directly applying statistical formulas to the questions raised, this essay tries to identify the sorts of questions that could, in theory, be addressed in a more rigorous fashion, and to get a sense of how useful such an approach could be. From this, it should be understood that when I use terms such as *confidence level* in the present work, they are intended with their everyday sense, and not as technical terms.

What are some of the factors we might want to compare between populations? The most obvious would seem to be which specific names were in use. Clearly, even if the statistical attributes of two name populations are identical, if the actual names involved are different, then we are dealing with distinct populations. The masculine and feminine names of a single population might be expected to show this type of relationship. Another factor related to the specific names would be their relative popularity. Apart from specific names, we might want to compare the size of the name pool: the number of different names available in use. We may also be interested in the skewing of popularity: the degree to which the more popular names dominate the name pool. In a case such as medieval Wales, where more than one naming tradition is present, we are also interested in the presence of "foreign" names—either representing the presence of an immigrant community or the introduction of the names into the existing population. (The two processes can be hard to distinguish for a particular record.) Going back to a previous notion, we may also be interested to know whether the masculine and feminine names in a population behave simi-

---

[3]For example, Prys Morgan, "The Rise of Welsh Hereditary Surnames," *Nomina* 10 (1986), 121–35; Gerald Morgan, "Naming Welsh Women," *Nomina* 18 (1995), 119–39.

larly, or whether there are more differences between them than the specific names involved.[4]

A study of the nature of, and changes in, the name pool and naming practices in historic Welsh records immediately brings up the problem of how one compares populations of extremely variable size and nature. But even with samples of equivalent size, there may be small-sample problems if random variation in the particular population being studied overwhelms any statistical trends that are being measured.[5] So a question of equal importance to the one of differently-sized data-sets is: what is the smallest population size that is reasonably representative of the whole, or at least that avoids the distortion of small-sample effects? Furthermore, does this optimum size differ depending on the statistic being studied? Can such factors as the size of the name pool and the skewing of popularity be described in terms of mathematical formulae that would make comparisons easier?

The ideal data for studying these questions would be a relatively large sample, taken randomly with respect to the names (and cultural background) of their bearers within the particular population, with each individual appearing only once. The available records that best fulfill these conditions are tax rolls (such as the lay subsidy records of 1292–93) and, to a lesser extent, tenantry surveys (such as the Extent of Bromfield and Yale of 1315).

Two assumptions must be made about records such as this that need to be questioned. The first is that the individuals appearing in the record are representative of the entire population. For example, in the case of a property-based tax roll, that property ownership does not select for or against particular names or naming practices.[6] In one important respect, this is clearly untrue. All the records used in this study preferentially select men's names over women's names by an order of magnitude. While this can be corrected for by analyzing men's and women's names separately, it has consequences for the usefulness of the feminine data (which, as noted, cannot be assumed to behave similarly to the masculine data, even apart from the question of

---

[4]Evidence against a default assumption of similarity in English contexts can be found in Clark, "Women's Names in Post-Conquest England," and Postles, "The Distinction of Gender?"

[5]Clark, "Women's Names in Post-Conquest England," and Norton, "The Vital Question," discuss small-sample problems in trying to identify trends.

[6]Morgan, "Naming Welsh Women," discusses this problem, as well as the difficulties posed by duplicate references in court records.

the specific names in use). A type of record that, by its nature, recorded masculine and feminine names equally would be preferable, but in most cases is not available. (An example of a record that approaches this standard would be the seventeenth-century birth, marriage, and death records in *Y Cwtta Cyfarwydd*,[7] but I have not yet had a chance to process these data.)

There is also the question of whether the type of record affects the "name community" it represents (by "name community" I mean a relatively homogeneous population using the same name pool in the same ways). A tax roll and a record of lawsuits may sample distinctly different subsets of the population. Do these subsets use different naming practices? An extreme example, in the historic Welsh context, might be the Anglesey Submissions of 1406, which select for the ethnically Welsh population in targeting supporters of Owein Glyndwr,[8] as compared with the lists of burgesses from Cardiff and Aberystwyth ca. 1300, where political policy, in theory, discouraged Welsh settlement.[9] Clearly, in making claims about what name community a document represents, one must be aware of which factors in that document affect a name's appearance there.

The second assumption made, at least for the sources used in the developmental part of this paper, is that the order in which names appear in the document (and hence, the nature of the subsets that are analyzed) is random with respect to the names. In rare cases, this may not be the case (as in the 1292–93 lay subsidy data from Monmouth, where names of Welsh origin appear disproportionately in the second half of the list) but because the basis of the ordering is not recoverable, this assumption is necessary. This problem could be overcome by choosing test subsets via an automated randomization process (which would be necessary for a more formal analysis in any case), but the current explorations are based on the above assumption. The assumption is irrelevant when whole populations are compared, as in Section 5.0 below.

---

[7]Thomas Rowlands, *Y Cwtta Cyfarwydd: The Chronicle Written by the Famous Clarke Peter Roberts, Notary Public, for the Years 1607–1646, with an Appendix from the Register Notebook of Thomas Rowlands, Vicar-Choral of St Asaph, for the Years 1595–1607 and 1646–1653* (London, 1883).

[8]Glyn Roberts, "The Anglesey Submissions of 1406," *Bulletin of the Board of Celtic Studies* 15 (1952), 39–61; R. R. Davies, *The Revolt of Owain Glyndowr* (Oxford, 1995), p. 306.

[9]I. J. Sanders, "The Boroughs of Aberystwyth and Cardigan in the Early Fourteenth Century," *Bulletin of the Board of Celtic Studies* 15 (1954), 282–92.

As noted above, in addition to the tax-roll type of record, a common source of names on an anecdotal level is records of law courts and similar legal proceedings. For statistical studies, these introduce the additional problem of multiple mentions of the same individual. Often these duplicates can be identified easily (e.g., when an individual is identified as "the same" or "the aforementioned" in the course of a single entry). In other cases the identification may be more difficult, depending on assumptions about the coincidence of complete name structures between separate individuals and about the consistency with which a particular individual will be identified. However, assuming that such duplicates can be identified at an acceptable level, the question can be addressed of how similarly an unedited record (with duplicates) behaves compared to a record with no duplicates. If the behavior is similar enough, then the unedited record could be used in comparisons.

2.0 METHODS AND SOURCES

The data used in this paper are taken from published legal records (tax rolls, court records, etc.) from the thirteenth through the sixteenth centuries in Wales. (These are listed in the Appendix below.) From each record, I have defined sample populations as the smallest geographically determined subset that could be identified from the published information, although the size of this division varies depending on the source (and editorial practices). Throughout, I will use *population* to describe the complete set of data from a source (and, by implication, the actual larger population it is believed to represent) and *sample* to describe a subset of the population. The developmental work here has been done only on populations of men's names from sources where the original order of the names has been preserved. For documents in which an individual's name may appear more than once, only the edited, non-duplicate version has been used. In order to consider the question of the optimum sample size for analysis, each population has been sampled in subsets of successive powers of two, with each sample taken from the beginning of the population. (That is, each subsequent sample includes the previous one, and an equal amount of material following it.) For reasons that will become clear, only populations equal to or greater than $N = 32$ have been used for developmental work. When all these selection factors are considered, forty-four populations are available. The largest number of them come from northern Wales, with a smaller group from the extreme Southeast and a single population from the Southwest.

For each statistic of interest, the purpose will be to identify the smallest sample that will reflect or predict the behavior of the whole population with an acceptable level of accuracy, to identify a numeric way of comparing the statistic between populations of different sizes, and to determine what magnitude of difference can be considered significant. For the first statistic, the process and reasoning is presented in detail. For other statistics, a more abbreviated version is given.

3.0 DEVELOPING THE STATISTICS

3.1 PROPORTION OF "FOREIGN" NAMES

The simplest factor that can illustrate the approach I will be using here is the proportion of "foreign" names in a population. The definition of a particular name in a record as "Welsh" or "foreign" is not at all straightforward,[10] and different criteria may be applied for different purposes. The foreign category can include names with a wide variety of histories: names such as *Addaf* (Adam) that were adopted at a fairly early period (as shown by the phonological changes), names such as *Gwilym* (William) adopted in the post-Conquest period but "naturalized" to some extent in form, post-Conquest names that show no "naturalization" but are clearly being used by the ethnically Welsh population, and names of the non-Welsh population resident in Wales. In addition, the recorded form of a name may be normalized in a way that obscures which category it belongs to (e.g., the use of *Johannes* versus *Ieuan*) or that obscures the ethnicity of the bearer (e.g., *Johannes filius Philipi* versus *Ieuan ap Philip*). Since the amount of normalization or latinization may differ greatly between documents, the only statistic that can be compared consistently is the linguistic origin of the names— however strange it may seem to count *Dafydd* as a "foreign" name in Wales. This will provide a guide to the degree to which names that are not linguistically Welsh have entered a particular population, but not to the fine distinctions of how and when those entries occurred.

The goal is to determine what sample size will reliably reflect the nature of the overall population. Table 1 (see tables beginning on p. 249) and Figure 1 show the way in which small-sample effects level out with in-

---

[10]See Morgan, "Naming Welsh Women," for an extensive discussion of the topic.

creasing sample size. Random variation ensures that even with very large subsets, the sample result will not be precisely the same as for the whole population, so an acceptable level of closeness must be determined. From an examination of graphs similar to Figure 1, the initial approximation is that populations under eight will show significant small-sample errors. But since a larger sample is needed to which to compare the subset, only populations of sixteen or larger would be useful for identifying the optimum size. I have gone further than this in the developmental work, and only used populations in which the comparison sample is at least four times the size of the sample being evaluated. If the optimum sample is, in fact, smaller than this, it will be apparent in the larger populations too. Table 2 shows the percentage of foreign names for each sample size in these populations. Table 3 shows the difference between the percent foreign for the largest available sample and the smaller samples.

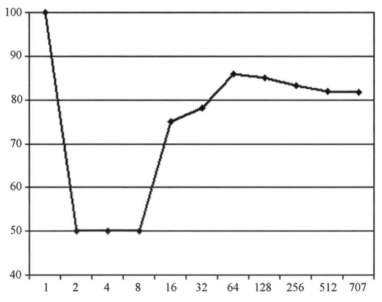

Figure 1. Percent foreign vs. N.

One can judge how well a sample size reflects the larger population by setting a cutoff for this difference and determining what proportion of sample differences fall within the cutoff. Table 4 shows the results for three possible cutoffs: 5%, 10%, and 15%. (Since the range of values for the statistic is from 0% to 100%, being able to identify a sample as falling within ±15% of the whole population is still useful. For some statistics considered later in this paper, where the range of values is much smaller, the acceptable range of variation would also need to be smaller.)

Since the size of the optimum sample is unknown, it makes sense to begin the analysis by looking at the largest populations ($N > 256$). Within this group, if a sample size of $N = 16$ is examined, 100% of the samples fall within range for the 15% cutoff, 71% for the 10% cutoff, and 57% for the 5% cutoff. Since an accuracy of ±15% provides useful information for this statistic, this could be acceptable as an optimum sample size. At a sample size of $N = 32$, the accuracy is considerably less at the two lower cutoffs, suggesting that the good results at $N = 16$ may be partly by chance. The samples at $N = 64$ show only minor improvement over $N = 16$. Based on these results, one could hypothesize a smallest optimum sample of $N = 16$, with the results most useful for an accuracy of ±15%. However, if this is a valid sample size, then there should be similar results for the next two size-ranks of populations. If all populations of $N > 128$ are considered, the accuracy at $N = 16$ is fairly comparable, slightly better or worse for different accuracy levels. If all populations of $N > 64$ are considered, then the accuracy is generally worse. This suggests that $N = 16$ may not be as valid a sample size as first appeared. If, instead, a sample of $N = 32$ is considered, then the populations at $N > 128$ are as accurate or more so than the larger group alone. The populations at $N > 64$ are excluded from consideration by the requirement that the comparison sample be at least four times the test sample.

The process above gives a reasonable first approximation for an optimum sample size and what levels of accuracy and precision can be expected from this statistic. Populations smaller than thirty-two can be considered too unreliable for use. Samples at or above the optimum size can be considered distinct populations with a high level of confidence if they differ by thirty percentage points or more (twice the 15% cutoff), and with somewhat less confidence, but still what is probably an acceptable level, if they differ by twenty percentage points or more. And while it has been useful to work through the process on an intuitive level, this sort of straightforward, one-variable measurement is exactly the sort that simple statistical tests are designed for. In combination with an automated procedure for generating random sub-samples, it would be easy to create a test that gave a more formal answer to the question of whether two populations differ in their content of foreign names.

3.2 SIZE AND SHAPE OF THE NAME POOL

Three factors together describe the general size and shape of the name pool: the popularity of the most common name(s), the overall skewing toward the most popular names, and the number of names in circulation in the population.[11] Before looking at actual populations, it makes sense to consider some hypothetical population models and how these statistics would work in them. The simplest model is a population in which each individual is uniquely identified. Each name appears only once. The early medieval saints' names in Morgan (1995) resemble this pattern, although it is difficult to know whether it represents an actual naming practice or an artifact of the data-survival process. Here, the most popular name does not represent a set percentage of the population; rather it will vary inversely with the size of the sample. There is no skewing toward the most popular names, because there are no "most popular names." In a particular sample, a linear plot of the top x most popular names versus the percentage of names they represent will be a straight line. The size of the name pool for the entire population is, in theory, infinite, but the size for any particular sample is easily calculated since it is identical to the size of the sample. As with the preceding statistic, it will be linear when plotted on a linear graph.

At what might be the opposite end of the scale, consider a pyramid-shaped model, where there are relatively few popular names but they are significantly more popular than the others. A very simple version of this would be a model in which each higher rank of names is twice as popular as the preceding rank but with half as many different names (e.g., one name with sixteen instances, two with eight, four with four, etc.). In a population like this the percentage represented by the most popular name will remain constant, no matter what the sample size, a plot of the top x most popular names versus the percentage of the total they represent will be linear if both are plotted on a logarithmic scale. The size of the name pool can be calculated from the sample size by a fairly complex formula, but the result is, in effect, linear on a linear graph.

Actual populations in Welsh records fall somewhere between these two, with a less regular progression of popularity and practical limits on the po-

---

[11]Morgan, "Naming Welsh Women," discusses similar factors in a Welsh context without the statistical analysis; Weiss et al., "Wherefore Art Thou, Romio," take a statistical approach to similar questions, although to a different end.

tential maximum size of the name pool that do not affect the models. What emerges is that the popularity of the top name does stabilize at a fixed proportion (in a large enough sample), the skewing of the most popular group of names is fairly linear when the log of x is plotted against the percentage represented by the x most popular names (on a linear scale), and the relationship between the size of the sample and the size of the name pool is complicated and not entirely linear in any standard plot, although certain useful approximations can be made.

The general questions being asked here have parallels in other fields, for example, the variety and distribution of vocabulary in a text, or the number and frequency of biological species in an environment. In each case, questions arise concerning the optimum sample size and how to compare results from samples of different sizes. A variety of attempts have been made in both fields to develop a single statistic that would describe both variety and distribution, but both the nature and the usefulness of such a formula are still debated.[12] I have chosen to describe the different factors separately rather than trying to develop a single formula.

3.2.1 *Percentage of most popular name(s).* The most straightforward of these three statistics is the popularity of the most common name. Here we are not concerned with whether the most popular name in the sample is identical to that of the entire population, but rather with the relative distribution. Table 5 shows the raw data for this statistic for a fairly typical population.

Table 6 shows the populations greater than thirty-two with the percentage given for the overall most popular name in each of the usual sample subsets of eight or more. The table also shows the range of results at each sample size. To determine whether a sample size is representative, the statistic is noted as being within five or ten percentage points of the statistic for the entire population. (I have not included a 15% cutoff due to the smaller range of results for this statistic.) The results of this test are found in Table 7, which shows the percentage of populations that fulfill the con-

---

[12]R. M. Frumkina, "The Application of Statistical Methods in Linguistic Research," in *Exact Methods in Linguistic Research*, ed. O. S. Akhmanova et al. (Univ. of California Press, 1963), pp. 96–118; Stuart H. Hurlbert, "The Nonconcept of Species Diversity: A Critique and Alternative Parameters," *Ecology* 52 (1971), 577–86; Anne E. Magurran, *Ecological Diversity and Its Measurement* (Princeton University Press, 1988); G. Udny Yule, *The Statistical Study of Literary Vocabulary* (Cambridge, 1944).

dition at a particular sample size. As usual, the first approximation comes from the largest populations ($N > 256$).

Using the ±10% limit, 100% of the populations fulfill the condition at $N = 64$, and results for smaller samples are fairly consistent around 75–80% for any size from $N = 8$ to $N = 32$. Clearly, $N = 64$ would be an ideal choice for a sample limit for this cutoff, although smaller samples may be acceptable with less confidence in the results. Using the ±5% limit, the best results occur at $N = 128$. But this presents practical problems. Only one population here has a comparison sample four times this size, and only eleven fall above it at all. The first means that the acceptability of a $N = 128$ sample size cannot be confirmed with any confidence, and the second means that setting such a requirement would interfere with the usefulness of the test. At $N = 64$ the confidence level is only around 75–80% (depending on what size population is considered) and this may still be usable. On the other hand, in the present data, a precision of ±10% in samples of sixty-four or larger demonstrates nothing useful: the entire range for this statistic is less than twenty percentage points, so no two populations could be shown to behave differently. Rather than this being a flaw in the statistic, it may simply be a testament to the remarkable consistency of Welsh practice with respect to this factor during the period studied, a possibility explored further in Section 3.2.4.

A similar analysis of the two most popular names taken together produces a more practical result. As Table 8 shows in summary, a ±10% cutoff at $N = 64$ has a fairly acceptable confidence level (around 90%) and as the range of results at this size is thirty percentage points, there is a fair confidence that populations falling at opposite ends of the range represent distinct name communities with respect to this factor. Even though the confidence level is slightly less, the precision is more useful.

3.2.2 *Skewing*. The second factor related to the size and shape of the name pool is the skewing of the population toward the most popular names. The most common one or two names may be unusual stand-outs in a population in which other names are relatively equal (a low skew) or may be part of a more steady "pyramid of popularity" (a moderate skew) or may be part of a small number of names with relatively similar popularity that utterly dominate the population (a high skew). The simplest way to represent this is to chart the percentage of the total sample taken up by the x most popular names, versus x itself. This plot could, in theory, take a number of forms, as seen in the discussion of population models (Sect. 3.2), but in the actual populations under consideration here, such a plot tends to be linear when x is between two and eight (or sixteen, depending on the size of the population) if x is plotted on a logarithmic scale.

The tables and graph (Tables 9, 10, Fig. 2) for the 1406 data from the commote of Menai show what a fairly "well-behaved" population looks like. As a rule, names that appear only once in a sample are more likely to produce erroneous results, and the measurements that include these are shown in parentheses in Table 10. As the graph (Fig. 2) shows, samples at or below four are clearly unrepresentative, the one at eight is somewhat less so, and successive sample sizes behave nearly identically to the whole population. Not all populations are this straightforward, and some of the problems with determining an optimum sample size by eyeballing alone can be seen in a similar graph for the commote of Talebolion in the same source (Fig. 3) which appears to settle into a pattern at $N = 16$ but then shifts significantly at $N = 64$.

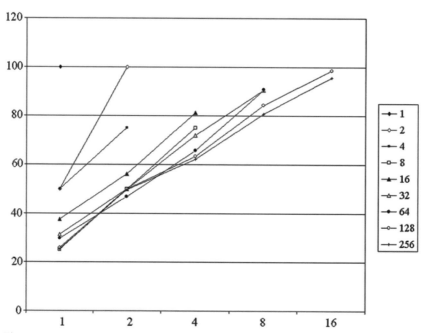

Figure 2. Skewing curve at all sample sizes (Menai 1406).

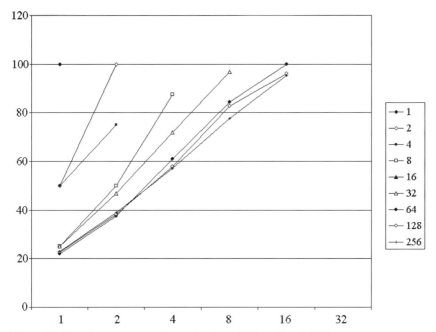

Figure 3. Skewing curve at all sample sizes (Talebolion 1406).

A means of quantifying this factor not only provides a number to use in comparisons but also one with which to identify the optimum sample size. The obvious quantification is the slope of the plot, taken from the most linear section. As seen in the preceding section, the percentage for the top two names produces a more useful statistic for identifying distinct behavior than that of the top name alone. And, as noted above, an x that includes one-item name listings will tend to produce more erratic results. As a general rule of thumb, populations above 128 will avoid this problem up to $x = 16$, those between 64 and 128 only to $x = 8$, and between 32 and 64 only to $x = 4$. Since the optimum minimum sample for the popularity statistics appears to be $N = 64$, the most reliable slope to calculate is between $x = 2$ and $x = 8$.

The slope is calculated as the difference between the percentages of the chosen name-sets divided by the difference between the logs of the magnitude of the name-sets (i.e., the number of names for which the percentage is taken). However, since only an index for comparison is required rather than the true slope of the line, and since the denominator is a constant, this formula can be simplified to the difference in percentage alone (i.e., the percentage of the total represented by names ranked 3 to 8).

Table 11 shows this skewing statistic for populations of 128 or greater, taken at $N = 32$, $N = 64$, and the largest available sample, as well as the difference between the skew at these points. There is relatively little drift between samples of adjacent sizes. The difference in skew between $N = 32$ and $N = 64$ is five or less in 88% of the populations, and the shifts between $N = 64$ and $N = 128$ are similarly small. For populations with a largest sample of 256 or greater, only 62% meet this condition, but for the whole set, 73% do. The confidence level is higher if a 10% cutoff is used (82% for all populations), but again the problem occurs that this sets the difference required for significance essentially identical to the range found for the statistic. Since larger sample sizes appear to be impractical, however, a smaller cutoff with a lower confidence level may be all that can be achieved. As with the statistic for the two most popular names, part of the difficulty in establishing a high-confidence test may simply be that all the populations studied are relatively consistent with respect to this factor.

3.2.3 *Size of the name pool.* The most difficult factor to measure, of those under discussion in this paper, is the comparative size of the name pool. Unlike the ecological sampling studies mentioned above, a sample of personal names cannot be arbitrarily large—even if perfect records were available, the number of names available for study is limited by the number of people in the population being studied, which often results in trying to compare small and large samples. Given the general distribution patterns involved, increasingly larger samples will net decreasingly smaller numbers of new names. Thus comparisons based simply on the average number of different names in a particular sample size will underestimate the variety in large populations and overestimate that of small populations.

An extreme case would be that of Roman *praenomina* in the first century CE. With approximately thirty different elements in use,[13] a sample of three hundred individuals might conceivably include all thirty. A sample of three thousand individuals would contain the same thirty. The first, at ten distinct names per hundred, appears more varied than the second at one distinct name per hundred, and yet both draw from exactly the same name pool.

---

[13]Stephen Wilson, *The Means of Naming: A Social and Cultural History of Personal Naming in Western Europe* (London, 1998), p. 5.

Anecdotal conclusions can be drawn when a larger sample contains fewer distinct names than a smaller one, given a difference greater than attributable to chance, but to interpret a larger sample with more distinct names we need a better system. Similarly, it is unclear how comparable are samples that are taken over different time periods. A sample taken over several generations (such as the genealogical material discussed in Morgan [1995]) during a period of significant change in name fashions will show more variation than a similarly sized sample from a single time point within that span. Clearly the most reliable comparisons would be based on limited timespans, and some formula must be developed to deal with samples of significantly different size.

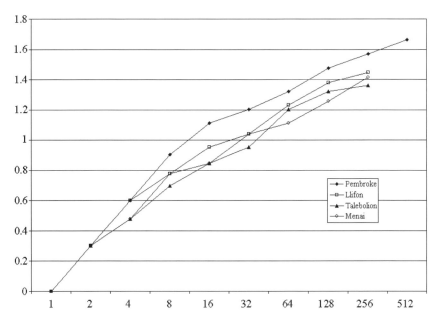

Figure 4. Size of name pool-log (*N*) vs. log (distinct names) for populations of 256 and over.

As a first approximation, the behavior of the name pool with increasing sample size can be seen in the raw data for Llifon (1406) in Table 12, and for this and several other sets of samples in Figure 4 with the log of the name pool plotted against the log of the sample size. The point at which the plot becomes roughly linear is the best guide to an optimum sample size for this factor, so the first approximation will be to look at populations with several samples larger than thirty-two. However, this does not identify a way to compare this statistic between populations of different sizes. Ideally, if there were an equation (using the pool and sample sizes) for which the linear portion of the graph were horizontal, then the intercept of this formula could provide the comparison statistic—one that would be identical no matter what size sample were used. My current methods of sampling have not identified a formula of this type (although this is the sort of question where automated random sampling could be useful); however, a formula dividing the square of the number of different names by the size of the population comes close enough for developmental work. There is a slight decrease in the plot with increasing size (which is accounted for in comparisons by a normalization process), but the curves remain roughly parallel. Figure 5 shows this formula plotted against the log of N for populations of 256 or greater. The erraticness of the curves between $N = 32$ and $N = 64$ suggests that the linear portion may begin above that point (although several of the curves are difficult to call linear at all). The remaining portions of the curves provide at least a rough comparison metric. The 1406 Anglesey populations, for example, cluster together (except for Llifon) at a fairly low pool-size index. Llifon (1406) and Monmouth (1292) fall more in the middle, with Pembroke (1600) higher.

Looking at the eight populations with samples for $N = 64$ to $N = 256$, the range of results is within 1.5 for 88% of the populations and within 2.0 in all cases. This means that a difference of 3.0 between two name-pool indexes is probably significant, and one of 4.0 is almost certainly so. This difference is relative to the slant of the plots shown in Figure 5, not an absolute difference. Figure 6 plots the name-pool indexes for all the populations studied (including ones not used in development) with 2.0 unit guidelines added to assist in comparing the results. (Comparisons of this statistic in Sect. 5.4 use a normalized figure based on projections parallel to these guidelines back to the $N = 64$ axis.)

3.2.4 *Interpreting the size and shape of the name pool.* These three numbers provide a way of describing the general parameters of the name pool in a population. The percentage represented by the top two names describes how significantly the pool is dominated by the favorites; the skew describes the distribution of the middle rank of names; and the name-pool index describes whether the "low-end" names include a large number of rare names or a smaller number of more common names.

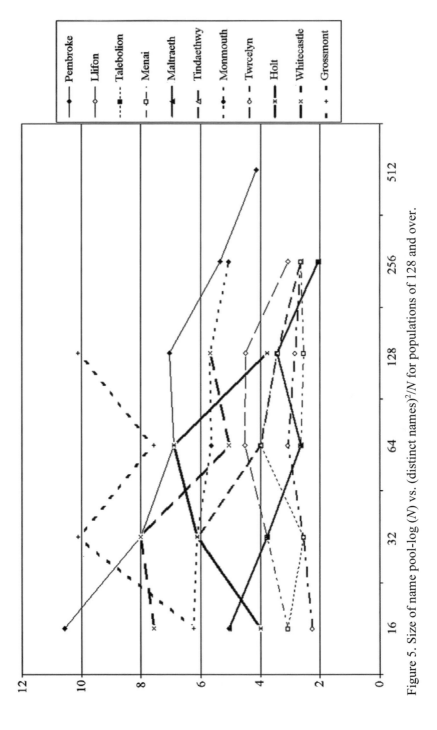

Figure 5. Size of name pool-log (*N*) vs. (distinct names)²/*N* for populations of 128 and over.

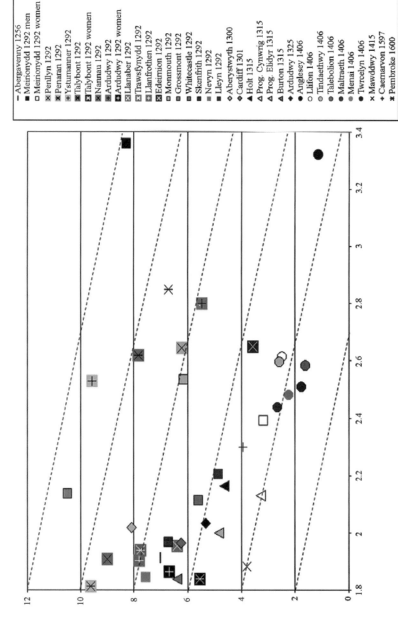

Figure 6. Size of name pool-log (N) vs. (distinct names)$^2/N$ for all populations.

One of the most striking aspects of the populations under study is how consistent the first two factors are. Even between populations that clearly represent different name communities (based, for example, on the percentage of foreign names) the overall shape of how names are distributed is remarkably similar. Is this a flaw in the test? A peculiarly Welsh phenomenon? Or perhaps a general European phenomenon in the medieval and early modern periods?

A brief survey of some non-Welsh data-sets, similarly focused in time and space and already processed such that the data are accessible, suggests that the last may be closest to the truth. Fernández (1997) provides data from the Centru PatRom d'Uviéu name database for the thirteenth through the fifteenth centuries in Asturias, taken in one-decade intervals.[14] For all populations, the percentage accounted for by the top two names and the skew fall within the same range as the Welsh material in the current study with only a couple of trivially different outliers, and the name-pool indexes fall either within or below the Welsh data.

Sample data from England in the thirteenth century[15] and sixteenth century[16] also fall completely within the Welsh ranges for the top two names and skew. The name-pool index for the sixteenth-century data is similar to the Welsh material, while the thirteenth-century index falls only slightly higher.

Two sets of Italian data, on the other hand, demonstrate the ability of these statistics to identify a significantly different pattern. A list of women's names from a 1285 tax roll from Perugia[17] shows top-two and skew sta-

---

[14]Xulio Viejo Fernández, *La conformanza hestórica de l'antroponimia asturiana: Tradición, modes y continuidá nos nomes medievales de persona* (Oviedo, 1997).

[15]*Feet of Fines for Essex*, ed. R. E. G. Kirk, Essex Archaeological Society (1899); Susan Carroll-Clark, *A Statistical Survey of Given Names in Essex Co., England, 1182–1272* (http://members.tripod.com/nicolaa5/articles/names.html).

[16]Stuart Flight, *King's Stanley Marriages to 1678: Parish Registers: Marriages*, 1: *1573–1677* (http://www.glosgen.co.uk/stanley/ksstart.htm); Kathleen M. O'Brien, *Name Distribution in King's Stanley Marriages: 1573–1600* (http://www.s-gabriel.org/names/mari/kingsstanley/).

[17]Alberto Grohmann, *L'Imposizione Diretta nei Comuni della'Italia Centrale nel XIII Secolo: La Libra di Perugia del 1285* (École Française de Rome, 1986); Josh Mittleman, *Feminine Given Names from Thirteenth-Century Perugia* (http://www.s-gabriel.org/names/arval/perugia/).

tistics lower than half of the bottom of the Welsh range (and significantly different from the majority of the individual values) and a name-pool index of over one hundred. Feminine data from the Florentine Catasto of 1427[18] show top-two and skew statistics falling between the Perugia data and the bottom of the Welsh range and a name-pool index (41.6) that, while lower than Perugia, is vastly higher than any of the Welsh data.

These comparison statistics are summarized in Table 13. (Only selected Asturias examples are given.) From the above, it is clear that while the top-two and skew statistics may be of limited usefulness in internal Welsh comparisons, it is due to internal consistency of practice rather than limitations of the statistic itself.

3.3 STABILIZATION OF THE MOST POPULAR NAME(S)

How large must a sample be to ensure that the names that are the most popular in the overall population appear among some selected subset of the most popular names in the sample? Table 14 shows the raw data on this question for the 1292 Monmouth data. Table 15 lists the populations with $N > 32$, showing the two most popular names in the overall sample. (If the top two are tied, this is indicated with an equals sign; if there is a tie for second place, no name is listed in that position and the population is not used for that statistic.) For each sample of eight or larger, the ranking for these names is shown.

Three parameters were examined: above what sample size does the overall number-one name consistently appear in either of the top two positions? (Very often, the top two names are very close, so this is a more useful test than requiring the name to appear in the number-one slot.) Above what size do the overall top two names consistently appear within the top five positions? And, similarly, above what size do the overall top two names appear in the top three positions? Table 16 shows the results in terms of the percentage of populations that fulfill the condition.

In the largest populations ($N > 256$), a sample size of sixty-four is the smallest one that satisfies all three parameters in all cases. If the scope is

---

[18]David Herlihy and Christiane Klapisch-Zuber, *Census and Property Survey of Florentine Dominions in the Province of Tuscany, 1427–1480* (Catasto of 1427 v.1.1; Brown University, 1996); Josh Mittleman, *Feminine Given Names from the Online Catasto of Florence of 1427* (http://www.s-gabriel.org/names/arval/catasto/).

restricted to populations where the comparison sample (the full population in this case) is at least four times that of the sample being tested, this is the only group relevant for a sample of $N = 64$. This same group at a sample of $N = 32$ shows only the second parameter at 100% accuracy, with the other two at 88%, which is still a usable result. If this is a valid sample size, then the results should be similar for all populations over 128 and, in fact, the results are very close, falling only slightly for the third parameter. At a sample size of $N = 16$, the results are also quite consistent for all relevant population sizes, but the accuracy rate becomes unacceptable for both the first and third parameters.

The use of the larger bracket (i.e., appearance within the top five names) suggests a way of quantifying the similarity between the most popular names in populations: the number of names that are shared among the top five names in each population. Based on the above results, two populations that are part of the same name community should never have a similarity score less than two, but the greater the similarity, the higher the score. Table 17 shows the five most popular names for all populations discussed in Section 5.0, from which similarity indexes can be calculated.

4.0 Summary of the Initial Analysis

Table 18 summarizes the results for all the previously discussed statistics. It should be remembered that these are based on a relatively small number of populations, but they provide a basis for making initial comparisons and for further refinement of the tests. From the preceding, it appears that the smallest sample that can reasonably predict the behavior of larger populations with an acceptable (although not perfect) level of accuracy for the factors studied is sixty-four. This has a number of significant consequences. Of the 197 separate local populations of men's names in my data, only twenty-five (around one-eighth) satisfy this condition. The eight "super-populations" composed of geographic groupings within a particular document all satisfy the requirement as well. Of the 112 separate local populations of women's names, none satisfy the size requirement, although three of the super-populations do. This means that it may be impossible to draw useful conclusions about certain statistical comparisons of names on the level of the community, and of women's names at all except on a fairly large scale. The size constraint may also lead to a comparison of larger super-populations that are more likely to be heterogeneous, or to making arbitrary assumptions about which populations are likely to be part of the same "name community" in order to group them. (Of course, selecting populations purely on the basis of geography does not guarantee homogeneity of naming practices either.) Taking the minimum population size of sixty-four, some of the other questions raised at the beginning of the article can be addressed.

4.1 MASCULINE AND FEMININE NAME COMMUNITIES

To what extent do men's and women's names in the same population behave similarly? The only populations in my current data that contain sixty-four or more women's names are the super-population groupings from the commotes of Talybont and Ardudwy in the Merioneth Lay Subsidy of 1292–93, as well as the entire set of Merioneth data (Table 19).

The percentage of foreign names is higher for men in all groups, but only in the case of Ardudwy is the difference large enough to be significant (at 70–80% confidence). The specific names in the most popular slots are, of course, different, but the level of their popularity and the overall skewing of popularity are not demonstrably different. (On an anecdotal level the female populations are uniformly higher for these factors, but the difference is not large enough for confidence.)

The name-pool index provides the most interesting differences. The male and female name pools are not significantly different in size for Ardudwy, but in Talybont the male pool is probably significantly larger (at 80–90% confidence) and the male pool for all of Merioneth is demonstrably significantly larger than the corresponding female pool. It is also larger, although possibly not significantly so, than the male pools for Talybont and Ardudwy. The similarity index for the top five names is very high among the female populations (4 and 5 for Talybont and Ardudwy, respectively, when compared to the whole) and slightly lower for men (3 and 4, respectively). Taken together, this suggests that there is more regional variation in male name fashions than in female ones in these data. This topic is discussed further in Section 5.1.

So the overall influences that shape name popularity appear to be similar for men and women in the populations where it can be studied, but there may be some factor that keeps rare male names in circulation more than rare female names. The percentage of foreign names will be influenced in part by underlying fashions for particular names, so it is not surprising to see some differences between men's and women's names for this factor. There are insufficient examples to judge whether there is any general pattern relating the proportion of foreign names between the genders.

4.2 RECORDS WITH DUPLICATE NAMES

To what extent does a record with duplicate names behave similarly to the same data with no duplicates? That is, must a source such as a court record be edited to remove duplicate names in order to provide useful statistics about the population?

Five populations provide data for this question: the court records from Abergavenny (1256), Ardudwy (1325–26), and Mawddwy (1415–16), the list of burgesses of Cardiff (1301), and the toll records from Pembrokeshire (1599–1603) (Table 20). All the percentage-based statistics (percent foreign, top one and two names, and skew) differ by less than five percentage points in each pair—close enough to consider them functionally identical. The name-pool index, on the other hand, is higher (at some significant level of confidence) in three of the five pairs. This is only what would be expected. By definition, a sample including duplicates will have a larger count, but the same number of distinct names, compared with the same sample from which duplicate individuals have been removed. In all cases, the similarity index for the most popular names is 5.

Overall, this suggests that records that include multiple references to individuals can (in most cases) be used as is for all the statistics under consideration except the size of the name pool. This holds only when the duplication of reference is random across the population. If, for example, a document recorded pairs of individuals involved in transactions and one particular individual were present in all pairs, this would distort the results in an unacceptable fashion.

4.3 TAX VERSUS COURT RECORDS

The two populations from Ardudwy make an important point (Table 21). The two populations appear quite different at first glance, but show few significant differences when the statistical tests are applied. The nature of the most popular names is the most clearly different, although the similarity score for the top five names is 3—still a moderate similarity. The difference in percentage taken up by the top two names has a 70–80% confidence level of being significant. The quarter-century difference between the samples could, in theory, have produced this shift, if it marked a period of rapid transition between different fashions in names, but a more likely cause is that the two types of records are netting slightly different populations. A pair of records set even more closely in time would address this question less ambiguously.

5.0 MISCELLANEOUS COMPARISONS

Now that a set of comparisons and an optimum sample size have been established, various interesting sets of populations (including those not used for the developmental work) can be compared.

5.1 INTERNAL CONSISTENCY WITHIN SUPER-POPULATIONS

Since the usefulness of populations is dependent on their size, we want some idea of how to judge the validity of combining smaller populations in a source in order to have a statistically reliable super-population. One test would be to compare the populations for $N \geq 64$ for that source to determine if any clearly represent distinct name communities. The five of these available for the 1292 Merioneth data are found in Table 22 and the four for the 1415 Bromfield and Yale data in Table 23 (as well as super-populations for each source).

In the Merioneth data, the five local populations show a range of similarity in the most popular names from a score of 1 to 4, with eight out of ten possible pairs scoring 2 or 3 and an average of 2.5, but between the local populations and their respective commotes the similarity is slightly greater, with a range of 2–4 and an average of 3. The five commotes are more similar to each other than the local populations are to the commotes (a range of 3–5 and average of 3.8), and they are even more similar to the population of Merioneth as a whole, with a range of 3–5 and an average of 4. The populations falling at the extremes for skew (Nannau and Llanaber) and for the size of the name pool (Penaran and Llanaber) have some confidence for significant difference, but there is no significant difference when they are compared with the respective super-populations. Compare this with the results for Bromfield and Yale, where Holt is clearly a different name community, on the basis of percent foreign and the nature of the most popular names (similarity scores of 0–1), while the other three local populations show no significant differences from each other (similarity scores of 2–4 and no significant difference in percent foreign). The results for the whole Bromfield and Yale document resemble the second group in the nature of the top two names and fall between the two groups with respect to foreign names. The similarity index between the local populations and the whole in the top five names ranges from 1 to 4, with Holt the least similar and the Progenies Elidyr group the most similar.

Looking back to Table 22, there are few significant differences for any statistics between the local populations and the commotes they fall in, or between the five commotes when compared to each other, with the exception of the size of the name pool, where Edeirnion has a significantly lower pool size than the others (and than Merioneth as a whole). At a lower confidence level, Penllyn may have a lower pool size than Ystumanner and the whole of Merioneth. This might be sufficient basis for not pooling the commotes into a single analysis.

It is interesting that the pool index for the entire document falls higher (relative to the comparison guidelines, see Fig. 6) than all the separate commotes (two at significant levels of confidence, the other three by possibly non-significant amounts). It is also interesting that there is more similarity among the most popular names on a commote level than on a local level. To interpret this dynamic, consider two models: in model A, two identical populations are combined; in model B, two completely distinct populations are combined. Assuming that the basic populations are all of the same size (N) and each has the same number of distinct names (n), model A will have a pool index of $n^2/(N+N) = .5(n^2/N)$ or half that of each of the components, while model B will have a pool index of $(n+n)^2/(N+N) = 2(n^2/N)$ or twice that of each of the components. That is, the more similar the populations are that are being combined, the more likely the combined index is to be lower than the components; the more different they are, the higher it will be in comparison. In Model A, the similarity index for the component popular names will be 5, in model B it will be 0. The similarity to the combined population in Model A will also be 5, and in Model B will be 3 (assuming identical distributions). That is, the more similar the component populations are, the higher and more similar the two similarity indexes will be, while the more distinct they are, the lower and more dissimilar the two comparisons will be. Both factors suggest there is more variation within the commotes than between them, at least among the men's names. Looking back at the limited results for women in the same document (Sect. 4.1), there is no significant difference (but an anecdotal decrease) in the pool index for all of Merioneth compared to the individual commotes. This suggests that the female name communities in the document may be more similar to each other than the male name communities are.

For samples at or above the $N = 64$ cutoff, either a significant difference in percent foreign names or the size of the name pool may argue against combining populations for analysis, but what of smaller populations—the more usual case? The measurement of percent foreign is fairly reliable for populations of thirty-two or more (and possibly smaller), but relying on this factor alone would miss distinctions such as in the Merioneth data, so it is mostly useful for arguing against, rather than for, such combined populations. For example, there are eight populations falling in size between thirty-two and sixty-four in the Bromfield and Yale data. One (Wrexham) has a foreign percentage significantly different (at 100% confidence) both from Holt and from the three low-foreign large populations. The other seven fall in a thirty-point range with these latter three, although not within a twenty-point range. Based on this, Holt and Wrexham should be analyzed separately, but the most that could be said for the other local populations would be that this test provides no reason not to combine them for analysis.

5.2 THE ANGLESEY SUBMISSIONS OF 1406

The results from the 1406 Anglesey records (Table 24) are an example of an extremely homogeneous name community. Although, on an anecdotal level, the commote of Menai is a slight outlier with respect to percent foreign (somewhat higher) and skew (somewhat lower), the only statistic for the group that falls within the significance parameters is the percentage for the top two names between Menai and Talebolion (at 70–80% confidence). Otherwise, there is no significant local variation. The same two names occupy the top slots in all cases, and the similarity index for the top five names ranges from 3 to 5 with an average slightly over 4. The relationship on the name-pool graph between the cluster of commote results and the result for the whole population is exactly what is expected if the whole Anglesey population were a single, homogeneous name community. (Compare this specifically with the internal variability in the 1292 Merioneth data in the preceding section.)

5.3 POPULATIONS CA. 1300

There are enough data from various sources for the quarter century around 1300 that an overall picture can begin to be developed, at least for the limited group of locations included in the data. This group includes records for the 1292–93 lay subsidy from eleven different commotes or boroughs (Table 25), records of burgesses for two towns, and four populations from the 1315 tenantry survey of Bromfield and Yale (Table 26).

The proportion of foreign names falls into three significantly distinct clusters: High (79–98), all six urban settlements associated with fortifications (some explicitly identified as borough towns); Low (11–31), eight populations comprising the Merioneth commotes and non-borough regions of Bromfield and Yale; and three falling in the middle (46–66) of no particular type. The populations at the edges of the middle group are not significantly different from those at the respective edges of the extremes, but the way in which the results cluster suggest these groupings.

The percentages taken up by the top one and two names show a moderate significant difference between the high and low ends of the range, but there is no clear grouping within that range. However, when correlated with the percent-foreign results, the Low foreign group tends to have a lower percentage for the top two names.

The skew statistics are clustered in the 36–47 range (with little or no confidence in distinguishing between them) except for Grossmont, at 26, which shows a significantly lower skew than the rest. (That is, even though it has one of the highest top two values, the popularity of the next rank of names drops off more precipitously. It also has one of the higher name-pool indexes, which also contributes to the flattening of the skew.)

The size of the name pool varies considerably within these samples, but does not correlate noticeably with any other attribute except the top-two percentage, which varies inversely. This is a general correlation only (and not a surprising one), and there is statistically significant variation in the name-pool index at any given level of the other statistic. Interestingly enough, Grossmont once again bucks this trend. So in Grossmont there is a comparatively large and less-skewed name pool where only the most popular one or two names are disproportionately more common than the usual.

The similarity in the top five names is fairly complex to analyze with so many populations, but by grouping them both according to their similarity to each other and by patterns of similarity (or lack thereof) to other populations, eight groups emerge. For example, the group of urban populations in the Monmouth and three castles record plus Aberystwyth are all similar to each other with a range of 3–4 and an average of 3.7, but Abergavenny (geographically next to the Monmouth group) has similarities of 1–2 when compared to any of them. Cardiff and Holt have a moderate similarity to each other (3.0) and are fairly similar to the Monmouth group (mostly 2–3 with a single score of 1) but have no other resemblances higher than 1. The non-urban populations show a moderate level of similarity to each other (2–4), although internal groupings could be identified if desired, and generally a low resemblance to the urban populations (0–2), but even here there are outliers, such as the Progenies Cynwrig group, which not only has zero resemblance to any of the urban populations but fairly low resemblance to any population, going as high as three in only one case (Burton, a geographic neighbor in the same document).

5.4 CHANGE IN NAMING PRACTICES OVER TIME

As demonstrated in the preceding section, there could be considerable variety among name communities within a narrow timespan. So, to address questions of long-term change in naming practices, factors associated with this sort of variation must be controlled for. Ideally, the comparison would be of statistics for the same location, from documents of the same type, over a range of time periods. In practice, this sort of document sequence may not be available. Among the current data, only the pair of data-sets from Ardudwy (compared in Sect. 4.3) and three data-sets from the Caernarvonshire area (Table 27) provide a look at changes in the same region over time. The 1597 data cover a larger area that includes Nefyn and Lleyn.

There is a significant increase in the proportion of foreign names between the thirteenth and the sixteenth centuries. There is some decrease in the proportion of names accounted for by the most popular name (although only compared with Lleyn at an acceptable level of confidence), but this difference is not significant when the top two names are considered, nor is there a significant change in the skew. The name-pool index for the sixteenth-century population is anecdotally lower than the thirteenth-century ones, but the difference is not large enough to be considered significant at any acceptable level of confidence. In fact, once the population size has been adjusted for, there is more difference between the size of the two thirteenth-century name pools than between the lower of those and the sixteenth-century pool. Of the most popular names, only *John* is consistently present among the top five names. *David* has dropped to eighth place in the sixteenth-century record, and *Einion* does not appear at all, while *Robert* does not appear at all in the thirteenth-century records.

In the absence of sequences of records from the same location over time, general trends and correlations can be traced by examining the behavior of all the populations taken together. Figures 7–12 plot all the results for percent-foreign, percent for the top two names, and the normalized name-pool index (as defined in Sect. 3.2.3) against the century of the data, and against each other.

One problem in interpreting Figures 7–9 (change over time) is the relatively small number of populations available for the fifteenth–sixteenth centuries. (The internal consistency of the 1406 Anglesey data means that there are really only two distinct populations studied for this century, although the Anglesey commotes have been plotted separately.) Figure 7 shows the shift in appearance of foreign names as a progression from a wide range of results to a much narrower range in the high end of the scale. More samples would be needed for the later centuries to confirm this, but if it is an accurate picture it could, in theory, be explained by various hypotheses: as a change in name fashions among still distinct communities; by a change in the proportions of distinct communities with static name fashions; or a homogenization of communities accompanied by an overall shift in fashion. Other tests (aside from knowledge of the historic context) would be needed to distinguish among the possibilities, such as a study of the appearance of foreign and native names together in patronyms.

Figure 8, plotting the top two statistics by century, shows the danger in drawing conclusions from small samples. If the fifteenth-century data were absent, the graph would clearly indicate a narrowing of the range of results over time toward the middle of the earlier range. But if the sixteenth-century data were absent, the graph would just as clearly indicate an overall increase in results over time, but with only a slight narrowing of the range. Clearly this is a statistic where no trend can be traced without more data.

The trend in the name-pool index (Fig. 9) is similarly inconclusive without more data in the later centuries, but the current data do not support a strong conclusion that the size of the Welsh name pool declined between the medieval and the early modern periods. Using the pool index developed here, we can examine the data from which Morgan (1995) suggests such a conclusion. Table 28 shows data from five groupings of genealogical sources

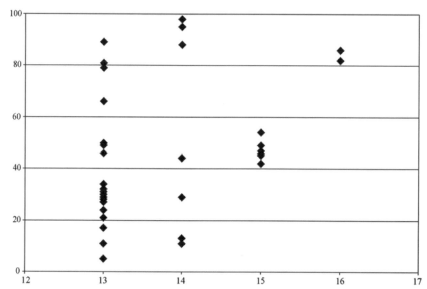

Figure 7. Century vs. % foreign.

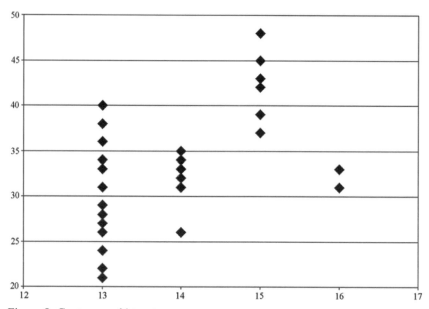

Figure 8. Century vs. % top two.

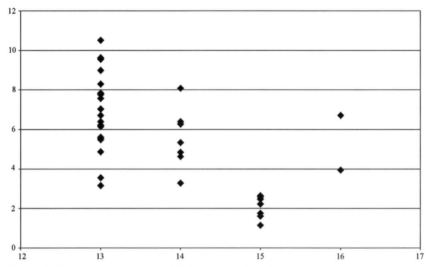

Figure 9. Century vs. name-pool index (normalized).

and a set of wills. While the earliest two groupings do show a significantly higher name pool, the samples from the thirteenth through the sixteenth centuries show no significant difference in the normalized name-pool indexes. Observed differences in the raw data may reflect statistically insignificant sampling differences or be difficult to interpret due to large differences in sample size.

The proportion of foreign names correlates with the proportion taken by the top two names in an interesting fashion (Fig. 10). Populations in which foreign and native names are roughly equal in proportion are, as a group, more concentrated among the most popular names, while populations that are more homogeneous with respect to the origin of the names (in either direction) are less concentrated. If the proportion of foreign names were due solely to differing proportions of two distinct name communities in the sample, then this should correlate with a lower concentration, not a higher one. (Consider a hypothetical case involving the mixture of distinct native and foreign name cultures where the top two names in each represents 20% and 15%, respectively. In a homogeneous population of either type, the top two names represent 35% of the whole, but in a fifty-fifty mixture of both, the top two names will only represent 20%.) This indicates that the presence of foreign names is not solely a matter of mixing name communities in different proportions, but that some more complex dynamic is involved. This might seem to be an obvious conclusion from a historical

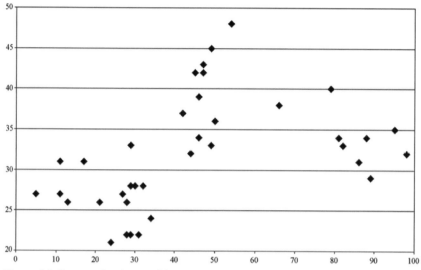

Figure 10. Percent foreign vs. % top two.

perspective, but the ability of the analysis to predict expected results sup-
plies more confidence when considering unexpected ones.

The correlation of the proportion of foreign names with the size of the
name pool (Fig. 11) produces no clear trends, except possibly a tendency
at the extremes of the scale for more homogeneous populations to have
smaller pools. If this is a valid trend (rather than a random artifact), then at
least those extremes do behave as if they were mixtures of distinct populations. In such a case, the introduction of small numbers of a distinct name
community would increase the size of the overall name pool disproportionately. However, while this dynamic may exist in the earlier populations
(and it still appears if only the ca. 1300 populations are charted), it is unlikely to be the case for the later populations. And once again the populations with more equal proportions of name origins do not behave as a
mixture of distinct name cultures.

In Section 5.3 the ca. 1300 data showed a general inverse correlation
between concentration among the top two names and the size of the name
pool. Figure 12 shows this same correlation for all populations and, as noted
before, it is not surprising if there is a "normal" pattern for the distribution
of names in this general region and era. While this correlation is not noteworthy in itself, it can help identify populations worthy of closer exami-

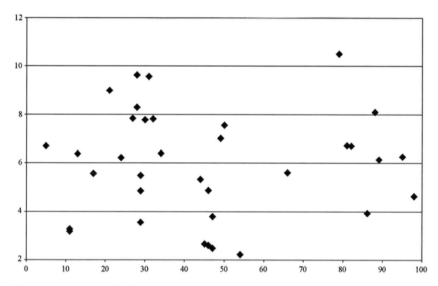

Figure 11. Percent foreign vs. name-pool index (normalized).

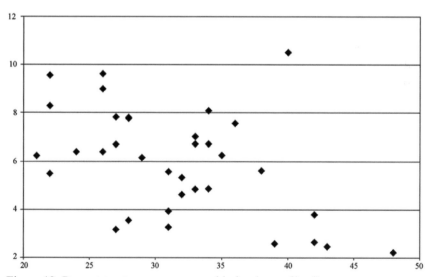

Figure 12. Percent top two vs. name-pool index (normalized).

nation if they fall outside the general trend (such as Grossmont in the upper right, which has previously been noted as unusual).

5.5 CONCLUSIONS

As noted above in the introduction, Wales in the medieval and early modern periods is of particular interest for studying the ways in which cultural contact and mixing can affect naming practices. The dynamics of this process can be seen most clearly in the presence and prevalence of linguistically non-Welsh names. Although the use of such names in Wales is not related solely to the presence of English immigration and influence, there is a strong correlation in the early records between a high proportion of foreign names and populations identified with English settlements (boroughs and fortifications). With time, this correlation fades as incoming names are adopted in increasing numbers by the native population and become numbered among some of the most popular name choices. By the end of the medieval period, local variation appears to express itself in the details of name choice rather than in the broad patterns of origin.

Through the entire period studied, the distribution of name popularity remains remarkably consistent, both between native and immigrant communities in the earliest samples and between the earliest and latest populations. Even those differences in distribution that can reasonably be considered significant pale when compared to a radically different distribution pattern (as in the Italian populations mentioned in Sect. 3.2.4). Even the size of the available name pool is relatively consistent, with local fashion varying more (in the available data) than the fairly subtle trends over time. These local fashions are most strongly illustrated by the nature of the most popular names, providing one of the clearest measures both of changes in fashion over time and of geographic shifts in the name community.

Perhaps most important, a statistical approach to the study of the above topics suggests caution when dealing with anecdotal impressions of trends and practices, as well as leading to a careful consideration of the types of data being compared, and the types of conclusions that can reasonably be drawn from them.

Appendix

SAMPLE POPULATIONS

Only local populations of thirty-two or more are listed separately, although the un-listed ones are included in the super-populations. The last column lists the identi-fications used in the tables and figures.

Location	Men	Women	Identification

A. J. Roderick and William Rees, eds., *Ministers' Accounts for the Lordships of Abergavenny, Grosmont, Skenfrith and White Castle: Part I—The Lordship of Aber-gavenny*, South Wales and Monmouth Record Society No. 2 (Abergavenny Court Records, 1256).

All records	94		1256 Abergavenny All
No duplicates	82		1256 Abergavenny (Unique)

Keith Williams-Jones, *The Merioneth Lay Subsidy Roll 1292–3* (University of Wales Press, 1976).

Location	Men	Women	Identification
Merioneth	2296	247	1292 Merioneth
Penllyn	441	39	1292 Mer Penllyn
Penaran	65		1292 Mer/Pen Penaran
Rhywedog	57		1292 Mer/Pen Rhywedog
Gwernefail	34		1292 Mer/Pen Gwernefail
(plus 24 smaller local populations)			
Ystumanner	339	37	1292 Mer Ystumanner
Cefnrhos	38		1292 Mer/Yst Cefnrhos
(plus 29 smaller local populations)			
Tal-y-Bont	416	69	1292 Mer Talybont
Nannau	81		1292 Mer/Tal Nannau
Peniarth	47		1292 Mer/Tal Peniarth
Rhyd-cryw	38		1292 Mer/Tal Rhydcryw
Brithdir	33		1292 Mer/Tal Brithdir
(plus 15 smaller local populations)			
Ardudwy	632	73	1292 Mer Ardudwy
Llanaber	90		1292 Mer/Ard Llanaber
Trawsfynydd	87		1292 Mer/Ard Trawsfynydd
Llanfrothen	80		1292 Mer/Ard Llanfrothen
Penrhyndeudraeth	49		1292 Mer/Ard Penrhyn.
Llanfair	45		1292 Mer/Ard Llanfair

Maentwrog	42	1292 Mer/Ard Maentwrog
Llandanwg	32	1292 Mer/Ard Llandanwg
Llandecwyn	32	1292 Mer/Ard Llandecwyn
(plus 11 smaller local populations)		
Ederinion	447	1292 Mer Ederinion
Gwyddelwern	48	1292 Mer/Ed Gwyddelwern
Cynwyd	40	1292 Mer/Ed Cynwyd
(plus 30 smaller local populations)		

Anthony Hopkins, "The Lay Subsidy of 1292: Monmouth and the Three Castles," *Studia Celtica* 30 (1996), 189–96.

Monmouth	344	42	1292 Monmouth
Grossmont	137		1292 Grossmont
Whitecastle	130		1292 Whitecastle
Skenfrith	93		1292 Skenfrith

T. Jones-Pierce, "Two Early Caernarvonshire Accounts: I. Lay Subsidy Account 242/50B [A.D. 1293]," *Bulletin of the Board of Celtic Studies* 5 (1930), 142–48. [Nevyn in Dinllaen]

Nevyn	70	1292 Nevyn

T. Jones-Pierce, "A Lleyn Lay Subsidy Account," *Bulletin of the Board of Celtic Studies* 5 (1929), 54–71.

Lleyn	161	1292 Lleyn
(15 local populations, all less than 32)		

I. J. Sanders, "The Boroughs of Aberystwyth and Cardigan in the Early Fourteenth Century," *Bulletin of the Board of Celtic Studies* 15 (1954), 82–292.

Aberystwyth	104	1300 Aberystwyth
Cardiff		
All records	128	1301 Cardiff All
No duplicates	92	1301 Cardiff (Unique)

T. P. Ellis, *The First Extent of Bromfield and Yale A.D. 1315* (London: The Honourable Society of Cymmrodorion, 1924).

Borough of Holt	146	1315 BY Holt
Progenies Cynwrig	135	1315 BY Prog Cynwrig
P.C. Group 4	48	1315 BY Prog Cynwrig 4
(plus 5 smaller groups)		
Progenies Elidyr	100	1315 BY Prog Elidyr
P.E. Group 4	54	1315 BY Prog Elidyr 4
(plus 3 smaller groups)		

Burton	69	1315 BY Burton
Trefydd Bychain	58	1315 BY Tref. Bychain
Allington Gresford	53	1315 BY Allington
Wrexham	52	1315 BY Wrexham
Pickhill	42	1315 BY Pickhill
Eyton	40	1315 BY Eyton
Llandynnan	37	1315 BY Llandynnan
(plus 27 smaller populations)		

E. A. Lewis, "The Proceedings of the Small Hundred Court of the Commote of Ardudwy in the County of Merioneth from 8 October, 1325, to 18 September, 1326," *Bulletin of the Board of Celtic Studies* 4 (1928), 153–66.

| All records | 130 | 1326 Ardudwy All |
| No duplicates | 108 | 1326 Ardudwy (Unique) |

Glyn Roberts, "The Anglesey Submissions of 1406," *Bulletin of the Board of Celtic Studies* 15 (1952), 39–61.

Anglesey	2099	1406 Anglesey
Llifon	414	1406 AS Llifon
Tindaethwy	396	1406 AS Tindaethwy
Talebolion	385	1406 AS Talebolion
Maltraeth	325	1406 AS Maltraeth
Menai	304	1406 AS Menai
Twrcelyn	275	1406 AS Twrcelyn

Keith Williams-Jones, "A Mawddwy Court Roll, 1415–16," *Bulletin of the Board of Celtic Studies* 23 (1970), 329–45.

| All records | 154 | 1415 Mawddwy All |
| No duplicates | 76 | 1415 Mawddwy (Unique) |

Emyr Gwynne Jones, "Caernarvonshire Subsidy Roll, 1597/8," *Bulletin of the Board of Celtic Studies* 8 (1937), 336–44.

| Caernarvonshire | 199 | 1597 Caernarvon |
| (12 local populations, all under 32) | | |

E. A. Lewis, "The Toll Books of some North Pembrokeshire Fairs (1599–1603)," *Bulletin of the Board of Celtic Studies* 7 (1934), 284–318.

| All records | 1088 | 1600 Pembroke All |
| No duplicates | 707 | 1600 Pembroke (Unique) |

Summary of Populations (including those not listed separately)

Sample	Total	< 8	8–15	16–31	32–63	64–127	128–255	256–511	>511
Men									
Local populations	197	45	59	49	19	13	4	7	1
Super-populations							2	4	1
Women									
Local populations	112	96	13	2	1				
Super-populations			2	1	2	2			

TABLE 1. DATA FOR FOREIGN NAMES IN PEMBROKE 1600

Sample Size	1	2	4	8	16	32	64	128	256	512	707
Non-Welsh	1	1	2	4	12	25	55	109	212	420	577
%	100	50	50	50	75	78	86	85	83	82	82
John	—	—	—	1	3	6	14	23	53	116	153
David	—	—	—	1	1	3	9	17	34	58	80
William	—	—	—	—	—	1	4	12	28	50	70
Thomas	—	—	—	—	—	4	8	14	25	50	67
Lewis	—	—	1	1	1	2	3	7	13	23	31
Philip	—	—	—	—	1	2	5	7	9	17	25
Richard	—	—	—	—	1	1	3	5	9	16	25
Henry	—	—	—	—	—	—	1	5	9	18	22
James	1	1	1	1	2	2	2	3	4	9	17
Moris	—	—	—	—	—	—	1	2	3	8	16
Hugh	—	—	—	—	—	—	—	2	5	11	14
Robert	—	—	—	—	—	—	—	2	3	9	11
George	—	—	—	—	—	—	—	—	1	4	6
Nicholas	—	—	—	—	—	—	—	1	2	5	6
Roland	—	—	—	—	—	1	1	1	1	2	4
Edward	—	—	—	—	—	—	—	—	1	2	3
Arnold	—	—	—	—	—	—	—	—	1	2	2
Ellis	—	—	—	—	—	—	—	1	1	2	2
Frances	—	—	—	—	—	—	—	—	—	1	2
Laurence	—	—	—	—	—	—	—	—	—	2	2
Mathias	—	—	—	—	—	—	—	—	—	1	2
Matthew	—	—	—	—	—	—	—	—	—	1	2
Peter	—	—	—	—	—	—	—	1	1	2	2
Rinold	—	—	—	—	1	1	1	1	2	2	2

Table 1, continued

Sample Size	1	2	4	8	16	32	64	128	256	512	707
Roger	—	—	—	—	1	1	1	1	1	1	2
Alban	—	—	—	—	—	—	—	1	1	1	1
Anthony	—	—	—	—	—	—	—	—	1	1	1
Balthasar	—	—	—	—	1	1	1	1	1	1	1
Gilbert	—	—	—	—	—	—	—	—	—	1	1
Humphrey	—	—	—	—	—	—	—	1	1	1	1
Melchior	—	—	—	—	—	—	1	1	1	1	1
Miles	—	—	—	—	—	—	—	—	1	1	1
Patrick	—	—	—	—	—	—	—	—	—	—	1
Walter	—	—	—	—	—	—	—	—	—	1	1
Welsh	—	1	2	4	4	7	9	19	44	92	130
Rhys	—	—	—	1	1	3	3	6	12	25	39
Gruffudd	—	—	1	1	1	1	1	3	8	20	31
Owein	—	—	—	—	—	—	—	—	8	15	24
Morgan	—	1	1	1	1	1	1	2	5	9	10
Hywel	—	—	—	—	—	—	—	1	1	5	7
Einion	—	—	—	1	1	2	2	3	4	6	6
Llywelyn	—	—	—	—	—	—	—	—	—	3	4
Rhydderch	—	—	—	—	—	—	1	2	3	3	3
Maredudd	—	—	—	—	—	—	1	1	1	2	2
Cadwaladr	—	—	—	—	—	—	—	—	—	1	1
Iorwerth	—	—	—	—	—	—	—	—	1	1	1
Meilyr	—	—	—	—	—	—	—	—	—	1	1
Trahaearn	—	—	—	—	—	—	—	1	1	1	1

TABLE 2. PERCENT FOREIGN NAMES—POPULATIONS 32 FOR SAMPLES 8

		Sample Size						
		8	16	32	64	128	256	512
Range		0–100	0–100	6.2–100	12.5–100	11.7–97.7	43.0–88.3	
N	Population							
707	1600 Pembroke	50.0	75.0	78.1	85.9	85.2	83.2	82.0
344	1292 Monmouth	100.0	100.0	100.0	100.0	96.1	88.3	
304	1406 AS Menai	37.5	56.2	50.0	50.0	56.2	55.9	
325	1406 AS Maltraeth	37.5	50.0	43.8	50.0	50.8	49.6	
396	1406 AS Tindaethwy	37.5	43.8	56.2	53.1	47.7	48.4	
275	1406 AS Twrcelyn	50.0	56.2	59.4	54.7	48.4	44.9	
385	1406 AS Talebolion	50.0	43.8	53.1	40.6	43.0	43.0	
146	1315 BY Holt	100.0	100.0	96.9	95.3	97.7		
92	1301 Cardiff	100.0	92.8	96.9	93.8	95.3		
137	1292 Grossmont	100.0	100.0	93.8	92.2	80.5		
128	1292 Whitecastle	62.5	62.5	68.8	64.1	66.4		
108	1325 Ardudwy	50.0	43.8	53.1	46.9	44.4		
414	1406 AS Llifon	25.0	37.5	37.5	34.4	39.1		
135	1315 BY Prog. Cynwrig	0.0	6.2	15.6	12.5	11.7		
104	1300 Aberystwyth	87.5	93.8	87.5	89.1			
93	1292 Skenefrith	50.0	75.0	84.4	82.8			

Table 2, continued

		Sample Size						
		8	16	32	64	128	256	512
Range		0–100	0–100	6.2–100	12.5–100	11.7–97.7	43.0–88.3	
N	Population							
76	1415 Mawddwy	50.0	37.5	40.6	46.9			
80	1292 Mer/Ard Lanfrothin	50.0	43.8	34.4	35.9			
82	1256 Abergavenny	75.0	62.5	50.0	34.4			
90	1292 Mer/Ard Llanaber	25.0	37.5	28.1	32.8			
64	1292 Mer/Pen Penaran	25.0	25.0	25.0	26.6			
87	1292 Mer/Ard Trawsfynydd	12.5	18.8	15.6	26.6			
81	1292 Mer/Tal Nannau	0.0	12.5	18.8	20.3			
100	1315 BY Prog. Elidyr	0.0	0.0	6.2	17.2			
69	1315 BY Burton	25.0	12.5	15.6	12.5			
52	1315 BY Wrexham	75.0	68.8	62.5				
49	1292 Mer/Ard Penrhyn.	62.5	50.0	40.6				
38	1292 Mer/Yst Cefnrhos	50.0	43.7	37.5				
33	1292 Mer/Tal Brithdir	50.0	31.2	34.4				
42	1315 BY Pickhill	25.0	50.0	31.0				
38	1292 Mer/Tal Rhydcryw	25.0	43.8	25.0				
48	1292 Mer/Ed Gwyddelwern	25.0	25.0	25.0				

Table 2, continued

		Sample Size						
		8	16	32	64	128	256	512
Range		0–100	0–100	6.2–100	12.5–100	11.7–97.7	43.0–88.3	
N	Population							
40	1292 Mer/Ed Cynwyd	25.0	25.0	25.0				
32	1292 Mer/Ard Llandegwyn	0.0	12.5	25.0				
47	1292 Mer/Tal Peniarth	37.5	37.5	25.0				
58	1315 BY Tref. Bychain	0.0	12.5	21.9				
37	1315 BY Llandynman	25.0	25.0	21.9				
53	1315 BY Allington	50.0	31.2	21.9				
45	1292 Mer/Ard Llanfair	25.0	25.0	18.8				
34	1292 Mer/Pen Gwernefail	25.0	12.5	18.8				
42	1292 Mer/Ard Maentwrog	12.5	12.5	18.8				
32	1292 Mer/Ard Landanwg	25.0	25.0	15.6				
40	1315 BY Eyton	0.0	12.5	12.5				
57	1292 Mer/Pen Rhywedog	0.0	6.2	9.4				

TABLE 3. PERCENT FOREIGN NAMES (POPULATIONS AS IN TABLE 1)—DIFFERENCE BETWEEN SAMPLE AND MAXIMUM SAMPLE

		Sample Size					
N	Population	8	16	32	64	128	256
707	1600 Pembroke	32.0	7.0	3.9	-3.9	-3.2	-1.2
344	1292 Monmouth	-11.7	-11.7	-11.7	-11.7	-7.8	
304	1406 AS Menai	18.4	-0.3	5.9	5.9	-0.3	
325	1406 AS Maltraeth	12.1	-0.4	5.8	-0.4	-1.2	
396	1406 AS Tindaethwy	10.9	4.6	-7.8	-4.7	0.7	
275	1406 AS Twrcelyn	-5.1	-11.3	-14.5	-9.8	-3.5	
385	1406 AS Talebolion	-7.0	-0.8	-10.1	2.4	0.0	
146	1315 BY Holt	-2.3	-2.3	0.8	2.4		
92	1301 Cardiff	-4.7	2.5	-1.6	1.5		
137	1292 Grossmont	-19.5	-19.5	-13.3	-11.7		
128	1292 Whitecastle	3.9	3.9	-2.4	2.3		
108	1325 Ardudwy	-5.6	0.6	-8.7	-2.5		
414	1406 AS Llifon	14.1	1.6	1.6	4.7		
135	1315 BY Prog. Cynwrig	11.7	5.4	-3.9	-0.8		
104	1300 Aberystwyth	1.6	-4.7	1.6			
93	1292 Skenefrith	32.8	7.8	-1.6			
76	1415 Mawddwy	-3.1	9.4	6.3			
80	1292 Mer/Ard Lanfrothin	-14.1	-7.9	1.5			
82	1256 Abergavenny	-40.6	-28.1	-15.6			
90	1292 Mer/Ard Llanaber	7.8	-4.7	4.7			
64	1292 Mer/Pen Penaran	1.6	1.6	1.6			
87	1292 Mer/Ard Trawsfynydd	14.1	7.8	11.0			

Table 3, continued

N	Population	Sample Size					
		8	16	32	64	128	256
81	1292 Mer/Tal Nannau	20.3	7.8	1.5			
100	1315 BY Prog. Elidyr	17.2	17.2	11.0			
69	1315 BY Burton	-12.5	0.0	-3.1			
52	1315 BY Wrexham	-12.5	-6.3				
49	1292 Mer/Ard Penrhyn.	-21.9	-9.4				
38	1292 Mer/Yst Cefnrhos	-12.5	-6.2				
33	1292 Mer/Tal Brithdir	-15.6	3.2				
42	1315 BY Pickhill	6.0	-19.0				
38	1292 Mer/Tal Rhydcryw	0.0	-18.8				
48	1292 Mer/Ed Gwyddelwern	0.0	0.0				
40	1292 Mer/Ed Cynwyd	0.0	0.0				
32	1292 Mer/Ard Llandegwyn	25.0	12.5				
47	1292 Mer/Tal Peniarth	-12.5	-12.5				
58	1315 BY Tref. Bychain	21.9	9.4				
37	1315 BY Llandynnan	-3.1	-3.1				
53	1315 BY Allington	-28.1	-9.3				
45	1292 Mer/Ard Llanfair	-6.2	-6.2				
34	1292 Mer/Pen Gwernefail	-6.2	6.3				
42	1292 Mer/Ard Maentwrog	6.3	6.3				
32	1292 Mer/Ard Landanwg	-9.4	-9.4				
40	1315 BY Eyton	12.5	0.0				
57	1292 Mer/Pen Rhywedog	9.4	3.1				

TABLE 4. PERCENT FOREIGN NAMES—PERCENTAGE OF POPULATIONS OF A
GIVEN SIZE FALLING WITHIN CUTOFF

Population Size	Cutoff	Sample Size					
		8	16	32	64	128	256
$N > 512$ (1 population)	± 5.0	0.0	0.0	100.0	100.0	100.0	100.0
	± 10.0	0.0	100.0	100.0	100.0	100.0	100.0
	± 15.0	0.0	100.0	100.0	100.0	100.0	100.0
$N > 256$ (7 populations)	± 5.0	0.0	57.1	14.3	57.1	85.7	
	± 10.0	28.6	71.4	57.1	85.7	100.0	
	± 15.0	57.1	100.0	100.0	100.0	100.0	
$N > 128$ (14 populations)	± 5.0	21.4	64.3	42.9	71.4		
	± 10.0	42.9	78.6	71.4	85.7		
	± 15.0	71.4	92.9	100.0	100.0		
$N > 64$ (25 populations)	± 5.0	24.0	52.0	52.0			
	± 10.0	40.0	80.0	72.0			
	± 15.0	68.0	88.0	96.0			
$N > 32$ (44 populations)	± 5.0	22.7	43.2				
	± 10.0	50.0	79.6				
	± 15.0	70.5	88.6				

TABLE 5. DATA FOR MOST POPULAR NAME—1292 MER/ARD LLANABER

Sample Size	1	2	4	8	16	32	64	90
Most Common	1	1	1	1	3	5	10	11
% of Total	100	50	25	12	19	16	16	12
Adam	—	—	—	—	3	5	10	11
Madog	—	—	—	—	1	2	8	11
David	—	—	—	1	1	2	5	10
Gronw	1	1	1	1	2	2	6	8
Iorwerth	—	—	—	—	2	5	6	8
Einion	—	—	—	1	1	3	5	6
John	—	—	—	—	—	—	2	6
Gwion	—	—	—	1	1	4	5	5
Ednyfed	—	—	—	—	—	1	1	4
Gwyn	—	—	1	1	1	1	3	4
Cadwgan	—	—	1	1	1	1	2	2
Cynwrig	—	—	—	—	—	2	2	2
Gruffri	—	—	—	—	—	—	1	2
Benedict	—	—	—	1	1	1	1	1
Cogan	—	1	1	1	1	1	1	1
Deheuwynt	—	—	—	—	—	—	1	1
Isaac	—	—	—	—	—	—	1	1
Ithel	—	—	—	—	—	—	—	1
Meilyr	—	—	—	—	—	—	—	1
Morfran	—	—	—	—	—	—	—	1
Osborn	—	—	—	—	1	1	1	1
Philip	—	—	—	—	—	—	1	1
Tale	—	—	—	—	—	1	1	1
Tudur	—	—	—	—	—	—	1	1

TABLE 6. PERCENTAGE FOR MOST POPULAR NAME—POPULATIONS 32 FOR SAMPLES 8

		All	Sample Size						
			8	**16**	**32**	**64**	**128**	**256**	**512**
Range			12–50	12–50	12–34	14–30	17–29	16–25	23
N	**Population**								
707	1600 Pembroke	22	12	19	19	22	18	21	23
414	1406 AS Llifon	24	25	25	22	17	19	23	
396	1406 AS Tindaethwy	20	25	25	22	22	20	22	
385	1406 AS Talebolion	21	25	25	25	22	23	23	
344	1292 Monmouth	16	25	19	22	19	20	16	
325	1406 AS Maltraeth	23	25	25	25	25	27	23	
304	1406 AS Menai	25	25	38	31	30	26	25	
275	1406 AS Twrcelyn	21	50	50	34	28	24	21	
146	1315 BY Holt	16	25	19	19	14	17		
137	1292 Grossmont	27	38	31	22	25	29		
128	1292 Whitecastle	26	25	19	28	30			
108	1325 Ardudwy	18	25	19	22	20			
104	1300 Aberystwyth	22	25	25	16	17			
93	1292 Skenefrith	22	38	19	28	20			
92	1301 Cardiff	23	50	31	22	23			
90	1292 Mer/Ard Llanaber	12	12	19	16	16			
87	1292 Mer/Ard Trawsfynydd	14	38	19	16	14			
82	1256 Abergavenny	24	38	25	34	28			
81	1292 Mer/Tal Nannau	14	38	31	19	14			
80	1292 Mer/Ard Lanfrothin	15	25	25	16	16			
76	1415 Mawddwy	21	38	25	22	22			
69	1315 BY Burton	14	25	19	19	14			
64	1292 Mer/Pen Penaran	14	38	19	19				

Table 6, continued

		Sample Size						
	All	**8**	**16**	**32**	**64**	**128**	**256**	**512**
Range		**12–50**	**12–50**	**12–34**	**14–30**	**17–29**	**16–25**	**23**
N	**Population**							
58	1315 BY Tref. Bychain	21	38	19	19			
57	1292 Mer/Pen Rhywedog	16	25	12	19			
54	1315 BY Prog. Elidyr 4	20	25	25	16			
53	1315 BY Allington	15	25	19	16			
52	1315 BY Wrexham	19	25	19	19			
49	1292 Mer/Ard Penrhyn.	16	38	19	19			
48	1292 Mer/Ed Gwyddelwern	19	25	19	19			
48	1315 BY Prog. Cynwrig 4	12	25	12	12			
47	1292 Mer/Tal Pennarth	21	25	19	25			
45	1292 Mer/Ard Llanfair	22	25	25	22			
42	1292 Mer/Ard Maentwrog	21	25	19	16			
42	1315 BY Pickhill	24	25	38	22			
40	1292 Mer/Ed Conryt	22	38	25	28			
40	1315 BY Eyton	20	25	19	25			
38	1292 Mer/Yst Cefnrhos	18	38	19	16			
38	1292 Mer/Tal Rhydcryw	24	25	31	19			
37	1315 BY Llandynnan	16	25	19	16			
34	1292 Mer/Pen Gwernefail	15	25	19	12			
33	1292 Mer/Tal Brithdir	15	38	25	16			

TABLE 7. PERCENTAGE FOR MOST POPULAR NAME—PERCENTAGE OF POPULATIONS OF A GIVEN SIZE FALLING WITHIN CUTOFF

Cutoff	Population Size	Sample Size				
		8	**16**	**32**	**64**	**128**
± 5%	$N > 256$ (8 populations)	62	75	62	75	100
	$N > 128$ (10 populations)	50	80	70	80	100
	$N > 64$ (22 populations)	36	68	73	91	—
	$N > 32$ (42 populations)	36	76	83	—	—
± 10%	$N > 256$ (8 populations)	88	75	75	100	100
	$N > 128$ (10 populations)	80	80	80	100	100
	$N > 64$ (22 populations)	59	86	91	100	—
	$N > 32$ (42 populations)	62	90	95	—	—

TABLE 8. PERCENTAGE FOR TWO MOST POPULAR NAMES—PERCENTAGE OF POPULATIONS OF A GIVEN SIZE FALLING WITHIN CUTOFF

Cutoff	Population Size	Sample Size				
		8	**16**	**32**	**64**	**128**
± 5%	$N > 256$ (8 populations)	38	50	62	62	100
	$N > 128$ (10 populations)	30	50	70	70	100
	$N > 64$ (22 populations)	23	45	64	86	—
	$N > 32$ (42 populations)	14	55	69	—	—
± 10%	$N > 256$ (8 populations)	75	75	75	87	100
	$N > 128$ (10 populations)	70	80	80	90	100
	$N > 64$ (22 populations)	45	82	82	95	—
	$N > 32$ (42 populations)	36	86	90	—	—

TABLE 9. RAW DATA FOR SKEWING—1406 AS MENAI

Sample	1	2	4	8	16	32	64	128	256
Rank									
1	1 Einion	1 Einion	2 Einion	2 David	6 David	10 David	19 David	33 David	65 David
2		1 Madog	1 John	2 Einion	3 Gr'	6 Gr'	11 John	31 John	62 John
Top 2 (%)		**2 (100)**	**3 (75)**	**4 (50)**	**9 (56)**	**16 (50)**	**30 (47)**	**64 (50)**	**127 (50)**
3			1 Madog	1 Gronw	2 Einion	4 John	6 Gr'	9 Hywel	18 Hywel
4				1 Gr'	2 John	3 Einion	6 Madog	8 Einion	14 Madog
5				1 John	1 Gronw	2 Gronw	5 Einion	8 Gr'	14 Gr'
6				1 Madog	1 Madog	2 Madog	5 Hywel	8 Madog	13 Einion
7					1 Matthew	1 Adam	3 Gronw	6 Gronw	11 Iorwerth
8						1 Hywel	3 Ll'	5 Iorwerth	10 Gronw
Top 3–8 (%)						**13 (41)**	**28 (44)**	**44 (34)**	**80 (31)**
9						1 Iorwerth	2 Iorwerth	5 Ll'	10 Ll'
10						1 Matthew	1 Adam	5 Matthew	10 Matthew
11						1 Rhys	1 Mared'	2 Adam	6 Cynwrig
12							1 Matthew	2 Rhys	3 Mared'

Table 9, continued

Sample	1	2	4	8	16	32	64	128	256
13							1 Rhys	1 Bleiddyn	3 Tudur
14								1 Cynwrig	2 Adam
15								1 Elidr	2 Ithel
16								1 Ithel	2 Rhys
17								1 Mared'	2 Simon
18								1 Simon	1 Bleiddyn
19									1 Conws
20									1 Cynddelw
21									1 Ednyfed
22									1 Elidr
23									1 Gwyn
24									1 Heilyn
25									1 Henry
26									1 William

Gr' = Gruffudd
Ll' = Llywelyn
Mared' = Maredudd

TABLE 10. SUMMARY DATA FOR SKEWING—PERCENTAGE OF NAMES
REPRESENTED BY TOP x NAMES (1406 AS MENAI)

	x				
Sample Size	**1**	**2**	**4**	**8**	**16**
1	(100)				
2	(50)	(100)			
4	50	(75)			
8	25	50	(75)		
16	38	56	81		
32	31	50	72	(91)	
64	30	47	66	91	
128	26	50	63	84	(98)
256	25	50	62	81	96

TABLE 11. SKEWING—ALL POPULATIONS FOR N 128, SAMPLED AT 32, 64, AND
MAXIMUM DIFFERENCE IN SKEW FROM MAXIMUM

Population	**Skew at** $N = 32$	**Skew at** $N = 64$	**Max.** N	**Skew at Max.**	**Diff. at 32**	**Diff. at 64**
1600 Pembroke	44	41	512	36	-8	-5
1406 AS Llifon	50	50	256	39	-11	-11
1406 AS Talebolion	50	47	256	39	-11	-8
1406 AS Menai	41	44	256	31	-10	-13
1406 AS Maltraeth	50	42	256	39	-11	-3
1406 AS Tindaethwy	41	41	256	43	+2	+2
1292 Monmouth	41	38	256	39	-2	+1
1406 AS Twrcelyn	38	36	256	41	+3	+5
1315 BY Holt	47	44	128	41	-6	-3
1292 Whitecastle	34	38	128	38	+4	0
1292 Grossmont	28	30	128	25	-3	-5

TABLE 12. DATA FOR SIZE OF NAME POOL—1406 AS LLIFON

Sample	Names	No. of Names	$(Names)^2/N$
1	David	1	1
2	(preceding +) Madog	2	2
4	(preceding +) Ednyfed Gruffudd	4	4
8	(preceding +) Iorwerth Morris	6	4.5
16	(preceding +) Hywel John Tudur	9	5.06
32	(preceding +) Einion Maredudd	11	3.78
64	(preceding +) Caradog Cynwrig Gronw Matthew Rhys Tegwared	17	4.52
128	(preceding +) Llywelyn Heilyn Adam Cona Hwfa	24	4.50

Table 12, continued

Sample	Names	No. of Names	$(Names)^2/N$
	Meurig		
	William		
256	(preceding +)	28	3.06
	Ithel		
	Richard		
	Conws		
	Bleiddyn		

TABLE 13. SUMMARY OF COMPARATIVE MATERIAL FOR THE SIZE AND SHAPE OF THE NAME POOL

Location	Date	Sex	N	Top 2%	Skew %	Pool Index
Asturias	1200	m	387	24.5	43.7	5.23
Asturias	1300	m	1125	30.0	42.9	2.40
Asturias	1400	m	941	32.8	46.2	1.53
Asturias	1490	m	995	38.0	41.9	1.69
Asturias	1200	f	65	43.1	40.0	4.98
Asturias	1300	f	116	42.5	43.4	3.54
Asturias	1400	f	249	50.2	34.5	1.77
Asturias	1490	f	123	38.2	43.9	2.63
Essex	13th	m	4001	23.0	30.2	12.2
Essex	13th	f	1407	21.3	27.1	15.8
King's Stanley	16th	m	125	32.8	44.8	6.27
King's Stanley	16th	f	125	30.4	50.4	3.53
Perugia	1285	f	612	8.8	16.8	102.9
Florence	1427	f	1562	14.9	19.3	41.6

TABLE 14. DATA FOR STABILIZATION OF MOST POPULAR NAMES—1292 MONMOUTH

Ranking					Sample Size				
	1	2	4	8	16	32	64	128	256
1	Edmund	Edmund =	Edmund =	John	Elias =	William	William	William	John
2		William	John =	Edmund =	John	John	John	John	William
3			Richard =	Elias =	Hugh =	Elias	Adam =	Richard	David
4			William	Nicholas =	William	Adam =	Thomas	Adam	Adam
5				Richard =	Clement =	Gilbert =	Elias =	Robert =	Richard
6				Thomas =	Edmund =	Hugh =	Richard	Walter	Walter
7				William	Gilbert =	Robert =	Gilbert =	Thomas	Robert
8					Nicholas =	Thomas	Philip =	Gilbert =	Thomas
9					Richard =	Clement =	Robert =	Henry	Gronw =
10					Thomas	Edmund =	Walter	David =	Henry =
11						Henry =	Henry =	Elias =	Meurig =
12						Nicholas =	Hugh	Philip	Philip
13						Richard =	Andrew =	Hugh	Nicholas
14						Walter	Clement =	Andrew	Gilbert
15							Edmund =	Clement =	Elias
16							Matthew =	Cneitho =	Gruffudd =
17							Nicholas =	Edmund =	Hugh
18							Peter =	Felemon =	Andrew =
19							Roger	Gronw =	Ithel =
20								Gruffudd =	Madog =
21								Ithel =	Matthew =
22								Matthew =	Peter =

Table 14, continued

Ranking	Sample Size								
	1	2	4	8	16	32	64	128	256
23								Meurig =	Rhiryd =
24								Nicholas =	Seisyllt
25								Peter =	Alexander =
26								Radulph =	Clement =
27								Roger =	Cneitho =
28									Edmund =
29									Einion =
30									Felemon =
31									Gwyn =
32									Jacob =
33									Iorwerth =
34									Morfran =
35									Radulph =
36									Roger
Comparison Index Relative to Largest Sample									
	na	na	na	2	2	3	4	4	5

First-ranked name in largest sample is **bold** in all samples.
Second-ranked name in largest sample is <u>underlined</u> in all samples.
Other top five names in largest sample are *italicized* in all samples.
An equals sign (=) following a name indicates that it is tied in rank with the following name(s).

TABLE 15. MOST POPULAR TWO NAMES—RANKING OF OVERALL MOST POPULAR NAMES WITHIN ALL SAMPLES 8 FOR POPULATIONS OF $N > 32$

N	Population	Names		Sample Size						
		#1	#2	8	16	32	64	128	256	512
707	1600 Pembroke	John	David	–/1	1/1	1/2	1/2	1/2	1/3	1/3
414	1406 AS Llifon	David	John	3/–	1/5	1/4	1/3/	1/2	1/2	
396	1406 AS Tindaethwy	John	David	–/1	3/1	1/2	2/1	2/1	2/1	
385	1406 AS Talebolion	David	John	4/4	6/1	2/1	1/2	1/2	1/2	
344	1292 Monmouth	John	William	1/2	1/3	2/1	2/1	2/1	1/2	
325	1406 AS Maltraeth	John =	David	–/3	1/3	1/3	1/2	1/2	2/1	
364	1406 AS Menai	David	John	1/3	1/3	1/3	1/2	1/2	1/2	
275	1406 AS Twrcelyn	John	David	1/–	1/5	1/2	1/2	2/1	2/1	
146	1315 BY Holt	Robert	William	1/1	1/1	2/4	1/2	1/3		
137	1292 Grossmont	John	William	1/–	1/2	1/2	1/2	1/2		
92	1301 Cardiff	John	Philip	1/–	1/4	1/3	1/4			
128	1292 Whitecastle	John	David	2/2	1/5	1/3	1/3			
108	1325 Ardudwy	John	David	–/2	6/1	1/2	1/2			
104	1300 Aberystwyth	John	David	3/3	2/5	2/4	1/2			
93	1292 Skenefrith	John	Nicholas	1/–	1/3	1/3	1/2			
90	1292 Mer/Ard Llanaber	Adam =	Madog	–/–	1/4	1/5	1/2			
87	1292 Mer/Ard Trawsfynydd	John =	Iorwerth	–/–	–/–	7/2	2/1			
82	1256 Abergavenny	John	Philip	1/2	1/2	1/2	1/2			
81	1292 Mer/Tal Nannau	Mad	Einion	1/2	1/2	1/2	1/2			
80	1292 Mer/Ard Lanfrothin	John	tie	3/	3/	2/	1/			
76	1415 Mawddwy	David =	John	1/–	1/4	1/2	1/2			

Table 15, continued

N	Population	#1	#2	8	16	32	64	128	256	512
		Names		**Sample Size**						
69	1315 BY Burton	Iorwerth	Madog	1/—	2/2	1/3	1/2			
64	1292 Mer/Pen Penaran	Einion	David	—/2	—/2	5/2				
58	1315 BY Tref. Bychain	Madog	tie	—/	3/	1/				
57	1292 Mer/Pen Rhywedog	Einion	tie	—/	1/	1/				
54	1315 BY Prog. Elidyr 4	David =	Madog	3/3	4/4	1/1				
53	1315 BY Allington	David	Madog	1/—	2/2	4/1				
52	1315 BY Wrexham	John	Madog	—/—	4/2	1/1				
49	1292 Mer/Ard Penrhyn.	Adam =	John	2/2	1/3	1/2				
48	1292 Mer/Ed Gwyddelwern	Madog	Iorwerth	1/3	1/1	1/2				
48	1315 BY Prog. Cynwrig 4	Hwfa =	Iorwerth	1/—	1/3	1/3				
47	1292 Mer/Tal Pennarth	Madog	David	1/1	1/1	1/2				
45	1292 Mer/Ard Llanfair	Iorwerth	tie	1/	1/	1/				
42	1292 Mer/Ard Maentwrog	Madog	tie	2/	2/	1/				
42	1315 BY Pickhill	Iorwerth	John	1/1	2/1	1/1				
40	1292 Mer/Ed Cynwyd	Madog	Iorwerth	1/—	1/5	1/4				
40	1315 BY Eyton	Madog	Iorwerth	1/2	1/2	1/2				
38	1292 Mer/Yst Cefnrhos	John	Ithel	—/1	4/1	2/1				
38	1292 Mer/Tal Rhydcryw	Einion	David	1/3	2/1	1/1				
37	1315 BY Llandynman	Einion =	Madog	—/4	—/1	1/1				
34	1292 Mer/Pen Gwernefail	Madog	David	—/1	1/2	1/1				
33	1292 Mer/Tal Brithdir	John	Madog	1/2	1/2	1/2				

An equals sign (=) following a name indicates it is tied in rank with the following name(s).

TABLE 16. MOST POPULAR TWO NAMES—PERCENTAGE OF POPULATIONS OF A
GIVEN SIZE SATISFYING THE CONDITIONS AT A PARTICULAR SAMPLE SIZE

	Sample Size			
Population Size	**8**	**16**	**32**	**64**
Top #1 Name Appears in Top Two Slots				
$N > 256$ (8 populations)	50	75	88	100
$N > 128$ (14 populations)	64	71	86	100
$N > 64$ (22 populations)	59	77	91	—
$N > 32$ (43 populations)	58	72	—	—
Top #1 and 2 Names Appear in Top Five Slots				
$N > 256$ (8 populations)	38	88	100	100
$N > 128$ (14 populations)	36	86	100	100
$N > 64$ (21 populations)	33	86	95	—
$N > 32$ (38 populations)	42	84	—	—
Top #1 and 2 Names Appear in Top Three Slots				
$N > 256$ (8 populations)	25	62	88	100
$N > 128$ (14 populations)	26	50	79	86
$N > 64$ (21 populations)	19	48	71	—
$N > 32$ (38 populations)	32	53	—	—

TABLE 17. FIVE MOST POPULAR NAMES—ALL POPULATIONS

Population	1	2	3	4	5
Masculine					
1256 Abergavenny unique	John	Philip	Caradog	Gronw	Ithel
1256 Abergavenny all	John	Caradog	Ithel =	Philip	Gronw = Seisyllt
1292 Monmouth	John	William	David	Adam	Richard
1292 Grossmont	John	William	David	Richard	Philip = Walter
1292 Whitecastle	John	David	Philip	William	Adam
1292 Skenfrith	John	Nicholas	Adam	David	Philip
1292 Merioneth	Madog	David	Einion	Iorwerth	John
1292 Mer Ardudwy	Iorwerth	Madog	Adam	John	Einion
1292 Mer/Ard Llanaber	Adam =	Madog	David	Gronw =	Iorwerth
1292 Mer/Ard Llanfrothen	John	Iorwerth =	Madog	Adam	Gwyn
1292 Mer/Ard Trawsfynydd	John =	Iorwerth	Ithel	Cynwrig =	Einion
1292 Mer Edeirnion	Madog	David	Iorwerth	John	Einion
1292 Mer Penllyn	Madog	Einion	David	Iorwerth	Gronw
1292 Mer/Pen Penaran	Einion	David	Gwyn	Iorwerth	Adam
1292 Mer Talybont	Madog	David	Einion	Ithel	Adam
1292 Mer/Tal Nannau	Madog	Einion	John	Gwyn	Iorwerth
1292 Mer Ystumanner	Madog	David	Adam =	Einion	John
1292 Nevyn	David	Einion	John	Adam	Madog
1292 Lleyn	John	David	Iorwerth	Adam	Einion
1300 Aberystwyth	John	David	Philip =	Richard =	William
1301 Cardiff unique	John	Philip =	Walter	William	David
1301 Cardiff all	John	Philip	Walter =	William	Thomas
1315 Bromfield & Yale	Madog	Iorwerth	John	David	Einion

Table 17, continued

Population	1	2	3	4	5
1315 BY Burton	Iorwerth	Madog	Llywelyn	David =	Ednyfed
1315 BY Holt	Robert	William	John	Richard	Thomas
1315 BY Prog. Cynwrig	Iorerth	Madog	Hywel	Hwfa	Llywelyn
1315 BY Prog. Elidyr	Madog	Iorwerth	David	Ednyfed	John = Cynwrig
1325 Ardudwy unique	John	David	Adam	Iorwerth	Gronw
1325 Ardudwy all	John	David	Adam =	Iorwerth	Gronw
1406 Anglesey	David	John	Iorwerth	Hywel	Madog
1406 AS Llifon	David	John	Iorwerth	Gruffudd	Hywel
1406 AS Maltraeth	John	David	Iorwerth	Gruffudd	Einion
1406 AS Menai	David	John	Hywel	Iorwerth	Gruffudd = Madog
1406 AS Talebolion	David	John	Iorwerth	Madog	Hywel
1406 AS Tindaethwy	John	David	Iorwerth	Hywel	Einion
1406 AS Twrcelyn	John	David	Hywel	Madog	Iorwerth
1415 Mawddwy unique	David =	John	Gruffudd	Madog	Llywelyn
1415 Mawddwy all	John	David	Gruffudd	Madog	Llywelyn = William
1597 Caernarvon	John =	Robert	William	Richard	Hugh
1600 Pembroke unique	John	David	William	Thomas	Rhys
1600 Pembroke all	John	David	William	Thomas	Rhys
Feminine					
1292 Merioneth	Angharad =	Gwenllian	Gwladus	Dyddgu	Eva = Generys = Tangwystl
1292 Mer Ardudwy	Gwenllian	Angharad =	Dyddgu =	Gwladus	Tangwystl
1292 Mer Talybont	Angharad	Eva	Dyddgu =	Gwladus	Tangwystl

An equals sign (=) following a name indicates it is tied in rank with the following name(s).

TABLE 18. SUMMARY OF STATISTICS

Statistic	Precision	Accuracy at $N = 64$	Accuracy at $N = 32$
% Foreign	30	100%	100%
	20	70–80%	70–80%
% Top 1	20	100%	inaccurate
	10	80–90%	inaccurate
% Top 2	20	80–90%	inaccurate
	10	70–80%	inaccurate
Skew	20	80–90%	inaccurate
	10	70–80%	inaccurate
Pool	4.0	100	inaccurate
	3.0	80–90%	inaccurate
Top 1 in 2	n.a.	100%	80–90%
Top 2 in 5	n.a.	100%	100%
Top 2 in 3	n.a.	100%	80–90%

TABLE 19. MASCULINE VS. FEMININE NAME COMMUNITIES

	N	% Foreign	% Top 1	% Top 2	Skew	Pool
1292 Merioneth men	2296	28	13	22	42	8.29
1292 Merioneth women	247	11	13	27	50	3.17
1292 Mer Talybont men	415	27	16	27	39	7.83
1292 Mer Talybont women	72	17	18	31	47	5.56
1292 Mer Ardudwy men	631	29	11	22	44	6.70
1292 Mer Ardudwy women	73	5	16	27	53	5.48

TABLE 20. RECORDS WITH DUPLICATE NAMES

	N	% Foreign	% Top 1	% Top 2	Skew	Pool
1256 Abergavenny all	94	45	23	32	37	6.13
1256 Abergavenny unique	82	49	24	33	35	7.02
1301 Cardiff all	128	95	27	39	41	4.50
1301 Cardiff unique	92	95	23	35	42	6.26
1326 Ardudwy all	128	43	17	32	45	4.50
1326 Ardudwy unique	108	44	18	32	44	5.33
1415 Mawddwy all	154	49	21	42	45	2.10
1415 Mawddwy unique	76	47	21	42	43	3.80
1600 Pembroke all	1088	82	20	31	36	4.17
1600 Pembroke unique	707	82	22	33	37	6.71

TABLE 21. ARDUDWY RECORDS—1292 LAY SUBSIDY VS. 1325 COURT RECORDS

	N	% Foreign	% Top 1	% Top 2	Skew	Pool
1292 Mer Ardudwy	631	29	11	22	44	6.70
1325 Ardudwy	108	44	18	32	44	5.33

TABLE 22. MERIONETH—LOCAL POPULATIONS AND SUPER–POPULATIONS

	N	% Foreign	% Top 1	% Top 2	Skew	Pool
1292 Merioneth	2296	28	13	22	42	8.29
1292 Mer Ystumanner	340	31	11	22	38	9.56
1292 Mer Edeirnion	449	29	16	28	43	3.56
1292 Mer Talybont	415	27	16	27	39	7.83
1292 Mer/Tal Nannau	81	21	14	26	37	9.00
1292 Mer Penllyn	434	24	11	21	42	6.23
1292 Mer/Pen Penaran	65	28	14	26	39	9.62
1292 Mer Ardudwy	631	29	11	22	44	6.70
1292 Mer/Ard Llanaber	90	34	12	24	48	6.40
1292 Mer/Ard Trawsfynydd	87	30	14	28	45	7.77
1292 Mer/Ard Llanfrothen	80	32	15	28	44	7.81

TABLE 23. BROMFIELD AND YALE

	N	% Foreign	% Top 1	% Top 2	Skew	Pool
1315 Bromfield & Yale	1062	36	13	25	38	3.17
1315 BY Burton	69	13	14	26	41	6.39
1315 BY Holt	146	98	16	32	47	4.63
1315 BY Prog. Cynwrig	135	11	19	31	39	3.27
1315 BY Prog. Elidyr	100	24	19	33	46	4.84

TABLE 24. ANGLESEY SUBMISSIONS OF 1406—COMMOTES AND SUPER-POPULATION

	N	% Foreign	% Top 1	% Top 2	Skew	Pool
1406 Anglesey	2099	47	22	42	38	1.14
1406 AS Llifon	414	47	24	43	37	2.47
1406 AS Maltraeth	325	49	23	45	38	1.77
1406 AS Tindaethwy	396	46	20	39	41	2.59
1406 AS Menai	304	54	25	48	33	2.22
1406 AS Talebolion	385	42	21	37	40	1.62
1406 AS Twrcelyn	275	45	21	42	40	2.65

TABLE 25. LAY SUBSIDY OF 1292–93

	N	% Foreign	% Top 1	% Top 2	Skew	Pool
1292 Mer Ardudwy	631	29	11	22	44	6.70
1292 Mer Edeirnion	449	29	16	28	43	3.56
1292 Mer Penllyn	434	24	11	21	42	6.23
1292 Mer Talybont	415	27	16	27	39	7.83
1292 Mer Ystumanner	340	31	11	22	38	9.56
1292 Monmouth	344	89	16	29	38	6.15
1292 Grossmont	137	79	27	40	26	10.5
1292 Whitecastle	130	66	25	38	38	5.61
1292 Skenfrith	93	81	22	34	39	6.72
1292 Nefyn	70	50	26	36	36	7.56
1292 Lleyn	161	46	21	34	45	4.87

TABLE 26. OTHER POPULATIONS FROM CA. 1300

	N	% Foreign	% Top 1	% Top 2	Skew	Pool
Burgesses 1300–01						
1300 Aberystwyth	104	88	22	34	40	8.09
1301 Cardiff	92	95	23	35	42	6.26
Extent of Bromfield & Yale 1315						
1315 BY Burton	69	13	14	26	41	6.39
1315 BY Holt	146	98	16	32	47	4.63
1315 BY Prog. Cynwrig	135	11	19	31	39	3.27
1315 BY Prog. Elidyr	100	24	19	33	46	4.84

TABLE 27. TAX RECORDS FROM CAERNARVONSHIRE

	N	% Foreign	% Top 1	% Top 2	Skew	Pool
1292 Nefyn	70	50	26	36	36	7.56
1292 Lleyn	161	46	21	34	45	4.87
1597 Caernarvon	199	86	16	31	44	3.94

TABLE 28. NAME-POOL INDEXES FOR DATA FROM MORGAN (1995)

Source	Date	N	Names	Raw Index	Normalized Index
Genealogy	< 895	250	85	28.9	> 29
Genealogy	895–1215	480	86	15.4	> 15
Genealogy	1215–1350	1680	78	3.62	7
Genealogy	1350–1415	2124	72	2.44	7
Genealogy	15th c.	10,778	94	0.82	6
Wills	1550–1620	371	47	5.91	7

RESISTANT, DIFFUSED, OR PERIPHERAL? NORTHERN PERSONAL NAMES TO CA. 1250

Dave Postles

During the twelfth century a general transformation in English naming processes and patterns occurred.[1] It has also been suggested that this transformation was more precocious for the *nomina* of males, whereas female names tended towards a higher corpus of traditional names, since either female names remained a repository of traditional culture or female role models were persistently of Insular origin.[2] Amongst males, Insular personal names—mainly, but not exclusively OE and AScand items—were rapidly supplanted by newly introduced forms of personal name, mainly, but again not exclusively, CG and Christian names. More women, however, continued to be given Insular personal names, because, first, the new aristocracy was predominantly male, so that intermarriage with indigenous females was inevitable (but was equally an important strategy for legitimation of the acquisition of estates by "conquest") and thus female exemplars for naming bore traditional names. Second, as a result, women remained the repository of a traditional culture.

---

[1]Cecily Clark, "Women's Names in Post-Conquest England: Observations and Speculations," *Speculum* 53 (1978), 223–51, repr. in C. Clark, *Words, Names and History: Selected Writings of Cecily Clark*, ed. Peter Jackson (Cambridge, 1995), pp. 117–43 and above (pp. 65–102); M. T. Clanchy, *England and Its Rulers, 1066–1272: Foreign Lordship and National Identity* (London, 1983), p. 57.

[2]Clark, "Women's Names in Post-Conquest England."

This transformation should be problematized, nevertheless, for it was complex. One of the potential complexities is regional variation and, not least, how regional differences should be interpreted. It seems clear that Insular names persisted in some regions, such as some parts of the West Midlands, longer than elsewhere, even amongst the naming of males.[3] It is, however, the North, however defined, which might present the greatest ambiguity. It might be helpful to present an analysis of the evidence of personal naming in the North up to ca. 1250 and then to consider the possible interpretations of that evidence.

In the late eleventh century, some localized parts of the North were an intense confusion of naming etymologies, a commingling of Norman, Breton, Godoillic, Scottish, OE, and AScand name forms—thus betraying persistent Insular as well as exogamous influences from a variety of directions.[4] Such a confusion of naming and thus cultural processes has been identified in the North in the late eleventh century in the upper levels of free society. It will be suggested here that the persistence of the Insular tradition in naming extended longer, well into the late twelfth century, and that it endured at lower social levels.

The importance of Insular actors at some levels of society has also been more recently established.[5] For example, the English provided the substantial number of the Domesday jurors. Moreover, reliance on English officials was significant into the 1130s.[6] It has also long been recognized that there was a stronger survival of Insular families, paradoxically, in the regions where resistance to new overlordship was most intense, including, and perhaps especially, the North.[7] An example of the continuation of Insular male

---

[3]Dave Postles, "Cultures of Peasant Naming in Twelfth-Century England," *MP* 18 (1997), 25–54.

[4]John Insley, "Some Aspects of Regional Variation in Early Middle English Nomenclature," *Leeds Studies in English. Studies in Honour of Kenneth Cameron*, n.s. 18 (1987), pp. 183–99. This paper is reprinted above (pp. 191–209), and my debt to it will be obvious; my limited intention here is to assess the persistence of these names over a wider area of the "North" and for a longer continuum.

[5]C. P. Lewis, "The Domesday Jurors," *Haskins Society Journal* 5 (1993), 17–44 (reprinted below, pp. 307–39).

[6]A. Williams, *The English and the Norman Conquest* (Woodbridge, 1995), pp. 71–125.

[7]F. M. Stenton, "English Families and the Norman Conquest," repr. in his *Preparatory to*

role models in the North is the descent of the family of Gospatrick, succeeded by Uchtred (de Alverstain), then Thorphin (de Alverstain), the *nomen* in the family becoming "new" only with the accession of Alan *filius Torphini* in the late twelfth century, and then assuming a Breton *nomen*.[8]

DURHAM

For the Durham episcopal estates in the twelfth century, we are fortunate to have a manorial survey, Boldon Buke of 1183.[9] Unlike contemporary surveys from southern estates, however, it largely omits the names of tenants, but with exceptions. A proportion of tenants is named, but in itself that inconsistency raises questions about the status of these named tenants. By and large, it might be assumed that these tenants are more significant, but it is not exclusively so, for some cottagers were attributed names. Despite this inconsistency, it is possible to present the evidence of Insular names in tabulated form (Table 1).

TABLE 1. INSULAR PERSONAL NAMES IN BOLDON BUKE, 1183

Manor	Names	Tenure	Other description
Bedick	Ulkill	sixth of a knight's fee	
Clevedon	Ketel	2 bovates	riding service
Clevedon	Osbert *filius Leising'*	80 acres	
Burdon	Elfer de Birdena	2 bovates	riding service
Houghton	Leveric *prepositus*	2 bovates	
Sutton	Saddoc	1 bovate	
N. Shirburn	Ulkill	2 bovates	riding service

Anglo-Saxon England, ed. D. M. Stenton (Oxford, 1970); Williams, *The English and the Norman Conquest*, pp. 96–97.

[8] *Cartularium Abbathiae de Whiteby*, 1, ed. John Christopher Atkinson, Surtees Society 69 (1879), pp. 35–37 (nos. xxix–xxx), Alan's benefaction being ca. 1174.

[9] *Boldon Buke: A Survey of the Possessions of the See of Durham made by Order of Bishop Hugh Pudsey in the Year M.C.LXXXIII*, ed. William Greenwell, Surtees Society 25 (1852).

Manor	Names	Tenure	Other description
Shireburn	Arkill	2 bovates	previous tenant
Shireburn	Watling and his wife Sama	4 bovates	
Middleham	Arkil	4 bovates	
Stockton	Elwin	toft	cotmannus
Stockton	Godwin	toft	cotmannus
Stockton	Suan *faber*	toft	
Preston	Orm *filius Toki*	½ carucate	
Quesshow	Toki	2 bovates	
Quesshow	Orm	2 bovates	brother of Toki
Midridge	Ulkill	1 bovate	cotmannus [*sic*]
Midridge	Anketill	2 bovates	
Thickley	Ail	?	cotmannus
Escombe	Ulf Raning	6 acres	former tenant
West Auckland	Aldred	1 bovate	
West Auckland	Uchtred *forestarius*	1 bovate	
West Auckland	Godmund	1 bovate	
West Auckland	Edwin	toft	
West Auckland	Elstan *drengus*	4 bovates	dreng
Stanhope	Bernulf de Pec	60 acres	
Stanhope	Gamel *filius Godrici*	60 acres	
Stanhope	Thore	60 acres	
Stanhope	Ethelred	15 acres	
Stanhope	Osbert	15 acres	
Stanhope	Aldred *faber*	12 acres	
Stanhope	Arkill Hubaldus	9 acres	
Stanhope	Collan	6 acres	

Manor	Names	Tenure	Other description
Stanhope	Meldred *faber*	toft and croft	
Stanhope	Ilving	4 acres	
Stanhope	Meldred	toft	
Langchester	Liulf	60 acres	
Langchester	Ulkill	20 acres	
Langchester	Meldred	20 acres	
Langchester	Orm	8½ acres	
Crawcrock	Meldred *filius Dolfini*	land	previous tenant
Westlikburna	Turkill		owed rent of hens
Westlikburna	Eadwin		owed rent of hens
Westlikburna	Patrick		owed rent of hens
Norham	Suartbrand	1 carucate	
Norham	Elfald Langstirap	½ carucate	

The size of many of the tenements of these tenants with Insular personal names suggests that they were substantial tenants, some of whom were of free status. Moreover, some tenants bearing CG personal names represented a transitional generation, such as William *filius Uttingi*, who held half a carucate at Preston, William *filius Ormi* with a carucate in Carlton, Walter *filius Sigge*[10] with two bovates at Great Halghton, Richard *filius Ulkilli* with half a carucate at Norham, and Robert *filius Gospatricii* and Arnald *filius Uctredi* who owed rents of hens at Netherton. Furthermore, the bishop had leased Little Slickburn to a group of peasant *firmarii* including Edmund *filius Edmundi*, John *filius Patricii*, Laurence *filius Edmundi*, and Thomas *filius Edmundi*, which reflect (in the first name) the persistence of Insular names and (in the case of the other three) recent change.

---

[10]*Boldon Buke*, p. 19: but one wonders whether this represents confusion of long *s* and *f*, so that the patronym is derived from *Figgi*.

NORTHUMBERLAND

Material for Northern naming during the twelfth century occurs in un-
systematic sources in the sense that it survives less in manorial surveys than
in documents which necessarily provide only an impression of naming:
charters; miracle narratives; and the pleas recorded in "criminal" jurisdiction in royal courts. The earliest, but perhaps most eclectic, of these
sources are the miracle narratives surrounding Godric of Finchale. Of 237
narratives, however, only 133 stated the names of the pilgrims to the numi-
nous place. Moreover, 153 of the supplicants were female. The narratives
extend through the middle of the twelfth century, perhaps to ca. 1175.[11] By
and large the supplicants were of lower status, although the overall com-
plexion was mixed. From the narratives some fifty-five different female
names emerge, of which the most frequent were the ambiguous *Adeliz*
(seven occurrences), followed by the new *Matilda* (six), *Eda* (five), and
Agnes (four). Amongst the non-Insular names were also *Mabilia* (twice),
and, once each, *Wimarc, Avelina, Hawise, Emelina, Beatrice, Emelotha,
Emma, Cecily, Isabel, Johette,* and *Margaret*. Whilst such a purposive
sample might be considered unrepresentative, it did comprehend a considerable element of new forms of female name. Nevertheless, the Insular
forms also remained extensive, if none was as frequent as *Alice, Matilda,
Eda,* or *Agnes*. *Sierith* (thrice) exhibited some popularity, reflected in its later
persistence, alongside *Heccoc* and *Siwine* (both also three), followed by,
twice each, *Sungiva, Tunnoc,* and *Eluuiua*. Some names perceived to be
frequent were reflected only once each, such as *Goda, Brictiva,* and *Edith*.
Overall, the corpus of female names continued to include a high proportion
of Insular forms but was obviously already in transition.

Amongst male pilgrims to the holy *locus*, CG names had already
established a more considerable presence: *Hugh, Robert,* and *William* three
incidences each, *Gilbert, Elias, Henry,* and *Richard* two each, with single
appearances of *Ralph, Baldwin, Gervase,* and *Roger*. Christian names were
represented by two *John*s, Breton by a single *Alan*, and Crusading by
Jordan (if such be its etymology). It is, nevertheless, important to provide
a further context for these names, for the two *Gilbert*s were of higher status,

---

[11]Reginald of Durham, *Libellus de Vita et Miraculis S Godrici, Heremitae de Finchale*, ed.
J. Stevenson, Surtees Society 20 (1847), p. 463 (ccx) is dated 1175 (hereafter cited as Godric).

dispensator and *clericus*, although one of the *Hugh*s was a shepherd, another was a *minister*, and the third the *homo* of Fulk Painel. Of the three *William*s, one was a monk of Durham and another a priest. One of the *Henry*s was a *clericus*, as was Gervase, whilst Alan was of knightly status, a lord. Jordan was son of Elias Escollande, a benefactor of Finchale Priory, and equally both *Richard*s were of wealthy status (a *primogenitus* of a *dives* and the other *dominium possidens*). In fact, the preponderance of newer forms of names is comprehended by higher status.

In contrast, Alsi was a reeve, but we have little evidence of the status of the other bearers of Insular names, except for Waltheof, who was of seignorial status, lord of a vill. Those names comprised *Crin, Wilgrun, Edric, Acke, Edulf, Godric, Elsi, Gamel, Iggi,* and *Uchtred,* all once each. Moreover, some belonged to youths, thus reflecting the persistence of the names: Edulf, for example, was a *juvenis*. Acke was the son of Pace and Gamel the offspring of Carl. One of the *Henry*s was son of Uchtred, as was one of the *Robert*s, and one of the *John*s a son of Sigar, so reflecting recent generational change.

On balance then, male Insular *nomina* continued to be as prominent at the lower social levels as female, it seems, although the sizes of the two samples are disparate. It is possible to examine some of these individuals in a little more detail, particularly the women. In some cases, it is certainly true that males with new forms of name had taken in marriage females with Insular names: thus Walter *minister episcopi* was the husband of one of the Sieriths, whose daughter was named Aviza, as William de Waltham had married Eccoc, their offspring being William.[12] Another Sierith, a *matrona*, was the wife of the reapreeve, Elias, a Sungiva wife of Norman, Emma wife of Leofric, but equally Edoc was married to Seman *faber*, Avelina to Richard, Agnes to Gospatrick (with the status of a lady), and Margaret was the daughter of the lord Waltheof. One Eda was the daughter of a Durham man, an Alice was a *puella*, an Eleuuiua a servant (*ancilla*), Emelotha a young girl (*puellela* or *juvencula*), and Aldusa poor, Eda a young woman (*femina*) aged twenty-three, Tunnoc the daughter of Ferthan, Agnes a young girl (*puella*), Alice another *puella*, and Bothilda also poor. Ekke of Hardwick was of similar lowly status, for she had only two lambs. No discernible pattern seems to emerge from this prosopography.

---

[12]*Godric*, pp. 422–23 (clii, cliv).

On the other hand, the persistence of Insular names amongst males was itself propagated by the saint's cult. As a result of her child's swollen body, Emelotha de Wideslade conveyed the boy to Finchale, and in gratitude for his recovery renamed her child Ralph Godric.[13]

YORKSHIRE

By the early thirteenth century, the North was characterized in part by the persistence—at whatever level—of a corpus of distinctive Insular personal names.[14] Incidentally, how paradigmatic some of these names became of northern society is perhaps reflected in the Benedictine monk Uchtred of Bolton, a monk of Durham Cathedral Priory who studied at Oxford in the 1360s.[15] Such names recur amongst those involved in the Crown Pleas held at York in 1218–19, whether as plaintiffs, those appealed, or convicted felons. In the majority of cases it is likely that those involved are from lower social groups. Thus, when Utting de Folifant was found guilty of killing Elias de Lidel', his chattels were appraised at only 17d.[16] Many of the males involved in these pleas still held Insular names, whilst other pleas reveal a recent generational change in naming in patronymic descriptions.

When Orm and William, men of the abbot of Beauchief, were murdered, Uchtred de Brincliffe found the perpetrators. When Walter son of Gamel de Farnl' was found drowned, it was his father, Gamel, who discovered the body, illustration of the recent transition from Insular OE and AScand personal names.[17]

---

[13]Godric, pp. 434–35 (clxxvii).

[14]G. W. S. Barrow, "Northern English Society in the Twelfth and Thirteenth Centuries," *Northern History* 4 (1969), 1–28.

[15]G. L. Ripple, "Uchtred and the Friars: Apostolic Poverty and Clerical Dominion between FitzRalph and Wyclif," *Traditio* 49 (1994), 235–58.

[16]*Rolls of the Justices in Eyre, Being the Rolls of the Pleas and Assizes for Yorkshire in 3 Henry III (1218–19)*, ed. Doris Mary Stenton, Selden Society 56 (1937), p. 272.

[17]*Rolls of the Justices in Eyre . . . for Yorkshire, 1218–19*, p. 242 (no. 649).

TABLE 2. INSULAR PERSONAL NAMES IN YORKSHIRE CROWN PLEAS 1218–19

Actor	Event
Arkell de Breddal'	found murdered
Auty *plumbarius* (of Leeds)	found murdered
Auty le paumer	appealed as accessory to murder
Gamel Gosenoll	accessory to battery/robbery
Gamel *filius Gamelli*	held a messuage, had been pilgrim to Jerusalem
Gamel *garcio*	
Gamel (a certain Gamel)	found dead
Leolf	accessory to robbery
Leofric	fell from his cart and died
Ketel de Saghe	convicted murderer
Orm de Grinlinton'	accessory to murder
Swan de Criggleston'	
Swan de Bretton'	appealed for murder but acquitted
Swan de Stodfeld	accessory to battery
Swan de Hesinton'	fell from his horse and died
Swan de Chinkel'	appealed for murder
Swan de Wadinton'	accessory to murder
Uchtred de Bramle	found murdered
Ukeman	found murdered
Utting de Folifant	convicted of murder
Utting *nepos* of Ukeman	appealed for robbery
Utting scutehod	outlawed for robbery
Utting *filius* Leuer'	fell from his cart and died
Utting de Ilketon	was appealed for rape

Transition is reflected in many other pleas, as when William *filius Saxi* was appealed for murder or when Bernard *filius Bernolfi* appealed Robert *filius Ukeman'* and his nephew, Utting, for robbery. The two sons of Ulf, Walter and Adam, were outlaws for the same offense of theft. Thomas *filius Eylsi* was a pledge. Agnes daughter of Uchtred de Nid was an appellor for rape, and Hugh son of Aylsi de Drictlington' was another appellor. Walter *filius Derman* brought an appeal for battery, and Emma *filia Edric'*, even more seriously, for homicide. The two sons of Heremer, Thomas and Gilbert, were appealed. The pledges found in another case were Robert *filius Dolfin'* and Peter *filius Auty*, but Geoffrey *filius Grimkell'* was attached.

TABLE 3. PATRONYMS WITH INSULAR PERSONAL NAMES
IN THE YORKSHIRE CROWN PLEAS

Actor	Event
Walter *filius Toly*	pledge
Thomas *filius Siwardi*	appealed for rape
William *filius Edrici*	appealed for battery
Alan *filius Uctred'*	fell from cart and died
Adam *filius Waldef'*	appealed for theft
Nicholas *filius Bernolfi*	plea of waste
Anketin *filius Wulmer'*	his body found dead
William *filius Dolfini de Spanton'*	appellor for the murder of his son
Hugh *filius Ukeman'*	outlawed for murder
Thomas *filius Akkeman'*	outlawed for battery
Thomas *filius Elsi le poter*	outlawed for murder
Thomas *filius Eylsi*	his body found dead
Galiena daughter of Kenwald' de Wusseburc'	appellor for rape
Robert *filius Gemelli de Wusseburc'*	appealed for rape
Henry *filius Ormi*	appealed for murder

Actor	Event
William *filius Edwardi de Claverle*	his body found dead
Robert *filius Arkelli*	ditto
Richard *filius Dolfini*	ditto
Alan and Thomas *filii Alsy*	
Richard *filius Dolfini de Elmesh'*	
Robert *filius Ulfi*	
John *filius Swani de Upton*	
Ralph *filius Ormi*	
Herbert *filius Herewardi de Sutton'*	
Geoffrey *filius Herewardi de Barnebi*	appellor
Simon *filius Aki de Hetele*	appellor for robbery
Stephen *filius Gospatricii de Preston'*	outlawed for murder

Of higher position were Peter the son of Wulmar, who held nine acres in Greasborough, and Henry the son of Eylsy, who held twenty-two acres in Wombwell. In litigation about four bovates in Melmerby, six daughters, Golle, Maud, Emma, Beatrice, Isolda, and Agnes, were the offspring of Ulf de Westone. Adam *filius Waldef'* was encountered again as the defendant in a plea of dower relating to two bovates in Carlton Husthwaite.[18]

These names appeared in the earlier Crown Pleas and Assizes for the county, fragments of which have been published. So in 1204 Gernegan de Tanfeld impleaded Landric, Dolfin, Elvric, and William *filius Patricii* along with others concerning common of pasture in Tanfield.[19] Haldan *filius Willelmi* was appealed as an accessory and Gamel de Winkesleye acted as a

---

[18]*Rolls of the Justices in Eyre . . . for Yorkshire, 1218–19*, pp. 26–27 (no. 57), 29 (no. 60), 35–36 (no. 80), and 70–71 (no. 172).

[19]*Select Pleas before the King or His Justices*, 3, ed. Doris Mary Stenton, Selden Society 83 (1967), p. 125 (no. 895).

pledge, in 1208.[20] The recent transition is reflected in some of the assizes of *mort d'ancestor* which depended on establishing the previous tenant who died seised of the land: Uchtred *pater Arnaldi* in half a carucate in Follifoot in 1204; Horm *pater Ricardi de Torp* in seven acres; Ketel *pater Willelmi de Doctton'* in two bovates in Grafton in 1204; all these cases represent Insular personal names held at the end of the twelfth century by free tenants of considerable land.[21] In a plea of *novel disseisin* between two more free tenants in 1205, the litigants were Geoffrey *filius Lefwini* and Roger *filius Lefwini*.[22] Robert *filius Uctred'*, moreover, introduced a plea about a substantial amount of land, six bovates in Langton, in 1204.[23] These assizes confirm that Insular personal names continued amongst the substantial free tenantry, were not marked out as deficient in social honor, and were not confined to the unfree tenantry or the lowest social groups.

The corpus of the names is expanded, however, by the Crown Pleas, for David *filius Siward'* was appealed of a breach of the peace in 1208.[24] Alan *filius Dering'* killed Benedict the clerk and he was probably of low status, for he held no chattels.[25] Two unfortunate incidents involved the accidental deaths of William *filius Harding'* in the River Wiske and William *filius Forn'*, who fell from his horse, both in 1208.[26]

The proliferation of such names in the Crown Pleas suggests a strong survival of male Insular personal names into the late twelfth, if not the early thirteenth, century. Consequently, Richard de Claiton's sons, Alan and Walth[eof], were provided with names from both cultural traditions, perhaps at the very end of the twelfth century, for on the death of Waltheof, Alan brought an appeal, before the war, but he was found to be underage.[27] Such names were becoming encapsulated in bynames, as when Roger Tosty of

---

[20]*Select Pleas before the King or His Justices*, 4, ed. Doris Mary Stenton, Selden Society 84 (1967), p. 103 (no. 3448).

[21]*Select Pleas* 3:141–42 (nos. 936–37).

[22]*Select Pleas* 3:140 (no. 934).

[23]*Select Pleas* 3:156.

[24]*Select Pleas* 4:101 (no. 3439).

[25]*Select Pleas* 4:101 (no. 2440).

[26]*Select Pleas* 4:108 and 111 (nos. 3465 and 3481).

[27]*Rolls of the Justices in Eyre . . . for Yorkshire, 1218–19*, p. 214 (no. 536).

Marton appealed Robert Tosty of battery.[28] In that same year Robert *filius Copsi* was appealed for wounding, his accessory allegedly Hugh *filius Copsi*, and John *filius Walding'* was also appealed in that session.[29]

The evidence provided by cartularies is likely to be different and perhaps even more eclectic. Charters legally involve only free tenants and, when the charters represent mainly benefactions to religious houses, the donors are potentially of a stratum which has some disposable land. What charters do reveal is the persistence of Insular personal names amongst the free and also amongst the significant free tenants. Thus Henry de Willardby, whilst giving to Bridlington Priory half a carucate, also confirmed the previous benefaction by Adelard, his father, of the advowson of Willardby and half a carucate. Charters of Henry's successors divulge that he had three children, Adelard, his son and heir, Henry, and Agnes.[30] Thus the OE personal name *Adelard* had continued in a knightly family and was further extended by the naming of a son for his grandfather, whilst the second son assumed the father's name. In another gift by Adelard de Willard' to Bridlington, the land provided abutted on the toft of Alemann *faber* and mention was made of the croft of Adelard Cuuing.[31] In the early thirteenth century, Beatrice de Killom married, first, John de Brigham, and second, Edulf de Killum.[32] Beatrice held at least two bovates and a toft. In Burton Fleming, Eilward *filius Edwaldi* received three bovates and two tofts from Theobald de Wikham, part of a knight's fee.[33]

Warter Priory acquired two bovates from Adam Murdac, which two bovates Ailwin used to hold ("Quas Ailwinus aliquando tenuit") and, in the same benefaction, a messuage was described as lying between that of Peter *clericus* and Reginald *filius Bonde*.[34] Warter also received a toft and furlong in Seaton from Gilbert *filius Edrici de Seton'* as well as an exchange of

---

[28]*Rolls of the Justices in Eyre . . . for Yorkshire, 1218–19*, p. 382 (no. 1062).

[29]*Select Pleas* 4:113 and 117 (nos. 3488 and 3505), but Walding is a problematic name: see the Appendix, below.

[30]London, British Library Add. MS 40,008, fols. 76r–83r.

[31]BL Add. MS 40,008, fol. 88r.

[32]BL Add. MS 40,008, fols. 141r–142r.

[33]BL Add. MS 40,008, fol. 43r.

[34]Oxford, Bodleian Library, Fairfax MS 9, fol. 9v.

lands with German de Hay, lord of Acton.[35] Drax Priory received a bovate and toft from Colswann de Happlesthorp'.[36] Such transactions suggest that Insular personal names were not undignified nor confined to the unfree peasantry and that they were persistently used amongst males into the early thirteenth century.

For Yorkshire it is not possible to quantify the persistence of Insular personal names, but there is sufficient evidence to affirm that these names continued to the end of the twelfth century at all levels of peasant society, including amongst substantial free tenants. The material suggests that they persisted at a fairly high numerical level. Since substantial free tenants constantly bore these forms of name, it seems unlikely that any social dishonor was attached to the names before the early thirteenth century. It is important to note that the names were retained by males as well as females, with no apparent distinction by gender.

DONORS TO ST. BEES AND FURNESS

Other expositions of the general transformation of naming practices in England in the twelfth century have suggested the importance of downwards cultural conflation, predicated on cultural imitation of superiors. Below it will be maintained that such conflation was by no means the only influence on cultural situations, but here it will be demonstrated that at a middling level of society Insular personal names persisted into the late twelfth century. Whilst Stenton, Williams, and Lewis, respectively, have demonstrated the revival of the fortunes of English families in the early twelfth century or the significance of a level of an English administrative cadre in the realm generally, through to the 1130s, in the North Insular personal names continued in use at the same level into the late twelfth century. Donors and witnesses to charters to religious houses in the North included numerous who still bore Insular personal names, represented, for example, in charters to St. Bees and Furness in the further North. As one instance, in 1165x1177, Waltheof *filius Edmundi* made a benefaction to Furness of Newby, his charter witnessed *inter alia* by Elias *filius Gamelli*, Thomas *filius Swani*, Uchtred de Austwyk, Ulf *filius Ormi* and Dolfin

---

[35]Bodl. Lib., Fairfax MS 9, fols. 44r–45r.

[36]Bodl. Lib., Top Yorks. MS c 72, fols. 70v–71r.

brother of that Ulf.[37] Some degree of status is represented by Torfin, who made a benefaction to Easby Abbey before the honorial baronage of the court of the honor of Richmond in 1162x1194.[38] In ca. 1200, the benefaction of Robert de Stalmine and his son, Peter, to Furness Abbey, of a carucate in Stalmine, was attested as the first five witnesses by Osbern *filius Ethmundi*, Ralph *filius Bernulfi*, Hucc *prepositus*, Robert *filius Hucce*, and Ulv (Ulf) *filius Uvieti*.[39] In this case, an important transaction, transferring a considerable amount of land for this time, was witnessed by a group of freemen who either had Insular personal names or whose immediate predecessors had borne Insular personal names, so that persons with Insular personal names retained some status locally, and there had been no complete transformation from Insular to newer forms of personal name by the turn of the century.

TABLE 4. INSULAR PERSONAL NAMES IN CHARTERS TO SOME RELIGIOUS HOUSES

Actor	Date(s)	Action	Beneficiary	Page(s)	Number(s)
Uccheman de Chertmel	1170x1180	witness	Furness	303	15
William *filius Uchtredi*	1170x1180	ditto	ditto	ditto	15
Uchtred *filius Gamelli*	1170x1180	ditto	ditto	ditto	15
Hutred de Austwic	ca. 1177, 1177x1193	ditto	ditto	301, 304	12, 16
Waltheof	12th cent.	ditto	St. Bees	28, 30, 32, 34–36, 39	1–3, 5–7, 9–10
Ketel	ditto	ditto	ditto	ditto	ditto
Siward *presbiter*	ditto	ditto	ditto	ditto	ditto
Chetell	ditto	ditto	ditto	ditto	ditto

[37] *The Coucher Book of Furness Abbey*, 2/2, ed. John Brownbill, Chetham Society, ser. 2, 76, (1887), p. 296 (no. 5).

[38] *Early Yorkshire Charters*, 5, ed. Charles T. Clay, Yorkshire Archaeological Society, e.s. 11 (1936), p. 59 (149): "coram baronibus in placitis Richem' recitari feci."

[39] *Furness*, 2/1, Chetham Society, n.s. 74 (1915), p. 232 (1).

Actor	Date(s)	Action	Beneficiary	Page(s)	Number(s)
Gospatrick *filius Ormi*	1145x1179	donor	St. Bees	60, 62	32–33
Elwin de Egremundia	1185x1201	witness	ditto	65–67	35–36
Thomas *filius Gospatricii*	1185x1201	ditto	ditto	ditto	ditto
Alan *filius Gospatricii*	1185x1201	ditto	ditto	ditto	ditto
Adam *filius Gospatricii*	1185x1201	ditto	ditto	ditto	ditto
Gamel *prepositus*	1158x1160	ditto	ditto	84	53
Orm de Yreby	1185x1201	ditto	ditto	92	61
Waltheof	ca. 1185	ditto	ditto	113	84
Orm *filius Rogeri*	late 12th cent.	ditto	ditto	113	85
Waltheof de Dena	ca. 1185	ditto	ditto	117	88
Waltheof *filius Thome clerici de Dene*	1178x1184	ditto	ditto	137	100

Moreover, the importance of these lay freemen inheres also in their attestation of charters of knightly families such as the de Boivilla and Morevilla families, or in the case of Waltheof, Ketel, Siward *presbiter*, and Chetell, a charter of William Meschin. Gospatrick *filius Ormi*'s conferring of the vill of Salter on St. Bees, in 1145x1179, reflects his substance. Not only did Insular personal names persist amongst the English families of middling status, however, for elements within the secular clergy continued to bear Insular personal names in the late twelfth century: Gospatrick *sacerdos de Keltona* (1145x1179); Dolfin *presbiter de Camertona* (1145x1179); Gospatrick *clericus de Derann'* (1158x1160); Waltheof *persona de Briggaham* and Waltheof *decanus* (both 1178x1184), as examples.[40]

---

[40]*The Register of the Priory of St Bees*, ed. J. Wilson, Surtees Society 126 (1915), pp. 62 (no. 32), 84 (no. 52), 137 (nos. 100–01).

In some of the instances of Latin patronymic forms of naming, whilst the father's name was CG or Christian, the son's renewed an Insular personal name. Even in the early thirteenth century, Insular personal names were entirely socially acceptable, as is represented, for example, in Gospatrick *filius Willelmi de Fel*, who made a benefaction of a toft in Lancaster to Cockersand in 1200x1240, or Grimbald son of Herbert de Ellale, who provided a rent of 100s. to the same religious house in 1209x1235.[41] Indeed, Grimbald, the son of Herbert, had as issue Walter, whose son was another Grimbald (1240x1268).[42] Similarly, some families felt no social or cultural impetus to discontinue Insular personal names: Grimbald de Soureby confirmed to the same religious house the land which had been donated by his father, Grimbald, the status of the younger Grimbald reflected in his further benefaction of a bovate with his body for burial.[43]

In the Northwest, the transition from Insular personal names to CG and Christian names appears to have been firmly located in the late twelfth century rather than earlier, according to the evidence in the charters to Cockersand. Illustrative of this process is Bernard *filius Akke*, who made several benefactions to Cockersand between 1205 and 1230, comprising 15 acres 3 roods and unspecified land in nine separate charters.[44] Similarly, between 1190 and 1230, Waltheof de Pulton conveyed to this religious house by five separate charters twelve acres, six selions, a messuage and toft.[45] These benefactions were confirmed by Waltheof's son, William, in 1220x1268.[46] The manner in which freemen with Insular personal names were still predominant into the early thirteenth century is reflected in a memorandum in the house's cartulary describing the provenance of lands in a gift by a certain Ralph (fl. 1236x1246), for his immediate predecessors in the lands had been attributed Insular personal names:

---

[41]W. Farrer, *The Cartulary of Cockersand Abbey . . .* , 3/1, Chetham Society 56 (1905), pp. 770–71 (10) and 823 (5).

[42]*Cockersand* 3/1:779 (22) and 783 (28).

[43]*Cockersand* 3/1:771–75.

[44]*Cockersand* 3/2, Chetham Society, n.s. 57 (1905), pp. 931–37 (2–10).

[45]*Cockersand* 2/1, Chetham Society, n.s. 40 (1898), pp. 453–57 (8–13).

[46]*Cockersand* 2/1:457 (13).

Habemus etiam cartam Suani filii Michaelis factam dicto Radulpho de ista terra
et cartam Suani filii Roberti de Hoton factam Suano filio Michaelis de ista terra.[47]

In this area, therefore, there was no cultural stigma against Insular personal names in the early thirteenth century, as is exemplified by Gospatrick
filius Roberti filii Sigge, who had issue four sons, Robert (named for his
grandfather), Gospatrick (named for his father), Hugh, and Ranulph.[48]

The cartulary thus reflects the continuation of some of these names
amongst the free tenantry of the region, and that persistence is evident at
lower social levels, for example in the cursory rentals of the house in 1251,
where the tenants enumerated included Uchtred Kempedale, Grimme Stanis-
trete, Grimbald de Barton, another Uchtred, Uchtred de Warton, Brun de
Mora, Uchtred de Loxum, Brun de Bonka, Grimbald de Forton, Uchtred de
Hildreston, Waltheof *filius Rogeri*, Swain de Katon, Grimbald de Elhale,
and Orm *filius Astini* as well as those reflecting a recent transition in the
early thirteenth century, such as Dikre *filius Alwardi*, Dothe *filius Uchtredi*,
John *filius Ulfi*, Dobbe *filius Dolphini*, William *filius Uchtredi*, and William
filius Thorphini.[49]

TABLE 5. INSULAR PERSONAL NAMES IN THE COCKERSAND CARTULARY

Actors	Event	Date	Reference
Uchtred *filius* Haldani	tenant of at least half an acre	1205x1225	3/2:931 (2)
Alan Hardingsun	tenant of land	1210x1226	3/2:398–99 (63)
Robert *filius* Gilmichael de Lathebot'	donor (6 separate charters)	1194x1219	3/2:940–44 (1–7)
Waltheof *filius* Alfredi	tenant of land	1194x1219	ibid.
Gospatrick	tenant of land	1194x1219	ibid.
Waltheof *albus*	tenant of an assart	1194x1219	ibid.

[47]*Cockersand* 2/1:421 (15).

[48]*Cockersand* 3/2:1017 (2).

[49]*Cockersand* 3/3, Chetham Society, n.s. 64 (1909), 1219–29.

Actors	Event	Date	Reference
Benedict *filius Waldevi filii Anketini de Bland*	donor	1235x1268	3/2:961 (11)
German de Bland	donor	1200x1250	3/2:962 (12)
Orm [*filii Thor'*]	(i) tenant of 7.5 acres (ii) donor	1200x1250 1184x1190	3/2:962–63 (12–13), 997 (1), 1010–11 (1)
Orm *filius Ade de Kellet*	donor	1222x1229	3/2:984–85 (9)
Uchtred *filius Osolfi*	donor	1184x1190	3/2:1001–02 (2–3)
Gospatrick *filius Gilmichael' de Burton*	quitclaim	1200x1220	3/2:1008 (5)
Gospatrick *filius Roberti filii Sigge*	donor	1190x1210	3/2:1017 (2)
Uchtred de Kempedale	donor	1220x1250	2/1:422 (18)
Gamel *filius Sesar de Thorp'*	donor	1184x1212	2/1:478–79 (11–13)
Siward de Longetre	donor	1190x1219	2/1:513 (3)
Gospatrick *filius Warini de Kiuerdale*	donor	1190x1220	2/1:518 (1)
William *filius Hutredi filii Suani*	donor	1242x1268	1/2 (Chetham Society, n.s. 39, 1898), 190 (1)
Suan *filius Osberti de Frekelton'*	donor	1200x1212	1/2:199 (5); his son was Richard: ibid., 199 (6)
Orm *filius Rogeri*	donor	early 13th century	1/2:214
Grimbald *filius Willelmi de Slen'*	donor	1230x1268	1/2:260 (13)

Actors	Event	Date	Reference
Jordan *filius* Torphini de Gairstang	donor	1246	1/2:276 (6); Torphin had held 1 bovate and 6 acres from the rectory of Garstang
Siward *filius Uccke*	donor	1185x11901	1/2:114 (1); his son was Richard, who fl. 1205x1233: ibid., 116

The persistence of Insular personal names is perhaps exemplified by the charter of Edgar in favor of his sister Juliana, who married Ranulph de Merlay, the two siblings being children of Earl Gospatrick. Edgar's charter was attested by Ostred *presbiter*, Grimbald de Merlay, William *filius Elef'*, Sewert *filius Liolf'*, Liolf *filius Liolf'*, Cospatric *filius Leuenoc'*, and Cospatric de Horsley. The witness list represents a different and vital Insular culture at the time of the event, ca. 1167.[50]

INTERPRETATION

From this evidence, it is apparent that there was no cultural homogeneity in the North for much of the twelfth century, but that different cultural traditions of naming co-existed and persisted for some generations into the late twelfth century and with residual levels amongst the peasantry into the early thirteenth. Considering the spatial aspects, one possible explanation might be center (core) periphery differences, with naming processes changing more rapidly in the core areas but exhibiting residual traces in the peripheral areas. Such an interpretation is problematic, however, because of the relationship between core and periphery and defining each in relation to the other. Viewed from inside, the north of England might have retained a greater affinity with southern Scotland for much of the twelfth century. Peripheral areas might also be considered to be creative because of their liminality, rather than culturally residual.[51]

---

[50]*Chartularium Abbathie de Novo Monasterio*, ed. J. T. Fowler, Surtees Society 66 (1878), pp. 268–69.

[51]These issues which are much exercising geographers are succinctly explained now by

Since naming processes and patterns continued to represent cultural heteroglossia over several generations and perhaps a century after the Conquest, cultural theories which are constituted around an homologous culture seem inappropriate, thus excluding, for example, Geertzian interpretive anthropology, which depends on "thick description" from single cultural variables, such as names, to elicit the total nature of a culture. Although Geertz, in one statement, requires only a minimum of cultural coherence, yet it is apparent that his interpretation does predicate an homologous culture. That extensive degree of cultural coherence manifestly did not exist in the twelfth-century North. Rather than "thick description," a more appropriate conceptualization might be William Sewell's "thin coherence," which allows beneath a "dominant" discourse of culture, cultural variants which might be residual, oppositional, or resistant, allowing space for those cultural undercurrents perceived by cultural materialists.[52] Nevertheless, the question remains as to the precise nature of these cultural expressions: residual, oppositional, or resistant? Attractive as is the temptation to regard them simply as residual, perhaps some case might be advanced for their oppositional or resistant nature to a dominant discourse of culture, that of the new overlords. It is, of course, possible that recursive repetition of names (in the manner of Bourdieu's *habitus* or Giddens's structuration) might have sustained cultures that were entirely residual, but the process of naming is in itself an act of considerable agency. It is inherently intentional and is an expression of wider allegiances and associations, if not identities. On the other hand, the strategies available to the northern peasantry for resistance were limited and circumscribed; indeed, it is probable, as de Certeau maintained, that such social groups do not have access to strategies, only tactics, and so naming is a tactic of resistance, the only form of cultural resistance available to the Northern peasantry.[53]

R. A. Dodgshon, *Society in Time and Space: A Geographical Perspective on Change* (Cambridge, 1998), esp. pp. 1–20.

[52]William H. Sewell, "The Concept(s) of Culture," in *Beyond the Cultural Turn*, ed. V. E. Bonnell and L. Hunt (Berkeley, 1999), pp. 35–61.

[53]M. de Certeau, *The Practice of Everyday Life* (Berkeley, 1984); for a slightly more action-centered resistance, James C. Scott, *Domination and the Arts of Resistance: Hidden Transcripts* (New Haven, 1990).

Appendix

THE CORPORA OF INSULAR PERSONAL NAMES
IN THREE NORTHERN COUNTIES IN THE TWELFTH CENTURY

Name	Northumberland	Durham	Yorkshire
Acke, Aki[54]	•		•
Adelard[55]			•
Ailwin			•
Akkeman[56]			•
Aldred		•	
Arketill[57]		•	
Arkill[58]		•	•
Auty[59]			•
Bernolf, Bernulf[60]		•	•
Bond[61]			•

---

[54]John Insley, *Scandinavian Personal Names in Norfolk: A Survey Based on Medieval Records and Place-Names*, Acta Academiae Regiae Gustavi Adolphi 62 (Uppsala, 1994), pp. 2–3 (hereafter, *SPNN*); Gillian Fellows Jensen, *Scandinavian Personal Names in Lincolnshire and Yorkshire*, Navnestudier 7 (Copenhagen, 1968), pp. 3–5 (hereafter *SPNLY*).

[55]Otto von Feilitzen, *The Pre-Conquest Personal Names of Domesday Book*, NG 3 (Uppsala, 1937), p. 184 (*PCPNDB*); T. Forssner, *Continental-Germanic Personal Names in England in Old and Middle English Times* (Uppsala, 1916), p. 8: possibly CG.

[56]Insley, *SPNN*, p. 8; Fellows Jensen, *SPNLY*, pp. 5–6.

[57]Insley, *SPNN*, pp. 19–23; Fellows Jensen, *SPNLY*, pp. 14–16.

[58]Insley, *SPNN*, pp. 22–23, for this contracted form of *Ar(n)ketil* and the difference of syncopated and unsyncopated forms.

[59]Insley, *SPNN*, pp. 86–88; Fellows Jensen, *SPNLY*, p. 44.

[60]Feilitzen, *PCPNDB*, p. 200: possibly either OE or AScand.

[61]Insley, *SPNN*, pp. 98–107; Fellows Jensen, *SPNLY*, p. 60. *Bóndi* as a personal name is not frequent in Yorkshire.

Name	Northumberland	Durham	Yorkshire
Colswann[62]			•
Copsi			•
Crin[63]	•		
Dering			•
Derman[64]			•
Dolfin[65]		•	•
E[a]dwin[66]		•	
Edmund[67]		•	
Edric	•		•
Edulf[68]	•		•
Edwald			•
Edward			•
Elfald		•	
Elfer		•	
Elgi[69]		•	
E[y]lsi/Aylsi	•		•
Elstan		•	
Elvric			•

---

[62]Insley, *SPNN*, p. 279; Fellows Jensen, *SPNLY*, pp. 179–80.

[63]Feilitzen, *PCPNDB*, p. 219: OIr etymology.

[64]Feilitzen, *PCPNDB*, p. 233: OE etymology.

[65]Feilitzen, *PCPNDB*, pp. 22–26: AScand etymology.

[66]Feilitzen, *PCPNDB*, p. 233: OE etymology.

[67]Feilitzen, *PCPNDB*, p. 233: OE.

[68]Feilitzen, *PCPNDB*, p. 242: OE *Ealdwulf.*

[69]Prior's Kitchen, Durham, 1 Finc 1 (1197x1217): Elgi held 2 bovates.

Name	Northumberland	Durham	Yorkshire
Elwin		•	•
Ethelred		•	
Figge[70]		•	
Forn[71]			•
Gamel[72]	•	•	•
Godmund[73]		•	
Godric[74]	•	•	
Godwin[75]		•	
Gospatrick	•	•	•
Grimkell[76]			•
Grund			•
Haldan[77]			•
Harding[78]			•
Hauell			•

[70]Presumably from AScand *Feggi*: Insley, *SPNN*, p. 121; Fellows Jensen, *SPNLY*, p. 81.

[71]Insley, *SPNLY*, pp. 124–25; Fellows Jensen, *SPNLY*, p. 85. Apparently frequent in Yorkshire.

[72]Insley, *SPNN*, pp. 129–31; Fellows Jensen, *SPNLY*, pp. 89–95. Frequent in Yorks. and Lincs., less so in Norfolk.

[73]Insley, *SPNN*, pp. 154–56, where AScand and OE etymons are considered.

[74]Feilitzen, *PCPNDB*, pp. 266–69: OE.

[75]Feilitzen, *PCPNDB*, pp. 269–73.

[76]Insley, *SPNN*, pp. 142–43; Fellows Jensen, *SPNLY*, pp. 107–08. More frequent in northern Danelaw than in East Anglia.

[77]Insley, *SPNN*, pp. 186–92; Fellows Jensen, *SPNLY*, pp. 126–28. Widespread in England.

[78]Feilitzen, *PCPNDB*, pp. 287–88: OE.

Name	Northumberland	Durham	Yorkshire
Heremer[79]			•
Hereward[80]			•
Iggi	•		
Ilving		•	
Kenwald			•
Ketel[81]		•	•
Landric			•
Lefwin[82]			•
Leising		•	
Leofric		•	•
Leolf[83]			•
Meldred		•	
[H]Orm[84]		•	•
Oswald[85]			•
Osward[86]			•
Pace	•		
Patrick		•	

---

[79]Feilitzen, *PCPNDB*, p. 290.

[80]Feilitzen, *PCPNDB*, p. 290.

[81]Insley, *SPNN*, pp. 256–63; Fellows Jensen, *SPNLY*, pp. 166–70. Frequent throughout England.

[82]Feilitzen, *PCPNDB*, p. 317: OE.

[83]Insley, *SPNN*, pp. 289–90; Fellows Jensen, *SPNLY*, pp. 188–89.

[84]Insley, *SPNN*, pp. 314–15; Fellows Jensen, *SPNLY*, pp. 204–06. More frequent in northern England.

[85]Feilitzen, *PCPNDB*, p. 340: OE.

[86]Feilitzen, *PCPNDB*, pp. 340–41.

Name	Northumberland	Durham	Yorkshire
Saddoc		•	
Saxi[87]			•
Seman[88]	•		
Sigar[89]	•		
Siward			•
Snell[90]			•
Suartbrond[91]		•	
Swa[i]n[92]		•	•
Thore		•	
Toki[93]		•	
Toly[94]			•
Turkill[95]		•	
Uchtred[96]	•	•	•
Ukeman			•
Ulf[97]		•	•

---

[87]Insley, *SPNN*, pp. 323–24; Fellows Jensen, *SPNLY*, pp. 227–28; Feilitzen, *PCPNDB*, p. 352.

[88]Feilitzen, *PCPNDB*, p. 353: OE.

[89]Insley, *SPNN*, pp. 325–26; Fellows Jensen, *SPNLY*, pp. 230–31.

[90]Feilitzen, *PCPNDB*, p. 368, had only Snelling.

[91]Insley, *SPNN*, p. 354; Fellows Jensen, *SPNLY*, pp. 274–75.

[92]Insley, *SPNN*, pp. 356–60; Fellows Jensen, *SPNLY*, pp. 276–82.

[93]Insley, *SPNN*, pp. 371–76; Fellows Jensen, *SPNLY*, pp. 287–88.

[94]Insley, *SPNN*, pp. 377–79; Fellows Jensen, *SPNLY*, pp. 289–90.

[95]Insley, *SPNN*, pp. 414–19; Fellows Jensen, *SPNLY*, pp. 309–11.

[96]Feilitzen, *PCPNDB*, p. 398: OE.

[97]Insley, *SPNN*, pp. 437–39; Fellows Jensen, *SPNLY*, pp. 321–24.

Name	Northumberland	Durham	Yorkshire
Ulkill[98]		•	
Utting		•	•
Walding[99]			•
Waltheof	•		
Watling		•	
Wulmer			

---

[98]Insley, *SPNN*, pp. 433–37; Fellows Jensen, *SPNLY*, pp. 325–27. Syncopation of the second element to *-kel/-kil* predominated in the northern Danelaw, whereas the uncontracted form *-ketel* was concentrated in East Anglia.

[99]Feilitzen, *PCPNDB*, p. 408, but also Forssner, *Continental-Germanic Personal Names*, p. 240, and thus possibly CG.

PART IV—CHRONOLOGIES AND IMPACTS

THE DOMESDAY JURORS

C. P. Lewis

Much attention has been paid recently to the effects of the Norman Conquest on land ownership in England.[1] Peter Sawyer's bold view that "the changes in tenurial structure after the Norman Conquest were less than revolutionary" depended on carefully sifting evidence from Domesday Book that some pre-Conquest estates were transferred *en bloc* to Norman owners. He inferred that other such estates have not and cannot be recognized only because Domesday Book did not make a systematic record of AS lordships.[2] That suggestion has been given greater substance by David Roffe's demonstration that many of the legal and tenurial characteristics of pre-Conquest thegnly lordship continued in being as part of Norman baronial lordship.[3] On the other hand, Robin Fleming has restated the case for a massive upheaval in aristocratic tenure by marshaling the Domesday material to map

This article, originally published in *Haskins Society Journal* 5 (1993), 17–44, is reprinted with permission of the author, with minor changes.

[1] My warmest thanks go to Prof. Robin Fleming, whose detailed comments on an earlier draft of this paper helped me to strengthen the argument. In order to facilitate reference to any of the editions of Domesday Book, citations are in the form GDB (for Great Domesday Book), followed by the folio number, recto or verso, 1 or 2 (for the column), and either the place name or a line number.

[2] Peter Sawyer, "1066–1086: A Tenurial Revolution?" in *Domesday Book: A Reassessment*, ed. Peter Sawyer (London, 1985), pp. 71–85, quotation at p. 85.

[3] David Roffe, "From Thegnage to Barony: Sake and Soke, Title, and Tenants-in-chief," *A-NS* 12 (1989), 157–76.

out with greater precision the substantial changes in the recorded pattern of estates between 1066 and 1086.[4] First reactions to Professor Fleming's book suggest that the argument is not yet close to being settled.[5]

A further dimension, perhaps a crucial one, can be added to the debate by considering the fate of English landowners in and after 1066. On the face of it, that is to say in the folios of Domesday Book, they all but disappeared. The common supposition is that the thousands of thegns and freemen who were named as holders of land in the time of King Edward (TRE) had been killed in battle or rebellion or driven into exile or simply dispossessed by the Normans. By 1086 there were only two English landowners in the top flight of two hundred or so laymen, and the proportion was little larger among all those holders of land recorded in Domesday. However, there is good evidence that Domesday Book did not describe the whole of landed society as it existed in 1086, indeed that large sections of the landowning classes were omitted. When account is taken of them, the question of English survival as landowners looks very different. The new evidence is the Domesday jurors.

Jurors were regularly impaneled on solemn oaths in early Norman England to declare the facts during the course of legal pleadings. Around 1081, for instance, the king ordered the great assembly which was to inquire into the losses suffered by Ely Abbey to elect Englishmen who knew how the land was held before 1066.[6] Again, sometime between 1077 and 1082, twelve Englishmen of the shire court of Cambridge confirmed on oath a disputed decision about a manor at Isleham.[7] Once more, perhaps about 1080, twelve Englishmen and six Normans stood witness to the customary rights of the archbishop in York.[8]

---

[4]Robin Fleming, *Kings and Lords in Conquest England* (Cambridge, 1991), pp. 107–231.

[5]Apparent in conversation at the Chequers public house, Battle, 17–19 July 1992; I am particularly grateful to Dr. David Bates and Dr. John Hudson for sharing their views of the book with me.

[6]*Inquisitio Comitatus Cantabrigiensis and Inquisitio Eliensis*, ed. N. E. S. A. Hamilton (London, 1876), p. xviii (no. 3); E. Miller, "The Ely Land Pleas in the Reign of William I," *EHR* 62 (1947), 438–56 at 446–50.

[7]*Textus Roffensis (Part 2)*, ed. P. H. Sawyer, in *Early English Manuscripts in Facsimile*, 11 (Copenhagen, 1962), fols. 175v–176v. I am grateful to Dr. Ann Williams for this reference.

[8]"An English Document of about 1080," ed. F. Liebermann and M. H. Peacock, *Yorkshire*

The presentation of facts on oath was an especially important part of King William's survey of England in 1086, and Domesday Book contains hundreds of instances of the men of a shire or a hundred giving evidence by validating or contradicting information presented to them.[9] Perhaps in some shires the whole body of oath-worthy freemen who formed the hundred court had a say; but in the only ones for which there is certain evidence, Cambridgeshire and part of Hertfordshire, there was a smaller jury acting on behalf of the hundred, and it is reasonable to suppose that there were juries in other counties. The responsibilities of the Domesday jurors were onerous: the rightful possession of land might depend on what they said; their neighbors who were not on the jury looked to them to maintain the good reputation of the hundred; the Domesday commissioners must surely have been in a hurry; and there was bound often to have been pressure by the parties interested in a case. The Isleham jurors mentioned above became pawns in a contest between the sheriff of Cambridgeshire and the bishop of Rochester, were accused of perjury, tried in London, and had to pay a heavy financial penalty. For all those reasons, jurors can never have been names drawn at random; they must have been the men best qualified by local land ownership, status, residence, and personal qualities to speak on behalf of others, and they may often have had connections with the great barons and churches of their shire.

The jurors of 1086 whose names are known appear in two of the Domesday satellites: the *Inquisitio Comitatus Cantabrigiensis* (*ICC*) and the *Inquisitio Eliensis* (*IE*). Both documents have fuller-than-Domesday manorial returns arranged by hundred.[10] *ICC* covered all Cambridgeshire (apart from the king's manors) and gives the names of the jurors as a series of prefaces to the returns for each hundred. They appear in the form "In the hundred of X these men swore, viz. A, B, C, D, E, F, G, and H, and all the other

Archaeological Journal 18 (1905), 412–16; D. M. Palliser, *Domesday York*, Borthwick Paper 78 (York, 1990), pp. 6–8, 19, 25.

[9]R. Welldon Finn, *The Domesday Inquest and the Making of Domesday Book* (London, 1961), pp. 99–109; *Domesday Book*, ed. John Morris, 38: *Index of Subjects*, ed. J. D. Foy (Chichester, 1992), s.vv. County, evidence; Hundred, evidence.

[10]H. B. Clarke, "The Domesday Satellites," in *Domesday Book: A Reassessment,* pp. 50–70, at p. 53; V. H. Galbraith, *The Making of Domesday Book* (Oxford, 1961), pp. 123–45; R. Welldon Finn, "The Inquisitio Eliensis Re-considered," *EHR* 75 (1960), 385–409.

Frenchmen and Englishmen."[11] Three sets of jurors are missing because some of the folios of the only manuscript are lost. *IE* described the abbot of Ely's manors in the six counties where he held land. The description begins with the names of all the jurors, cast in a form similar to *ICC* for the hundreds in Cambridgeshire and Hertfordshire where the abbot had estates.[12] There are no jurors' names for Essex, Norfolk, Suffolk, or Huntingdonshire. Taking the two documents together, there are lists for all fifteen hundreds in Cambridgeshire and three in Hertfordshire. Each hundred had eight jurors, and each double hundred (of which there was one in each county) had sixteen. The 160 names represent 158 individuals, since Walter de Clais and Ralph de Banks each swore in two separate Cambridgeshire hundreds. The jurors were all men; in each hundred precisely half were French and the rest English; and the Frenchmen were normally listed first.

Almost nothing has been written about the Domesday jurors, and this paper is the first published systematic attempt to identify who they were.[13] The first objective was to trace them elsewhere in Domesday Book in order to establish whether they were landowners and how much land they held. The appendix [below] summarizes the results, and it will be apparent from a glance that far fewer than half the jurors can be identified with Domesday landowners. Establishing why that should be so led to other questions. First, what sort of landowners, if landowners at all, were the jurors who were not named in Domesday? Second, did the jurors as a whole, whether named in Domesday or not, represent a distinct social group (or, perhaps, more than one group) in early Norman England? The answers will occupy the greater part of this paper. Beyond them lies a further question: what do the Cambridgeshire and Hertfordshire jurors, eighty Englishmen and seventy-eight Frenchmen, tell us about the double-headed question of English survival and French colonization in conquered England and so about changes in land ownership?

*   *   *

---

[11] *ICC and IE*, ed. Hamilton, pp. 1, 9, 11–12, 17, 25, 28–29, 38, 43, 51, 68, 83, 93.

[12] *ICC and IE*, ed. Hamilton, pp. 97–101.

[13] A start was made in *Domesday Book*, ed. Morris, 12: *Hertfordshire*, ed. John Morris (Chichester, 1976), appendix; *Domesday Book*, ed. Morris, 18: *Cambridgeshire*, ed. Alexander Rumble (Chichester, 1981), appendix.

The names borne by the Domesday jurors are important; if carefully and cautiously analyzed, they can be shown to be comparable with the names of members of some well-defined social groups in early Norman England, and conversely, to be different from the names of men belonging to other groups. I shall start with their surnames. Some of those in the jury lists were of the standard types recognized in personal name studies: the main categories are patronymics like "fitz Brian" and "son of Grim," toponymics like "de Noyers" and "of Horseheath," and adjectival bynames describing place of origin or some personal characteristic like "the Lotharingian" and "framward."[14] Other jurors had descriptive identifications which were not surnames in the accepted sense, though they performed the same function of distinguishing them from other men of the same forename. Those quasi-surnames fall into two main groups, those which named an individual's lord ("William, man of Walter") and those which stated his own rank ("Ralph, reeve of this hundred"). What jurors were called could vary according to circumstances and the surnames recorded in the lists were not necessarily what they called themselves. The man called Ralph de Banks in Wetherley Hundred was called Ralph of Barrington in Thriplow. The phenomenon is not unknown in Domesday Book itself (where, for example, Albert the Lotharingian was also called Albert the clerk and Albert the chaplain), but it was far commoner among the jurors. In fact, of the eighty-seven jurors appearing in both *ICC* and *IE*, twenty-two were named differently in the two documents. Not many of them had alternative true surnames, and most of the differences were between a true surname and no surname (Leofwine of Bottisham/Leofwine), a true surname and a quasi-surname (Fulk Waruhel/Fulk, man of the sheriff), or no surname and a quasi-surname (Richard/Richard, reeve of this hundred). In particular, *IE* tended to give a fuller name by adding a description to a simple forename and especially by defining a man by naming his lord. That practice stemmed from the nature of the document: *IE* was compiled for the greatest of the Cambridgeshire lords, the abbot of Ely, and naturally tended to define individuals both within and without the abbot's lordship in terms of whose men they were; *ICC*, by contrast, had a more official and public character and was less interested in lordship.

In comparing the types of surname borne by the French jurors with other groups of Frenchmen in Domesday England, it is desirable to exclude

---

[14]Gösta Tengvik, *Old English Bynames*, NG 4 (Uppsala, 1938).

the quasi-surnames, and the figures in Table 1 are therefore drawn only from *ICC*. The forty-six French jurors concerned make an instructive comparison with the lesser tenants-in-chief of Domesday Book, arbitrarily defined as those with land in only one shire and fewer than ten manors. In some important respects their naming patterns were virtually identical, as the second and third columns of the table demonstrate: the percentages with no surname, with French toponymics, and with bynames are practically the same. There are also some differences. Less than half as many jurors as minor tenants-in-chief had patronymics. Less than one third as many jurors as minor tenants-in-chief had quasi-surnames referring to their rank. Those jurors known as "the man of X" had no equivalent among the tenants-in-chief, who were by definition all the king's men. The biggest difference is that the jurors were far more likely than the lesser tenants-in-chief to be surnamed from places in England. The second point to emerge from the table (comparing the first and second columns) is that greater and lesser

TABLE 1. NAMING PATTERNS OF TENANTS-IN-CHIEF AND JURORS

Type of surname	Greater t-in-c %	Lesser t-in-c %	French jurors %	English jurors %
No surname	5	16	16	10
True surname:				
Patronymic or other family relationship	21	16	7	10
French toponymic	36	18	18	0
English toponymic	7	3	24	65
Byname	20	15	16	2
Quasi-surname:				
Own rank	10	32	9	6
'Man of X'	0	0	9	4
Double surname	0	0	2	2
Total percent	99	100	101	99
Number in sample	201	145	46	48
Source	Domesday Book	Domesday Book	*ICC*	*ICC*

tenants-in-chief had very different sorts of surnames indeed and (comparing the first and third columns) that the jurors' surnames were also very different from the names borne by the greater tenants-in-chief. Their surnames thus allow the French jurors as a group to be placed closer to the lesser than to the greater tenants-in-chief. At the same time there was an orientation among the French jurors, which is not found among the lesser tenants-in-chief, toward an association with one particular place in England.

The surnames of the English jurors are much less helpful in locating them socially because there is no other large enough socially specific group of Englishmen whose surnames are known.

Useful comparative evidence can also be drawn from the jurors' fore-names. On the French side, all the types of name in use in Normandy and neighboring regions of northern France are represented.[15] They were mostly of Old Germanic origin but also included ones derived from ON, Breton, Latin, and biblical traditions. All the common Norman names are there: *Ralph*, *William*, *Geoffrey*, *Richard*, *Robert*, *Roger*, and *Walter*; but there was also a tendency towards much less common names. *Aleran*, *Firmin*, *Letard*, *Matfred*, *Rodri*, *Sefrid*, *Sturmid*, *Tancred*, and *Tehard* are not found at all among Domesday landholders; *Everard*, *Farman*, *Germund*, *Giffard*, *Gosbert*, *Huard*, *Lovet*, *Nicholas*, *Riculf*, *Rumold*, and *Tiel* were borne by only a handful of men each, always among the lowest orders; and except for a few bigger men, the same was true of the names *Albert*, *Brian*, *David*, and *Warin*.[16] A helpful parallel is the name stock of the tenants of undertenants who were recorded in Cheshire and Shropshire, who were another relatively humble group of landowners. Many of their names were common ones but there were also in Cheshire men with the much rarer names of *Ascelin*, *David*, *Lambert*, and *Odard*, and in Shropshire a *Berner*, an *Ingelrann*, a *Sasfrid*, and a *Widard*. In all, perhaps a quarter of the French jurors had names which were not borne by anyone among the upper ranks of AN society represented by the tenants-in-chief and the greater honorial barons. There is one obvious explanation: that the rarer jurors' names were representative of naming traditions among the lesser families of Normandy and

---

[15]E. G. Withycombe, *The Oxford Dictionary of English Christian Names,* 3rd ed. (Oxford, 1977); Ernst Förstemann, *Altdeutsches Namenbuch*, 1: *Personennamen* (Bonn, 1900).

[16]The evidence here was assembled by using *Domesday Book*, ed. John Morris, 37: *Index of Persons*, ed. J. McN. Dodgson and J. J. N. Palmer (Chichester, 1992).

northern France who formed the rank-and-file of the Conqueror's army in 1066, but not of naming patterns in the families of the great barons of Normandy who led and most profited from the invasion of England. That idea needs testing from Continental sources far beyond the scope of this paper.

The forenames of the English jurors are also instantly recognizable: predominantly OE in derivation; dithematic (that is, with two elements, like *Earnwig*); and rather conventional in the choice and combination of elements. In other words, they were exactly the same sort of names which had been borne by the mass of landowners in the two shires in King Edward's time.[17] Well over half the jurors had extremely common names: there were three *Alweard*s, three *Godwine*s, and three *Wulfric*s, four *Almær*s and four *Ælfwine*s, and no fewer than eight *Ælfric*s. But there were also some uncommon names which were enjoyed by only a handful of pre-Conquest landowners anywhere in England, like *Boia*, *Frawine*, *Huna*, and *Wine*; and three (*Godlive*, *Leofhun*, and *Sigeheah*) which no TRE landowner was called.[18] Pre-Conquest landowners as a whole encompassed the entire social range from peasants to aristocrats, and many of them, especially among the lower ranks, had unique names (in the sense that there was only one man of that name in Domesday Book). For example, about fifty of the roughly five hundred thegns and freemen in Cheshire, Shropshire, and Herefordshire had unique names. In other words, the mix of names among the English jurors was broadly representative of the stock of names common to all landed Anglo-Saxons in the mid-eleventh century.

Conversely, the names of the English jurors can be distinguished from what is known about the sorts of names carried by eleventh-century peasants and slaves. The nearest substantial body of evidence in time and place to the Domesday jurors comes from the will of the noble lady Æthelgifu.[19] Although it was made right at the start of the century, thus in the lifetime of the great-grandfathers of the English jurors, it named people who lived along the Hertfordshire/Bedfordshire border not far from the jurors' homes. Aristocratic personal names were much the same in the late tenth century as they were in the mid-eleventh, so there is some justification for supposing

---

[17]Olof von Feilitzen, *The Pre-Conquest Personal Names of Domesday Book*, NG 3 (Uppsala, 1937), esp. pp. 11–18.

[18]Ibid.

[19]*The Will of Æthelgifu*, ed. D. Whitelock, Roxburghe Club (Oxford, 1968), pp. 6–15, 58–60.

that peasant and servile names were too. The forty-nine named male slaves whom Æthelgifu manumitted or bequeathed included some with names common among the landholding classes (an *Ælfric*, an *Eadric*, and two *Wulfric*s) and even in the families of kings and earls (*Eadmund, Eadwine*, and *Leofric*). But half the names were either never borne by a TRE landowner or were carried only by men at the very lowest levels of landed society (those with half a hide of land or less). Names like *Boga, Cuthmund, Domic, Heremod, Mangod, Siduman*, and *Tatulf* were heard down on the farm in the eleventh century, but not in the manor house or at the meetings of the hundred court.

The evidence of forenames points to an inescapable conclusion about the social origins of the English jurors. The class which formed the rank-and-file of thegns and greater freemen in pre-Conquest Cambridgeshire and Hertfordshire also provided the jurors. The reason ought to be plain: in a few cases they were the same men, known survivors of the Conquest; in many more there is a strong presumption that they were their sons, brothers, nephews, and cousins.

The names of both French and English jurors can thus be used to locate them within late eleventh-century society, since it is clear that the stock of personal names in use varied greatly across the social range. Some English names were common to earl and slave, some French ones to count and foot-soldier, but there were others which were socially distinctive. Even more than that, the shape of the total name stock of the jurors—its precise balance of different types of names and of rare and common names—places the jurors firmly in the middle ranks of society. The French jurors broadly speaking shared a stock of names with the lesser Domesday landowners; their English colleagues on the hundred juries were indistinguishable in their personal nomenclature from the pre-Conquest landowners.

The most important point to emerge from a consideration of the jurors' names is the high proportion who took their surnames from some place in England. Table 1 shows the evidence for the *ICC* jurors alone. Even among the Frenchmen, English toponymics were the commonest type. More examples could be added from the hundreds in Cambridgeshire and Hertfordshire for which *IE* alone survives. Altogether exactly one third (twenty-six out of seventy-eight) of the French jurors had an English toponymic. Among the English jurors the use of English toponymic surnames was overwhelming. Of those named only in *ICC* (the fourth column in Table 1), they accounted for nearly two thirds of the total stock, and the proportion among all the

English jurors (also counting those named in *IE*) was virtually identical. English toponymic surnames are above all a sign of some connection with one particular place in Cambridgeshire or Hertfordshire. Some of the jurors who were so surnamed are known to have been landowners in the place which gave them their name, like Nicholas of Kennett, who held the entire manor of Kennett (Cambs.) under William de Warenne;[20] but it was more common for there to be no trace of a juror in the Domesday entry or entries for the place from which he was surnamed. There were Cambridgeshire jurors called Bernard of Hill and Hervey of Sawston, but no Bernard at the abbot of Ely's manor of Hill, and no Hervey at any of the three manors in Sawston.[21] I shall return to this problem below.

Evidence also can be deployed about the social status of the jurors from the circumstances of those who can be identified in Domesday Book, but bearing in mind that the very fact that they were Domesday landowners makes them unrepresentative of the jurors as a whole. J. H. Round's view of their social status was that most of the Englishmen were villeins and so lower in the social scale than the French.[22] That was simply on the grounds that far fewer of them were to be found in Domesday, a criterion which misses the point entirely (something which one can rarely say of Round). The appendix [below] identifies as Domesday landowners thirty-five out of the seventy-eight French jurors and eleven out of eighty English (besides four who are named only as pre-Conquest owners): 45% and 14%, respectively. A majority of even the French jurors are untraceable in Domesday Book. If Round had followed his logic of deducing social status from presence or absence in Domesday Book, he ought to have written that half the French jurors and most of the English were of lower status than the rest.

Most of the identifiable jurors appear in Domesday by name, usually just the forename and in a few cases under a slight variant. Three men, however (Manfred, Rumold, and Tibbald), were identical with unnamed Domesday knights. Although that might raise hopes that all the jurors apparently "missing" from Domesday Book could be identified with other specified but unnamed landowners (knights, sokemen, and others), in reality that is not

---

[20]GDB 196v1 Chenet.

[21]GDB 192r1 Helle; 193r2 Salsiton; 197r1 Salsiton; 197v1 Salsitone.

[22]J. H. Round, *Feudal England* (London, 1895), pp. 120–23.

a possibility since the unnamed landowners for the most part simply did not hold land in the right places to be the unidentified jurors, many of whom had toponymic surnames; and all can be located within a particular hundred. In short, most jurors are not just unnamed in Domesday Book but not mentioned at all.

Round's view of the differential status of English and French jurors can be attacked from another direction, since the landed wealth of those who can be identified is closely comparable. On average, the French had just over five and a half hides, the English just over four hides; the French twenty demesne plow oxen, the English, fifteen; and the Frenchmen's estates were worth on average about 130 shillings a year, the Englishmen's about 90 shillings. The identified French jurors were thus more prosperous than their English counterparts, but not much more. Broadly speaking, they belonged to the same class. In fact, their class was spread out over a fairly wide economic spectrum. At the extremes the identified jurors ranged from Humphrey d'Anneville, who had over twenty-five hides and a dozen plow teams worth over £40 a year, to Lovet, a man with only three quarters of a hide worth 8s. 8d. More typical estates at the top of the range were in the order of ten hides and four to six teams worth £10 to £15. At the bottom of the range, few had less than one and a half hides and a plow team worth 20 shillings or so. There were Englishmen at the top of the scale and Frenchmen at the bottom. These assessments and values stretched across the middle and lower bands of all Cambridgeshire landowners in 1086. The identified jurors could hardly match the estates of the great feudal lords like Count Alan and Picot the sheriff, but they were closely comparable with many of the out-of-county barons and the purely local men. The most important point to notice is that there was no significant difference in economic status between the identified French and the identified English jurors.

Nor was there any great difference in social status. The identified jurors can be characterized socially in various ways. Only one was a tenant-in-chief (Gosbert the Beauvaisien), and he on the tiniest scale possible. They were not the substantial honorial barons, the sort who on some honors held a swathe of manors across England. They did include a couple of that interesting group of undertenants who held land from more than one lord: Humphrey d'Anneville held as much as he did because he was tenant of two great lords. They almost invariably held land in the hundred for which they swore and were normally resident there, judging residence from their largest estate (where there was more than one). For example, Geoffrey de Mandeville's English steward Sigar was a juror in Thriplow Hundred and probably lived at Foxton, the largest of his four manors in 1086, which had two demesne plows.[23] Several were named from their place of residence, like William of Letchworth in Hertfordshire.[24] Two fifths also held lands outside the hundred for which they swore, almost half of them in another nearby county. The identified jurors tended above all to be the middle-ranking tenants of the greater barons and the greater tenants of the middling barons. Some Cambridgeshire examples will help to show what factors made a man a juror. Count Eustace had three identifiable tenants on his Cambridgeshire fee. The wealthiest, Arnulf d'Ardres, was not a juror; nor was the poorest, an unidentified knight at Grantchester; but the middle one, Rumold of Coton, was. Walter Giffard's two Cambridgeshire tenants, Hugh de Bolbec and Walter fitz Aubrey, were great honorial barons with land halfway across England and did not serve as jurors; on the other hand, Aubrey de Vere's men Everard, Firmin, and Norman owned nothing outside Cambridgeshire but were figures of some substance within the county and sat on the juries for the hundreds where they held land.

A great deal can thus be said about those jurors who can be found in Domesday Book, but the majority who are missing from Domesday remain a puzzle. In respect of the types of names which they bore, there is nothing to distinguish them from the identified jurors, especially as both groups included many men, French and English, who were named from places in Cambridgeshire and Hertfordshire. That takes us to the heart of the difficulty in defining their tenurial standing. What sort of a connection with a place might have given them a surname but not a mention in Domesday Book? Why call a man Gilbert of Histon or Frawine of Kirtling if he did not live and own land there? Why make him a juror for the hundred if he had no position among the landowners of the district? To answer those questions it is necessary to explore the ways in which a man might hold a significant landed estate without being entered in Domesday Book as a tenant. One possibility which can be rejected is that jurors did not need to be landowners. That is clearly what Round had in mind for the supposedly low-status English jurors, whom he regarded as peasants. That explanation cannot hold

---

[23]GDB 197r1 Foxetune.

[24]GDB 137v2–138r1 Leceworde.

good for the French jurors (no one has ever suggested that the Normans colonized England as peasants), and there is no compelling reason why it should apply to the English, partly because their name stock identifies them more closely with landowners than with peasants and partly because some individuals among them were demonstrably of comparable standing with the French. Instead I shall suggest some ways in which jurors could have been landowners without being mentioned as such in Domesday Book. The arguments necessarily proceed from a few individual cases where it is virtually certain that a juror held land without being named in Domesday.

The first group of cases consists of jurors who can be shown to have been the unrecorded tenants of named Domesday undertenants. In other words, they were landholders at tenurial level three, counting tenants-in-chief as level one and their undertenants as level two. Except in Cheshire and Shropshire, Domesday Book systematically omitted the whole third tenurial level. Five of the Cambridgeshire jurors can be assigned confidently to tenurial level three on the basis of how they were named and described in the jurors' lists. Wulfmær, man of Wighen, was an English juror in Cheveley Hundred. The Wighen who was his lord (the only Wighen in the whole of Domesday Book) was the Wighen of "Mara" who held a manor at Woodditton in Cheveley Hundred under Count Alan and who was himself a juror in that hundred, though mistakenly called William in the jurors' lists.[25] Wulfmær must therefore have been Wighen's man at Woodditton, holding some or all of the manor from him. The manor was later not held directly by Wighen's descendants, but under them by another family, the Valognes, though the earliest record of their tenure is not until 1206.[26] The second example is the French juror William, man of Walter, in Radfield Hundred. The only Walter who held land in the hundred was Walter de Grandcourt, who was undertenant of William de Warenne at Carlton and Weston Colville.[27] Again, the juror William must have held some or all of Walter's holding under him. Third, one of the English jurors in Staploe Hundred was Ælfric of Snailwell. There was only one manor at Snailwell in 1086, which was held by Hugh de Port as part of the fief of the disgraced Bishop Odo of

[25] GDB 195r2 Ditone.

[26] *VCH Cambs.*, vol. 10, *North-Eastern Cambridgeshire*, ed. A. F. Wareham and A. P. M. Wright (Oxford, 2002), p. 87.

[27] GDB 196r2–v1 Carlentone, *ll.* 1–5; Westone, *l.* 11.

Bayeux.[28] Ælfric may have been Hugh's tenant. A fourth example is Ralph de Cluny, juror in Radfield Hundred. There was no Ralph named as a Domesday landholder in the hundred, but a manor at Carlton belonged to the abbot of Cluny as the undertenant of William de Warenne, and it is very likely that Ralph was the abbey's tenant or perhaps the manager of its estate.[29] The fifth case is the most conclusive. The Chesterton Hundred juror Giffard of Drayton was surnamed from Dry Drayton. Although there is no trace of him at Dry Drayton in Domesday Book, by ca. 1160 and until 1302 half a knight's fee there was held by a family with the surname Giffard, who were presumably his descendants. The overlordship of the fee shows that it was the manor which in 1086 was held under the tenant-in-chief Robert Fafiton by a man named Avesgot.[30] Giffard the juror must have been Avesgot's unrecorded undertenant. Furthermore, it is very likely that the whole three-hide manor was in his hands, judging from the amount of land later held as the Giffards' home farm and by their tenants and grantees.[31]

Those five jurors, Wighen's man Wulfmær, Walter de Grandcourt's man William, Ælfric of Snailwell, Ralph de Cluny, and Giffard of Drayton, were thus all in actual occupation of manors in 1086 as tenants of undertenants. Their position was unrecorded in Domesday simply because the survey confined its attention to the first two levels of tenure, and they were in the third. There were probably other jurors like them. Hervey of Sawston was presumably the unrecorded tenant of the undertenant of one of the three manors at Sawston.[32] Hardwin de Scalers's man Richard in Papworth Hundred (Cambs.) and Bishop Odo's men Boia and Hugh in Odsey Hundred (Herts.) must have held estates under the men whom Hardwin and Odo had enfeoffed with all their manors in those hundreds.[33] The pre-Conquest owners Godwine the priest, Grim of Wratting, and Thurbert of Orwell, all jurors in 1086, may have survived the Conquest at tenurial level three. Domesday's

---

[28]GDB 199r2 Snellewelle.

[29]GDB 196r2 Carlentone, *ll.* 6–9.

[30]GDB 202r1 Draitone.

[31]*VCH Cambs.*, vol. 9, *Chesterton, Northstowe, and Papworth Hundreds (North and North-West of Cambridge)*, ed. A. P. M. Wright and C. P. Lewis (Oxford, 1989), pp. 76–78.

[32]GDB 193r2 Salsiton; 197r1 Salsiton; 197v1 Salsitone.

[33]GDB 199r1; 134v1.

blanket omission of the tenants of undertenants leaves room for a great many men, both French and English, from precisely the social and economic class most likely to be made hundred jurors in 1086.

The second place in the tenurial system where jurors apparently absent from Domesday Book might be located is as holders of part of a manor. There are three certain cases which deserve exploration. The juror Rumold of Coton, man of Count Eustace, swore in Wetherley Hundred in Cambridgeshire. He was a tenant of Count Eustace on three Hertfordshire manors not far away. Coton was not itself named as a separate manor in Domesday because it was part of Count Eustace's manor of Grantchester, held from the count by two unnamed knights. One of the two holdings was clearly Coton and one of the unnamed knights Rumold.[34] The second example is from Flendish Hundred (Cambs.), where Fulcard of Ditton, man of the abbot of Ely, was a juror. The Ditton from which he took his name was Fen Ditton. Like Coton, Fen Ditton was not described in its own Domesday entry, but under another manor, in this case the abbot of Ely's manor of Horningsea. From the Domesday entry alone one would not know that it covered two places. "Fen Ditton with Horningsea" was the name of an Ely manor right through the Middle Ages and into modern times, but it covered two parishes which had come into the church's hands by different means and were still distinct about 1030. Again in 1166 Fen Ditton was held separately within the larger manor as a knight's fee in the possession of one William Muschet, and it later descended in the Muschet family.[35] There are therefore strong grounds for thinking that Fen Ditton also had a separate tenurial identity in 1086 which was disregarded in the Domesday survey and that Fulcard of Ditton was then its tenant. He may even have been the ancestor of the Muschets. The third example is from Hertfordshire, where the juror Humphrey of Kinsbourne took his surname from a place not named in Domesday Book, but which was part of the abbot of Westminster's manor of Wheathampstead and was later treated as a separate manorial entity.[36] Again, there is a presumption that Humphrey held Kinsbourne as part of Wheathampstead in 1086, just as Rumold held Coton and Fulcard held Ditton.

---

[34]GDB 196r1 Grantesete; *VCH Cambs.*, vol. 5, ed. C. R. Elrington (Oxford, 1973), pp. 190, 202.

[35]GDB 19lr1 Horningesie; *VCH Cambs.* 10:123.

[36]GDB 135r2 Watamestede; *VCH Herts.*, vol. 2, ed. William Page (London, 1908), p. 297.

Rumold, Fulcard, and Humphrey are locatable in the tenurial structure because they were surnamed from places which can be identified as un-named components of Domesday manors. Most unidentified jurors with English toponymic surnames, however, were named from places which were themselves Domesday manors. Some of them might well also have held part of the estate, but where their share did not comprise a separate settlement or a later manor (like Coton, Fen Ditton, and Kinsbourne), it is impossible to identify what part of the Domesday estate they held. If they had toponymic surnames they would have been known by the name of the parent manor.

In some cases it is possible that what jurors held was part of an estate which had a separate pre-Conquest tenurial identity but in 1086 was rolled up into the description of the parent manor. There were a great many more pre-Conquest tenurial units in Cambridgeshire than were recorded as sep-arate entities in 1086. For example, Geoffrey de Mandeville's unitary ten-hide manor of Chippenham comprised five hides which had been in the king's farm, three hides belonging to Ordgar the sheriff, and two hides held from King Edward by two sokemen.[37] It might look as if the holdings of Ordgar and the sokemen had lost their separate identity by 1086, but that appearance is merely a function of the way that Domesday Book was com-piled. The fact that Ordgar had mortgaged his holding for seven marks and two ounces of gold, as Geoffrey's men testified in 1086, shows that it re-mained separate under the Normans. Thus William of Chippenham, Geof-frey de Mandeville's man and a juror, may have held one of the pre-Conquest holdings there. Only a very few pre-Conquest portions of Cambridgeshire manors received separate notice in 1086, like the hide of land at the royal manor of Fordham, which Brunmann held under both King Edward and King William,[38] or the nine and three quarter hides of Histon, which nine of the bishop of Dorchester's sokemen had held before the Conquest and which had passed by 1086 to Picot the sheriff as undertenant of (by then) the bishop of Lincoln.[39] Many more were ignored. One of the reasons may have been that they were usually not physically separate areas of the manor. Even Picot's holding at Histon, the later manor of Histon Denny, was not

---

[37]GDB 197r2 Chipeham.

[38]GDB 189v1 Fordeham, *ll.* 10–13.

[39]GDB l90r2–v1 Histone, *ll.* 9–15.

distinct on the ground, but a collection of houses and arable strips inter-mingled with the other main manor in Histon.[40]

Another reason for the concealment of pre-Conquest holdings in 1086 is that many of them were held TRE by groups of sokemen whom the Normans regarded as tenurially subordinate to the manor in which their lands were located. Only occasionally does Domesday Book for Cambridge-shire give a glimpse of what happened to such groups of sokemen, as on Gilbert of Ghent's fief. Gilbert was the successor of the king's thegn Ulf Fenisc, and his possessions in six parishes in northwest Cambridgeshire were an outlying part of Ulf's large and valuable manor of Fenstanton just over the Huntingdonshire border.[41] Ulf had held some land in Cambridge-shire himself, and the rest belonged to his sokemen: two at Elsworth, eight at Conington, six at Boxworth, and one at Fen Drayton. In 1086 all the sokemen remained in possession of their estates, while Gilbert kept Ulf's former demesne holdings in his own hands. The only change in twenty years was that Gilbert had given Ulf's demesne holding at Papworth St. Agnes to an Englishman called Ælfwold. Domesday Book reveals the existence of the sokemen in 1086 probably because their holdings were the sokelands of a manor in Huntingdonshire, a county where the owners of outlying soke-lands were recorded fairly systematically. The holdings in question were well-established tenurial units, and at Boxworth and Conington they were still in existence two hundred years later.[42] The jurors in Papworth Hundred in 1086 included two of Gilbert of Ghent's men, the Englishmen Beorhtstan and Osmund, who might well have been among his unnamed sokemen. Other jurors too could perhaps have been recruited from the ranks of those who held parts of larger estates. Fulk Waruhel, a man of Picot the sheriff and a juror in Wetherley Hundred (Cambs.), might have been one of the two men who held Comberton from Picot in 1086; the two holdings had appar-ently been distinct before the Conquest, since they were assigned to two separate groups of sokemen.[43] Bruning of Chesterton, a juror in Chesterton Hundred, might have held a small unrecorded estate on that royal manor similar to his near namesake Brunmann's hide at the other royal manor of

---

[40]*VCH Cambs*. 9:90, 95, 102.

[41]GDB 197r2–v1; 207r1.

[42]*VCH Cambs*. 9:273, 281–82.

[43]GDB 200v1 Cumbertone.

Fordham.[44] Eudes fitz Hubert's reeve Ælfric, who swore in Longstowe Hundred, was perhaps one of (or a successor to one of) the nine sokemen who had held part of Eudes's manor of Gamlingay.[45] All in all, the structure of landed estates in both Cambridgeshire and Hertfordshire was such that some of the jurors in 1086 might have been the holders of fragments of manors which were not separately mentioned in Domesday Book.

A third potential home for homeless jurors is as unrecorded lessees of manors. Leasing is well documented on the estates of Benedictine abbeys in the eleventh and twelfth centuries and especially on that of Ely. It is also the case that Ely's manors provided surnames for a large number of jurors who cannot be found in Domesday Book, and in general terms it seems likely that the two features are connected: that many of Ely's jurors were its lessees. That general case can be substantiated by looking at Ely's leasing policy before and after 1066.

The pre-Conquest abbots leased manors on standard terms, namely that the lessee could not sell or otherwise alienate and that the property should return to the church on his death. Lessees included grandees such as Archbishop Stigand and Asgar the staller, besides local men like Abbot Wulfric's brother Guthmund, the thegn Toki, the freeman Beorn, and the abbot's steward Æthelbeorht.[46] The estates leased included anything from large manors down to fifty acres. All the leases that were recorded are known because Ely had lost control of them since the Conquest and was claiming them in 1086, often by reference to the witness of the hundred court about the circumstances of the case. For instance, when Stigand died his two Cambridgeshire leases at Snailwell and Woodditton were taken by the king, while Toki's estate at Trumpington passed first to the Fleming Frederic and after his death to his Norman brother-in-law William de Warenne.[47]

When the abbey first began to reclaim its lost estates at a plea held sometime between 1072 and 1075, it divided its losses into three categories: demesne (*de dominio*), soke (*de soca*), and held by knight service (*ad ser-*

---

[44]GDB 189v2 Cestretone.

[45]GDB 197v2 Gamelinge.

[46]E. Miller, *The Abbey and Bishopric of Ely* (Cambridge, 1951), pp. 24–25, 51–53.

[47]GDB 189v2 Ditone; 196v1 Trumpinton; 199r2 Snellewelle.

vitium).[48] The demesne group included six Cambridgeshire holdings which Domesday Book shows were actually held on leases at Histon, Stetchworth, Swaffham Bulbeck, Trumpington, Little Gransden, and Milton.[49] They were not all retrieved by Ely before 1086, but one that clearly was, half a hide of meadow at Stetchworth which Earl Ralph had taken, went back into the demesne. Ely regarded its lost leases as part of the abbey's demesne. It follows that any leased manors which were still secure in 1086 would have been described then as demesne manors. The lack of any explicit reference in Domesday Book to manors on lease in 1086 is therefore not evidence that there were none. There are two further considerations. In view of the difficulties which Ely had in the early 1070s in keeping control of manors leased for life terms before the Conquest, the Norman abbots after 1073 may have switched to leases for shorter and definite terms. Second, Ely's manors in the Isle of Ely itself had probably long been managed in a flexible way which made them available in years of shortage to meet any deficiencies in the abbey's food rents from its other estates, but at other times would have left them free to generate a cash income on whatever terms could be negotiated with lessees.[50] Significantly, the island of Hainey, just south of Ely, had at some unspecified time before 1086 been held by a servant of the abbot for payment (*in presto*), presumably some kind of lease. That piece of information was omitted from Domesday Book and appears in the *Inquisitio Eliensis* probably only because Hainey had the unusual status of being neither geldable nor a manor.[51] Its uniqueness as a leasehold is only that we know about it.

There is also the important case of the abbey's man Osmund, who with his son Æthelmund gave up a holding at Witcham in the Isle of Ely to Abbot Symeon early in William II's reign.[52] The nature of Osmund's tenure is uncertain: Witcham was described simply as "a certain estate (*quandam ruris partem*)." It appears in Domesday Book as if it were a demesne manor of

---

[48]*ICC and IE*, ed. Hamilton, pp. 192–95.

[49]GDB 190v1, *ll*. 11–17; 190v1 Stuuicesworde, *ll*. 4–3 from end; 196r1 Suafham, *ll*. 6–8; 196v1 Trumpinton; 197v2 Gamelinge, *ll*. 7–9: holding at Grantedene; 20lv1 Middeltone, *ll*. 6–9.

[50]Miller, *Abbey and Bishopric of Ely*, pp. 37–43.

[51]*ICC and IE,* ed. Hamilton, 119; GDB 192r1–2 Haneia.

[52]*Liber Eliensis*, ed. E. O. Blake, Camden 3rd ser., 92 (London, 1962), pp. 218–19.

the abbey, though Osmund must then have been in possession.[53] Osmund was apparently of high social standing, since he was able to dispose of his estate and since he and his son left Witcham in order to fight in the king's army. They may even have been part of the contingent of Ely knights which Abbot Symeon sent to the king's aid in 1088. The way that their departure was described would not rule out Osmund's interest in Witcham being a leasehold which he was giving up before the term had expired. The important point about Osmund, however, is that he was a juror, the Englishman Osmund of Witcham who swore in the two hundreds of Ely in 1086. Here for certain is a man who held an estate of some kind at Witcham, was surnamed from Witcham, and was called as a juror for the hundred in which it stood, but who went unnoticed in Domesday Book.

Ely's manors as described in 1086, especially in the Isle, were remarkably bare of undertenants, as indeed were the Cambridgeshire estates of other abbey churches. Ramsey's return named tenants on only two manors, not its other nine; none were listed for the ten manors belonging to Thorney, Crowland, and Chatteris; Ely itself named virtually no tenants apart from its three baronial predators, Hardwin de Scalers, Picot the sheriff, and Guy de Reimbeaucourt, who had probably been enfeoffed in Cambridgeshire in order to provide part of the knight service which the abbot owed the king but were already treating the lands as their own.[54] In the case of Ramsey there is some evidence for leasing immediately after Domesday: of its seven estates in Northstowe and Papworth Hundreds, Over was leased for a life term in 1088; Girton was granted or leased after 1091 and recovered in 1114; and three quarters of a hide at Elsworth had been granted out and taken back by 1129.[55] It may be that Ramsey began leasing its manors only in 1088, but it is more likely that it was not then a new policy and that its leased manors were regarded in 1086 as demesne, as Ely's were. There are two general reasons for that view. The first is that there was a real practical difference between a manor granted for military service to fulfil an abbot's obligations to the king and a manor granted to produce a rent in cash or kind for the support of the monastic community. The second is that the leases that we know about at both Ramsey and Ely are the ones where the abbey had a

---

[53]GDB 192r2 Wiceham.

[54]GDB 190v1–193r1; Miller, *Abbey and Bishopric of Ely,* pp. 165–71.

[55]*VCH Cambs.* 9:118, 307, 343.

struggle to regain possession at the end of the term. We know nothing about any grants which reverted to the church in due order and at the proper time. There are thus grounds for supposing that many of the unidentified jurors could have been lessees as opposed to tenants by knight service. A great many of them were surnamed from places which were ecclesiastical manors or in townships where such a manor was one of several.

There is thus evidence from both Domesday Book and other sources that tenurial structures in 1086 were more complicated than they appear at first sight. Domesday provides comprehensive evidence only for tenurial levels one and two: tenancies-in-chief and undertenancies. It reported almost none of the holdings within manors which had been separate tenurial entities TRE and arguably largely remained so in 1086. It said nothing of leases which were still in being. Sokemen, tenants of undertenants, lessees, and holders of portions of manors were all actual occupiers of land, a concept well understood in late eleventh-century England. The English word for them was used in the Anglo-Saxon Chronicle for 1086: *landsittende* men.[56] There were thus many ways in which jurors could have been occupiers of land but not had their tenures recorded in Domesday Book. The categories of landholder described here overlap with the lower end of the spectrum formed by the identified jurors. Many of them will have been of comparable economic standing with men who held a single small manor at tenurial level two and were named in Domesday Book, but they also extended downwards into the upper ranks of the free peasantry.

If I am right in believing that the jurors in general, both French and English, were occupiers of land rather than peasants or unbeneficed household knights, then the jury lists for Cambridgeshire and Hertfordshire are a highly significant corrective to any picture of the landed settlement of England derived from Domesday Book alone. They add a substantial number to the landowners whom we know about in Cambridgeshire and Hertfordshire in 1086. In Cambridgeshire, where the jury lists are complete, Domesday itself names some 116 individual landowners, of whom ninety-six were French and twenty English. The jury lists add no fewer than ninety-nine names, of whom forty were French and fifty-nine English. Taking into account unnamed French knights and others, they thus add 28% to the

---

[56] *Two of the Saxon Chronicles Parallel*, ed. C. Plummer and J. Earle, 2 vols. (Oxford, 1892–99), 1:217.

contingent of French settlers in the county and nearly quadruple the named English survivors that we know something about. Those figures are only for unrecorded landowners revealed directly by the jury lists. Presumably, there were other French settlers who had acquired similar landed estates but were not called on to act as jurors in 1086. Presumably, there were other Englishmen besides the jurors who had leases of church estates, or who remained on their ancestral manors but were pushed out of sight into the third tenurial level by incoming tenants-in-chief and undertenants, or who had retained their own or their father's sokelands. Even the minimum additions suggest that Domesday underestimates by a significant proportion the number of newcomers and by a huge factor the number of surviving Englishmen of some account in local society. Note that I say *local* society. If the jury lists argue for greater English survival in 1086 than has previously been reckoned with, it was nevertheless survival at a low level. It is undoubtedly significant that far fewer English jurors than Frenchmen can be identified by name in Domesday as undertenants, since the undertenants were almost certainly mainly knights. At the next tenurial level down, among the actual occupiers of manors, it is likely that England remained very largely English in 1086 or at least that Cambridgeshire and north Hertfordshire did.

In conclusion, the jury lists highlight the incompleteness of the Domesday record of land ownership in 1086 and might tempt those already skeptical enough of Domesday numerology to dismiss even Domesday prosopography as a delusive waste of time. That would be a pity. Like so much else about Domesday, any sense of certainty, even about Domesday's uncertainties, is misleading. The jurors are a warning that certain types of landowner are likely to be unrecorded: specifically life tenants of ecclesiastical manors who were not (or not yet) breaking the terms of their tenure and claiming as their own; tenants of undertenants; and Englishmen with tenures on terms other than military service. There is no evidence that Domesday set out to record such tenures. When the Inquest asked of each manor "Who holds it now?" it expected straightforward answers: either the tenant-in-chief held it in demesne or he had subinfeudated it. If Sir James Holt is right (and I think that he is) about deducing the purpose of the Domesday Survey from the final form of Domesday Book,[57] then all lower levels of tenure mattered not one bit to the commissioners. Domesday was not asking for the

---

[57]J. C. Holt, "1086," in *Domesday Studies*, ed. J. C. Holt (Woodbridge,1987), pp. 41–64, esp. 50–55.

name of every Tom, Dick, and Ælfgar with some interest in the land of the manor. It reflects a particular view of English landed society in the late eleventh century, looking from its summit down only as far as the under-tenants. The usefulness above all of the jury lists is that they give a quite different perspective upwards from the bottom of landed society, from where, paradoxically, both the intensity of the Norman settlement and the degree of English survival look more substantial than is commonly acknowledged.

Appendix

LIST OF JURORS

NB: The "=" sign indicates the jurors who can be identified in Domesday Book and is followed by a note of their manors, concluding with totals for assessments in hides (h.) or carucates (c.) and acres (a.); plow teams in demesne and with the peasants (in the form 1:3 pl.); and values in shillings and pence (in the form 50/1; [est.] means that the value is estimated).

French Jurors

Albert de "Sansona" (Odsey, Herts.)
Albert, man of the abbot of Ramsey (Papworth, Cambs.)
Aleran the Frenchman [*ICC*]; Aleran [*IE*] (Staine, Cambs.)
Anketil de Herouville (Whittlesford, Cambs.)
Baldwin with the beard [*ICC*]; Baldwin the cook [*IE*] (Flendish, Cambs.)
Bernard of Hill (Ely, Cambs.)
Brian de Scalers (Chilford, Cambs.)
    = Brian, tenant of Count Alan in Cambs. at Babraham (Chilford Hund.), later held by Scalers fam. [*VCH Cambs*. 6:21]
    2 h. 84 a.; 1:3 pl.; 50/-
David of Balsham (Radfield, Cambs.)
Everard fitz Brian [*ICC*]; Everard, man of Aubrey de Vere [*IE*] (Cheveley, Cambs.)
    = Everard fitz Brian, tenant of Aubrey de Vere in Cambs. at Ashley and Saxon Street (Cheveley Hund.)
    8 h. 60 a.; 5:6 pl.; 260/-
Farman (Staine, Cambs.)

Firmin (Chilford, Cambs.)

    = Firmatus, tenant of Aubrey de Vere in Cambs. at Great Abington and Babraham (Chilford Hund.)

    6 h. 15 a.; 2:4 pl.; 161/8

Fulcard of Ditton [*ICC*]; Fulcold, man of the abbot of Ely [*IE*] (Flendish, Cambs.)

Fulk waruhel [*ICC*]; Fulk, man of the sheriff [*IE*] (Wetherley, Cambs.)

Fulk, man of Gosbert the Beauvaisien (Odsey, Herts.)

    = Fulk, tenant of Gosbert de Beauvais in Herts. at Wallington (Odsey Hund.)

    3 h. 40 a.; 2:2 pl.; 50/-

Geoffrey of Chesfield (Broadwater, Herts.)

    = Godfrey, tenant of Peter de Valognes in Herts. at Graveley and Chells (Broadwater Hund.): Chesfield was a manor in Graveley parish which can be identified with Godfrey's holding there [*VCH Herts*. 3:87]; DB's "Godefridus" is probably the correct forename, mistaken or corrupted by *IE* into the more familiar "Goisfrid," perhaps under the influence of the next name in the list, another "Goisfrid"

    3 h. 105 a.; 3:1 pl.; 70/-

Geoffrey of Westbrook (Broadwater, Herts.)

Geoffrey, constable of the abbot [of Ely] (Ely, Cambs.)

Geoffrey, reeve of these hundreds (Ely, Cambs.)

Gerard the Lotharingian (Whittlesford, Cambs.)

    = Gerard, tenant of Count Alan in Cambs. at Whittlesford and Duxford (Whittlesford Hund.)

    6 h. 15 a.; 2:4 pl.; 102/-

Germund de Saint-Ouen (Odsey, Herts.)

    = Germund, tenant of Geoffrey de Mandeville in Herts. at Ashwell and "Hainstone" (Odsey Hund.) and "Stivicesuuorde" (Hertford Hund.); outside Herts. at Ivinghoe Aston (Bucks.) and Birchanger (Essex); no evidence from the descents that he was the same as the Germund(s) who held of Walter Giffard in Beds., of Richard fitz Gilbert in Essex and Suff., and of Ralph Baynard in Essex

    Herts.: 3 h. 37½ a.; 2:½ pl.; 33/-

    Bucks.: 4 h. 30 a.; 2:1½ pl.; 50/-

    Essex: 60 a.; 1:0 pl.; 10/-

    Total: 8 h. 7½ a.; 5:2 pl.; 93/-

Giffard of Drayton (Chesterton, Cambs.)

Gilbert of Histon (Chesterton, Cambs.)

Gilbert of Linden (Ely, Cambs.)

Gosbert the Beauvaisien (Broadwater, Herts.)

    = Gosbert de Beauvais, tenant-in-chief in Herts. of Wymondley and

Graveley (Broadwater Hund.) and Wallington (subinfeudated to Fulk, q.v.)
5 h. 30 a.; 3:2 pl.; 100/-

Guy, man of the abbot of Ramsey [*IE*]; Guy, man of the abbot of St. Benedict's
[*ICC*] (Longstowe, Cambs.)
= Guy, tenant of Ramsey in Cambs. at Longstowe (Longstowe Hund.);
probably Guy d'Eu: Abbot Reynold (1114–30) granted or confirmed
Longstowe to Guy d'Eu [*VCH Cambs.* 5:121]
2 h.; 2:3 pl.; 50/-

Hervey of Sawston (Whittlesford, Cambs.)

Huard de Noyers (Edwinstree, Herts.)
= Huard, tenant of Geoffrey de Mandeville in Herts. at Bengeo (Hertford
Hund.); same as Hugh, tenant of Geoffrey de Mandeville in Herts. at
Barkway (Edwinstree Hund.), which belonged in the 1140s to the Noyers
(*Noeriis*) fam. [*VCH Herts.* 4:30]; presumably DB mistook "Huardus" for
the more common Hugo, or wrongly extended Hu'
6 h. 30 a.; 4:6 pl.; 165/-

Hugh Farsit [*IE*]; Hugh Farsi [*ICC*] (Northstowe, Cambs.)

Hugh Pedefold [*IE*]; Hugh Petuuolt [*ICC*] (Armingford, Cambs.)
= Hugh, tenant of Hardwin de Scalers in Cambs. at Meldreth (Armingford
Hund.) and Shepreth (Wetherley Hund.); the two manors probably
descended together [*VCH Cambs.* 5:255–56; 8:87]
1 h. 75 a., 0:2 pl.; 42/-

Hugh of Exning (Staploe, Cambs.)

Hugh, man of the bishop of Bayeux (Odsey, Herts.)

Humphrey d'Anneville (Armingford, Cambs.)
= Humphrey d'Anneville, tenant of Eudes fitz Hubert in Cambs. at Clopton,
East Hatley, and Croydon (Armingford Hund.), Wimpole (Wetherley
Hund.), Kingston (Longstowe Hund.), and in Herts. at Knebworth (Broad-
water Hund.) and an unnamed place in Hertford Hund.; tenant of Guy de
Raimbeaucourt in Cambs. at Barton and Haslingfield (Wetherley Hund.)
and Eversden (Longstowe Hund.); holder of two houses in Hertford
borough; all of which descended to the Andeville fam. [*VCH Cambs.* 5:60,
113, 162, 266; 8:34; *VCH Herts.* 3:114]
Cambs.: 16 h. 68 a.; 9:13 pl.; 560/8
Herts.: 8 h. 90 a.; 3:9 pl.; 260/-
Total: 25 h. 38 a.; 12:22 pl.; 820/8

Humphrey of Kinsbourne (Broadwater, Herts.)

Letard, man of the abbot [of Ely] (Broadwater, Herts.)

"Livet," man of G. de Bec (Broadwater, Herts.)
probably = Lovet, tenant of Geoffrey de Bec in Herts. at Theobald Street
(Dacorum Hund.) and Rodhanger (Broadwater Hund.)
90 a.; 0 pl.; 8/8

Manfred [*IE*]; Matfred [*ICC*] (Radfield, Cambs.)
> = one of two unnamed knights, tenants in Cambs. of Count Alan at Dulling-
> ham (Radfield Hund.); the manor was later called Matfreys and was held ca.
> 1125 by Ralph son of Mafred (the son of the juror?) and later by his
> descendants, the Madfrey fam. [*VCH Cambs*. 6:162]
> 1 h. 5 a.; 1 pl.; 22/- [est.]

Nicholas of Kennett (Staploe, Cambs.)
> = Nicholas, tenant of William de Warenne in Cambs. at Kennett (Staploe
> Hund.) and outside Cambs. at Elveden, Herringswell, and Tunstall (Suff.)
> Cambs.: 3 h. 60 a.; 5:5 pl.; 240/-
> Suff.: 3 c. 30 a.; 2:1 pl.; 78/4
> Total: 6 h. 90 a.; 7:6 pl.; 318/4

Norman of Nosterfield (Chilford, Cambs.)
> = Norman, tenant of Aubrey de Vere in Cambs. at Shudy Camps and Horse-
> heath (Chilford Hund.); Nosterfield was in Shudy Camps parish [*VCH
> Cambs*. 6:52]
> 2 h.; 1:3 pl.; 100/-

Osmund of Stretham (Ely, Cambs.)
> probably = Osmund, tenant of Picot the sheriff in Cambs. at Waterbeach
> (Northstowe Hund.), which adjoined Stretham
> 1 h. 70 a.; 1:0 pl.; 20/-

Osmund the small (Flendish, Cambs.)

Pain, man of Hardwin [*ICC*]; Pain, steward of Hardwin [*IE*] (Whittlesford,
Cambs.)
> = Pain, tenant of Hardwin de Scalers in Cambs. at Duxford (Whittlesford
> Hund.), Papworth, Elsworth, Conington, Boxworth (Papworth Hund.), and
> Dry Drayton (Chesterton Hund.), which descended together [*VCH Cambs*.
> 6:207; 9:77, 271, 282, 308]
> 16 h. 15 a.; 6:8¼ pl.; 219/-

Ralph Baynard (Edwinstree, Herts.)
> probably = Ralph Baynard, nephew of Ralph Baynard, the substantial
> tenant-in-chief [Richard Mortimer, "The Baynards of Baynard's Castle," in
> *Studies Presented to R. Allen Brown,* ed. Christopher Harper-Bill,
> Christopher J. Holdsworth, and Janet L. Nelson (Woodbridge, 1989),
> pp. 241–53 at 244–46]

Ralph de Banks (Wetherley, Cambs.) alias Ralph of Barrington (Thriplow,
Cambs.)
> = Ralph de Banks, tenant of Picot the sheriff in Cambs. at Pampisford
> (Chilford Hund.), Barrington, Wratworth, Whitwell (Wetherley Hund.), and
> Kingston (Longstowe Hund.); tenant of Count Alan in Cambs. at Pampis-
> ford (Chilford Hund.); tenant of Guy de Raimbeaucourt in Cambs. at Orwell

and Wratworth (Wetherley Hund.); holder of two houses in Cambridge borough

from Picot: 7 h. 116 a.; 3:7¾ pl.; 168/-

from Alan: 71 a.; ½:½ pl.; 15/-

from Guy: 70 a.; 0:⅝ pl.; 22/-

Total: 9 h. 17 a.; 3½:8⅞ pl.; 205/-

Ralph de Cluny (Radfield, Cambs.)

Ralph de Feugeres (Papworth, Cambs.)

    = Ralph, tenant of Hardwin de Scalers in Cambs. at Over (Papworth Hund.), which descended in the Feugeres fam. [*VCH Cambs.* 9:344]; not the same as Ralph de Fougères, tenant-in-chief in Surr., Berks., Devon, Bucks., Norf., and Suff.

    2 h. 30 a.; 0:2½ pl.; 30/-

Ralph de Hotot (Cheveley, Cambs.)

Ralph of Shephall (Broadwater, Herts.)

Ralph, reeve of this hundred (Thriplow, Cambs.)

Reynold of Downham (Ely, Cambs.)

Richard of Morden (Armingford, Cambs.)

    = Richard, tenant of Geoffrey de Mandeville in Cambs. at Guilden Morden (Armingford Hund.)

    90 a.; 1:1 pl.; 20/-

Richard, man of Hardwin (Papworth, Cambs.)

Richard, reeve of this hundred [*IE*]; Richard [*ICC*] (Cheveley, Cambs.)

Richard, reeve of this hundred [*IE*]; Richard [*ICC*] (Staine, Cambs.)

Riculf, man of the bishop of London (Edwinstree, Herts.)

    = Riculf, tenant of the bishop of London in Herts. at Pelham (Edwinstree Hund.)

    2 h.; 2:2 pl.; 100/-

Robert of Hinton (Flendish, Cambs.)

    = Robert, tenant of Count Alan in Cambs. at Teversham (Flendish Hund.), part of which was assessed with Cherry Hinton

    1 h.; 0:1 pl.; 10/-

Robert fitz Warin (Northstowe, Cambs.)

    = Robert, tenant of Picot the sheriff in Cambs. at Lolworth (Northstowe Hund.) and Childerley (Chesterton Hund.)

    9 h. 60 a.; 2:3 pl.; 83/4

Robert the chamberlain (Ely, Cambs.)

Rodri, man of the bishop [of London] (Edwinstree, Herts.)

    = Rodri, tenant of the bishop of London in Herts. at Chaldean (Edwinstree Hund.) and Thorley (Braughing Hund.)

    1 h.; 2:0 pl.; 50/-

Roger of Childerley (Chesterton, Cambs.)
>   = Roger, tenant of the bishop of Lincoln in Cambs. at Little Childerley
>   (Chesterton Hund.), ancestor of the Childerley fam. [*VCH Cambs.* 9:42–43]
>   3 h.; 1:1 pl.; 50/-

Roger fitz Morin (Northstowe, Cambs.)

Roger, man of Walter Giffard [*IE*]; Roger [*ICC*] (Staine, Cambs.)

Rumold of Coton [*ICC*]; Rumold, man of Count Eustace [*IE*] (Wetherley,
    Cambs.)
>   = one of two unnamed knights, tenants of Count Eustace in Cambs. at
>   Grantchester (Wetherley Hund.), which included Coton [*VCH Cambs.*
>   5:190, 202]; Rumold was also tenant of Count Eustace at Throcking,
>   Eckington, and Beauchamps (Herts.)
>   Cambs.: 1 h. 45 a.; 1½:1½ pl.; 80/- [est.]
>   Herts.: 2 h. 78 a.; 2 pl.; 52/-
>   Total: 4 h. 3 a.; 5 pl.; 132/-

Sefrid the reeve [*ICC*]; Sefrid, reeve of this hundred [*IE*] (Wetherley, Cambs.)
>   = Sefrid, tenant of Picot the sheriff in Cambs. at Haslingfield and Harlton
>   (Wetherley Hund.)
>   5 h. 90 a.; 2:2 pl.; 100/-

Sturmid of Cottenham (Chesterton, Cambs.)

Tancred of Sutton (Ely, Cambs.)

Tehard, man of the abbot of Ely (Papworth, Cambs.)

Tibbald, man of Hardwin (Thriplow, Cambs.)
>   = unnamed knight, tenant of Hardwin de Scalers in Cambs. at Shepreth
>   (Wetherley Hund.); and = Tibbald, tenant of Hardwin de Scalers in Herts. at
>   Luffenhall, Clothall, Broadfield, Ashwell, Hinxworth, Barley, Hodenhoe,
>   Throcking, Eckinton, Wakely, and Berkesden, all of which passed to his
>   descendants the FitzRalph fam. [*VCH Cambs.* 5:256; *VCH Herts.* 3:202,
>   210, 234; 4:20–21, 39–40, 42, 84, 111]
>   Cambs.: 2 h. 15 a.; 2¼ pl.; 42/-
>   Herts.: 12 h. 15½ a.; 2:9½ pl.; 215/-
>   Total: 14 h. 30½ a.; 13¾ pl.; 257/-

Tiel, reeve of the abbot of Ely (Longstowe, Cambs.)

Walter de Clais (Chilford, Cambs., and Northstowe, Cambs.)
>   probably = Walter, tenant of Picot the sheriff in Cambs. at Impington
>   (Northstowe Hund.)
>   3 h. 60 a.; 0:3 pl.; 60/-

Walter the monk (Armingford, Cambs.)
>   = Walter the monk, tenant of Azeline Talboys in Cambs. at Tadlow (Arming-
>   ford Hund.) and outside Cambs. at Old Warden and Chicksands (Beds.)
>   Cambs.: 1 h. 30 a.; 1:1 pl.; 40/-

Beds.: 1 h. 60 a.; 1 pl.; 30/-

Total: 2 h. 90 a.; 3 pl.; 70/-

Warin of Soham (Staploe, Cambs.)

Warin the priest (Longstowe, Cambs.)

William de Cailly (Thriplow, Cambs.)

= William de Cailly, tenant of William de Warenne in Cambs. at Trumpington (Thriplow Hund.) and outside Cambs. at Hillington (Norf.); evidently
not the same as William de Cailly, tenant-in-chief of Sulham (Berks.) and
tenant of Miles Crispin in Berks., Bucks., and Oxon., ancestor of the
Sulham fam. [*VCH Oxon.* 6:94–95]

Cambs.: 4 h. 60 a.; 2:3 pl.; 120/-

Norf.: 1 c.; 2:1 pl.; 60/-

Total: 5 h. 60 a.; 4:4 pl.; 180/-

William of Chippenham [*ICC*]; William of Chippenham, man of Geoffrey [*IE*]
(Staploe, Cambs.)

William of Letchworth (Broadwater, Herts.)

= William, tenant of Robert Gernon in Herts. at Ayot St. Peter, Graveley,
Chells, Woolwicks, Little Wymondley, Letchworth (Broadwater Hund.),
Wallington (Odsey Hund.), Hyde Hall, "Sapeham," and Bozen (Edwinstree
Hund.)

20 h. 70 a.; 4½:13½ pl.; 280/-

William of "Mara" (Cheveley, Cambs.)

= Wighen of "Mara," tenant of Count Alan in Cambs. at Woodditton
(Cheveley Hund.); Wighen is probably the correct name

5 h.; 4:6 pl.; 200/-

William, man of Picot the sheriff [*IE*]; William [*ICC*] (Longstowe, Cambs.)
perhaps = William, tenant of Picot the sheriff in Cambs. at Girton (Northstowe Hund.)

3 h. 90 a.; 1:1½ pl.; 60/-

William, man of Walter (Radfield, Cambs.)

English Jurors

Alan of Burwell (Staploe, Cambs.)

= Alan, tenant of Count Alan in Cambs. at Burwell (Staploe Hund.)

2 h. 60 a.; 2:3 pl.; 80/-

Almær cild (Longstowe, Cambs.)

= Almær of Bourn, tenant of Count Alan in Cambs. at East Hatley and
Croydon (Armingford Hund.), Kingston, Bourn, Caldecote, Longstowe, and
Hatley St. George (Longstowe Hund.); TRE had held much of this from

Eadgifu the beautiful
   8 h.; 3:8¼ pl.; 195/-
Almær of Cottenham (Chesterton, Cambs.)
Almær of Weston (Broadwater, Herts.)
Almær son of Blæc (Wetherley, Cambs.)
Alnoth of Sutton (Ely, Cambs.)
Alweard framward (Broadwater, Herts.)
   perhaps = Alweard, tenant of Count Alan in Herts. at Reed (Odsey Hund.)
   1 h.; 0:1 pl.; 20/-
Alweard of Mardley (Broadwater, Herts.)
   = Alweard of Mardley, tenant of Robert Gernon in Herts. at Mardley (Broadwater Hund.) and tenant-in-chief of Rodhanger (Broadwater Hund.); TRE
   had held both manors, then worth 55/-; TRE one or more Alweards also held
   three manors as man of Archbishop Stigand, five as thegn of Earl Harold,
   four as man of Earl Ælfgar, one as man of Ælfstan of Boscombe, and one as
   man of Almær of Benington: some of these might be Alweard of Mardley
   1 h. 90 a.; 1:2 pl.; 35/-
Alweard of Munden (Broadwater, Herts.)
   probably = Alweard, tenant of Peter de Valognes in Herts. at Libury (Broad-
   water Hund.) and (jointly with Deorman) tenant-in-chief of Watton
   (Broadwater Hund.)
   2h. 75 a.; 1:2¼ pl.; 51/4 [est.]
Azor (Northstowe, Cambs.)
Ælfgar of Dullingham (Radfield, Cambs.)
Ælfric of Horseheath (Chilford, Cambs.)
Ælfric of Snailwell (Staploe, Cambs.)
Ælfric of Thriplow (Thriplow, Cambs.)
Ælfric of Wilbraham (Staine, Cambs.)
Ælfric of Wymondley (Broadwater, Herts.)
Ælfric serdere (Ely, Cambs.)
Ælfric wordepund (Ely, Cambs.)
Ælfric, reeve of Eudes (Longstowe, Cambs.)
Ælfwine of Hinton (Ely, Cambs.)
Ælfwine of Rushden (Odsey, Herts.)
Ælfwine of "Werlaio" (Broadwater, Herts.)
Ælfwine son of Oda (Armingford, Cambs.)
Æthelmær his [Colsveinn's] son (Armingford, Cambs.)
Æthelstan of Weston (Radfield, Cambs.)
Beorhtheah of Barton (Wetherley, Cambs.)
Beorhtstan, man of Gilbert of Ghent (Papworth, Cambs.)
Boia, man of the bishop (Odsey, Herts.)
Bruning of Chesterton (Chesterton, Cambs.)

Carl of Cheveley [*IE*]; Carl of Cheveley, son of Brun [*ICC*] (Cheveley, Cambs.)
Colsveinn (Armingford, Cambs.)
    = Colsveinn, tenant of Count Alan in Cambs. at Whaddon, Meldreth, and
    Melbourn (Armingford Hund.); TRE had held same three manors of Eadgifu
    the beautiful, and was lord of a man at Whaddon
    1 h. 60 a.; 1:3 pl.; 70/- (TRE 120/-)
Eadwine the priest (Flendish, Cambs.)
Earnwig of Childerley (Chesterton, Cambs.)
Frawine of Kirtling (Cheveley, Cambs.)
Godlive of Stanton [*ICC*]; Godlive [*IE*] (Northstowe, Cambs.)
Godmær of Girton (Northstowe, Cambs.)
Godric of Croxton (Longstowe, Cambs.)
Godric of Fowlmere (Thriplow, Cambs.)
Godwine of Fulbourn [*IE*]; Godwine son of Nabbe [*ICC*] (Flendish, Cambs.)
Godwine of Hormead (Edwinstree, Herts.)
    = Godwine, tenant of Edgar atheling in Herts. at Barkway and Hormead
    (Edwinstree Hund.)
    8 h. 30 a.; 5:6 pl.; 200/-
Godwine the priest (Papworth, Cambs.)
    TRE Godwine the priest, man of the abbot of Ely, held 45 a. in Cambs. at
    Papworth (Papworth Hund.), worth 10/-
Grim of Wratting [*IE*]; Grip of Wratting [*ICC*] (Radfield, Cambs.)
    TRE Grim, man of Eadgifu the beautiful, held 60 a. in Cambs. at Stetch-
    worth (Radfield Hund.), worth 10/-
Hag' of Linton (Chilford, Cambs.)
Harald, man of Hardwin de Scalers [*IE*]; Harald [*ICC*] (Staine, Cambs.)
Healfdene (Broadwater, Herts.)
    = Healfdene, tenant of Peter de Valognes in Herts. at Tewin, which he held
    TRE as a king's thegn, worth 80/-
    5 h. 60 a.; 1:3½ pl.; 60/-
Huna of Ely (Ely, Cambs.)
Huscarl of Swaffham (Staine, Cambs.)
    TRE Huscarl, man of King Edward, held 90 a. worth 55/- and was one of
    three sokemen of Ely with 2 h. 70 a., worth [est.] 68/2, both in Swaffham,
    Cambs. (Staine Hund.)
Leodmann the priest (Ely, Cambs.)
Leodmær of Drayton (Chesterton, Cambs.)
Leodmær of Whittlesford (Whittlesford, Cambs.)
Leodmær of Witchford (Ely, Cambs.)
Leofgeat, man of the count (Chilford, Cambs.)
Leofhun of Duxford (Whittlesford, Cambs.)

Leofmær of Hinxton (Whittlesford, Cambs.)

Leofric son of Grim (Whittlesford, Cambs.)

Leofsige, man of the abbess of Chatteris (Edwinstree, Herts.)

Leofwine gric (Papworth, Cambs.)

Leofwine of Bottisham [*ICC*]; Leofwine [*IE*] (Staine, Cambs.)

Ordmær of Badlingham (Staploe, Cambs.)

> = Ordmær, tenant of Count Alan in Cambs. at Badlingham (Staploe Hund.);
> TRE Ordmær, man of Eadgifu the beautiful, had held Badlingham and
> Swaffham (Staine Hund.), together 7 h. 60 a. worth 300/-
>
> 3 h. 60 a.; 2:4 pl.; 60/-

Osmund of Witcham (Ely, Cambs.)

Osmund, man of Gilbert of Ghent (Papworth, Cambs.)

Robert the Englishman of Fordham [*IE*]; Robert of Fordham [*ICC*] (Staploe, Cambs.)

Sæweard of Harlton (Wetherley, Cambs.)

Sigar (Sigegar) the steward (Thriplow, Cambs.)

> = Sigar, tenant of Geoffrey de Mandeville in Cambs. at Thriplow and Fox-
> ton (Thriplow Hund.), and Shepreth and Orwell (Wetherley Hund.); TRE
> Sigar had held those four manors with Sawston (Whittlesford Hund.) and
> Haslingfield (Wetherley Hund.) from Asgar the staller, altogether 13 h. 60
> a. worth 373/-; and perhaps also Fulbourn (Flendish Hund.), Dry Drayton
> (Chesterton Hund.), and Caldecote (Longstowe Hund.) from other lords,
> altogether a further 6 h. 50 a. worth 210/- [est.]
>
> 6 h. 60 a.; 3:5½ pl.; 148/-

Sigeheah of the same vill [Teversham] [*ICC*]; Sigeheah [*IE*] (Flendish, Cambs.)

Sigeric, man of Count Eustace (Edwinstree, Herts.)

Sigeweard of Hormead (Edwinstree, Herts.)

> perhaps = Sigeweard, tenant of Geoffrey de Mandeville and of Hardwin
> de Scalers in Herts. at Wallington (Odsey Hund.)
>
> 1 h. 116 a.; 1 pl.; 30/-

Stanheard of Hauxton (Thriplow, Cambs.)

Stanheard of Silverley (Cheveley, Cambs.)

Thorkil of Digswell (Broadwater, Herts.)

> = Thorkil, tenant of Geoffrey de Mandeville in Herts. at Digswell (Broad-
> water Hund.); had held it TRE as a man of Asgar the staller, when worth
> 80/-; TRE also held Bengeo as a man of Asgar the staller; TRE total:
>
> 5h. 30 a. worth 160/-
>
> 2h.; 2:6½ pl.; 80/-

Thorulf (Armingford, Cambs.)

Thurbert of Orwell (Wetherley, Cambs.)

> TRE Thurbern held 105 a. in Cambs. at Orwell (Wetherley Hund.) under
> Eadgifu the beautiful, worth 30/-

Wihtgar of Orwellbury (Odsey, Herts.)

    = Wihtgar, tenant of Hardwin de Scalers in Herts. at Orwell and Therfield (Odsey Hund.)

    2 h. 25 a.; 1½ pl.; 38/-

Wine of Balsham (Radfield, Cambs.)

Wulfmær, man of Wighen (Cheveley, Cambs.)

Wulfric of Girton (Northstowe, Cambs.)

Wulfric of Teversham (Flendish, Cambs.)

Wulfric (Chilford, Cambs.)

Wulfsige of Therfield (Odsey, Herts.)

Wulfwig of Hatley [*IE*]; Wulfwig of "Doesse" [*ICC*] (Longstowe, Cambs.)

NAMES AND ETHNICITY
IN ANGLO-NORMAN ENGLAND

Stephanie Mooers Christelow

When Eadmer composed his *Historia Novorum* during the late eleventh and early twelfth centuries, he alluded to the fate of the English after the Conquest: "So William became king. What treatment he meted out to those leaders of the English who managed to survive the great slaughter, as it could do no good, I forbear to tell."[1] The response reflects a combination of avoidance and reticence, for Eadmer, although an Englishman, served a representative of the Norman regime. Other survivors of the Norman Conquest, such as Orderic Vitalis, an English-born monk at the Norman monastery of Saint-Évroul, offer similarly oblique references to suffering followed by adjustment: at Henry I's death in 1135: "English and Normans were living peacefully together in boroughs, towns and cities, and were intermarrying

---

[1]Eadmer, *Historia Novorum in Anglia*, trans. G. Bosanquet (London, 1964), p. 9; also, Henry, archdeacon of Huntingdon, *Historia Anglorum,* ed. and trans. Diana Greenway (Oxford, 1996), and Orderic Vitalis, *Historia Ecclesiastica*, ed. and trans. Marjorie Chibnall, 2 (Oxford, 1969 and 1983) (hereafter, OV). The lament in *The Anglo-Saxon Chronicle*, ed. G. N. Garmonsway (London, 1955), *sub anno* 1066, is an exception. French historians describe the slaughter of Englishmen in more enthusiastic terms: William of Jumièges, *Gesta Normannorum ducum*, ed. J. Marx (Rouen and Paris, 1914), pp. 135–36, and William of Poitiers, *Histoire de Guillaume le Conquerant*, ed. Raymonde Foreville (Paris, 1962), pp. 180–204.

341

with each other."[2] By the late twelfth century, Richard son of Nigel could claim, "nowadays, when English and Normans live close together and marry and give in marriage to each other, the nations are so mixed that it can scarcely be decided (I mean in the case of the freemen) who is of English birth and who of Norman."[3]

These observations, and others like them, raise questions of sentiment and ethnicity perceived by free people in England after 1066. They pertain as well to the processes of cultural adaptation and cultural syncretism, and to assertions of identity.[4] A person's identity can be guessed by place of birth and status, by appearance or race,[5] by her or his name(s), and by religious practice, gastronomic styles, and costume, but is established primarily through the language and dialect that she or he speaks, and her/his accent. Ethnicity is demonstrated through one's considered emphasis on origin, kin, and nomenclature.[6] Whereas on the Continent the affirmation of lineage through naming patterns was well established,[7] family and kin ties were rarely emphasized in England before 1066. Instead, surnames, when they

---

[2]OV 2:257. See also Ann Williams, *The English and the Norman Conquest* (Woodbridge, 1996).

[3]Richard son of Nigel, *Dialogus de Scaccario*, ed. Charles Johnson (London, 1950), p. 53. On the recovery of economic influence by people of English descent in the late twelfth century, see K. S. B. Keats-Rohan, "The Making of Henry of Oxford: Englishmen in a Norman World," *Oxon.* 54 (1989), 289–309.

[4]See John Edwards, *Language, Society, and Identity* (Oxford, 1985) and Ronald Wardhaugh, *An Introduction to Sociolinguistics* (Oxford, 1986).

[5]Racial distinctions were applied on Europe's frontiers but were less important within Europe, where homogenization among different groups was rapid: Robert Bartlett, *The Making of Europe: Conquest, Colonization, and Cultural Change, 950–1350* (Princeton, 1993), pp. 197 ff.

[6]Joshua A. Fishman, *Language and Ethnicity* (Clevedon, 1989).

[7]Members of French and German comital families can be identified through the prolonged and restricted use of one or two personal names. Recent examples are explicated in Christian Settipani, "Les Comtes d'Anjou et leurs alliances aux Xe et XIe siècles," in *Family Trees and the Roots of Politics: The Prosopography of Britain and France from the Tenth to the Twelfth Century*, ed. K. S. B. Keats-Rohan (Woodbridge, 1997), pp. 211–67, and Kathleen Thompson, "The Formation of the County of Perche: The Rise and Fall of the House of Gouet," ibid., pp. 299–314.

were used, indicated place of residence, rank, and occupation.[8] As we will see, the Norman Conquest complicated native nomenclature by encouraging the assertion of English ethnicity through the prolonged use of Insular personal names and/or by adopting patronymics indicating English ancestry. Normans and many other French immigrants expressed their identity by utilizing, primarily, French place names as surnames. Bretons retained Breton personal names, but, it will appear below, were less concerned with indicating ethnicity either through a patronymic or a toponymic.

All of these groups shared a North Sea culture and environment, and before 1066 they knew something of one another through information gleaned from trade, immigration, and marriage. Brittany was involved, if peripherally, with Frisian and English trade during the Viking Age: quern stones found in excavations of North Sea emporia, for example, originated in Norway, Northern France, and Brittany.[9] But members of Breton noble houses emigrated to England during the tenth and eleventh centuries, partly to escape the physical threat of Northmen and partly to participate in the multi-ethnic court of Edward the Confessor (1042–66).[10] Edward's first cousins, to whom he gave land in England, were Bretons; his uncles were Normans and Flemings; his friends were Scandinavians.[11] Although they established an interest in the English economy and political structure, they may not have perceived themselves as distinctly English but rather as members of a North Sea community.

Rouen, which had been a comital and episcopal seat before the Viking Age, recovered its former status soon after its incorporation into the county of Normandy in 911. By the mid-tenth century its mint was reestablished, and Norman coins were distributed throughout markets in Scandinavia, England, and the Continent.[12] Personal and family ties among royal, ducal, and comital houses reinforced trade relationships. Normans had been represented in the English royal court with the marriage of Emma, daughter of

---

[8]Eleventh-century royal charters provide some evidence of this: see Frank Barlow, *Edward the Confessor* (Berkeley, 1970), Appendix F, "Some Unpublished Royal Charters," pp. 328–35.

[9]Richard Hodges, *Dark Age Economics: The Origins of Towns and Trade, AD 600–1000* (New York, 1982), pp. 105 ff.

[10]Patrick Galliou and Michael Jones, *The Bretons* (Oxford, 1991), pp. 166–68.

[11]Barlow, *Edward the Confessor*, pp. 40–41.

[12]David Bates, *Normandy before 1066* (London, 1982), pp. 2–43.

Richard I, duke of Normandy, to Æthelred, king of England (d. 1016). Emma, who died in 1052, outlived her English spouse and married Cnut, king of Denmark and England (d. 1035), only to survive him as well. Emma's successive marriages are only one example of intermarriage among Europe's elite: her daughter Godgifu married, first, Dreux, count of Nantes, and second, Eustace II, count of Boulogne; these marriages underscore the commonality among English and Norman, Breton and Fleming. Gunnhilde, the child of Emma and Cnut, married Henry III, king of Germany. Emma's grandchildren, like those of Queen Victoria centuries later, sat on the thrones of nearly all northern European states.[13] But while cultural borrowing occurred among North Sea neighbors, it may have been limited to the societies influenced by royal women.[14]

While the choice of name in one's own language may reflect either whim or design, the bestowing of a foreign name on one's child would rarely occur without a pressing, personal reason.[15] Cosmopolitan English people today, for example, are familiar with European culture, language, and styles through the media and easy travel, but such familiarity would not ordinarily cause them to call their children Birgit or Olaf (Scandinavian), Ludmilla or Klaus (German), Claudine or Jean-Paul (French). If one's spouse was Scandinavian, German, or French, one might be inclined to choose an obviously "alien" name out of respect and love.

Because NFr names are now synonymous with English names, we assume that they were perceived as such in the eleventh and twelfth centuries by native English persons. Yet there is a marked difference between *Wulfwine* and *Robert* or *Godgifu* and *Maud*. The choice of an OE or OFr personal name for a child by a non-native speaker would therefore represent an extraordinary departure from accepted customs and practices. The naming of his son Sweyn by Robert fitzWimarc, a Breton who settled in England under the Confessor,[16] is explained by his likely marriage to an English woman.

---

[13]Barlow, *Edward the Confessor*, genealogy following p. 375.

[14]John Carmi Parsons, *Medieval Queenship* (New York, 1993).

[15]V. Cook, *Linguistics and Second Language Acquisition* (London, 1993).

[16]I. J. Sanders, *English Baronies: A Study of Their Origin and Their Descent, 1086–1327* (Oxford, 1960), p. 139.

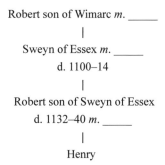

Figure 1. The Genealogy of Sweyn of Essex.

Ethnicity is a subject of interest for anthropologists and folklorists, but most historians have dealt casually and tangentially with issues of group identity.[17] Few studies of ethnicity in eleventh- and twelfth-century England have been undertaken by historians, although nomenclature, the act of naming individuals, has received thoughtful attention for this epoch.[18] Yet Anglo-Norman society lends itself to the twinned analysis of ethnicity and nomenclature because extant sources—which include Domesday Book, the pipe roll of 1130, and subsequent pipe rolls, as well as numerous records of civil disputes—contain the names of thousands of petitioners, litigants, and witnesses. When the names of such people are scrutinized systematically, then sorted according to language, type, and region, naming patterns reveal a complex process of syncretism in which the English were only gradually Normanized, and in which Normans eventually relinquished a Continental identity. Examining mid-twelfth-century naming patterns in a comprehen-

---

[17]An important, recent exception is Hugh M. Thomas, *The English and the Normans: Ethnic Hostility, Assimilation and Identity 1066–c.1220* (Oxford, 2003). But see Alfred P. Smyth, *Medieval Europeans: Studies in Ethnic Identity and National Perspectives in Medieval Europe* (New York, 1998), and *Concepts of National Identity in the Middle Ages*, ed. Simon Forde, Lesley Johnson, and Alan V. Murray (Leeds, 1995).

[18]See D. M. Hadley, "'And they proceeded to plough and to support themselves': The Scandinavian Settlement of England," in *A-NS XIX*, Proceedings of the Battle Conference 1996, ed. Christopher Harper-Bill (Woodbridge, 1997), pp. 69–96. For onomastic trends in medieval England, and many of whose studies concentrate on AN England, see Cecily Clark, *Words, Names and History: Selected Writings of Cecily Clark*, ed. Peter Jackson (Cambridge, 1995), and "Onomastics," in *The Cambridge History of the English Language*, 2: *1066–1476*, ed. Norman Blake (Cambridge, 1992), pp. 542–606.

sive fashion can reveal aspects of mentality barely disclosed by individual records that attest simply to the appearance of a person at court. The process also enables us to move beyond the identification of mainly aristocratic landholders whose nomenclature has been elegantly discussed by J. C. Holt, to lesser landholders and to urban dwellers, such as those of Battle, King's Lynn, and Canterbury, analyzed by Cecily Clark, or of London, by E. Ekwall.[19]

Here, comprehending cultural adaptation and the formation of altered identities can be served by determining the nomenclature prevalent in the mid-twelfth century, nearly one hundred years after the Norman Conquest, and by comparing English tendencies with those of French families. Difficulties in interpretation were created by scribes, who sometimes regularized and simplified variant name forms, who wrote the same name in different ways, or who abbreviated a name so that it could not be distinguished from other like forms. OE and NFr names were latinized. *Odda*, *Oda*, and *Eudes* were all transcribed as *Odo* by Latin scribes, even when people bearing such names must have referred to themselves in the OE or NFr manner. *Alberic* and *Albritus* were Latin variations on the French name *Aubrey* as well as the OE *Ælfric*.[20] OE *Alfred*, ON *Alvric*, and OBret *Alvred* were all rendered *Alured* in Domesday Book and in the pipe roll of 1130. *Alfred* is a name with broad associations, typically English but also reaching to the Continent.[21] After the Norman Conquest, aristocratic bearers of the name *Alured* were probably Breton rather than English, as in the case of Alvred of Lincoln,[22] a justiciar of Henry I who received the barony of Winterbourne St. Martin in Dorset upon his purchase of the land and the widow of

---

[19] J. C. Holt, *What's in a Name? Family Nomenclature and the Norman Conquest*, University of Reading, Stenton Lecture (1981), and E. Ekwall, *Early London Personal Names* (Lund, 1947), and "Some Early London By-names and Surnames," *English Studies* 46 (1965), 113–18.

[20] *Domesday Book* [hereafter *DB*], ed. John Morris, 34 vols. (London, 1976–86), vol. 9: Devon, n. 16, 36.

[21] Olof von Feilitzen, *The Pre-Conquest Personal Names of Domesday Book* (Uppsala, 1937), p. 176 and n. 3. I appreciate the insights of David Dumville on the transmission of *Alfred* to Brittany in the tenth and eleventh centuries.

[22] K. S. B. Keats-Rohan, "Le rôle des Bretons dans la politique de colonization normande de l'angleterre (vers 1042–1135)," *Mémoires de la Société d'Histoire et d'Archéologie de Bretagne* 74 (1996), 181–215.

Hugh fitzGrip.[23] When a name was latinized, the ethnicity of the bearer is difficult to determine, unless other information concerning origin exists.[24] In doubtful cases the person is not included in this study.

Emma was bestowed upon Norman and English daughters from the eleventh century, and women with this name possess an ambiguous ethnicity. The daughter and heiress of Grimbald *medicus*, who is assumed to be English, was named Emma.[25] Within the North Sea cultural milieu, too, there were similarities among Old German and OE names. Some ON names, such as *Ansketill* (or *Anschetill*), had taken hold in both England and Normandy, where the name became *Ansketil*.

It is true that the Norman Conquest altered English nomenclature by substituting personal names current in France for OE ones, and by encouraging the adoption of non-hereditary surnames. But the development was extended and haphazard, even within a single family. For example, a property dispute between St. Paul's Cathedral and the citizens of London, which reached court between 1138 and 1150,[26] lists among its witnesses eminent Londoners who indicated descent from English forebears. Many had only recently

---

[23]Sanders, *English Baronies*, p. 99. John Horace Round, *Feudal England* (London, 1909), p. 328, argued that Alvred was Breton, and the fact that one of his sons was named Alan suggests that this was the case, although there may have been an English connection as well. Alvred was highly favored by Henry I, not only in his fortuitous marriage and in his trusted position but also in the area of fiscal patronage. The pipe roll of 31 Henry I shows him to be excused a hefty £6 payment of danegeld on his Dorset lands and to be awarded the life tenancy of the honor of Pulham Cirencester; although Alfred contracted to pay 60 silver marks (£40) for the privilege, none was demanded by the Exchequer court (*The Pipe Roll of 31 Henry I, Michaelmas 1130*, ed. Joseph Hunter, henceforth cited as *PR*, facsimile from the 1833 edition [London, 1929], pp. 15–16). At the same time, Robert son of Alvred of Lincoln was exempted payment of £5 *murdrum* in Dorset (ibid., p. 15). Because the danegeld exemption was listed among the roll's New Pleas, and because Robert was not awarded an exemption, I suspect that Alvred was still alive in September 1130.

[24]Ann Williams, "A West-Country Magnate of the Eleventh Century: The Family, Estates and Patronage of Beorhtric Son of Ælfgar," pp. 41–68 in Keats-Rohan, *Family Trees and the Roots of Politics*; and C. P. Lewis, "Joining the Dots: A Methodology for Identifying the English in Domesday Book," ibid., pp. 66–88.

[25]*Regesta Regum Anglo-Normannorum*, ed. H. W. C. Davis et al., 4 vols. (Oxford, 1913–69); *Regesta* 3:579. Emma relinquished her rights to her family's land before King Stephen in 1137/38.

[26]H. M. C. Reports, *Ninth Report*, Appendix (London, 1883), p. 62; *English Lawsuits*, trans. R. C. Van Caenegem, 2 vols., Selden Society 106–07 (London, 1990–91), 1:286–88.

taken Norman names, and their parents had apparently vacillated between English and French choices. Two of the litigants were listed as brothers, Alfwin (Ælfwine, possibly the elder) and Robert, sons of Lefstan (Leofstan). Of the known family members, Robert is the sole bearer of a French name (see Figure 2 below). Robert son of Lefstan appeared before the Exchequer court in 1130, where he rendered account of £16 for the London Weaver's Guild.[27] Alfwin is mentioned as holding the London husting in which Wulfnoth of Walbrook sold land in Walbrook to Ramsey Abbey in 1113x1131,[28] which suggests that he was a man of importance. His brother, Witson son of Lefstan, rendered account in 1130 of one-half gold mark for the land and office of his father[29] but is not a witness to the later resolution. Witson's Flemish name suggests that his mother or grandmother was a member of London's Flemish community of merchants, just as Robert's name may have indicated intermarriage with a Norman family. Lefstan's father and aunt had English names, *Orgar* (*Ordgar*) and *Eadhild*, but his mother, who is never named, may have had an Anglo-French parent. Lefstan's sons bore Flemish, OE, and NFr personal names. The family therefore reflects both adaptation and cultural preservation in a socially diverse environment, even in the face of economic and physical challenges.

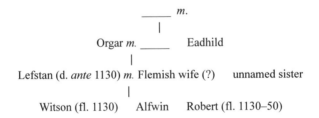

Figure 2. Genealogy of the sons of Lefstan.[30]

---

[27]*PR*, p. 144.

[28]*Cartularium Monasterii de Rameseia*, ed. W. H. Hart and P. A. Lyons, 2 vols., Rolls Series (London, 1884–93), no. 61, 1:139.

[29]Ibid.

[30]Van Caenegem, *English Lawsuits* 1:228, no. 270, and 1:286, no. 329. Lefstan is addressed in *Regesta* 2:898, and he may have been one of four sheriffs of London; the editor's note suggests that Lefstan died in 1115, but his sons' activities in 1130 indicate that he survived for at least another decade.

A key source in this endeavor is *The Pipe Roll of 31 Henry I*, a lengthy and informative account of royal income and expenses for the Anglo-Norman fiscal year of 1129/30. Among lists of danegeld and *murdrum* exemptions, petitions to recover land, relief payments, and proffers for favors are over two hundred people with English names or with known Anglo-Scandinavian heritage.[31] They make up roughly 7% of 1,450 individuals making cases or presenting accounts in person or by proxy before the Exchequer court of Henry I (1100–35). Analysis of nomenclature and its implications is contained below;[32] here, it is interesting to note the contexts in which people with English names appear in post-Conquest records. Among the military vassals entitled to danegeld exemptions and landholders excused of *murdrum* payments in 1130 were Aluric the fat, Algar the prior of Bodmin, Ralph son of Algot, William son of Ansered, Siward of Arden, William son of Aylward, Godric of Beelsby, Thierry son of Deormann, Herbert son of Dudeman, Osmund the cupbearer, Anschetill of Rye, Richard son of Wiglac, Robert fitzSiward, Robert of Essex son of Sweyn, Robert son of Toli, Hugh son of Ulger, Ulric the huntsman, William son of Warmund, and Robert son of Wimund. Others of probable English descent obtained their right to disputed manors in 1130 as well. Ernwi of Misterton, Derbyshire, paid 40s. toward a 10-mark debt *pro recto de terra sua*.[33] Godereda daughter of Gospatric son of Aldret (Ealdred) purchased a writ of right for her father's land, as did Thorfin son of Thorfin for his ancestral estates.[34] Ælfwold son of Ælfwold Child rendered account of relief for his father's land.[35] Yves son of Forne rendered account of 100s. (£5) for his father's land.[36] Forne son of Sigulf (d. 1129–30) had been lord of Greystoke,

---

[31] Anglo-Scandinavian is used throughout to denote people with either English or Scandinavian ancestry as well as people with a mixed heritage, such as those found in the former Danelaw. For the influence of ON on personal names see Gillian Fellows Jensen, "On the Identification of Domesday Tenants in Lincolnshire," *Nomina* 9 (1985), 31–40.

[32] Below, pp. 360 ff.

[33] *PR*, p. 10.

[34] *PR*, pp. 31 and 32.

[35] Ibid., p. 132.

[36] Ibid., p. 25. Aylward of Chislehampton's (Wilts.) intent to pay his relief in knights to the bishop of Lincoln demonstrates his liability to knight service (ibid.).

Cumberland.[37] Similar transactions secured landed title: the widow of Walter son of Godwine and Robert brother of Godwine obtained custody of the land and the small sons of Walter.[38] Ælfric son of Godric rendered account of fifteen silver marks for the land and office of his father.[39] William son of Aylward rendered account before the Exchequer of five silver marks for his father's office and land in Berkshire, of which he paid all but £2.[40] Adam son of Sweyn petitioned the Exchequer court meeting at Michaelmas 1130 for his mother's dowry.[41]

Descendants of pre-Conquest landholders sometimes fined before the court in order to avoid lawsuits.[42] Avicia, Coleman's wife, and her son rendered account of one-half gold mark to hold their land in peace.[43] Turbert son of Gamel rendered account of a writ to recover land unjustly seized: "ut rex faciat ei habere saisitionen de terra sua de Willelmo de Albamara."[44] Twelfth-century Anglo-Normans, like their post-Conquest forebears, were relentless in pursuit of land to add to their estates: William of Pont de l'Arches, Henry I's sheriff of Hampshire, purchased the custody of the land of Walter son of Ulric the huntsman until Ulric's heirs were able to hold the land.[45] Robert de l'Isle sought a writ of right to the land which Ulric of Stanton held.[46] The process of acquiring an English wife with her land is revealed in part through a pipe roll entry recording Hervey of Vesci's debt of £10 for the widow of Sweyn fitzÆlfric with her land.[47] Charges of false claims, false testimony, and defaulting on duels or payments owed to the king against people with IG names were common. Native moneyers were

---

[37]Sanders, *English Baronies*, p. 50.

[38]*PR*, p. 66.

[39]Ibid., p. 78.

[40]Ibid., p. 124.

[41]Ibid., p. 25.

[42]Ibid., p. 118.

[43]Ibid., p. 50.

[44]Ibid., p. 33.

[45]Ibid., p. 37.

[46]Ibid., p. 41.

[47]Ibid., p. 142.

in frequent trouble: Osgot the priest of *Duimfeld*, Ælfric *nepos* Saieti, Saieti himself, and Brand were among those fined for counterfeiting.[48]

By 1130 several English landholders and townspeople had become impoverished and, perhaps because of their earlier importance, were pardoned their considerable debts by the Exchequer court meeting at Michaelmas. Among the Wiltshire men owing money to the king via his justiciar, Ralph Basset, were Hubert son of Anganilde, Gospatric, Alfred son of Huri, Duncan, Turbert son of Chembel, and Robert fitzSweyn.[49] Each was pardoned for his poverty ("pro paupertate sua"). The latter case is a familiar, and thus sad one: Robert fitzSweyn of Essex had inherited his father's land and shrievalty and had married a Norman woman of high status. The pipe roll of 1130 reports his presence before the Exchequer court: "Robert son of Sweyn renders account of 29s 2d for treasury pleas [undifferentiated fines]. In pardon to the same Robert 29s 2d because he is ill and has nothing." In Yorkshire, Benedict son of Aldret of York rendered account of fifteen silver marks for the land and debts of his father. He paid £4.8.4 into the treasury, but owed £5.6.4.[50] Benedict's case demonstrates four tendencies of the post-Conquest era: an Anglo-Scandinavian father (Aldret) bestowing a name without ethnic color (*Benedict*) on his son, the son's choice of an ethnic patronymic, the maintenance of family lands well beyond the Conqueror's reign, and the failing economic circumstances of native families.

More important than its evidence for the continued presence of English men and women in the political landscape of the late eleventh and early twelfth centuries is the statistical sample of a cross section of Anglo-Norman society which the pipe roll provides. People of almost every occupation, from villein to chancellor to queen, and of varied backgrounds, both Insular and Continental, are represented in the roll. Virtually all of them were given a personal name and a second name—only the most well-known among them were casually described by a single name, and then usually only if a full reference was made earlier. Presumably, an individual was named by the sheriff presenting the account, or he introduced himself, much as would have occurred at court proceedings requiring the testimony of jurors and the signing of witnesses. The pipe roll of 1130 therefore facilitates a compar-

---

[48]Ibid., pp. 9, 40, and 42.

[49]Ibid., p. 19.

[50]Ibid., p. 26.

ison of nomenclature among Anglo-Norman families who flourished from the early to the mid-twelfth century.

Records of lawsuits reflect a similar cultural pluralism and so enable us to establish naming patterns as well. The witness lists of charters and resolutions of conflicts do not allow the kind of comprehensive analysis that the pipe roll does, but they do provide a check on conclusions drawn from it. It is interesting, however, that although Englishmen attended the courts of Norman barons and ecclesiastics, they were relegated to a lower status than their French fellows, appearing at the ends of witness lists or excluded entirely. Many of the more weighty cases, in which barons and important churches contested one another's claims to land, have no obviously English jurors or witnesses. The proportion of English to Continental names on witness lists is, therefore, ordinarily very low. The resolution of the contest between the abbey and cathedral at Canterbury, for example, relied on natives to testify to the claims of each, but only six of the thirty-six men listed as witnesses were clearly English: Asketur of Rettlynge, Wulfric, Geldewine, Leofwine, Wikemonde, and Sprot.[51] The negotiations concerning gifts to the newly founded Augustinian priory of Kenilworth were witnessed by eighteen men, only three of whom were English.[52] Bernard the scribe's 1121x1130 contest with the son of Elwi Gold over land in Trecharl, Cornwall, was witnessed by thirteen men, two of whom had English names: Edmund of *Cuhic*[53] and Ordgar of St. Stephen, even though Bernard himself was English.[54]

But some records contain long lists of Anglo-Scandinavians among their witnesses. Of the sixteen witnesses to the 1086 agreement between Bishop Wulfstan of Worcester and Abbot Walter of Evesham, eight were English.[55] The 1122 settlement between St. Stephen's Caen and the men of Bridport listed sixteen witnesses, of which thirteen were English.[56] The record of the

---

[51]Doris Mary Stenton, *English Justice between the Norman Conquest and the Great Charter, 1066–1215* (London, 1965), Appendix I, pp. 116–22.

[52]BL Harley MS 3650 (Kenilworth cartulary), fol. 10v.

[53]*Cuhic* is not found in Domesday Book, but it may have been a rendering for *Carewrge* or *Chori* (*DB*, vol. 1, fols. 120c and 123d).

[54]J. H. Round, "Bernard the King's Scribe," *EHR* 14 (1899), 421, nos. 15–16.

[55]M. M. Bigelow, *Placita Anglo-Normannica* (London, 1879), p. 288.

[56]F. Palgrave, *Rotuli Curiae Regis*, 7 (London, 1835), pp. 249–51, and *Regesta* 2:1341.

purchase of land from Lefstan's sister and sons by St. Paul's, London, contained forty-two witnesses, half of whom had English first names or patronymics.[57] The agreement between Robert of Ferrers and Geoffrey abbot of Burton reached between ca. 1121 and 1127 contained over twenty-three witnesses, seven of whom were clearly English.[58] In 1136x1137, twenty-one Englishmen attested to the claims of Aschuil, custodian of the Tower of London, against Norman the prior of Holy Trinity, London.[59] And the claims of Reginald abbot of Ramsey to land in Cranfield and Crawley were attested by numerous people bearing English and French names.[60]

The oaths sworn by predominantly native men legitimized the claims of respective churches and other corporate groups, and English witnesses were often described in respectful terms by Norman scribes. Among the "senior and noble people" who spoke to the claims of the bishop of Worcester and the abbot of Evesham in 1079x1083 were Kineward sheriff of Worcester, Siward "a rich man in Shropshire," and Thurkill of Arden,[61] for example. Twelve king's men of Dover and twelve men of Sandwich—"mature, wise old men of good repute"—were witnesses to the resolution of disputes between the archbishop of Canterbury and St. Augustine's Canterbury in 1127; these men bore mainly English names.[62] The 1106 dispute between Osbert the sheriff and the archbishop of York brought "the wisest Englishmen . . . to say the truth about those customs" before Henry I's justiciars. Their testimonies were interpreted by Ansketil of Bulmer, the Anglo-Scandinavian reeve of Yorkshire's North Riding, whose son, Bertram of Bulmer, figured prominently in the pipe roll of 1130.[63]

Neither the pipe roll of 1130 nor records of lawsuits were consistent in the rendering of names for the same individual, which suggests that different scribes had a hand in the work of recording business, and that spelling

---

[57]Van Caenegem, *English Lawsuits* 1:286–87.

[58]G. F. Warner and H. J. Ellis, *Facsimiles of Royal and Other Charters in the British Museum* (London, 1903), i no. 9.

[59]*Regesta* 3:506; printed and trans. in Van Caenegem, *English Lawsuits* 1:244.

[60]*Cartularium . . . Rameseia*, no. 69, p. 143.

[61]William Dugdale, *Monasticon Anglicanum*, 6 vols. in 8 (London, 1817–30), 1:602, no. 38.

[62]Stenton, *English Justice*, Appendix I, pp. 116–22.

[63]A. F. Leach, *Visitations and Memorials of Southwell Minster* (London, 1891), pp. 190–96; trans. and printed in Van Caenegem, *English Lawsuits* 1:138–43.

itself was variable. Lawsuits, in particular, could be prolonged over months or years of conflict, claims, and counterclaims, and records were kept by a succession of scribes. The same person could be described in various fashions according to the writer's understanding of the dispute and his familiarity with those involved, or the individual's manner of describing himself. In a case between the abbot of Thorney and Ralph son of Segbold of Lowick, Ralph is referred to in 1113 with a tripartite name.[64] Later, possibly in the same year, when an agreement was reached, Ralph (or the chronicler) dropped "son of Segbold" and simply attached "of Lowick" to Ralph's personal name.[65] As people inherited manors, acquired work or moved, their names changed, and their identities shifted to outward observers.

ANALYSIS

Post-Conquest naming styles fall into a number of categories: (1) a single (personal) name; (2) a personal name with a byname;[66] (3) a personal name with an occupational surname; (4) a personal name with a patronymic, metronymic, or other indicator of relationship; (5) a personal name with a toponymic; and (6) a tripartite name involving a combination of these parts. While most of the 1,450 names recorded in the pipe roll of 1130 have CG or French forms, 217 suggest an English identity in personal names or patronymics. They represent locally and regionally active free men and women with ties to the royal court in Henry I's later reign, and people with a wish to preserve and announce native ethnicity.[67] The naming styles evident among many of them suggest that while English parents bestowed a variety of personal names upon infants born after 1066—OE, NFr, classical, and biblical—their grown children identified themselves (or were identified by scribes) primarily by an English patronymic. Seventy-six men and women carried names of the *son of* form, e.g., Robert son of Toli, Adam son of

[64]Cambridge University Library Add. MS ii fol. 416v (Thorney Abbey 'Red Book').

[65]Ibid., fol. 420.

[66]See Gösta Tengvik, *Old English Bynames* (Uppsala, 1938), and Gillian Fellows Jensen, "On the Study of Middle English By-Names," *Namn och Bygd* 68 (1980), 102–15.

[67]Dave Postles, "Cultures of Peasant Naming in Twelfth-Century England," *MP* 18 (1997), 25–54, discusses the contrasting influences of fashion and tradition.

Sweyn, Walter son of Ulfketil, and Godric son of Leoflæd.[68] Some people with bipartite names were recognized as the wives, brothers, or nephews of an English person, as were Ulverona wife of Ulf, Aiulf brother of Edward, and Aluric *nepos* Saieti. Some tripartite names included English patronymics as well: *Hamo son of Atsor (Azor) of Marlborough, Thomas of York son of Ulviet, Hugh son of Ailric of Yarmouth,* and *Ralph son of Godwine of Hall* are examples.[69] In all, ninety-nine bipartite and tripartite names contained an English patronymic.

Ethnic markers reflect a similar distribution among witnesses to lawsuits. In the 1127 case of the archbishop of Canterbury *vs.* St. Augustine's, Canterbury, where the witnesses were mostly English, nine were identified by an English patronymic: Wulfwine son of Beornwig, Wulfwig son of Wulfnoth, Brunman son of Lemay, Goldstan son of Bruning, Baldwine son of Fike, Alfward son of Elwold, Alfward son of Blackman, Siric son of Godwine, and Wulfwine son of Cake. Of the twelve Anglo-Scandinavians who spoke to the customs of the archbishopric of York, all but two, Northmann and Frenger the priests, used English patronymics.[70]

While people with AScand personal names sometimes combined them with native patronymics (in twenty-six of the ninety-seven pipe roll cases), they more often chose toponyms for surnames. Ulviet of Hornecastle (Lincolnshire), Godwine of Taversham (Cambridgeshire) and Orm of Derlaston (Staffordshire) exemplify a widespread practice. Sixty-seven people with English given names utilized a surname which was a place name: fifty-three carried bipartite names and fourteen adopted tripartite ones. Most toponymics were manorial names, suggesting ownership or stewardship: the Gamel of Hawkswick who was one of Stephen count of Richmond's "lesser men" in 1130 may have been the namesake of the Gamel who held three carucates at Hawkswick, Yorkshire, from Roger of Poitou in 1086.[71] But names of hundreds and wapentakes were included as well—Chislehampton (Oxfordshire), Chafford (Essex), and Walshcroft (Lincolnshire) were car-

---

[68]Godric, whose account was rendered in Lincolnshire, was probably the son of the Leoflaed who held land here before 1086 (*DB* i 357c and 368c).

[69]See also P. H. Reaney and R. M. Wilson, *A Dictionary of English Surnames*, 3rd ed. (London, 1991), p. xii.

[70]Cited above, n. 63.

[71]*PR*, p. 28, and *DB* 332b.

ried as surnames by English local officials who presented judicial pleas before the Exchequer court. Towns such as Newcastle, York, Caerleon, Salisbury, Yarmouth, Ipswich, and Lincoln were used by a handful of Englishmen as surnames. Exchequer officials and scribes seem to have encouraged the use of place names as surnames, however, as people with manorial, hundredal, and urban surnames were viewed as representatives for these areas. They may have been known by a patronymic or an occupational surname by their neighbors rather than by a generic place name which many could claim. In most cases, their pre-1130 status is impossible to detect.

Nonetheless, place names were chosen as surnames by mid-twelfth-century witnesses to charters as well—Leofmar of Barningham, Osmund of Langford, and Ordgar of St. Stephen, for example—but they were never as common as patronymic surnames. Toponymic surnames were rare in settings where everyone shared the same residence, and were used only when outsiders testified to the claims of a particular litigant. Among the twenty-one Anglo-Scandinavian Londoners who confirmed the statements of prior Norman and Holy Trinity, London, in 1136x1137, none used toponymic surnames, because they were unnecessary. Instead, they indicated an occupation, a byname, or, simply, a personal name.[72]

Occupational surnames were used by Exchequer officials to explain payments made from the treasury for completed work and for stipends or tax exemptions to household servants, engineers, porters, and falconers. People whose land was held in sergeanty, such as royal foresters, moneyers, priests, archers, crossbowmen, and clerks were specified as such. Twenty-seven men were identified by an English personal name combined with an occupational surname in the pipe roll of 1130. While the use of an occupational surname is more likely to have been used within one's locale than a place name, its appearance, too, may have been a means of identification imposed by the Exchequer court. But records of lawsuits show that witnesses distinguished themselves by occupation, even when they were well-known by their fellows. In the case mentioned above, of the archbishop of Canterbury *vs.* St. Augustine's Canterbury, two of the English witnesses were known by their occupations: Godwine the smith and Eadwine the clerk.[73]

In fact, relatively few people used only a personal name. Some of the pipe roll's twenty-one Englishmen in this category possessed uncommon

---

[72]Above, n. 59.

[73]Above, n. 51.

names, such as *Schipeman, Spracheling, Damiot*, and *Scorfani*, which may have been sufficient to identify them. But others had traditional and quite ordinary names, such as *Edward, Ælfgar*, and *Edmund*. Some were amerced by the Exchequer court for legal infractions, and the use of only one name—a personal name—may have been an indicator of low status. Unfree, or recently freed, English people whose names appear in records of purchase and manumission tended to utilize only one name or crude bynames—Wulfric pig and Edith daughter of Godric cock's throat.[74] "Rustics," both unfree and free, did utilize surnames, and these frequently indicated a family connection: "Eadmær, Spernægl's son, released Leofhild, his kinswoman, from the estate at Topsham, for twenty-four pence."[75] Several men whose lands were transferred from the earl of Lincoln to the church of Nunburnholme, Yorkshire, in 1142 were known by their personal names with a by-name or a patronym: Ælfric son of Sweyn, Uccha son of Bruni, Ralph son of Ansketill, Haldan Bola, Rainald son of Siric, Ascan son of Jeffe, Ralph son of Ketel, and Ralph byscop.[76] Bynames were less common than patronymics; only seven men with English names in 1130 exhibited this sort of descriptive marker, a negligible percentage of the whole: Leofwine *chidde*, Leofric *locc*, Aluric *gross*, and Walter *anglicus* are fairly unambiguous examples.[77] Other names—Ulric *bulehals*, Godwine *quachehand*, and Alfwine *futerill*[78]—may be occupational names rather than bynames. *Bulehals* may be a steerherd or cowman; *quachehand* may refer to a baker of a kind of bread. In contrast, nicknames seem to have been common among some urban groups of varied or mixed origin by 1200,[79] but this may reflect a wish to appear fashionable (see Table 1).

---

[74]David A. E. Pelteret, *Catalogue of English Post-Conquest Vernacular Documents* (Woodbridge, 1990), nos. 103 and 111. Witnesses to vernacular documents were presumably free, and they emphasized their occupation in their choices of surname. Nonetheless, imaginative bynames were applied by these English people as well: *Algar oxbelly, Æthelweard saddlehook*, and *Algar tramp* (nos. 93, 94, and 104).

[75]Ibid., no. 123.

[76]*Early Yorkshire Charters*, vols. IV to XII, ed. Sir Charles T. Clay (Yorkshire Archaeological Society Record Series e.s. 1–10, 1935–65), 10:114–45, no. 66.

[77]*PR*, pp. 10; 107; 148 and 151; and 108.

[78]Ibid., 48, 146, and 154.

[79]Cecily Clark, "People and Languages in Post-Conquest Canterbury," in *Words, Names and History*, ed. Jackson, pp. 179–206.

TABLE 1. NOMENCLATURE AMONG PEOPLE WITH ENGLISH NAMES IN 1130

Personal Name Only	Byname	Occupational Surname	Patronymic	Toponymic	Tripartite Names	Totals
21	7	27	76	53	33	217
10%	3%	12.5%	35%	24.5%	15%	100%

Occupational surnames were occasionally used in conjunction with bynames or patronymics to produce tripartite names. Their application was infrequent enough to suggest deliberate usage on the part of scribes (as in the 1136x1137 appearance of one Ordgar the monk the prudent)[80] or affectation by the holder himself (as in Baldwin brother of Algar the priest and Ralph the chaplain son of Algot).[81] The elaborate nomenclature identified an obscure person with a locally-known figure: Alfwine son of Onwin of Burton, Andrew son-in-law of Orm or Ocker, and Bernard son of Aylward of Blackmarston emphasized their relationship to older Englishmen in order to lend force to their testimonies. Bernard, for instance, was one of the relative few to win his lawsuit against a church. In 1133 he won his right to land over the efforts of Hereford Cathedral through his insistence on a tenure held by his father, Aylward, of the manor of Blackmarston.[82]

While people with Continental names chose from the same pool of name forms as those with English names, they were far less interested in patronyms than in toponyms. Patronymics may have been employed when a child's sire was in doubt because his mother had married more than once. Geva, the daughter and heiress of Serlo of Burg (or Burcy),[83] married, first,

---

[80]*Regesta* 3:502.

[81]D. C. Douglas, *Feudal Documents from the Abbey of Bury St. Edmunds* (London, 1932), pp. 127–28, no. 135.

[82]D. Walker, "Some Charters Relating to St. Peter's Abbey, Gloucester," *A Medieval Miscellany for Doris Mary Stenton*, ed. P. N. Barnes and C. F. Slade (London, 1962), p. 259, no. 2.

[83]*Serlo* was the latinized form of the OE *Searle*; the man's ethnicity may well be impossible to determine, but he is usually thought to be a Norman. In the pipe roll of 1130 his toponymic was rendered *burg*, the scribes' term for the English towns of Knaresborough and Aldborough (*PR*, pp. 24 ff.). Serlo's personal name, his surname, and the fact that one of his daughters entered Shaftesbury Abbey suggest that he might instead have been English.

one Martin, and after his premature death in 1086, William of Falaise. Her son and heir by her first marriage took the name *Robert fitzMartin*, to avoid the assumption that his father was William.[84] In this case and in others where *filius* was later rendered *fitz* the patronymic was carried by a legitimate child. In other cases, when patronymics were preferred over toponymics, as in *fitzJohn* or *fitzRichard*, sons had inherited an official role or status rather than land. Brian fitzCount was the landless natural son of Alan Fergant count of Brittany. After his spectacular promotion by his patron, King Henry I, Brian retained the prestigious surname *fitzCount*, even though he now possessed the vast honor of Wallingford by right of his wife, Maud.[85]

Of the ninety people listed in Oxfordshire's accounts for 1130, eighty-four utilized French names. Only a small percentage of Normans utilized patronymics, as Table 2 suggests. In Oxfordshire, Ralph fitzAlmaric, Brian fitzCount, Richard fitzUrse, Robert fitzWalter, William son of Manasses, Walter son of Ragan, and Payn fitzJohn boasted patronymics. The ethnic tag of greatest significance was the place of origin rather than the progenitor: a full 50% of people (forty-two out of eighty-five) utilized personal names and a toponym. A handful of toponyms represent English places—Evesham, Wallingford, Salisbury, for instance—but most were northern French. Henry of Lamare, Hubert of Sainte-Suzanne, Walter of Ansgrevill, William of Ferrers, and Geoffrey of Mandeville are among the numerous bearers of both Continental personal names and Continental toponymics.

Only two of the fifty-seven names inscribed among Surrey's brief records suggest English ethnicity, those of Gundwine the tentkeeper and Avicia (who may have been French) wife of Coleman. Most of the people with Continental names used toponyms, indicating the same striking imbalance in AN naming patterns that we observed in Oxfordshire. Again, most of the toponymic surnames were French rather than English, although here, as elsewhere, a few very powerful Anglo-Norman earls and prelates identified with their English seats of power: the earl of Gloucester, the archbishop of Canterbury, and the bishops of Salisbury and Winchester. Lawrence of Rouen, Humphrey of Bohun, Robert of Pont-Echanfray, William

---

[84]Sanders, *English Baronies*, p. 15.

[85]R. W. Southern, *Medieval Humanism and Other Studies* (Oxford, 1970), pp. 206–33, and K. S. B. Keats-Rohan, "The Devolution of the Honour of Wallingford," *Oxon.* 63 (1989), 311–18.

TABLE 2. NOMENCLATURE AMONG CONTINENTAL INHABITANTS OF ENGLAND IN 1130

COUNTY	Personal Name Only	Byname	Occupational Surname	Patronymic	Toponymic	Tripartite Names	TOTALS
Oxfordshire	2	15	14	7	42	4	84
Surrey	0	5	7	5	33	2	52
Lincolnshire	0	14	3	22	50	17	106
Yorkshire	1	14	1	14	47	6	83
TOTALS	3	48	25	49	172	29	324
PERCENTS	1%	14.5%	7.5%	15%	53%	9%	100%

of Curzon, Ingelrann of Abernon, William of Balliol, Reginald of Dunstanville, and William of Pont de l'Arche are examples of men consciously perpetuating French ethnicity in the early to mid-twelfth century.

The preference for French toponymic surnames was not as marked in Lincolnshire, where the twelfth-century Anglo-Scandinavian population was influential and assertive. A full one fourth of the names appearing in Lincolnshire's pipe roll accounts were English. And although among the rest toponymic surnames were the most popular, patronymics (in twenty-two cases) and surnames which combined patronyms and toponyms (in eight cases) were carried as well. In Lincolnshire, men and women with Continental personal names were inclined to identify themselves with a close male relative, as in the cases of Walter son of Remy and Gilbert his brother, Walter son of Eudes, Ralph son of Nigel, and Lambert son of Peter, or Robert son of Ralph son of Norman and Adeliza wife of Roger Bigod.

Moreover, when toponyms were applied they tended to represent English rather than French places. Some people with Continental personal names and English toponymics may well have been English. Those affirming French ethnicity through a connection with a French place were Walter of Gant (Ghent); Ranulf of Bayeux; Humphrey, Ralph, and William of Aubigny; Alan of Craon; Roger of Montbegon; Alan of Monceaux (Limousin); Robert of Lacselles (Ardeche); William of Alost (Burgundy); and the daughter of Richard of Montpinchon (Normandy). Not only are French toponymics rare, but their affiliations are sometimes of the most general and tenuous kind, as in the examples of Walter of Gant and Ranulf of Bayeux, who shared their surnames with countless other Anglo-Normans.

The kind of cultural blending apparent in Lincolnshire was avoided in Yorkshire, where the extreme ethnic conflict of 1069/70 was probably bitterly remembered in 1130. Here, nearly all people utilizing a toponymic surname combined a non-English personal name with a Continental place name: Oilli, Aubigny, Percy, Lonvilers, Warenne, Escures, Cancy, Flamenville, Brittany, Lacselles, Lamare, Busli, Arques, Monceaux, Mowbrai, Balliol, Laval, Ver, Lovetot, Mesnilwarin (later Mainwaring), and Oberville were places proudly asserted by Yorkshire's colonists.

Whereas the English offered evidence of their ethnicity through either an English personal name or an English patronymic, they rarely utilized both. The French, however, reinforced the ethnic suggestion of their personal names with an ethnic surname. For the English, a toponymic signified domicile. For the French, the use of a toponymnic surname may have been a statement of dominance utilized by people of originally landless status. Given this status, one suspects that the use of a Continental place name as a surname signified geographical origin rather than lordship. Whereas 53% of French immigrants of varied statuses and occupations utilized toponymic surnames, Continental holders of English baronies used French toponyms in 65.5% of cases: among the Anglo-Norman elite, the preponderance of French toponymic surnames is extraordinary. Where status and ethnicity were entwined, the French toponymic became hereditary, even when the name of the barony was English. Thus Keynes, Percy, Port, Curcy, and Chaworth (Sourches), Chandos, de Scales (l'Escalerie), Lacy, Cause (Caux), Beauchamp, and Beaumont were perpetuated by AN magnates. J. C. Holt's conviction that the English nobility emphasized kinship while the French aristocracy stressed patrimony is thus borne out, but also extended to lesser and middling landholders and to urban dwellers.[86] Nonetheless, as they acquired both land and the status associated with it, ordinary Frenchmen seem to have abandoned Continental toponymics during the course of the twelfth century, and to have used English toponymics,[87] or they retained by-names as hereditary surnames.

People with Norman backgrounds were more likely to use bynames than were Englishmen: in four counties where French names have been analyzed, nearly 15% of men carried bynames. Among Anglo-Norman barons the proportion is nearly the same, with 14.5% using bynames. Bynames attached to personal names called attention to individual traits, skills, temperament, and appearance. Unlike patronymics and toponymics, names such as *Fossard* (the digger) and *Tourniant* (the turner) were transformed into hereditary surnames, even when they were no longer appropriate, thus revealing a dilution of French ethnicity as their families were absorbed into English society. Hereditary bynames were essentially patronymics, commemorating the first person to hold the name. Some bynames were latinized forms of OFr words denoting occupation, which may suggest that Anglo-Norman barons were descended not only from landless knights but also from skilled craftsmen. In the twelfth century, such surnames as *Tourniant* and *Peverel*

---

[86]J. C. Holt, "Feudal Society and the Family in Early Medieval England I: The Revolution of 1066," *Transactions of the Royal Historical Society*, 5th ser., 32 (1982), 193–212, esp. pp. 200–01.

[87]Ian Short, "*Tam Angli Quam Franci*: Self-Definition in Anglo-Norman England," in *A-NS XVIII*, ed. Christopher Harper-Bill (Woodbridge, 1996), pp. 153–76.

(a maker or seller of pepper, implying spicy or lascivious)[88] were red flags waved in front of native people to signal the flamboyant rise in status enjoyed by these men, who had either been granted or had stolen English land.

Many Frenchmen carried bynames indicating an infamous past. Soubriquets like *Maleteche* (evil), *Malregard* (ugly), *Maltravers* (evil traveler), *Coterel* (bandit, pillager), *Basset* (low), *Esturmit* (reckless), and *Musard* (fool, rogue, rascal)[89] suggest the violence and non-conformity that we might associate with knights of the Conquest and the immediately post-Conquest generation. Unflattering bynames such as *Poynant* (stinging, biting) and *Pancevolt* (pot-bellied or paunch-face) reinforce the suggestion that it was scribes (and possibly English ones at that) who were responsible for affixing surnames. (The same scribes were no doubt responsible for attaching offensive names to English people of low status, as well.)

It is also possible, since the holders of occupational bynames were sometimes heirs in fairly important families, that their usage was intended to be amusing. It may also have reinforced an impression of importance. The Breton hereditary stewards of the counts of Richmond were Geoffrey Boterel (the second son of Alan son of Aimeri) and his sons, William Boterel (the eldest, who died in 1154) and Peter Boterel (the second son).[90] The third son, Haimo, was referred to only by his given name during Henry I's reign; by 1154, he too was described as Haimo Boterel.[91]

Breton colonizers of England often, but not always, dispensed with names denoting origin or status: Spirewic, a Breton tenant-in-chief of Tattershall, Lincolnshire (d. 1118) gave his son the name *Eudes*. His grandson was Hugh fitzEudes.[92] None of Spirewic's descendants took names that referred either to their progenitor or to his barony. Tihel *brito*, the Domesday

---

[88]Cecily Clark, "Socio-Economic Status and Individual Identity: Essential Factors in the Analysis of Middle English Personal Naming," in *Words, Names and History*, ed. Jackson, pp. 100–13, esp. 111.

[89]For these and other AN surnames refer to Marie-Thérèse Morlet, *Dictionnaire etymologique des noms de famille* (Paris, 1995). William Rothwell, Louise Stone, and T. B. W. Reid, *Anglo-Norman Dictionary* (London, 1992), consider mainly late twelfth- and thirteenth-century vocabulary, and offer definitions at variance with Morlet's.

[90]Keats-Rohan, "Le rôle des Bretons," p. 214.

[91]*The Pipe Rolls of 2-3-4 Henry II*, ed. Joseph Hunter (London, 1844), reproduced in facsimile from the 1844 edition in 1930, pp. 54, 56, 105–06 *bis* and 171–72.

[92]Sanders, *English Baronies*, p. 88.

lord of estates in Essex, called his son the NFr name *William*, who in turn used the surname *Helion*, which appears to be a byname but was in fact a place. Hellean, Brittany, was recalled in the name of the family's English barony, Helion Bumpstead.[93] Ansger *brito*'s son and heir was called Walter son of Ansger, while Ansger's grandson was Ansger *brito* the second.[94] Ansger himself was known by a variety of names, which were used as the occasion demanded.[95] William of Aubigny *brito*, Ansgar *brito*, and Mainfelin *brito* preserved their sense of otherness through the ethnic tag as well as, in Aubigny's case, through a toponymic. William of Aubigny's byname also distinguished him from the Norman William of Aubigny *pincerna*, who was Henry I's butler. Other people with Breton grandfathers or fathers, like Alan of Craon son of Guy of Craon,[96] perpetuated a tie through nomenclature with their progenitor's home long after the pre-Conquest connection had been weakened.

Witness lists of charters closely approximate the distribution of name forms revealed by the pipe roll of 1130 in the cases of toponymics. But there is variance in the other categories. The foundation charter for Kenilworth Priory, issued between 1122 and 1125, was attested by two Englishmen (Siward son of Thorkill and Herfast son of Godric) and fifteen Frenchmen. Among the latter, nine (or 60%) used toponymic surnames, six of which were French, five (30%) used patronymics (but two of the five acknowledged a brother instead of a father), one (or 5%) Geoffrey Lovet used a byname, and one (5%) Anschetil *dapifer* (or steward) of Geoffrey of Clinton was known both by his profession and by his employer, Kenilworth's founder.[97]

The decision following the 1127 claims of Gloucester Abbey, which were supported by Henry I and his court, was attested by fourteen Anglo-Normans. Here there are nine tripartite names, those indicating both position and seat by prelates, as in *William archbishop of Canterbury* and *Roger*

---

[93]Ibid., p. 121.

[94]Ibid., p. 132.

[95]*DB* Devon, n. 40.

[96]Round, *Feudal England*, p. 211. But Alan's family may have originated in Craon, Anjou (*Sir Christopher Hatton's Book of Seals*, ed. L. C. Loyd and D. M. Stenton [Oxford, 1950], p. 224).

[97]BL Harley MS 3650, fol. 10v.

bishop of Salisbury, and those using a patronymic with the father's full name, as in *William son of Adam of Port*. People with bipartite names specified an occupation twice, Geoffrey the chancellor and Robert *de sigillo*, toponymics twice, Miles of Gloucester and Walter of Ansfreville, while one, William Foliot, carried a byname. If we combine all references to places, then a full 57% fit into the category of surnames which use place names.[98] In the 1151x1154 account of Southwick Priory's wrangling with Herbert of Burhunt and his son, Alexander, eighteen witnesses with Continental given names used toponymics (albeit English ones) nine times, patronymics five times (although four of these were named as brothers of two of the witnesses), bynames twice, an occupational surname once, and a tripartite name, that of Henry cleric of Hambledon, which joined an occupational surname with a toponymic.[99] Fifty percent thus boasted toponymic surnames, 30% displayed patronymics, 10% bynames, 5% an occupation, and 5% elaborated on their identity by using a tripartite name.

Summary

Many Anglo-Scandinavians began early on to assign French names to their children in what seems to have been a deliberate attempt to conceal their origins.[100] So decisive was the process that OE names now seem ludicrous, unless they refer to English monarchs, even though they are roughly the same age as the more respectable Norman names. Sweyn of Essex, the son of Robert fitzWimarc (above, p. 345) called his heir to the shrievalty and to the family property, Robert. Edward of Salisbury, lord of Trowbridge and Chittern, Wiltshire, named his children and co-heirs Maud and Walter, even though his wife was probably English, like himself.[101] When these men gave their children French names as well, the written connection with the

---

[98]William of Malmesbury, *De Gestis Regum Anglorum*, ed. W. Stubbs, 2 vols. (London, 1887–89), 2:521–22.

[99]Hampshire Record Office, Winchester, M54/1, fols. 23v–24 (Southwick cartulary); printed and trans. in Van Caenegem, *English Lawsuits*, pp. 298–301.

[100]As suggested by Van Caenegem, *English Lawsuits*, p. 139 n. 6, with respect to the sons of Ulf son of Basing.

[101]Sanders, *English Baronies*, pp. 75, 91, and 112.

society of pre-Conquest England was severed, and people of English descent were perceived all around to be Norman.

The denial of English ethnicity after the country's disastrous defeat in 1066 was particularly apparent among thegnly families who had been almost entirely dispossessed. It is their children who were given NFr names in the generation after the Conquest. The thegn Wihtlac held several Hampshire manors from King Edward in freehold.[102] His manor at Stanpit, Hampshire, comprised one hide with a hall, which was thought worthy of comment, and his hide at Bolderfod was worth £10. Most of Wihtlac's land, however, was soon enforested, and his TRW holdings sharply reduced in size and value to four acres of meadow in Edgegate Hundred and two urban joint tenancies. Wihtlac's experience may have led him to bestow the respectable name *Richard* on one of his sons. But Wihtlac's pre-Conquest landed wealth and his continued post-Conquest status as a king's thegn may have prompted Richard, in turn, to acknowledge his English parent in his surname, for he was described as Richard son of Wihtlac by an Exchequer clerk in 1130.[103] Cultural compromises are apparent in the names of Adam son of Sweyn, Yves son of Forni, Walter and Henry sons of Ulfketil, Roger son of Rancher, and Osbert son of Edmund. The initial inclination to conceal coupled with later acceptance of native ethnicity can be found among several twelfth-century men whose fathers were locally powerful in 1066. Siric had been the TRE holder of the Essex manor of Dengie;[104] in 1086 he was a substantial undertenant of Sweyn of Essex, with three manors valued at £25.[105] In 1130, his son William used the surname *son of Siric*.[106] Odelard, who held Peasmore and Hodcott, Berkshire, of Ralph of Mortimer in 1086, seems to have named his son after his lord, Ralph.[107]

Other thegns continued, despite (or because of) the humiliation of the Conquest, to bestow English names on their offspring, while the latter recognized their English ethnicity as well. Sweyn son of Lesing (Leysingi) and Lesing his brother were sons of the Yorkshire thegn whose possessions had

---

[102]*DB* i 46b, 51b–d, and 54a.

[103]*PR*, p. 38.

[104]*DB* i 24a.

[105]Ibid., i 42a and 47b.

[106]*PR*, p. 53.

[107]*DB* i 62d and *PR*, p. 123.

included land at Westude, Newham, Tollesby, Acklam, Tunstall, Tanton, Allerton, Guisborogh, and Normanby.[108] Godwine of Witchingham, Norfolk, seems to have been the son of the Godwine who held Witchingham of count Eustace of Boulogne in 1086.[109] Godric of Grimsby may have been the son or grandson of Ælfric, who held one carucate and two bovates of land in Little Grimsby, Lincolnshire, in 1066.[110] Freseschin son of Oslac was the son of the Oslac who held a little over three virgates of land from the king at Fardon, Lincolnshire, in 1086.[111] Firm expressions of ethnicity occur in the mid-twelfth-century names of Thorfinn son of Thorfinn, Godric son of Ketilbert, Ailsi son of Ulf, and Uhtræd son of Waltheof, all Yorkshire men of local stature in 1130.[112] Nomenclature echoes regional traditions: areas with light Norman settlement and persistent native influence show healthy signs of English ethnicity. Records from areas of demoralization or dispossession, such as Yorkshire, Cambridgeshire, Surrey, and Devon disclose few people of obvious English identity by the mid-twelfth century.

In numerous instances, then, English men and women seemed reluctant to accept French names. Instead they retained English names, bestowed such names on their children, or acknowledged English parentage through chosen surnames. The family of Thurkill of Arden, whose name is Scandinavian, and who was a tenant-in-chief in Oxford and Warwickshire in 1086, continued to bear Insular names until well into the reign of Henry I (Figure 3). Thurkill's heir from a first marriage was Siward of Arden, who still held at least portions of the family lands in 1130, when he received danegeld exemptions totaling £2.[113] But Siward named his sons Henry and Hugh, and his daughters Cecily and Felicia. The family were tenants of Geoffrey of Clinton, and they attested his charters to Kenilworth Priory.[114] Yves son of

---

[108]*DB* i 300a–b, 301c, and 320c.

[109]*PR*, p. 93 and *DB* ii 151b.

[110]*DB* i 354a and *PR*, p. 112.

[111]*DB* i 229b and *PR*, p. 136.

[112]*PR*, p. 53.

[113]*PR*, pp. 6 and 108.

[114]*Thurkill* or *Thorkell* was ON, ODan, or OSwed (von Feilitzen, *Pre-Conquest Personal Names of Domesday Book*, p. 394). For his family, which included offspring from two marriages, see Loyd and Stenton, *Book of Seals*, nos. 46, 52, and 138 and n. 48. Siward may have been born before the Norman Conquest, for Thurkill did name his son by his second

Forni son of Sigulf rendered account of his father's land and of the pleas of Blythe before the same court.[115] Forni son of Sigulf and his wife may have given their son his French name in or slightly before 1100. Godwine the turner, who was presumably given his name in about 1110 by staunchly English parents, and his sons, Osmund and Robert, named in the 1130s, were witnesses to the claims of Southwick Priory in the early 1150s.[116]

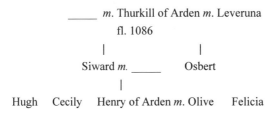

Figure 3. Genealogy of Thurkill of Arden.[117]

The inclination to retain English names up to the mid-twelfth century emerges most clearly in towns, which suggests that intermarriage brought with it the wish to preserve ethnicity rather than a desire to diminish it, for it was in towns that the English and French may have mingled most freely. Among the fifty-one tenants of St. Frideswide's Priory in Oxford, twenty-five used English personal names in the mid-twelfth century.[118] The occupations of Ernald the weaver, Thomas, William, and Philip the bakers, Nicholas, William, and Richard the priests, and Thomas the fuller hint at English identity as well, given the predominantly aristocratic nature of Norman settlement in England. Anglo-Scandinavians and their descendants formed sizeable and respected communities in Bury, Dover, London, Portchester, Sandwich, Oxford, and York well into Stephen's reign (1135–54). They tended to monopolize the more important guilds: in 1130 Thomas of

---

wife, Leveruna, Osbert, possibly at her wish. For the family's connections with Clinton see ibid., no. 36.

[115]*PR*, p. 25.

[116]Southwick, *Cartulary*, fols. 23v–24.

[117]*VCH Oxford*, p. 386.

[118]*Regesta* 3:640.

York son of Ulviet owed one hunting horse to be alderman of the Guild Merchant of York.[119] Lefstan, whom we have met, was prominent in the Weaver's Guild of London; after his death before Michaelmas 1130, his sons Robert and Witson continued his activity with the approval of the Exchequer court.

In urban contexts self-consciously English men were prominent local officials with responsibilities extending to Winchester. They served as local justices and deputies, collecting and presenting judicial pleas to the Exchequer court on behalf of royal justiciars such as Geoffrey of Clinton, Ralph Bassett, Walter Espec, and Eustace fitzJohn, among others. Robert son of Toli, Atsor of Wilton, Hubert son of Anganilde, Gospatric, Aluric son of Huri, Duncan, Turbert son of Chembel, Robert fitzSweyn, Accha son of Ernebrand, Godric son of Ketelbert, Payn son of Ocche, and Henry and Walter sons of Ulfketil presented moneys or were pardoned for their inability to do so by Henry I's barons of the Exchequer. Many sheriffs, whose tasks included rendering county tax farms, were English or half-English in 1130. Aiulf the chamberlain acted in a shrieval capacity when he rendered accounts for Dorset and Wiltshire.[120] Bertram of Bulmer son of Anschetill of Bulmer was sheriff of the unwieldy jurisdiction that comprised Yorkshire.[121] Odard son of Ligulf was, like his father before him, sheriff of Northumberland.[122] When Henry I's only extant pipe roll was compiled, few individuals lacked a surname. Thus, as early as 1130, if not well before, public figures generally carried two names: a personal name and a name indicating affiliation, either with kin or with a place, as in Gamel son of Grim and Morcar son of Ligulf or Ailric of Lewes and Edwin of Anningdon.[123] While the choice of surname varied, and expressed in different degrees background, parentage, or locale, the tendency to choose a surname grew more prevalent by the mid-twelfth century. Such shifts in nomenclature were expressions partly of ethnicity, but partly of the growth of literacy and the demands of

---

[119]*PR*, p. 34.

[120]Ibid., pp. 12 ff. and 16 ff.

[121]Ibid., p. 24: Bertram of Bulmer, sheriff of Yorkshire, rendered account of two hundred silver marks for the land and office of his father, Anschetil.

[122]Ibid., p. 35.

[123]Ailric of Lewes and Edwin of Anningdon appear in records dated between 1095 and 1115: H. E. Salter, *Facsimiles of Early Charters in Oxford Muniment Rooms* (Oxford, 1929), no. 1.

increasingly sophisticated governments for unambiguous references to litigants and plaintiffs in suits involving land.

Anglo-Scandinavians shifted their legal identity over time by assuming
non-English personal names, and after 1154, English personal names and
patronymics appear less frequently in the record sources.[124] This does not
mean that English people were absent at the events commemorated in these
same sources. The naming patterns of ambitious or disgraced families re-
volved around the adoption of Norman names, and even those with a sense
of ethnic solidarity—such as burgesses and other townspeople—evinced a
casual drift toward the use of Continental names.

But the increased use of surnames, in general, and of Continental personal names may not be the most instructive barometer of ethnicity. The
tendency of English people to utilize patronymics suggests that in many instances Continental personal names merely hide a disadvantageous or embarrassing identity. By the same token, since the use of bynames was often
discarded by ethnic Englishmen during the twelfth century, we may be reasonably sure that men with French first names and French bynames were
French. Nomenclature among natives and immigrants discloses willingness
to adapt, but not to completely mask, their eleventh-century origins.

Both French and English sought legitimacy in the century after 1066.
The new members of the upper aristocracy married natives, relied upon
them to manage their baronial and royal possessions, called upon them to
attest to their claims to land, adopted the English language, and eventually
referred to themselves as English. During the twelfth century, French holders
of small English estates and French urban dwellers began to abandon the
use of French toponymic surnames in favor of English place names and ambiguous surnames. Like English people, they occasionally acknowledged
a multi-generational allegiance. *William son of Ralph son of Anschetill* and
John son of Ralph son of Everard are examples of a tripartite nomenclature,
as are *Alwold son of Alwold Child*, in which one combined the use of a
patronymic with preservation of a byname; *Walter son of Robert of Caux*,
where the patronymic reflected ethnic origin; and *Thomas of York son of
Ulviet*. The expression of ethnicity through links maintained with one's kind,
or one's kin, became more difficult, and perhaps less desirable, with inter-

---

[124]In the pipe rolls produced by Henry II's revived Exchequer, less than one fifth had
English names: *PR 2-3-4 Henry II*, index.

marriage and cultural borrowing, even in towns after 1150, and nomenclature worked to deny origins among the English and French alike. Although ethnicity could be a source of pride and a political rallying point, it was advantageous to people of both English and French ancestry to abandon distinctions that prolonged ethnic conflict.

This analysis provides a snapshot of a moment in the shifting expressions of ethnicity in late Norman England. As descendants of English people accepted the styles and values of French people, they gave up aspects of their own culture, which to them may have seemed relatively unimportant—such as OE personal names—and retained those of cultural importance—such as the prolonged association with kin and ancestors. But at the same time as they acknowledged French cultural and political dominance, they drew Frenchmen into their own cultural orbit of everyday life. Their indigenous language and outlook survived, largely due to the women who perpetuated it and conveyed it to their children.[125] As intrusive and powerful as they were, Normans in 1150 were well on the way to becoming English.

Note

I am grateful to the Early Medieval Seminar at the Institute of Historical Research for suggestions and stimulating discussion following delivery of this paper in May 1997 and to Christopher Jones, Marjorie Chibnall, Emma Mason, and Dave Postles for their comments on subsequent drafts. The research for this paper was partially supported by Grant No. 777 from the Faculty Research Committee, Idaho State University, Pocatello, Idaho.

---

[125]Cecily Clark, "Women's Names in Post-Conquest England: Observations and Speculations," in *Words, Names and History*, ed. Jackson, pp. 117–43.

NOTES ON CONTRIBUTORS

Michael Bennett is Professor of History, School of History and Classics, University of Tasmania. He is the author of *Community, Class and Careerism: Cheshire and Lancashire Society in the Age of "Sir Gawain and the Green Knight"* (1983), *The Battle of Bosworth* (1985, rev. ed. 1993), *Lambert Simnel and the Battle of Stoke* (1987, rev. ed. 1993), and *Richard II and the Revolution of 1399* (1999). His most recent contributions to medieval studies include "Forms of Cultural Expression" in R. A. Griffiths (ed.), *The Short Oxford History of the Britain. IV. The Fourteenth and Fifteenth Centuries* (Oxford, 2003), and "*Mandeville's Travels* and the Anglo-French Moment," *Medium Aevum* 75 (2006).

Stephanie Mooers Christelow received her Ph.D. from the University of California, Santa Barbara, in 1983. After teaching at the University of Iowa and Western Washington University, she moved to Idaho State University in 1990. She is Professor of History and specializes in Anglo-Norman England. She has been a visiting member of Clare Hall, Cambridge, and is a life member of the University of Cambridge. Her articles on patronage and justice have been published in *American Historical Review*, *Speculum*, *Albion*, *Medieval Prosopography*, and the *Haskins Society Journal*. She is currently authoring a book on *Royal Patronage and Social Rank in Anglo-Norman England*.

Cecily Clark (1926–92) received the advanced degree of B.Litt. from the University of Oxford in 1952. After teaching at the Universities of London, Edinburgh, and Aberdeen, she was elected a Research Fellow of Newnham College, Cambridge (1966–69), and remained in Cambridge for the rest of her life as an independent scholar. Her initial research in Old and Middle English language and literature resulted in an edition of *The Peterborough Chronicle, 1070–1154* (Oxford, 1958; second ed., 1970) and in articles on the *Anglo-Saxon Chronicle*, *Ancrene Wisse*, and *Sir Gawain and the Green Knight*. From the mid-1970s, however, her attention turned increasingly to name-studies, in particular to personal naming patterns in post-Conquest England. An extended series of papers culminated in two substantial contributions on "Onomastics" to volumes 1 and 2 of *The Cambridge History of the English Language* (Cambridge, 1992). Many articles and reviews from across her career have been reprinted in *Words, Names and History: Selected Writings of Cecily Clark*, edited by Peter Jackson (Cambridge, 1995).

Virginia Davis is Senior Lecturer in the Department of History at Queen Mary, University of London. She completed her Ph.D. thesis at Trinity College, Dublin, worked at the University of Hull on the development of an electronic version of Domesday Book, and has published *The Medieval Seasons* (London, 1991), *William Waynflete, Bishop and Educationalist* (Woodbridge, 1993), and *Clergy in London in the Late Middle Ages: A Register of Clergy Ordained in the Diocese of London Based on Episcopal Ordination Lists* (London, 2000). Her interests are in late medieval English ecclesiastical and educational history and include the application of computer techniques to medieval history. She is currently completing a biography of William Wykeham.

Peter Franklin received his Ph.D. from the University of Birmingham in 1982/3 for his thesis on peasant society, landholding, and agriculture on the manor of Thornbury (Gloucestershire) in the fourteenth century. Using material from the thesis, he published articles on widows in *The Economic History Review* and on pre-1381 peasant movements in *Medieval Society and the Manor Court*, edited by Zvi Razi and Richard Smith (Oxford, 1996). He has additionally contributed articles on the taxpayers, malaria, heriots and deaths, and woodlands and deer parks in Gloucestershire. In 1993, he produced a new edition of the 1327 lay subsidy for the county: *The Taxpayers of Medieval Gloucestershire: An Analysis of the 1327 Lay Subsidy Roll, with a New Edition of its Text* (Stroud).

Louis Haas received his Ph.D. from the University of Illinois at Urbana-Champaign in 1990. After teaching at Duquesne University in Pittsburgh, he moved to Middle Tennessee State University in 2001. He is Associate Professor of History and specializes in medieval social history, especially in the late Middle Ages. He has published articles on godparenthood and childhood, and is author of *The Renaissance Man and His Children* (St. Martins, 1998).

John Insley was born in Preston in Lancashire (England) in 1947. He studied the Historical Tripos as Part 1 and the Anglo-Saxon, Norse, and Celtic Tripos as Part 2 at the University of Cambridge from 1967 to 1971. He subsequently completed a Ph.D. thesis at the University of Nottingham on Scandinavian personal names in Norfolk, this being published (in updated form) in Uppsala in 1994. He completed his Habilitation in Heidelberg in 2002. Having previously taught at the University of Erlangen-Nuremberg and at the Free University in Berlin, he is now employed by the University of Heidelberg, where he teaches Old and Middle English.

Heather Jones completed her Ph.D. thesis at the University of California, Berkeley in 2003, specializing in medieval Welsh. She has a B.Sc. from the University of California, Davis, in zoology. Since her Ph.D., she has returned to an intensive study of personal names in Welsh records of the thirteenth and fourteenth centuries, about which she has published several papers. She is employed as a conformance investigator in the pharmaceutical industry and continues to pursue a variety of historic topics as an independent scholar, both in the fields of onomastics and costume history.

C. P. (Chris) Lewis joined the staff of the Victoria County History in 1982, and since 2002 has been county editor for Sussex. His interest in the personal names of Domesday Book dates from his doctoral research on the Norman Conquest of the Welsh Marches.

Philip Niles is Professor Emeritus in History, Carleton College, Northfield, Minnesota, where he taught for 33 years. He retired in 1999. He is currently working on a biography of A. E. Doyle, the early twentieth-century architect of Portland, Oregon. As a medievalist his areas of interest were John Wyclif, Plague, and social structure in late medieval England.

Dave Postles has been Marc Fitch Research Fellow at the University of Leicester since 1988, as a contract researcher into naming patterns and processes in their cultural and social contexts. He has published two monographs for the Marc Fitch Fund, but has also published more widely on medieval naming cultures and also on medieval society.

Joel Rosenthal is Professor Emeritus in the History Department, State University of New York at Stony Brook. He co-edits *Medieval Prosopography* and was co-editor of *The Garland Encyclopedia of Medieval England*. He has published on Anglo-Saxon England, the social structure of fourteenth- and fifteenth-century England with particular interest in the study of women and widows, family structure, the social history of the Church and the episcopate, and old age.

GENERAL INDEX

Note: The index is divided into two parts: a general index, and, following that, a conspectus of personal names ("forenames").

CONSPECTUS OF *NOMINA* ("FORENAMES")

Note: Please bear in mind that this book is about names. Names consequently occur throughout the book. Particular names are indexed only if there is an expanded discussion of them in the text.

Typeset in 11 pt. Times New Roman
with Garamond display
Designed and composed by Julie Scrivener
at Medieval Institute Publications
Manufactured by Cushing-Malloy—Ann Arbor, Michigan

Medieval Institute Publications
College of Arts and Sciences
Western Michigan University
1903 West Michigan Avenue
Kalamazoo, MI 49008-5432
www.wmich.edu/medieval/mip

 WESTERN MICHIGAN UNIVERSITY